Managing the Legal Nexus Between Intellectual Property and Employees

ELGAR LAW AND ENTREPRENEURSHIP

Series Editors: Shubha Ghosh, *Vilas Associate and Professor of Law, Honorary Fellow and Associate Director, INSITE, University of Wisconsin School of Law* and Robin Paul Malloy, *E.I. White Chair and Distinguished Professor of Law and Director of the Center on Property, Citizenship and Social Entrepreneurism at Syracuse University, USA.*

The primary goals of this series are two-fold. The first is to develop the theoretical foundation for law and entrepreneurship. As to this goal, central research questions involve but are not limited to developing an understanding of the various meanings of entrepreneurship. Although superficially associated with the creation of a profit-making business enterprise, the concept of entrepreneurship extends to any motivation and effort to create something new. What does it mean to create? In what sense is an enterprise or project new? Is creation a process or an instantaneous, unpredictable event? What are the channels of creativity and in what venues do they occur? Is creativity in art, science, and business a coherent whole or a completely different exercise? These questions serve to define the contours of entrepreneurship and its relationship to law and legal institutions.

The second goal is to translate the theoretical understanding of law and entrepreneurship into concrete policy. At one level, this goal entails identifying key legal policy levers (taxation, property rights, competition policy, financial regulation, contract law) that structure and direct entrepreneurship. At a deeper level, the second goal mandates a detailed institutional analysis of successful and unsuccessful entrepreneurship activity. This deeper goal invites an inquiry into the definitions of success and its measures. These definitions and measures, in turn, provide a benchmark for accessing and defining implementable policies.

At its core, the Law and Entrepreneurship series examines the role of law and legal institutions in promoting and sustaining entrepreneurial activity.

Titles in the series include:

Managing the Legal Nexus Between Intellectual Property and Employees

Domestic and Global Contexts

Edited by

Lynda J. Oswald

Professor and Area Chair of Business Law, Stephen M. Ross School of Business, University of Michigan, USA

Marisa Anne Pagnattaro

Josiah Meigs Distinguished Teaching Professor and Director, Legal Studies Certificate Program, Terry College of Business, University of Georgia, USA

ELGAR LAW AND ENTREPRENEURSHIP

Cheltenham, UK • Northampton, MA, USA

Published by
Edward Elgar Publishing Limited
The Lypiatts
15 Lansdown Road
Cheltenham
Glos GL50 2JA
UK

Edward Elgar Publishing, Inc.
William Pratt House
9 Dewey Court
Northampton
Massachusetts 01060
USA

A catalogue record for this book
is available from the British Library

Library of Congress Control Number: 2015933351

This book is available electronically in the **Elgar**online
Law subject collection
DOI 10.4337/9781783479269

ISBN 978 1 78347 925 2 (cased)
ISBN 978 1 78347 926 9 (eBook)

Typeset by Columns Design XML Ltd, Reading
Printed and bound in Great Britain by T.J. International Ltd, Padstow

Contents

Contributors

Robert C. Bird is an Associate Professor of Business Law and the Northeast Utilities Chair in Business Ethics at the University of Connecticut. His scholarship focuses on employment law, legal strategy, intellectual property, and business and human rights. He has authored over seventy publications, including works in the *Journal of Law and Economics*, *American Business Law Journal*, *Law and Society Review*, *Connecticut Law Review*, and the *Harvard Journal of Law and Public Policy*. Bird is the recipient of the Academy of Legal Studies in Business Best International Paper Award, Distinguished Proceedings Award, Holmes-Cardozo Award, and various other best paper awards. He was editor in chief of the *American Business Law Journal* in 2012–13, designing and publishing the 50th anniversary issue of the journal's founding, and serving as its administrative editor, articles editor, senior articles editor, and managing editor from 2006 through 2012.

Norman D. Bishara is an Associate Professor of Business Law and Business Ethics at the Stephen M. Ross School of Business at the University of Michigan. His research interests include the areas of covenants not to compete as an obstacle to employee mobility and knowledge transfer, corporate governance and corruption as a constraint on business activity, and international legal reform and business ethics in the developing world. His recent research focuses on corporate governance and restrictive covenants, including in CEO contracts, and the implications of enforcement variations across the U.S. for highly skilled labor mobility. Bishara's current projects include a study of restrictive covenant legislation development and an extensive survey of employee perceptions of restrictive covenants.

Elizabeth A. Brown is an Assistant Professor in the Department of Law, Taxation and Financial Planning at Bentley University in Waltham, Massachusetts. She is a former partner in a global intellectual property law firm, and advised Fortune 500 companies on their legal strategies for more than twelve years before joining the Bentley faculty. Her research focuses on the intersection of intellectual property and emerging technology issues. Brown has published this research in the University of

Pennsylvania *Journal of Business Law*, the New York University *Journal of Intellectual Property and Entertainment Law*, and elsewhere. She received her undergraduate and law degrees with honors from Harvard University. She was named the 2011 Gaylord Jentz Scholar by the Academy of Legal Studies in Business. Brown is also the author of the best-selling book on alternative careers for lawyers, *Life After Law: Finding Work You Love with the JD You Have*.

Romain M. Lorentz is a Participating Adjunct Professor in the Ethics and Business Law Department, Opus College of Business, University of St Thomas, Minnesota. Prior to that, he taught U.S. law at the University of Paris II Panthéon-Assas, France. His research interests include intellectual property law, Internet law, European Union law, torts and comparative law. In 2006, he spoke on pure economic loss at the World Congress of the International Academy of Comparative Law, in Utrecht, the Netherlands. Lorentz was named 2012 Gaylord Jentz Scholar by the Academy of Legal Studies in Business. He has presented his research at academic conferences in the United States and at colloquia in London. His research has been published in law reviews and books. Lorentz holds a Maîtrise in Law (J.D.) from the University of Orléans (France), a D.E.A. (LL.M.) in Comparative Law, and a Doctorate in Comparative Private Law (J.S.D.) from the University of Paris II (Panthéon-Assas) (Paris, France).

Julie Manning Magid is an Associate Professor of Business Law and a Kelley Venture Fellow at the Kelley School of Business, Indiana University. Her primary areas of research include employment, trademark and governance issues and she has published this research in journals including the *American Business Law Journal*, *North Carolina Law Review* and the University of Pennsylvania *Journal of Business Law*. Magid has been recognized for her teaching excellence with several teaching awards and honors.

Susan J. Marsnik is a Professor and Chair of the Department of Ethics and Business Law, Opus College of Business, University of St. Thomas, Minnesota. Her research focuses on comparative and international intellectual property and data privacy law. She has been published in law and business journals, including the *American Business Law Journal*, in books and encyclopedias, and as part of legal practitioner and legal education programs. She has received the Hoeber Memorial Award for excellence in research. Marsnik has taught comparative intellectual property law in specialized graduate programs at European universities and as a Fulbright Specialist at Beni Suef University in Egypt. She has held visiting appointments at the University of Portsmouth, Université de Caen, Université de Poitier, and Novosibirsk State University. She regularly presents at academic conferences in the United States and has been invited to present her research in Europe and the Middle East. Prior to her academic career, she practiced law and has over a decade of other business experience.

David Orozco is an Associate Professor of Legal Studies and the MBA Program Director at Florida State University's College of Business. Orozco's research focuses on intellectual property management and legal strategy. His research has been published in leading law reviews and peer-reviewed journals.

Lynda J. Oswald is the Area Chair and Professor of Business Law at the Stephen M. Ross School of Business at the University of Michigan. She teaches and researches in the fields of intellectual and real property law, with a particular focus on standards of liability. Oswald has received numerous awards for her research, including the Hoeber Memorial Award and the Holmes-Cardozo Award for Research Excellence from the *American Business Law Journal.* Her work has been cited by numerous courts, including the U.S. Supreme Court in *United States v. Bestfoods.* She is also the author of a book entitled *The Law of Marketing,* co-editor of a book entitled *The Changing Face of U.S. Patent Law and its Impact on Business Strategy,* and the Editor of the *Michigan Real Property Review.* Oswald is a Past President of the Academy of Legal Studies in Business, and served on its Executive Committee from 2003–2008. She has held visiting appointments at the University of Florida Law School, the University of Michigan Law School, China University of Political Science and Law in Beijing, L'viv State University in Ukraine, the Hopkins-Nanjing Center in Nanjing, China, the University of Sydney in Australia, and the PKU School of Transnational Law in Shenzhen, China.

Marisa Anne Pagnattaro, J.D., Ph.D., is a Josiah Meigs Professor of Legal Studies at the University of Georgia's Terry College of Business. She is also the author of numerous articles on international trade and employment law issues. Her current research focuses on legal issues related to doing business in China, including the protection of trade secrets. Prior to teaching, Pagnattaro was a litigation associate with Kilpatrick & Cody (now known as Kilpatrick Townsend LLP) in Atlanta.

Stephen Kim Park is an Assistant Professor of Business Law at the University of Connecticut School of Business. His research focuses on international financial regulation, international trade law, and corporate governance and corporate social responsibility, particularly concerning the intersections between these areas of law and the roles of multi-national enterprises in transnational, and public-private governance regimes. Park holds a J.D. from Harvard Law School, an M.A.L.D. in international affairs from The Fletcher School at Tufts University, and a B.A. in Ethics, Politics, and Economics from Yale University.

Jamie Darin Prenkert is an Arthur M. Weimer Faculty Fellow and Professor of Business Law at the Indiana University Kelley School of Business, where he is the Chair of the Department of Business Law & Ethics. His research focuses on employment discrimination, whistle-blowing, and business' responsibility to respect human rights. He obtained his J.D., magna cum laude, from Harvard Law School and earned a B.A., summa cum laude with honors in Political Science, from Anderson University, Indiana. Prior to joining the Kelley School faculty, Prenkert was a senior trial attorney for the United States Equal Employment Opportunity Commission.

Christine M. Westphal holds a faculty appointment in the Management Department of the United States Coast Guard Academy teaching Human Resource Management and the Legal Environment of Business. Her research focuses on how government regulation affects labor markets. Westphal previously held the position of Program Director for the Graduate programs in Human Resources at Suffolk University, Boston, where she taught Global Human Resources and was a member of the Asian Studies faculty.

Table of cases

Administrative Proceeding Materials

Table of legislation

European Union

International Treaties, Conventions and other Instruments

Introduction

Lynda J. Oswald and Marisa Anne Pagnattaro

Surprisingly little research has been directed specifically at the impact of the new business environment on employee-employer relationships, domestically and globally. As the Industrial Age has been supplanted by the Information Age, we have seen a historic rise in inventive and creative activity.[1] The last half century has also seen a shift in firm behavior, from a highly structured model of vertical integration[2] to a networked form of organization that relies heavily on the use of supplier firms, outsourced or shared collaboration models of research and development, and internationally distributed workforces.[3] The implications of these shifts in business focus on both firm activity and employment patterns and behavior are profound. Patents, copyrights, trade secrets, and trademarks – the traditional four pillars of intellectual property law – have taken on increased import and firms must now concentrate on the protection of those assets in a more intense manner than they ever experienced in the past.

---

[1] PATENTING AND INNOVATION IN METROPOLITAN AMERICA, BROOKINGS INSTITUTION (Feb. 1, 2013), http://www.brookings.edu/research/interactives/2013/metro patenting. A collaboration between Cornell University, INSEAD, and the World Intellectual Property Organization (WIPO) has resulted in an index that attempts to measure global innovation. *See* SOUMITRA DUTTA, BRUNO LANVIN & SACHA WUNSCH-VINCENT, THE GLOBAL INNOVATION INDEX 2014: THE HUMAN FACTOR IN INNOVATION (2014), *available at* http://www.wipo.int/edocs/pubdocs/en/economics/gii/gii_2014.pdf.

[2] NEIL FLIGSTEIN, THE TRANSFORMATION OF CORPORATE CONTROL (1990).

[3] Walter W. Powell, *The Capitalist Firm in the Twenty-First Century: Emerging Patterns in Western Enterprise, in* PAUL DIMAGGIO, THE TWENTY-FIRST-CENTURY FIRM: CHANGING ECONOMIC ORGANIZATION IN INTERNATIONAL PERSPECTIVE (2003); MANUEL CASTELLS, THE RISE OF THE NETWORK SOCIETY: THE INFORMATION AGE: ECONOMY, SOCIETY, AND CULTURE (2009); Fred Niederman, *International Business and MIS Approaches to Multinational Organizational Research: The Cases of Knowledge Transfer and IT Workforce Outsourcing,* 11 J. INT'L MGT. 187 (2005).

This new environment raises many questions. How should courts, legislatures, and other policy-makers address issues of employee rights and obligations with regard to the intellectual property assets that they manage or create? How should firms manage their behavior so as to enhance both their intellectual property assets and their relationship with their workforce? And how do these issues change as firms increasingly engage in global activities, licensing intellectual property and know-how abroad, creating diverse, international workforces, and protecting themselves against the threats of global competitors, who may come from very different legal regimes and have very different notions of fair play in the intellectual property arena?

This book opens the dialogue on this topic of critical importance to modern firms, and so serves as a tool for firms and policymakers as they consider future actions and reforms. It provides insight into several of the potent issues that arise at the intersection between intellectual property and employees, and, we hope, serves as a catalyst for further research into the critical nexus between intellectual property and employees, in both the domestic and global contexts.

The shift in business activity from traditional manufacturing activities to intellectual property-intensive activities is well documented, both in the United States and at the global level. In the United States, manufacturing has declined as a share of Gross Domestic Product (GDP) from 24.3 percent in 1970 to 12.8 percent in 2010. This same pattern is reflected internationally, where manufacturing as a percentage of world GDP fell from 26.6 percent in 1970 to 16.2 percent in 2010.[4]

Meanwhile, intellectual property-intensive activity has grown as a leading contributor to the economic success of many nations, both in terms of jobs and in terms of value added to GDP. In 2012, the U.S. Commerce Department released a comprehensive report that found that intellectual property-intensive industries directly accounted for 27.1 million jobs in 2010 and supported over 12.9 million additional jobs (totaling 27.7 percent of all jobs in the U.S. economy). These industries contributed more than $5 trillion dollars to (or 34.8 percent of) U.S.

---

[4] *See* Mark J. Perry, Blog Post, *Manufacturing's Declining Share of GDP is a Global Phenomenon, and It's Something to Celebrate* (March 22, 2012), *available at* http://www.uschamberfoundation.org/blog/post/manufacturing-s-declining-share-gdp-global-phenomenon-and-it-s-something-celebrate/34261 (citing data from the United Nations National Accounts Main Aggregate Database, *available at* unstats.un.org/unsd/snaama/dnllist.asp).

GDP.[5] Similar trends hold true in other developed nations. The European Union, for example, reported in September, 2013 that between 2008 and 2010, intellectual property-intensive industries contributed almost 77 million direct or indirect jobs out of a total of 218 million jobs (35.1 percent), and that these industries generated almost 39 percent of GDP in the European Union, valued at €4.7 trillion.[6]

Moreover, the creation, protection, and exploitation of intellectual property, both at home and abroad, are important issues for all businesses, not just "high-tech" industries. The bulk of business assets today are held in the form of intangible property as opposed to the land, factories, and machines of earlier decades. The World Intellectual Property Organization (WIPO) notes that in 1982, almost two-thirds of corporate assets in the United States were physical assets (e.g., land or machinery); however, by 2000, 70 percent of all such assets were intangible.[7] A leading intellectual property merchant bank, Ocean Tomo, estimated in 2010 that 81 percent of the assets held by the S&P 500 were in the form of intangible assets, rather than tangible ones – a complete reversal from 1975, where only 17 percent of such assets were intangible and 83 percent were tangible.[8]

This growth in intellectual capital coincides with a growing understanding of the importance of human capital to the firm and the need to manage employees effectively. In 1973, in *The Coming of Post-Industrial Society*, Daniel Bell posited that the rapid rise of the computer industry in the 1950s and 1960s would lead to an increased dependence by business firms on highly skilled employees, such as scientists, engineers, and technicians, as the primary drivers of innovation.[9] In Bell's words:

---

[5]   U.S. DEPT. OF COMMERCE, INTELLECTUAL PROPERTY AND THE U.S. ECONOMY: INDUSTRIES IN FOCUS vi-vii (March 2012), *available at* http://www.uspto.gov/news/publications/IP_Report_March_2012.pdf.

[6]   EUROPEAN UNION, OFFICE FOR HARMONIZATION IN THE INTERNAL MARKET, INTELLECTUAL PROPERTY RIGHTS INTENSIVE INDUSTRIES: CONTRIBUTION TO ECONOMIC PERFORMANCE AND EMPLOYMENT IN THE EUROPEAN UNION (Sept. 2013), *available at* http://ec.europa.eu/internal_market/intellectual-property/docs/joint-report-epo-ohim-final-version_en.pdf.

[7]   KAMIL IDRIS, INTELLECTUAL PROPERTY: A POWER TOOL FOR ECONOMIC GROWTH 6-7 (2003), *available at* http://www.wipo.int/edocs/pubdocs/en/intproperty/888/wipo_pub_888_1.pdf.

[8]   Ocean Tomo, *Ocean Tomo's Intangible Asset Market Value Study*, INSIGHTS BLOG (Dec. 9, 2013, 12:00 AM), *available at* http://www.oceantomo.com/2013/12/09/Intangible-Asset-Market-Value-Study-Release/.

[9]   DANIEL BELL, THE COMING OF POST-INDUSTRIAL SOCIETY: A VENTURE IN SOCIAL FORECASTING (1973).

> If the dominant figures of the past hundred years have been the entrepreneur, the businessman, and the industrial executive, the 'new men' are the scientists, the mathematicians, the economists, and the engineers of the new intellectual technology.[10]

Bell's prediction has proven true. Even if ultimately owned by the firm, intellectual property today is created and managed by employees of the firm, who undertake research programs, develop new products, create promotional materials, foster confidential business relationships with suppliers, customers, and consumers, and engage in myriad other activities that promote the firm's economic position while simultaneously contributing to the firm's intellectual property holdings. As summarized in the foreword to a recent WIPO report:

> The fundamental driver behind any innovation process is the human factor associated with it. We observe that some nations take the lead in innovation capacity over others. A major factor for this disparity of innovation prowess is the quality of human capital linked to the innovation activities carried out in these nations. Other factors, such as technology and capital, also influence the innovation process; these directly correlate with the human factor. Hence nurturing human capital at all levels and in all sections of society can be crucial for developing the foundation for innovation.[11]

However, businesses must carefully balance this imperative of nurturing their human capital with the need to protect their intellectual property assets. Legal issues arise at various stages of the employment relationship, including the proper use of employment contracts to protect intellectual property, ownership of intellectual property created by the employee, personal liability issues relating to infringement or inadvertent or deliberate misappropriation or theft of trade secrets, and post-employment confidentiality and non-compete agreements. Moreover, these relationships, like modern business itself, may be global in reach. Mechanisms provided by U.S. trade laws are thus also important tools to protect intellectual property abroad.

The nexus, however, between protecting intellectual property, balancing employees' rights and responsibilities, and fostering fair trade practices has not been fully explored by scholars. This book is intended to highlight some of the pressing issues that arise at the intersection of intellectual property law and employment law, domestically and globally, including the impact that those issues have on managers and business

---

[10]   *Id.* at 344.
[11]   DUTTA ET AL., *supra* note 1, at vii.

practices. These issues can be broadly categorized into: (1) public policy considerations; (2) workplace ramifications; and (3) global intersections between intellectual property and employees. Individual chapters within this book provide detailed consideration of some of the critical issues that arise within these categories.

PUBLIC POLICY CONSIDERATIONS

There is a complex interplay between intellectual property protection and employee interests. On the one hand, businesses have a strong interest in ensuring the security of their intellectual property assets. On the other hand, while employees generally have an interest in (and duty to) protect the employer's business interests, the interests of the two parties may at times conflict. This gives rise to intricate and intertwined legal doctrines governing the employer-employee relationship, which generate concerns about how to balance competing and sometimes conflicting public policy goals.

In Chapter 1, Lynda J. Oswald considers the public policy issues raised by holding corporate officers personally liable for the patent or copyright infringements of their firms. The chapter begins by examining traditional corporate, agency, and tort law concepts that impose liability upon a corporate officer for his or her own wrongful acts, and agency rules of *respondeat superior* that impute that individual's actions to the corporation. It then contrasts those general officer liability concepts with the specialized rules that arise in intellectual property disputes, finding that in the patent and copyright areas, the federal courts have deviated from traditional doctrine and have inappropriately imposed liability upon corporate officers. In the patent area, the Federal Circuit has adopted a distorted application of the veil-piercing doctrine traditionally applied to corporate owners. In the copyright arena, the regional circuit courts of appeal apply a vicarious liability test that is not only inapposite to officer liability, but in some ways mimics the piercing analysis used by the Federal Circuit in the patent law arena and in other ways replicates the personal participation test of traditional doctrine. Oswald discusses why individual officer liability is so muddled in both patent and copyright law, and concludes that current case law reflects an instinctive rejection by the courts of the application of strict liability to individuals. The courts' subconscious efforts to reach liability standards and outcomes that are fault-based, rather than strict, for corporate officers have caused the courts to create *sui generis* officer liability rules that are at odds with traditional doctrine and that inappropriately expand the individual liability of corporate officers. The chapter concludes by proposing that the courts adopt a more direct approach to the imposition of personal liability on corporate officers that focuses on culpability and that more closely adheres to traditional legal doctrines.

In Chapter 2, Julie Manning Magid looks at another aspect of the conflicts that can arise between employees and their firm, examining the implications that the change in physician employment relationships – occasioned by the increasing consolidation of the U.S. health care industry – has had on physician ownership of health care-related inventions. One increasingly common mechanism that they have used to do this is to require physicians and other health care employees to sign invention assignment agreements that assign to the hospital system the intellectual property rights of any innovations created by those employees. But are invention assignment agreements the best means to motivate a culture of innovation? Magid finds that the health care industry's dependence on invention assignment agreements impedes rather than promotes a culture of innovation. The chapter examines the changes in the health care industry and the role of intellectual property in spurring those changes and then turns to the challenges of incentivizing innovation, noting that compensation alone does not accomplish innovation. The chapter concludes that the health care industry should engage employees in creating innovation to reduce health care costs and benefit patients by developing a process of employee-driven innovation.

In Chapter 3, Norman D. Bishara examines a broader issue of how firms with a globally diverse workforce can protect their important business knowledge. The misappropriation of proprietary business knowledge and trade secrets across international borders has received extensive attention from policy-makers, scholars, and commentators. There has been less consistent focus on an important underlying transfer mechanism of that commercial knowledge that companies can only partially control: the movement of knowledge across borders as a result of employee mobility. This chapter identifies a portfolio of legal options for businesses facing the dilemma of how to not only share business secrets with employees and cultivate employee skills for the benefit of both parties, but also how to protect those investments in human capital when there is an increased risk of the employee leaving for an overseas competitor. Bishara also discusses the contractual and non-contractual options firms can use to manage the knowledge held by key employees. He suggests a business and policy agenda related to successfully navigating the complex issues surrounding international employee mobility and knowledge transfer to competitors.

WORKPLACE RAMIFICATIONS

Part II of the book steps back from larger policy questions about how we should structure legal doctrine to protect intellectual property assets, incentivize innovators, and correctly attribute liability for infringement. It examines the ways in which intellectual property law and the rise of technology directly impact the workforce environment that employees face.

Chapter 4 looks at a special subset of trademark law: certification marks. Jamie Darin Prenkert examines the manner in which certification marks, which are sometimes used for the purpose of private regulation, may positively affect the employment relationship by providing for better working conditions. In particular, this chapter focuses on when certification is used to affect private ordering in the workplace to supplement existing employment or labor regulations or to fill regulatory voids. After describing the legal basis and history of certification marks and certification schemes, the chapter describes five exemplary uses of certification to regulate workplace conditions. Those descriptions provide a taxonomy to categorize certification according to the breadth of regulated conduct, the reliance on certification marks, the application to a particular product or service, and the type of regulation (supplemental versus new). Then the chapter raises four questions that relate to four characteristics of certification schemes that are likely to guide the inquiry into the likely regulatory effectiveness of a certification.

What happens when technology outstrips the law, creating detrimental impacts on employee working conditions? In Chapter 5, Robert C. Bird examines the impact that the rapid growth in technology can have on the modern workplace and considers the manner in which the law can seek to constrain the costs imposed on employees, using smartphone and related mobile technology as an example. Bird examines the impact of smartphone and related technology on modern fair labor standards, including the Fair Labor Standards Act (FLSA), finding that small increments of time, even when easily traceable and the source of frustrating interruptions, are not readily protected as compensable work. This chapter proposes a reform to the FLSA that narrows the *de minimis* exception that enables periods of time to remain unpaid. The narrowing of this exception, limited to what is available under reasonable business realities, will help employees be compensated for their full time worked regardless of location or length of time worked. The chapter also offers ways for employers to minimize administrative and other costs of such reform and presents opportunities for using such tracking information to add value to their organizations.

GLOBAL INTERSECTIONS

The last part of the book turns to the increasingly global nature of both modern business activity and intellectual property law, looking at the myriad of issues that are created when firms engage in business across borders. The cost and incidence of cross-border trade-secret misappropriation is rising, but current international protection measures often fall far short of companies' needs. Chapters 6 and 7 deal with this significant problem, but examine different mechanisms for addressing it. Chapters 8 and 9 look at the issues that global businesses face in confronting differing legal regimes around work, considering how firms address issues of copyright ownership and authorship and patent licensing when operating across borders. The final chapter of the book looks at intellectual property issues faced by firms doing business in China.

Specifically, in Chapter 6, Marisa Anne Pagnattaro and Stephen Kim Park explore trade-secret misappropriation in the context of Section 337 of the Tariff Act of 1930, analyzing how Section 337 can be used strategically to help trade-secret owners protect their valuable assets. For global employers, protecting trade secrets from employee disclosure is a common problem. When misappropriation occurs abroad, U.S. companies may find that it is difficult to obtain adequate redress. For such acts occurring outside of the United States, Section 337 of the Tariff Act offers another avenue of redress, as it can be used to block goods produced with misappropriated trade secrets from being imported into the United States. The chapter details the background of Section 337 and its use in the trade secret context. It explores several early cases, and then focuses on the *TianRui* case, which significantly expanded the potential use of Section 337, as well as a number of recent post-*TianRui* cases brought under Section 337. The chapter then turns to ongoing trends in trade-secret enforcement actions and addresses criticism about the use of Section 337 to address acts occurring entirely outside of the United States. Pagnattaro and Park conclude that, despite criticism, Section 337 is emerging as an important tool to protect the rights of trade-secret owners.

In Chapter 7, Elizabeth A. Brown addresses how the disparities among national and regional approaches to trade-secret protection and the lack of a central protection mechanism make it difficult for any company to secure its trade secrets effectively. Although this is a global problem, no consensus as to the best global solution has yet emerged. This chapter examines the risks of cross-border trade-secret misappropriation, the regional differences in approaches to trade-secret protection, the range of public and private remedies for trade-secret misappropriation, and the realistic strategies businesses can employ to protect their valuable trade secrets. It explores the differences between various countries' trade secret regimes and assesses the next wave of potential solutions, including both suggested efforts within the United States and proposed multi-national measures to increase global trade-secret protection.

In Chapter 8, Susan J. Marsnik and Romain M. Lorentz note that business functions best when the law is clear and predictable. However, clarity and predictability are notably lacking in the rules governing ownership of copyright when components of the work are contributed by authors in different countries. As U.S.-based companies source talent from employees or contractors in diverse countries to contribute to copyrighted products, it is important they understand that the U.S. work-for-hire rules will not ensure their corporate authorship or owner-ship. Depending on the country in which a particular task is performed, the rights of a U.S. company, and those of the individuals hired to complete the work, vary considerably. Moreover, moral rights in inter-national and foreign law are also at odds with the work-for-hire doctrine and can impact ongoing control of the work. This chapter explores these differences to facilitate understanding and management of copyright in a globally distributed work environment. It places the U.S. approach in the context of primary international agreements, the Berne Convention and the Agreement on Trade Related Aspects of Intellectual Property. The chapter presents approaches followed in four foreign jurisdictions, including three European Union member states and India, analyzing the conflicts among these foreign laws and demonstrating why a choice of law clause in employment or contractor agreements may not ensure application of the work-for-hire doctrine.

In Chapter 9, David Orozco examines the common practice of adding patent grant-back clauses in international license agreements, surveying U.S., Chinese, and Indian law to highlight important legal issues and differences with respect to this contentious licensing term. Patent grant-back clauses are used by patent owners to minimize competitive risks. The terms of these licenses can be so overly broad as to be an abusive practice that deprives the licensee of the incentive to innovate and the rewards of any such efforts. This chapter examines various international treatments of this issue to find a compromise that tempers the negative impacts of overly broad and restrictive grant-back clauses by offering a sample clause. This compromise represents an ethical solution that takes international norms and cultural differences into account.

Finally, in Chapter 10, Christine M. Westphal considers the political, economic, and public policy constraints on the use of employment contracts by Western firms to protect their intellectual property when doing business in China. The chapter considers the factors that Western firms must consider when evaluating the benefits of entering China against the risks of losing valuable intellectual property. The chapter concludes with a discussion of some of the steps that firms can take to protect their intellectual property assets in this challenging but economically important setting.

We are pleased to present this collection of research, which addresses a range of important issues arising at the intersection of intellectual property law, employment law, and global trade.

BIBLIOGRAPHY

BELL, DANIEL, THE COMING OF POST-INDUSTRIAL SOCIETY: A VENTURE IN SOCIAL FORECASTING (1973).

BROOKINGS INSTITUTION, *PATENTING AND INNOVATION IN METROPOLITAN AMERICA* (Feb. 1, 2013), *available at* http://www.brookings.edu/research/interactives/2013/metropatenting.

CASTELLS, MANUEL, THE RISE OF THE NETWORK SOCIETY: THE INFORMATION AGE: ECONOMY, SOCIETY, AND CULTURE (2009).

DUTTA, SOUMITRA, BRUNO LANVIN & SACHA WUNSCH-VINCENT, THE GLOBAL INNOVATION INDEX 2014: THE HUMAN FACTOR IN INNOVATION (2014), *available at* http://www.wipo.int/edocs/pubdocs/en/economics/gii/gii_2014.pdf.

EUROPEAN UNION, OFFICE FOR HARMONIZATION IN THE INTERNAL MARKET, INTELLECTUAL PROPERTY RIGHTS INTENSIVE INDUSTRIES: CONTRIBUTION TO ECONOMIC PERFORMANCE AND EMPLOYMENT IN THE EUROPEAN UNION (Sept. 2013), *available at* http://ec.europa.eu/internal_market/intellectual-property/docs/joint-report-epo-ohim-final-version_en.pdf.

FLIGSTEIN, NEIL, THE TRANSFORMATION OF CORPORATE CONTROL (1990).

IDRIS, KAMIL, INTELLECTUAL PROPERTY: A POWER TOOL FOR ECONOMIC GROWTH (2003), *available at* http://www.wipo.int/edocs/pubdocs/en/intproperty/888/wipo_pub_888_1.pdf.

Niederman, Fred, *International Business and MIS Approaches to Multinational Organizational Research: The Cases of Knowledge Transfer and IT Workforce Outsourcing*, 11 J. INT'L MGT. 187 (2005).

Ocean Tomo, *Ocean Tomo's Intangible Asset Market Value Study* (Dec. 9, 2013, 12:00 AM), *available at* http://www.oceantomo.com/ 2013/12/09/Intangible-Asset-Market-Value-Study-Release/.

Perry, Mark J., Blog Post, *Manufacturing's Declining Share of GDP is a Global Phenomenon, and It's Something to Celebrate* (March 22, 2012), *available at* http://www.uschamberfoundation.org/blog/post/manufacturing-s-declining-share-gdp-global-phenomenon-and-it-s-something-celebrate/34261.

Powell, Walter W., *The Capitalist Firm in the Twenty-First Century: Emerging Patterns in Western Enterprise*, *in* PAUL DiMAGGIO, THE TWENTY-FIRST-CENTURY FIRM: CHANGING ECONOMIC ORGANIZATION IN AN INTERNATIONAL PERSPECTIVE (2003).

U.S. DEPT. OF COMMERCE, INTELLECTUAL PROPERTY AND THE U.S. ECONOMY: INDUSTRIES IN FOCUS (March 2012), *available at* http://www.uspto.gov/news/publications/IP_Report_March_2012.pdf.

PART I

Public policy considerations

1. The individual liability of corporate officers under patent and copyright law

Lynda J. Oswald

The law encourages economic activity by limiting the personal liability of corporate owners through the corporate form. Not surprisingly, corporate officers are also concerned with personal liability. Unlike owners, officers do not participate to the full extent in the success of the corporation; correspondingly, they have little interest in assuming the risks. Imposition of officer liability should be fair, predictable, and further (rather than frustrate) important societal goals. Otherwise, corporate officers may be overcautious, make inefficient decisions, and forego economic activity that the corporate form was intended to encourage.

Patent and copyright law share certain fundamental characteristics: both encourage invention and creation but also provide for the public interest. In addition, the infringement of a patent or a copyright is a tort. The critical implication of this characterization is that general principles of tort and agency law apply to such infringement – a point that has important ramifications for infringement rules and individual liability. However, corporate officer liability doctrines under both the Patent Act[1] and Copyright Act[2] diverge markedly from traditional corporate, agency, and tort doctrines.

This chapter examines traditional corporate, agency, and tort law concepts that impose liability upon a corporate officer for his or her own wrongful acts, and agency rules of *respondeat superior* that impute that individual's actions to the corporation. In the patent infringement arena, the U.S. Court of Appeals for the Federal Circuit (Federal Circuit) has deviated from traditional doctrine and inappropriately imposed liability

---

[1] 35 U.S.C. §§ 1 *et seq.* (2012).
[2] 15 U.S.C. §§ 1 *et seq.* (2012).

upon corporate officers through a distorted application of piercing doctrine. In the copyright arena, the regional circuit courts of appeal apply a vicarious liability test that is not only inapposite to officer liability, but in some ways mimics the piercing analysis used by the Federal Circuit in the patent law arena, and in other ways replicates the personal participation test of traditional doctrine. This chapter discusses why individual officer liability is so muddled in both patent and copyright law, and concludes that current case law reflects an instinctive rejection by the courts of application of strict liability to individuals. The courts' subconscious efforts to reach liability standards and outcomes for corporate officers that are fault-based, rather than strict, have caused the courts to create *sui generis* officer liability rules that are at odds with traditional doctrine. This chapter proposes a more direct approach to the imposition of personal liability on corporate officers that focuses on culpability.

I. CORPORATE OFFICER LIABILITY UNDER TRADITIONAL DOCTRINE

When a corporation commits a tort or other wrongful act, that corporation is liable for the harm or injury that ensues. A corporation is a legal entity; it is separate and distinct from both its owners (whether individual shareholders or a parent corporation) and its corporate officers.[3] In the normal course of events, neither the corporate officers nor the corporate owners (i.e., shareholders) are liable for the debts or torts of the corporation.[4] However, in extraordinary circumstances, liability can attach to corporate officers or owners.

A.   Liability of Corporate Owners: Piercing of the Corporate Veil

Normally, shareholders are protected from the debts and liabilities of the corporation (beyond their contribution to capital) by the principle of limited liability.[5] The separateness of the corporate entity can be ignored, however, where respecting it would "defeat public convenience, justify wrong or protect fraud."[6] Typically, the courts employ piercing only

---

  [3]   *See, e.g.*, Walker v. Anderson, 232 S.W.3d 899, 918 (Tex. App. 2007).
  [4]   *See* FMC Finance Corp. v. Murphree, 632 F.2d 413, 421 (5th Cir. 1980).
  [5]   Krivo Indus. Supply Co. v. Nat'l Distillers & Chem. Corp., 483 F.2d 1098, 1102 (5th Cir. 1973), *modified per curiam,* 490 F.2d 916 (5th Cir. 1974).
  [6]   Fish v. East, 114 F.2d 177, 191 (10th Cir. 1940).

where: (1) "the corporation was formed or used for an illegal, fraudulent, or unjust purpose"; or (2) "the shareholders have ignored the corporate form and have used it to conduct their own affairs" (known as the "mere instrumentality" or "alter ego" theory).[7] Most courts require that piercing be supported by findings: "(1) that there be such unity of interest and ownership that the separate personalities of the corporation and the individual no longer exist and (2) that, if the acts are treated as those of the corporation alone, an inequitable result will follow."[8]

Although the term "piercing the corporate veil" is over 100 years old,[9] there are relatively few examples of it in action.[10] The act of piercing the corporate veil is considered an extraordinary event,[11] and veil-piercing doctrine has been described as "unpredictable, inconsistent, and largely unprincipled."[12] In practice, veil piercing is used only to reach the owners of closely held corporations or parent corporations – not to reach shareholders of large, publicly-held corporations – even though in theory corporations with a sole or few shareholders are protected by limited liability in the same manner as corporations with many shareholders.

B. Liability of Corporate Officers: Personal Participation

In some instances, the plaintiff may seek to hold individual officers liable, in addition to the corporation. There are a myriad of reasons why plaintiffs may sue individual officers: perhaps because the corporation has insufficient funds to fully compensate for the infringement and so additional pockets are sought; because the plaintiff is seeking access to director's and officer's insurance; because the individual's behavior is viewed as particularly culpable and in need of punishment; because the

---

[7] Lynda J. Oswald, *The Personal Liability of Corporate Officers for Patent Infringement*, 44 IDEA 115, 120 (2003) (citation omitted).

[8] Automotriz del Golfo de California S.A. de C.V. v. Resnick, 306 P.2d 1, 3 (1957) (citations omitted).

[9] *See* Mark J. Lowenstein, *Veil Piercing to Non-owners: A Practical and Theoretical Inquiry*, 41 SETON HALL L. REV. 839, 841 (2011) (phrase "first popularized" by Professor Maurice Wormser in early 1900s).

[10] *See* Robert B. Thompson, *Piercing the Corporate Veil: An Empirical Study*, 76 CORNELL L. REV. 1036, 1047-48 & table 1 (1991); Robert B. Thompson, *Piercing the Veil within Corporate Groups: Corporate Shareholders as Mere Investors*, 13 CONN. J. INT'L L. 379, 380 & n.4 (1999); Peter B. Oh, *Veil-Piercing*, 89 TEX. L. REV. 81, 110 (2010).

[11] *See* Dole Food Co. v. Patrickson, 538 U.S. 468, 475 (2003).

[12] Timothy P. Glynn, *Beyond "Unlimiting" Shareholder Liability: Vicarious Tort Liability for Corporate Officers*, 57 VAND. L. REV. 329, 333 (2004).

corporation is small or closely held and it is thus difficult to distinguish the various roles that the officer/employee/owner holds, or because the plaintiff seeks to create divisions between the corporation and its officers that will encourage settlement.[13]

Under traditional corporate law doctrine, piercing of the corporate veil is used to hold *owners* of a corporation liable,[14] not officers.[15] Officers generally are shielded from liability for the wrongful acts of their corporation unless they personally participated in a tort or other wrongful act (such as a statutory or regulatory violation)[16] "through affirmative actions of direction, sanction, or cooperation in the wrongful acts of commission or omission."[17] Thus, officers are not held liable based on their mere status as officers.[18]

The liability of corporate officers in such instances flows directly from traditional agency law principles that hold an agent personally liable for his or her own tortious conduct, even where the individual was acting in an official capacity as an agent of the corporation, or at the direction of his or her principal, and not on the agent's own behalf.[19] In such instances, the plaintiff may pursue the corporation, the individual officer, or both.[20]

An officer may also be a shareholder (even the sole shareholder) of a corporation, but in that instance, traditional doctrine dictates that the court should distinguish carefully the grounds on which liability is being imposed. In the leading case of *Donsco, Inc. v. Casper Corp.*, for example, the Third Circuit emphasized that while the individual at issue being held personally liable was both a shareholder and an officer, the individual's liability stemmed from his role "as an actor rather than as an owner."[21] The court noted that because officer liability is not rooted in a

---

[13]   *See* Dangler v. Imperial Machine Co., 11 F.2d 945, 947 (7th Cir. 1926); Oswald, *supra* note 7, at 121 n.32; Jason A. Wietjes and Michael D. Pegues, *Director and Officer Liability for Inducement of Patent Infringement*, 21 INTELLECTUAL PROPERTY LITIGATION, no. 2, at p. 3 (Winter 2010) (published by ABA Section of Litigation, Intellectual Property Litigation Committee).

[14]   Donsco, Inc. v. Casper Corp., 587 F.2d 602, 606 (3d Cir. 1978).

[15]   *See* Crigler v. Salac, 438 So.2d 1375, 1380 (Ala. 1983).

[16]   *See Donsco*, 587 F.2d at 606.

[17]   *See Oswald, supra* note 7, at 118.

[18]   *See* Murphy Tugboat Co. v. Shipowners & Merchants Towboat Co., 467 F. Supp. 841, 852 (N.D. Cal. 1979), *aff'd*, 658 F.2d 1256 (9th Cir. 1981).

[19]   *See* RESTATEMENT (SECOND) OF AGENCY § 343 (1958).

[20]   *See* Strang v. Hollowell, 387 S.E.2d 664, 666 (N.C. Ct. App. 1990) (citations omitted).

[21]   587 F.2d 602, 606 (3d Cir. 1978).

piercing of the corporate veil, it was "in no way dependent upon a finding that [the corporation] is inadequately capitalized, that the corporation is a mere alter ego [of the individual], that the corporate form is being used to perpetrate a fraud, or that corporate formalities have not been properly complied with."[22] Rather, "[t]he only crucial predicate" to officer liability is the individual's "participation in the wrongful acts."[23]

C. Liability of the Corporation for Acts of Corporate Officers

Under the well-known doctrine of *respondeat superior*, the wrongdoing of the officer, as agent, can be imputed to the corporation, rendering both the individual and the corporation liable.[24] This is a one-way street of imputed liability, however: the corporation is liable, as the principal, for the actions of the officer as agent. There is no rule holding the officer liable for the corporation's actions or liabilities merely because the individual holds the position of officer.

II. INDIVIDUAL OFFICER LIABILITY FOR PATENT INFRINGEMENT

The Federal Circuit has adopted a clearly inapposite doctrine – piercing of the corporate veil – to assess the personal liability of corporate officers for patent infringement. The statutory framework of the Patent Act and the court's desire to constrain the expansive strict liability of direct patent infringement most likely fuels adoption of this misplaced theory.

A. Patent Infringement Generally

A patent is a property interest of the patent holder,[25] infringement of the patent is a tortious taking of that property,[26] and the patent infringer is

---

[22] *Ibid.*

[23] *Ibid.*

[24] Poppenhusen v. New York Gutta Percha Comb Co., 19 F. Cas. 1059, 1063 (C.C.S.D. N.Y. 1858).

[25] *See* Dowagiac Mfg. Co. v. Minnesota Moline Plow Co., 235 U.S. 641, 648 (1915).

[26] *Ibid.*

thus a tortfeasor.[27] However, overlaid onto these common law character-istics is the specific statutory scheme of patent infringement found in the Patent Act.

In particular, Section 271(a) of the Patent Act imposes direct infringe-ment liability on "whoever without authority makes, uses, offers to sell, or sells any patented invention, within the United States or imports into the United States any patented invention during the term of the patent thereof … ."[28] Section 271(a) has no intent element and so direct patent infringement is a strict liability offense.[29] While a defendant's lack of willfulness or lack of bad faith may affect the availability of enhanced damages under the Patent Act,[30] it does not mitigate the imposition of liability itself.

The Patent Act also contemplates two forms of indirect infringement liability (only one of which, inducement of infringement, is relevant to officer liability).[31] Neither form of indirect infringement can exist in the absence of direct infringement by another.[32] Section 271(b) addresses inducement of infringement and provides: "Whoever actively induces infringement of a patent shall be liable as an infringer."[33] The courts interpret this language as encompassing a broad range of actions, such as licensing, indemnification of third parties for infringement, design or purchase of infringing items, and repair or maintenance of infringing items.[34] Unlike the strict liability of direct infringement, inducement of infringement has an intent element.[35]

---

[27]   *See, e.g.*, Carbice Corp. of Am. v. Am. Patents Dev. Corp., 283 U.S. 27, 33 (1931).

[28]   35 U.S.C. § 271(a) (2012).

[29]   *See, e.g.*, Global-Tech Appliances, Inc. v. SEB S.A., 131 S. Ct. 2060, 2065 n.2 (2011); Jurgens v. CBK, Ltd., 80 F.3d 1566, 1570 n.2 (Fed. Cir. 1996).

[30]   *See* 35 U.S.C. § 284 (2012).

[31]   Contributory infringement is addressed in 35 U.S.C. § 271(c). While it has a knowledge requirement, § 271(c) focuses more on the nature of the item sold than upon the status of the seller, and thus is not discussed further in this chapter.

[32]   *See, e.g.*, Limelight Networks, Inc. v. Akamai Techs., Inc., 134 S.Ct. 2111, 2117 and n.3 (2014).

[33]   35 U.S.C. § 271(b) (2012).

[34]   *See* 17 DONALD S. CHISUM, CHISUM ON PATENTS § 17.04[4] (2012) (citing cases).

[35]   *See Global-Tech Appliances*, 131 S. Ct. at 2068-69.

B. The Development of Officer Patent Infringement Doctrine

While most federal law issues go to the regional circuit courts of appeal, which have general jurisdiction,[36] patent cases fall under the specialized jurisdiction of the Federal Circuit. The creation of this specialized appellate court on October 1, 1982 has had profound effects upon the development of patent infringement doctrine, including officer liability doctrine.

Two characteristics in particular distinguish the Federal Circuit from its sister circuits. First, unlike the regional circuit courts, the Federal Circuit's jurisdiction is based solely on subject matter; geography plays no role. Second, the Federal Circuit has exclusive, nationwide jurisdiction over that subject matter. These subject matters include, in addition to patents, international trade, government contracts, certain trademark issues, federal personnel issues, veteran's benefits, and public safety officers' benefit claims.[37] Patent cases now form the largest segment of the Federal Circuit's caseload, comprising 47 percent, or almost one-half, of the appeals filed before the Federal Circuit in FY 2013.[38] The next largest category of cases pertained to personnel actions, which comprised only 17 percent of the total number of appeals filed.[39] It is not surprising, therefore, that the Federal Circuit is often viewed as a "patent court."[40]

The development of the rules pertaining to the individual liability of corporate officers for patent infringement can be broken into two temporal segments: before and after formation of the Federal Circuit in 1982. Pre-Federal Circuit doctrine coalesced around traditional agency, tort, and corporate law rules. Federal Circuit doctrine, by contrast, has taken a wrong turn toward holding corporate officers individually liable under theories more appropriately applied to corporate owners.[41]

---

[36] *See* www.uscourts.gov/FederalCourts.aspx (describing current configuration of federal courts) (last visited Sept. 8, 2014).

[37] 28 U.S.C. § 1295 (2012).

[38] *Statistics, Caseload by Category, Appeals Filed, 2013,* U.S. COURT OF APPEALS FOR THE FEDERAL CIRCUIT (2012), at www.cafc.uscourts.gov/the-court/statistics.html (last visited Sept. 8, 2014).

[39] *Ibid.*

[40] Paul R. Gugliuzza, *Rethinking Federal Circuit Jurisdiction,* 100 GEO. L.J. 1437, 1455 (2012).

[41] *See generally* Ronald B. Coolley, *Personal Liability of Corporate Officers and Directors for Infringement of Intellectual* Property, 68 J. PAT. & TM. OFF. SOC'Y 228 (1986); Oswald, *supra* note 7.

1. Pre-Federal Circuit liability rules

Prior to the creation of the Federal Circuit in 1982, the leading case on officer liability for patent infringement was *Dangler v. Imperial Machine Co.*,[42] decided by the Seventh Circuit in 1926. The *Dangler* court noted that the rules regarding personal liability of officers for patent infringement were confused and unclear.[43] Plaintiffs "seldom sought" to hold individual officers liable unless the corporation itself was insolvent,[44] and courts generally imposed liability only where the officers "acted outside the scope of their official duties."[45]

Dangler was the stereotypical case: the defendant corporation declared bankruptcy soon after the trial court found that the patent was valid and had been infringed, causing the patent owner to look for other parties from whom to recover. The two individual defendants were the president and secretary of the corporation; between them, they owned "nearly" 40 percent of the corporation's stock. The plaintiff contended that the individual officers should be held personally liable because they had operated the corporation as a shell.[46]

The Seventh Circuit disagreed, finding that managing officers of corporations were generally not liable for the patent infringement of the corporation even if the infringement was "committed under their general direction."[47] However, the *Dangler* court went on to state that an officer could be held jointly liable with the corporation based upon his or her own acts:

> It is when an officer acts willfully and knowingly – that is, when he personally participates in the manufacture or sale of the infringing article (acts other than an officer), or when he uses the corporation as an instrument to carry out his own willful and deliberate infringements, or when he knowingly uses an irresponsible corporation with the purpose of avoiding personal liability – that officers are held jointly liable with the company.[48]

The officers in *Dangler* were not held liable because the corporation was "a bona fide corporation" active in a field in which there were numerous patents (thus making it difficult for the corporation to evaluate whether

---

[42]   11 F.2d 945 (7th Cir. 1926).
[43]   *Ibid.* at 946.
[44]   *Ibid.* at 947.
[45]   *Ibid.*
[46]   *Ibid.* at 945–47.
[47]   *Ibid.* at 947.
[48]   *Ibid.*

its actions might infringe), and the corporation had sought appropriate legal counsel before proceeding.[49]

Subsequent courts[50] adopted *Dangler*'s general rule that "in the absence of some special showing, the managing officers of a corporation are not liable for the infringements of such corporation, though committed under their general direction."[51] The *Dangler* rule did not insulate officers from individual liability, however, and there were several cases in which an officer was held personally liable for infringement based upon his or her actions as a "moving force" behind the infringement,[52] or because of his or her deliberate participation in the infringing acts.[53]

2. Post-1982: the development of Federal Circuit doctrine

a. Early Federal Circuit cases: erroneous adoption of piercing analysis
Officer liability issues came before the Federal Circuit soon after its creation, and just as quickly took a wrong analytical turn that persists to today. In the first such case, Orthokinetics, Inc. v. Safety Travel Chairs, Inc.,[54] the Federal Circuit found that three individuals, all officers and shareholders of two corporations accused of infringement, could be held individually liable for direct infringement and for inducement of infringement.[55]

The *Orthokinetics* court began by examining the officers' liability for direct infringement under Section 271(a) of the Patent Act, making two conflicting statements with regard to such liability. On the one hand, the court correctly stated that "[i]nfringement is a tort and officers of a corporation are personally liable for tortious conduct of the corporation if they personally took part in the commission of the tort or specifically

---

[49]　*Ibid.* at 948.

[50]　*See, e.g.*, White v. Mar-Bel, Inc., 509 F.2d 287, 292-93 (5th Cir. 1975); Telling v. Bellows-Claude Neon Co., 77 F.2d 584, 586 (6th Cir. 1935); Dean Rubber Mfg. Co. v. Killian, 106 F.2d 316, 320 (8th Cir. 1939); Southwestern Tool Co. v. Hughes Tool Co., 98 F.2d 42, 46 (10th Cir. 1938).

[51]　11 F.2d at 947.

[52]　*See, e.g., White*, 509 F.2d at 292.

[53]　*See, e.g.*, Bewal, Inc. v. Minnesota Mining & Mfg. Co., 292 F.2d 159, 167 (10th Cir. 1961); Weller Mfg. Co. v. Wen Prods. Inc., 231 F.2d 795, 801 (7th Cir. 1956); Southwestern Tool Co. v. Hughes Tool Co., 98 F.2d 42, 45–46 (10th Cir. 1938).

[54]　806 F.2d 1565 (Fed. Cir. 1986).

[55]　*Ibid.* at 1578.

directed other officers, agents, or employees of the corporation to commit the tortious act."[56]

On the other hand, the *Orthokinetics* court went on to state that evaluating the personal liability of corporate officers "under § 271(a) requires invocation of those general principles relating to piercing the corporate veil."[57] In doing so, the court muddled doctrine relating to owner liability (piercing) with that relating to officer liability (personal participation). Moreover, the court's recitation of the facts indicated that the court did not give sufficient weight to the different roles that individuals can play within a corporation – i.e., as shareholders (owners) and managers (officers) – and the differing standards of liability that should apply to each such role. For example, the court emphasized that the individuals were the sole owners of the corporations at issue, yet did not discuss evidence of abuse of the corporate form that would permit the court to pierce the corporate veil and hold those individuals personally liable. Rather, the court emphasized that the individuals "were directly responsible for the design and production of the infringing [products] and that they were the only ones who stood to benefit from sales of those [products]."[58]

However, the mere fact that a corporate *owner* is in a position to financially benefit from the sale of an infringing device is insufficient grounds to impose liability upon him or her.[59] The relevance of monetary benefit is even more attenuated in the *officer* liability context, where every officer can be said to benefit from the corporation's profitability and financial stability, if only in the sense of an enhanced likelihood of employment, but where the officer has no direct claim on the corporation's profits, as would a shareholder.

The *Orthokinetics* court's consideration of the individual's "direct[] responsib[ility] for the design and production of the infringing"[60] items is equally perplexing. Although direct participation in a tortious act can lead to individual officer liability, the *Orthokinetics* court seemed to ground its analysis in the individuals' authority as officers to control the corporation's acts. In so doing, the *Orthokinetics* court opened the door to a broad statement of officer liability, as officers always have the authority to control the corporation.

---

[56]   *Ibid.* at 1579 (citation omitted).
[57]   *Ibid.*
[58]   *Ibid.*
[59]   *Oswald, supra* note 7, at 132.
[60]   806 F.2d at 1579.

The *Orthokinetics* court then turned its attention to the officers' liability for indirect infringement under Section 271(b), once again incorrectly interjecting corporate *owner* liability standards into corporate *officer* liability analysis. The court stated: "it is well settled that corporate officers who actively aid and abet their corporation's infringement may be personally liable for inducing infringement under § 271(b) regardless of whether the corporation is the alter ego of the corporate officer."[61] This, of course, suggests that an officer *can* be the alter ego of the corporation: the alter ego theory, however, requires a "unity of interest and ownership" held only by corporate owners.[62] Certainly, an officer can be liable for inducement of infringement under Section 271(b), but that liability is grounded in the officer's own acts of aiding and abetting direct infringement by the corporation, and requires a showing of intent.

The *Orthokinetic* court's erroneous adoption of piercing analysis and alter ego theory to reach corporate officers quickly took firm root in Federal Circuit case law. In *Manville Sales Corp. v. Paramount Systems, Inc.*,[63] in 1990, the court found that two corporate officers were not liable for direct infringement under Section 271(a) because the required "evidence to justify piercing the corporate veil" was not present,[64] and that the district court had erred in imposing individual liability upon the officers even though the district court had found that the officers were not the alter ego of the corporation.[65]

The Federal Circuit made an incomplete and short-lived attempt to correct its wrong course on officer liability in *Hoover Group, Inc. v. Custom Metalcraft, Inc.*[66] in 1996, where it noted that when an officer is acting within the scope of his or her responsibility, those acts "are not always sufficient grounds for penetrating the corporate protection and imposing personal liability,"[67] and that piercing the corporate veil to impose personal liability upon officers was appropriate "only in limited circumstances."[68] Rather, the *Hoover Group* court stated: "when a person *in a control position* causes the corporation to commit a civil wrong, imposition of personal liability requires consideration of the nature of the wrong, the culpability of the act, and whether the person acted in his/her

---

[61]   *Ibid.* at 1578–79.
[62]   *Automotriz*, 306 P.2d at 3–4.
[63]   917 F.2d 544 (Fed. Cir. 1990).
[64]   *Ibid.* at 552.
[65]   *Ibid.* (citation omitted).
[66]   84 F.3d 1408 (Fed. Cir. 1996).
[67]   *Ibid.* at 1411 (citing *Manville*, 917 F.2d at 553).
[68]   *Ibid.*

personal interest or in that of the corporation."[69] Rather than completely backing away from the statements in *Orthokinetics* and *Manville* that individual liability can only be based in a piercing of the corporate veil, however, the *Hoover Group* court found that individual officer liability for direct infringement under Section 271(a) could be based in either a piercing of the corporate veil or personal participation by the corporate officer[70] – effectively, getting only one-half of the analysis correct.

The Federal Circuit's next foray into officer liability, in *Al-Site Corp. v. VSI Int'l, Inc.*,[71] decided in 1999, returned Federal Circuit doctrine firmly back to the erroneous precedents set in *Orthokinetics* and *Manville*. According to the *Al-Site Corp.* court, "[p]ersonal liability under § 271(a) ... requires sufficient evidence to justify piercing the corporate veil,"[72] and "[t]he most common reason" for ignoring the corporate form is that the "corporation was merely the alter ego of its officers."[73] The court noted that the chairman and chief executive officer had "made the sole decision" to continue the allegedly infringing activity after the corporation had received a 'cease and desist' letter from the plaintiff,[74] but that he did so in "a good faith belief of noninfringement engendered by advice of counsel."[75] This, the Federal Circuit concluded, was insufficient to demonstrate that the corporation operated as the officer's "alter ego" or to support a piercing of the corporate veil.[76]

b.   Recent Federal Circuit decisions: solidifying incorrect officer liability doctrine   The damaging, and seemingly permanent, legacy of the wrong path initiated by the Orthokinetics court can be seen in recent Federal Circuit cases. For example, in *Wechsler v. Macke Int'l Trade, Inc.*,[77] decided in 2007, the Federal Circuit failed to explicitly discuss the distinction between owner and officer liability in evaluating individual patent infringement liability. Anthony O'Rourke was the president, sole stockholder, and sole employee of Macke International Trade, Inc.[78]

---

[69]   *Ibid.* (emphasis added) (citation omitted).
[70]   84 F.3d at 1411–12.
[71]   174 F.3d 1308 (Fed. Cir. 1999).
[72]   *Ibid.* at 1331 (citing *Manville*, 917 F.2d at 552).
[73]   *Ibid.* (quoting *Manville*, 917 F.2d at 552).
[74]   *Ibid.* at 1331.
[75]   *Ibid.*
[76]   *Ibid.*
[77]   486 F.3d 1286 (Fed. Cir. 2007), *appeal withdrawn*, 274 Fed. Appx. 870 (Fed. Cir. 2008).
[78]   *Ibid.* at 1289.

Because corporate, agency, and tort doctrines (including alter ego doctrine) are state law issues and not unique to patent law, the Federal Circuit applies the law of the regional circuit in which the case originated (here, the Ninth Circuit).[79] The Ninth Circuit, in turn, applies the law of the forum state (here, California).[80] California's jurisprudence regards application of the alter ego doctrine as an extraordinary measure and applies it "only reluctantly and cautiously,"[81] requiring both "a unity of interest and ownership [such] that the individuality, or separateness, of the said person and the corporation has ceased," and a finding that "an adherence to the fiction of the separate existence of the corporation would ... sanction a fraud or promote injustice."[82]

The plaintiff put forth five arguments in support of piercing: (1) the corporation was undercapitalized; (2) O'Rourke as an individual held the assets while the corporation held the liabilities; (3) O'Rourke treated corporate assets as his own; (4) O'Rourke held himself out as liable for the corporation's debts; and (5) O'Rourke used the corporate identity to defraud creditors.[83]

The *Wechsler* court's analysis correctly applied piercing analysis to O'Rourke in his role as a shareholder. However, the plaintiff lumped owner and officer liability together, and the court never drew the explicit distinctions that would clarify that: (1) piercing and alter ego doctrine were relevant to O'Rourke only in his status as a corporate owner; and (2) any liability that might attach to him in his role as a corporate officer would have to be based on personal participation. Ultimately, the appellate court found that none of these assertions raised a genuine issue of material fact,[84] and affirmed the trial court's grant of summary judgment.[85]

In 2010, a chink in the Federal Circuit's piercing doctrine emerged in *Wordtech Systems, Inc. v. Integrated Networks Solutions, Inc.*,[86] where the court hinted at the problematic nature of its precedent regarding application of piercing to officers. The corporation was a small family business, managed by two individuals, both of whom denied that they

---

[79] *Ibid.* at 1295 (citations omitted).
[80] *Ibid.* (citation omitted).
[81] *Ibid.* (citation omitted).
[82] *Ibid.* (citation omitted) (ellipses in *Wechsler*).
[83] *Ibid.*
[84] *Ibid.* at 1295.
[85] *Ibid.* at 1297.
[86] 609 F.3d 1308 (Fed. Cir. 2010).

were officers but admitted that they ran the company.[87] The Federal Circuit found that the trial court had erred in failing to provide jury instructions on piercing of the corporate veil[88] – and piercing, under Federal Circuit precedent, was necessary to impose direct liability upon individual officers under Section 271(a).[89] The *Wordtech* court noted in a footnote that commentators have argued that veil piercing does not apply to officers,[90] but found that it could not address that issue in the case before it because unless and until this issue is raised and addressed *en banc* by the Federal Circuit, panels are bound by previous precedential decisions. The *Wordtech* court then stated that "[t]he corporate veil can shield officers from liability under § 271(a),"[91] but that "corporate officers who actively assist with their corporation's infringement may be personally liable for inducing infringement *regardless* of whether the circumstances are such that a court should disregard the corporate entity and pierce the corporate veil."[92] The court highlighted, in a footnote, its discomfort with the differing rules for officer liability under Section 271(a) (which requires piercing) and Section 271(b) (which does not) as well as the differing treatment of officer and owner liability under existing precedent, but noted that the issues were "left for another day."[93]

The Federal Circuit's most recent discussion of individual officer liability for patent infringement came in *Hall v. Bed Bath & Beyond, Inc.*[94] in 2013. The plaintiff alleged inducement of infringement by the Vice-President/General Merchandise Manager. The plaintiff cited *Orthokinetics'* language that "it is well settled that corporate officers who actively aid and abet their corporation's infringement may be personally liable for inducing infringement under § 271(b) regardless of whether the corporation is the alter ego of the corporate officer."[95] However, the *Hall* court rejected the imposition of liability on the officer on the basis of New York veil-piercing doctrine, which requires a "two-part showing: (i) that the *owner* exercised complete domination over the corporation with respect to the transaction at issue; and (ii) that such domination was used to commit a fraud or wrong that injured the party seeking to pierce

---

87   *Ibid.* at 1311.
88   *Ibid.* at 1314.
89   *Ibid.* at 1313 (citing *Orthokinetics*, 806 F.2d at 1579).
90   *Ibid.* at n.2 (citing, *inter alia*, Oswald, *supra* note 7, at 130).
91   *Ibid.* at 1315–16.
92   *Ibid.* at 1316 (citing *Manville*, 917 F.2d at 553; *Hoover*, 84 F.3d at 1412).
93   *Ibid.* at 1316 n.3.
94   705 F.3d 1357 (Fed. Cir. 2013).
95   *Ibid.* at 1365 (quoting *Orthokinetics*, 806 F.2d at 1578-79).

the veil."[96] Thus, the New York doctrine itself revealed that veil-piercing relates to owner liability, not officer liability, and thus was inapposite to the case before the court. Ultimately, the Federal Circuit did not reach the merits of this argument but affirmed the district court's dismissal of the action against the individual on the grounds that the allegedly infringing activity by the individual had occurred *before* the patent had issued and thus was not actionable.[97]

III. INDIVIDUAL OFFICER LIABILITY FOR COPYRIGHT INFRINGEMENT

Individual officer liability in the copyright arena has received less scholarly attention than in the patent arena. This is likely to be at least in part because the courts house officer liability for copyright infringement in vicarious liability, which, on its face at least, appears to be a more doctrinally sound theory. However, closer examination reveals that the vicarious liability theory used for officer liability for copyright infringement also rests on shaky theoretical foundations.

In many ways, copyright infringement looks similar to patent infringement. Infringement of the copyright is a tort, and the copyright infringer is a tortfeasor.[98] However, while appeals in patent cases are heard by a specialized intermediate appellate court – the Federal Circuit – appeals in copyright cases go to the regional circuit courts of appeal. Because the regional circuit courts are generalist, not specialized, courts, they hear cases across a more diverse range of topics and are far more likely than the Federal Circuit to hear cases posing issues of traditional corporate, agency, and tort law concepts. This suggests that the regional circuits should be more adept than the Federal Circuit in correctly applying traditional doctrine to federal intellectual property issues. In fact, however, while courts seldom turn to application of the clearly erroneous piercing doctrine to hold corporate officers liable for copyright infringement, copyright infringement cases do reveal other articulations of officer liability that are at odds with traditional doctrine.

---

[96] *Ibid.* (emphasis added) (quoting Am. Fuel Corp. v. Utah Energy Dev. Co., 122 F.2d 130, 134 (2d Cir. 1997)).

[97] *Ibid.*

[98] *See* Ted Browne Music Co. v. Fowler, 290 F. 751, 754 (2d Cir. 1923).

A.   Infringement Liability under Copyright Law

As in patent law, it is not difficult in copyright law to impute infringement liability for the acts of officers to the corporation, invoking *respondeat superior* to hold the master (i.e., the corporation) liable for the infringing acts of the agent (i.e., the employee or officer).[99] The more difficult and provocative question in copyright law, like patent law, is under which circumstances should the *officer* be held individually liable for infringement.

The statutory language of the Copyright Act imposes direct infringement liability upon actors who engage in infringing actions under the Copyright Act,[100] such as reproduction, distribution, or copying.[101] Direct copyright infringement, like direct patent infringement, is a strict liability.[102]

However, unlike the Patent Act, the Copyright Act defines only direct infringement statutorily.[103] The absence of explicit statutory language has caused indirect copyright infringement to evolve through the courts in a messy and chaotic manner, as the courts have drawn upon both general tort and agency doctrine and have analogized to statutory patent infringement liability.[104] Indirect liability for copyright infringement now takes one of two forms: (1) "vicarious liability," which imposes liability upon a party who "has the right and ability to supervise the infringing activity and also has a direct financial interest in such activities,"[105] and (2) "contributory infringement," which imposes liability upon a party who has "knowledge of the infringing activity [and] induces, causes or materially contributes to the infringing conduct of another."[106]

---

[99]   *See* Fonovisa, Inc. v. Cherry Auction, Inc., 76 F.3d 259, 261-62 (9th Cir. 1996).

[100]   15 U.S.C. § 501(a) (2012) ("Anyone who violates any of the exclusive rights of the copyright owner... is an infringer of the copyright ... .").

[101]   *See ibid.* § 106.

[102]   *See* Educ. Testing Serv. v. Simon, 95 F. Supp. 2d 1081, 1087 (C.D. Cal. 1999).

[103]   *See* 15 U.S.C. § 501(a) (2012).

[104]   *See* Sony Corp. of Am. v. Universal City Studios, Inc., 464 U.S. 417, 439 (1984) (noting that it was "appropriate" to refer to patent liability rules in developing copyright vicarious liability rules "because of the historic kinship between patent law and copyright law").

[105]   Gershwin Publ'g Corp. v. Columbia Artists Mgmt., Inc., 443 F.2d 1159, 1162 (2d Cir. 1971) (citations omitted).

[106]   *Ibid.* (footnote omitted).

Overall, vicarious liability doctrine in the copyright cases "evidence[s] no grand principle in the making, nor even a distinct doctrine."[107] The modern articulation of vicarious liability as an explicit theory for indirect copyright infringement liability stems from the leading case of *Shapiro, Bernstein & Co. v. H.L. Green Co.*, decided by the Second Circuit in 1963.[108] Faced with an allegation that a store that allowed a concessionaire to sell infringing copies of musical recordings on its premises should itself be held liable for infringement, the court noted that its inquiry was one of having "to trace, case by case, a pattern of business relationships which would render one person liable for the infringing conduct of another."[109] Ultimately, the court concluded:

> When the right and ability to supervise coalesce with an obvious and direct financial interest in the exploitation of copyrighted materials – even in the absence of actual knowledge that the copyright monopoly is being impaired – the purposes of copyright law may be best effectuated by the imposition of liability upon the beneficiary of that exploitation.[110]

The courts have since condensed the *H.L. Green Co.* court's statement into a concise, two-pronged test for vicarious copyright liability, finding that vicarious liability attaches when the defendant has: (1) "the right and ability to supervise the infringing activities"; and (2) "a direct financial interest in those activities."[111]

B. Officer Liability for Copyright Infringement

Individual officer liability for copyright infringement can arise in one of two ways. The first is actual participation in direct infringement, which arises from the language of the Copyright Act. The second, vicarious liability, arises from the case law and shows a disturbing deviation from traditional legal doctrine.

---

[107] Craig A. Grossman, *The Evolutionary Drift of Vicarious Liability and Contributory Infringement: From Interstitial Gap Filler to Arbiter of the Content Wars*, 58 SMU L. REV. 357, 361 (2005).

[108] 316 F.2d 304 (1963).

[109] *Ibid.* at 307.

[110] *Ibid.* citations omitted).

[111] Roy Export Co. Establishment v. Trs. of Columbia Univ., 344 F. Supp. 1350, 1352 (S.D.N.Y. 1972).

1. Direct copyright infringement

Theoretically, an officer can be held directly liable for copyright infringement based upon his or her own culpable actions – a principle that arises out of traditional tort liability notions.[112] In practice, only a few courts have used personal participation by a corporate officer to support imposition of direct copyright infringement liability upon the individual, usually with little analysis.

Bangkok Broadcasting & T.V. Co. Ltd. v. IPTV Corp.,[113] decided in 2010, is a rare example of an officer being held personally liable for direct copyright infringement. The court applied traditional tort doctrine in assessing officer liability, noting: "Under Ninth Circuit precedent, 'a corporate officer or director is, in general, personally liable for all torts which he authorizes or directs or in which he participates, notwithstanding that he acted as an agent of the corporation and not on his own behalf.'"[114] The court further explained that cases imposing individual liability upon corporate officers "have typically involved instances where the defendant was the 'guiding spirit' behind the wrongful conduct ... or the 'central figure' in the challenged corporate activity."[115] Here, the individual: (1) had been the CEO since the corporation's founding; (2) personally hired all employees, selected programming, and arranged distribution agreements; and (3) personally negotiated the license renewal agreement at issue in the case.[116] Thus, the CEO was held jointly liable with the corporation for direct copyright infringement. The outcome in *Bangkok Broadcasting* is disturbing, for the acts of the officer that led to imposition of personal liability are the type of acts commonly undertaken by managers. Read on its face, the case would seem to be a troubling extension of personal liability to all officers engaged in normal officer activities: hiring, negotiating, and managing the firm.

The courts' reluctance to hold a corporate officer individually liable stems from the strict liability standard of direct copyright infringement. The implications of strict liability for corporate officers in the copyright area are much the same as in the patent area: the corporate officer, theoretically at least, can be held individually liable and without fault or intent for personal participation in the infringing behavior. This result is harsh, and so courts in the copyright area, as in the patent area, have

---

[112]   Screen Gems-Columbia Music, Inc. v. Mark-Fi Records, Inc., 256 F. Supp. 399, 403 (S.D.N.Y. 1966).
[113]   742 F. Supp. 2d 1101 (C.D. Cal. 2010).
[114]   *Ibid.* at 1114 (citations omitted).
[115]   *Ibid.* (citations omitted).
[116]   *Ibid.* at 1115.

turned to other mechanisms for assessing officer liability. While in patent law those alternative mechanisms are incorrect applications of piercing theory, in copyright law the mechanisms take the form of applying an expansive multi-factor test for evaluating such liability that is at odds with traditional doctrine.

2. Vicarious copyright infringement liability

In the copyright context, personal participation has become entwined in the vicarious liability standard, shifting personal participation from direct infringement liability to a form of indirect liability.

In 1976, the court in *Famous Music Corp. v. Bay State Harness Horse Racing & Breeding Assoc., Inc.*[117] identified the following situations in which the courts had imposed vicarious liability on individual officers for copyright infringement:

> (1) the officer personally participated in the actual infringement; or (2) the officer derived financial benefit from the infringing activities as either a major shareholder in the corporation, or through some other means such as receiving a percentage of the revenues from the activity giving rise to the infringement; or (3) the officer used the corporation as an instrument to carry out a deliberate infringement of copyright; or (4) the officer was the dominant influence in the corporation, and determined the policies which resulted in the infringement; or (5) on the basis of some combination of the above criteria.[118]

Interestingly, the *Famous Music* plaintiff was asserting that an officer should be held liable as a joint tortfeasor with the corporation for copyright infringement. Arguably, then, the *Famous Music* list should apply to *direct* copyright infringement – and certainly, some of the factors listed, such as personal participation, are more logical in that context. Subsequent cases, however, have transformed this list into a multi-factor test and have applied it to the evaluation of the *vicarious* liability of corporate officers, an indirect copyright infringement notion.[119]

On close examination, the *Famous Music* test is nonsensical. Because the factors are stated in the alternative – "*or*" – any one factor theoretically suffices to impose liability upon an individual actor. The

---

[117]   423 F. Supp. 341 (D. Mass. 1976), *aff'd*, 554 F.2d 1213 (1st Cir. 1977).

[118]   *Ibid.* at 344 (internal citations omitted).

[119]   *See, e.g.,* Emi Mills Music, Inc. v. Empress Hotel, Inc., 470 F. Supp. 2d 67, 74 (D. P.R. 2006); Marvin Music Co. v. BHC Lim Partnership, 830 F. Supp. 651, 655 (D. Mass. 1993).

implications of this are interesting. The first factor – personal participation – replicates the test for direct infringement liability, yet is adopted
here in the context of indirect infringement. The second factor – financial
benefit as a major shareholder – creates the potential for holding an
officer liable merely because he holds dual roles as an officer and an
owner. The third factor looks like a variant of the alter ego test, while the
fourth factor looks much like a "control" test. The second and fourth
factors, combined together, closely mimic the traditional two-pronged
test for vicarious liability.

In practice, the individuals against whom infringement liability is
sought under the *Famous Music* test tend to hold multiple roles within
the corporation. For example, in *Marvin Music Co. v. BHC Ltd. Partnership*,[120] BHC Corp. was the general partner of BHC Limited Partnership,
which in turn owned, controlled, and operated Club Café (at which
copyrighted music was performed and played without authorization).[121]
The defendant-officer held multiple roles; he was the president of the
corporation, a general partner of the limited partnership, and general
manager of Club Café.[122]

In analyzing the officer's vicarious liability as an individual, the court
adopted the *Famous Music* test, but also emphasized that he was, "at all
relevant times … an officer, shareholder and partner in the organizations
controlling" the club at which the allegedly infringing activities
occurred[123] (thus emphasizing the individual's multiple roles). The court
listed a number of activities the officer engaged in – control of day-to-
day operations, hire of musicians, direct engagement in licensing activities with ASCAP, knowledge of the license termination, and dominant
influence over club policies[124] – but did not discuss whether those
activities would suggest personal participation in the wrongful acts.

However, the *Marvin Music* court noted, the *Famous Music* test
addresses the scenario where an officer "derived financial benefit from
the infringing activities as either a major shareholder in the corporation,
or through some other means … ."[125] This factor does not rely upon a
piercing of the corporate veil, as does traditional corporate law doctrine
for imputing liability to shareholders. Rather, the inquiry focuses merely
on the financial benefit derived by the individual from the infringing

---

[120]   830 F. Supp. 2d 651 (D. Mass. 1993).
[121]   *Ibid.* at 653.
[122]   *Ibid.*
[123]   *Ibid.* at 655.
[124]   *Ibid.*
[125]   *Ibid.* at 654-55.

activity, regardless of the individual's role. In this instance, the court found, the *Famous Music* test was satisfied because the officer's "multiple roles in the club's management and ownership" provided him with "a substantial financial stake in the infringing activity."[126] Thus, the *Famous Music* test collapses the individual's separate roles as a shareholder and an officer into a single analysis that significantly broadens individual exposure to copyright infringement and significantly weakens the protections of the corporate form for small and closely-held corporations in particular.

By contrast, the district court in *Emi Mills Music, Inc. v. Empress Hotel, Inc.*,[127] found an officer vicariously liable under the *Famous Music* test without discussion of the source of the individual's financial benefit. The officer at issue was identified as the president and treasurer of a corporation accused of unauthorized public performance of copyrighted music; as such, he had "responsibility for the control, management operations and maintenance of the affairs" of the corporation.[128] However, he was not identified by the court as having any ownership interest in the corporation. Nonetheless, the court found him to be jointly and severally liable with the corporation for copyright infringement,[129] citing the second and fourth factors of the *Famous Music* test: (1) the individual's substantial financial stake in the infringing activity; and (2) the individual's dominant influence in the corporation and control over policies that led to infringement.[130] While under *Famous Music*, either element alone can suffice to support individual officer liability, it is unclear what financial benefit the *EMI Mills Music* court was looking to, other than mere employment by the hotel. To the extent that mere employment satisfies the second factor of the *Famous Music* test, all corporate officers are at risk of being held indirectly liable for copyright infringement.

Similarly, the individual at issue in *Disney Enterprises, Inc. v. Hotfile Corp.* was primarily a technical engineer, "responsible for implementing business ideas and functions" for the allegedly infringing corporation.[131] He actively participated in the corporation's management and decision-making,[132] although it was "undisputed" that he lacked "authority to

---

126   *Ibid.* at 655.
127   470 F. Supp. 2d 67 (D. P.R. 2006).
128   *Ibid.* at 74.
129   *Ibid.*
130   *Ibid.*
131   2013 U.S. Dist. LEXIS 172339, at *42 (S.D. Fla. Sept. 20, 2013).
132   *Ibid.* at *43.

make unilateral decisions regarding important aspects of [the corporation's] business or operations."[133] He held a power of attorney from the
corporation to act as manager of the company when "authorized to do so
by other shareholders,"[134] and wrote the source code that ran the
corporation's website and that was the basis for the allegations of
infringement against the corporation.[135]

The court acknowledged the individual's role as a shareholder of the
firm without discussing the relevance of such status.[136] Rather, the court's
analysis focused on actions that showed the individual's "participation,
control, and benefit" in the corporation's activities.[137] The court found
that the individual had both a "dominant influence upon the corporation"[138] and derived a financial benefit from the infringing activities,[139]
although it is unclear whether he derived those benefits in his role as a
shareholder rather than as an officer. If the financial benefit arose solely
from his status as a shareholder, that suggests that any active officer who
holds an ownership stake in the corporation is at risk of personal liability
– a substantial and unwarranted expansion of individual liability.

3.   Hints of piercing analysis in copyright cases

Noticeably absent from either the traditional two-pronged *H.L. Green*
vicarious liability test or the *Famous Music* test is any reference to a
piercing of the corporate veil. Thus, when the plaintiff in *White v.
Marshall*[140] argued that an individual should be held personally liable for
the corporation's allegedly infringing activities based upon "the role he
played – as an owner and manager in the corporation,"[141] the court
rejected the argument, explaining: "To 'pierce the corporate veil' is to
hold the *owners* of a corporation to be personally liable for the
corporation's liabilities."[142]

However, piercing notions seem to be creeping into a few copyright
officer liability cases. In 2010, in *Word Music, LLC v. Lynns Corp. of*

---

[133]   *Ibid.* at *44.
[134]   *Ibid.*
[135]   *Ibid.* at *43-44.
[136]   *Ibid.* at *141.
[137]   *Ibid.*
[138]   *Ibid.* at *144.
[139]   *Ibid.* at *143.
[140]   693 F. Supp. 2d 873 (E.D. Wis. 2009).
[141]   *Ibid.* at 885.
[142]   *Ibid.* (citations omitted) (emphasis added).

Am.,[143] for example, the officer argued that he could only be liable under a piercing analysis, citing *Orthokinetics*.[144] The court acknowledged that *Orthokinetics* was a patent infringement case, but then went on to apply it, noting that *Orthokinetics* recognized personal participation in a tort as grounds for liability, as well as piercing.[145] By comparison, the officer in *Word Music* was the "sole officer, director and shareholder" of the defendant corporation, was the "ultimate authority" for decision-making at the corporation with regard to advertising, distribution and sales, "personally participated" in the decision to sell infringing products, "personally benefitted financially" from the sales of infringing products, and was "the dominant influence in the corporation and determined the policies that resulted in infringement."[146] This, the *Word Music* court found, was sufficient to support imposition of direct infringement liability on the officer.

IV. OFFICER LIABILITY IN A STRICT LIABILITY REGIME

Something must be driving the appellate courts – both the regional circuits in the instance of copyright law and the Federal Circuit in the instance of patent law – down the wrong path. That "something" is mostly likely the courts' profound discomfort with the imposition of strict liability and its application to corporate officers. Direct infringement under both patent law and copyright law is based on strict liability and yet holding corporate officers strictly liable for infringement is fundamentally unfair and inconsistent not only with traditional corporate, agency, and tort law, but the underlying purposes of strict liability regimes.

A. Strict Liability Generally

Strict liability is generally defined as "liability that is imposed on an actor apart from either (1) an intent to interfere with a legally protected interest without a legal justification for doing so, or (2) a breach of a duty

---

143 2010 U.S. Dist. LEXIS 95559 (M.D. Tenn. Sept. 13, 2010).
144 *Ibid.* at *21.
145 *Ibid.* at *22.
146 *Ibid.* at *22-23.

to exercise reasonable care, i.e., actionable negligence."[147] Modern common law generally applies strict liability to very carefully defined actions, such as abnormally dangerous activities[148] or products liability.[149] Imposition of strict liability is guided by several policies and objectives, such as the promotion of fairness, economic efficiency, risk-spreading, and deterrence.[150] Although a full exploration of these policies is beyond the scope of this chapter, the basic principles underlying them can be summed up easily.

Fairness, in the strict liability setting, rests on the notion that where both parties are blameless, the one who created the risk of harm and enjoyed the benefit of the activity should bear any ensuing loss.[151] As explained by Richard Epstein, "as against an innocent plaintiff who has nothing to do with the creation of the harm in question, it is only too clear that the defendant who captures the entire benefit of his own activities should, to the extent that the law can make it so, also bear its entire costs."[152]

The economic efficiency arguments for strict liability rest on the notion that maximization of societal welfare and an efficient free market demand that firms and consumers bear the true costs associated with the activities that they undertake; i.e., costs should be "internalized."[153] Forcing a firm to bear all of the costs associated with its activities ensures that the price charged consumers will be a true price (e.g., costs will not be shunted off onto non-compensated injured parties), thus eliminating market distortions and inefficiencies.[154]

Strict liability can also assist in the spreading of risk. A firm forced to bear the costs of injuries occasioned by its activities can spread those risks among all consumers by raising prices enough to cover the liability. Each consumer can bear a small increase in price more easily than an

---

[147]   W. PAGE KEETON ET AL., PROSSER AND KEETON ON THE LAW OF TORTS § 75, at 534 (5th ed. 1984).

[148]   *See* RESTATEMENT (SECOND) OF TORTS § 519 (1) (1977).

[149]   *See* RESTATEMENT (THIRD) OF TORTS: PRODUCTS LIABILITY (1998).

[150]   *See* Lynda J. Oswald, *Strict Liability of Individuals Under CERCLA: A Normative Analysis*, 20 B.C. ENVT'AL AFF. L. REV. 579, 593-98 (1993).

[151]   This notion can be derived from the seminal case of *Rylands v. Fletcher*, 3 H. & C. 744, 159 Eng. Rep. 737, *rev'd*, L.R. 1 (Ex. 265), *aff'd*, L.R. 3 H.L. 330 (1868) (English & Irish Appeals).

[152]   RICHARD A. EPSTEIN, MODERN PRODUCTS LIABILITY Law 27 (1980).

[153]   *See* Barbara Ann White, *Economizing on the Sins of our Past: Cleaning up Our Hazardous Wastes*, 25 HOUS. L. REV. 899, 915-17 (1988).

[154]   *Ibid.* at 917.

injured party can bear the full costs of an uncompensated harm.[155] To the extent that the risk can be covered by insurance, it is generally easier (and thus more economically efficient) for the firm to obtain that insurance than the individual at risk of harm.[156]

Finally, strict liability is thought to promote deterrence. The party undertaking the activity that causes harm is in the best position to identify the accompanying risks and to take measures to minimize or eradicate that harm.[157] Thus, imposition of strict liability encourages these parties to structure their activities in such a way as to reduce the potential harm associated with their undertakings.[158] At a more pragmatic level, strict liability avoids the burdens of proof associated with a fault-based standard such as negligence.[159]

B. The Strict Liability of Officers for Patent or Copyright Infringement

These arguments for strict liability have limited applicability to the imposition of liability on corporate officers in the context of patent and copyright infringement. First, fairness dictates that where both parties are blameless, the party that created the harm and benefited from the activity should bear the risk. The benefit of copyright or patent infringement most directly accrues to the firm, not the corporate officer. Except for indirect benefits such as keeping his or her job or perhaps receiving compensation tied to the profits of the firm, the corporate officer does not receive the benefits of the activity that created the harm. Second, economic efficiency requires that the risk of harm be priced into a product so that the all costs are internalized. This is accomplished by imposing liability on the corporation and the imposition of additional or secondary liability on the corporate officer does not add to economic efficiency. Third, imposing liability on an individual corporate officer does not contribute to a sharing of risk. Risk sharing requires spreading the potential cost of harm among a wide class of beneficiaries (in this case, consumers and owners),

---

[155]   *See* Greenman v. Yuba Power Prods., Inc., 377 P.2d 897, 901 (Cal. 1963).

[156]   *See* Guido Calabresi, *Some Thoughts on Risk Distribution and the Law of Torts*, 70 YALE L. J. 499, 500-02, 543-44 (1961).

[157]   *See* Guido Calabresi and Jon T. Hirschoff, *Toward a Test for Strict Liability in Torts*, 81 YALE L. J. 1055, 1067-74 (1972).

[158]   *See* RICHARD A. POSNER, ECONOMIC ANALYSIS OF LAW § 6.5 (8th ed. 2011).

[159]   *See* Beshada v. Johns-Manville Prod. Corp., 447 A.2d 539, 548 (N.J. 1982); POSNER, *supra* note 158, § 6.5.

and is accomplished through pricing. Finally, imposing liability on corporate officers could promote deterrence, but only if the officer has both knowledge of the infringement and the ability to prevent it. Imposing strict liability on officers without knowledge or control can have no deterrent effect.

While the courts are willing to enforce the statutory strict liability schemes of direct patent and copyright infringement against corporations, they are more hesitant to impose such a harsh liability regime upon individual actors, such as officers. So, the courts have tried to devise alternatives that minimize the finding of direct infringement in both areas. In the patent law field, the courts have turned to concepts relating to piercing of the corporate veil to assess officer liability. The problem with this, of course, is that it not only rewrites traditional corporate doctrine, but it essentially eliminates the protection of the corporate form for small and closely-held firms, where individuals are likely to wear dual hats as owners and officers. In the copyright arena, the regional circuits have tended to avoid the application of direct infringement liability based on personal participation, and have instead turned to indirect forms of infringement liability. However, the courts analyze officer liability as a form of vicarious liability, yet vicarious liability is really a form of agency law that holds the master strictly liable for the torts of the servant. Moreover, the multi-factor test that the courts have articulated is a strange conglomeration of factors that suggests a desire to look to an officer's intent to infringe, yet is inartfully worded.

The correct result would be to avoid direct infringement liability in almost all instances for officer liability in both patent and copyright cases, on the ground that it is virtually impossible for an officer, in his or her role as an officer, to personally undertake the acts that result in patent or copyright infringement. The corporation is indeed the direct infringer in the vast majority of cases. That is not to say, however, that the officer should avoid liability in *every* instance. Rather, the officer's liability should be indirect, and should be supported by the appropriate test for such indirect infringement. In the patent arena, that is inducement of infringement, which has an explicit "intent" or *scienter* requirement. Similarly, officer liability for copyright infringement should be grounded in intent. The current, multi-factor, *Famous Music* test does a very poor job of teasing out the officer's intent, as it is not only framed in the alternative (as though only a single factor would suffice to establish liability), but it also seems to mix in notions of corporate ownership when it considers factors such as financial benefits as a major shareholder.

"Control" seems to offer the best proxy for evaluating the personal liability of an officer, and there are suggestions of the courts using this criterion in both the patent and copyright areas. To the extent that a corporate officer knew of the corporation's infringement or was "willfully blind" to it,[160] and the officer was in a position to direct and decide whether the corporation did in fact infringe, it would seem to fair to hold that officer personally liable. Indeed, the Federal Circuit seems to be implicitly seeking fairness by using piercing analysis, which, though inapposite in this context, is nonetheless an equitable doctrine, to assess personal liability.

It would not take a great leap in doctrine to reach this result under the existing "inducement of infringement" language in Section 271(b) of the Patent Act.[161] However, it would require a rewriting of the existing *Famous Music* vicarious liability test in the copyright field. Rewriting that test is warranted and easily accomplished. First, the *Famous Music* test is already specific to the corporate officer inquiry and is distinct from the general vicarious liability standard set forth in *H.L. Green Co.* The regional circuits have already established that officer liability requires a more specialized test than the general vicarious liability standard. In addition, there is already an established pattern of borrowing between patent and copyright doctrine; it seems eminently reasonable for copyright law to borrow from patent law in the officer liability area as well, particularly since there is no good reason to have different standards for evaluating officer liability in the patent and copyright fields. In short, the courts can reach the "fair" result they seem to be seeking in the officer liability field without completely jettisoning traditional doctrine.

V. CONCLUSION

The distinction between liability as a shareholder and liability as an officer seems clear on its face. However, in both the patent and copyright arenas, principles of officer liability deviate from traditional doctrine in ways that are inappropriate and that ignore the differences in the role of corporate officers and shareholders. While the differing statutory frameworks of patent and copyright law have caused officer liability in each area to devolve along different paths, in both areas, courts appear to have been motivated by a desire to limit inappropriate extension of strict

---

[160] Global-Tech Appliances, Inc. v. SEB S.A., 131 S. Ct. 2060, 2068-69 (2011).

[161] *See Oswald, supra* note 7, at 143–45.

liability to individual officers – but in both areas, they have gone about that effort in a manner that ignores traditional doctrine and that fails to provide corporate officers with appropriate protection from individual liability.

BIBLIOGRAPHY

Statutes and Codes

United States Code, 15 U.S.C. § 501(a) (2012).
United States Code, 28 U.S.C. § 1295 (2012).
United States Code, 35 U.S.C. § 271(a), (b), and (c) (2012).
United States Code, 35 U.S.C. § 284 (2012).
United States Code, Copyright Act of 1976, 15 U.S.C. §§ 1 *et seq.* (2012).
United States Code, Patent Act of 1952, 35 U.S.C. §§ 1 *et seq.* (2012).

Cases

Al-Site Corp. v. VSI Int'l, Inc., 174 F.3d 1308 (Fed. Cir. 1999).
Am. Fuel Corp. v. Utah Energy Dev. Co., 122 F.2d 130 (2d Cir. 1997).
Automotriz del Golfo de California S.A. de C.V. v. Resnick, 306 P.2d 1 (1957).
Bangkok Broadcasting & T.V. Co. Ltd. v. IPTV Corp., 742 F. Supp. 2d 1101 (C.D. Cal. 2010).
Beshada v. Johns-Manville Prod. Corp., 447 A.2d 539 (N.J. 1982).
Bewal, Inc. v. Minnesota Mining & Mfg. Co., 292 F.2d 159 (10th Cir. 1961).
Crigler v. Salac, 438 So.2d 1375 (Ala. 1983).
Dangler v. Imperial Machine Co., 11 F.2d 945 (7th Cir. 1926).
Dean Rubber Mfg. Co. v. Killian, 106 F.2d 316 (8th Cir. 1939).
Disney Enterprises, Inc. v. Hotfile Corp., 2013 U.S. Dist. LEXIS 172339 (S.D. Fla. Sept. 20, 2013).
Dole Food Co. v. Patrickson, 538 U.S. 468 (2003).
Donsco, Inc. v. Casper Corp., 587 F.2d 602 (3d Cir. 1978).
Dowagiac Mfg. Co. v. Minnesota Moline Plow Co., 235 U.S. 641 (1915).
Educ. Testing Serv. v. Simon, 95 F. Supp. 2d 1081 (C.D. Cal. 1999).
Emi Mills Music, Inc. v. Empress Hotel, Inc., 470 F. Supp. 2d 67 (D. P.R. 2006).
Famous Music Corp. v. Bay State Harness Horse Racing & Breeding Assoc., Inc., 423 F. Supp. 341 (D. Mass. 1976), *aff'd*, 554 F.2d 1213 (1st Cir. 1977).
Fish v. East, 114 F.2d 177 (10th Cir. 1940).
FMC Finance Corp. v. Murphree, 632 F.2d 413 (5th Cir. 1980).
Fonovisa, Inc. v. Cherry Auction, Inc., 76 F.3d 259 (9th Cir. 1996).
Gershwin Publ'g Corp. v. Columbia Artists Mgmt., Inc., 443 F.2d 1159 (2d Cir. 1971).
Global-Tech Appliances, Inc. v. SEB S.A., 131 S. Ct. 2060 (2011).
Greenman v. Yuba Power Prods., Inc., 377 P.2d 897 (Cal. 1963).
Hall v. Bed Bath & Beyond, Inc., 705 F.3d 1357 (Fed. Cir. 2013).
Hoover Group, Inc. v. Custom Metalcraft, Inc., 84 F.3d 1408 (Fed. Cir. 1996).
Jurgens v. CBK, Ltd., 80 F.3d 1566 (Fed. Cir. 1996).

Krivo Indus. Supply Co. v. Nat'l Distillers & Chem. Corp., 483 F.2d 1098 (5th Cir. 1973), *modified per curiam,* 490 F.2d 916 (5th Cir. 1974).

Limelight Networks, Inc. v. Akamai Techs., Inc., 134 S.Ct. 2111 (2014).

Manville Sales Corp. v. Paramount Systems, Inc., 917 F.2d 544 (Fed. Cir. 1990).

Marvin Music Co. v. BHC Lim Partnership, 830 F. Supp. 651 (D. Mass. 1993).

Murphy Tugboat Co. v. Shipowners & Merchants Towboat Co., 467 F. Supp. 841 (N.D. Cal. 1979), *aff'd,* 658 F.2d 1256 (9th Cir. 1981).

Orthokinetics, Inc. v. Safety Travel Chairs, Inc., 806 F.2d 1565 (Fed. Cir. 1986).

Poppenhusen v. New York Gutta Percha Comb Co., 19 F. Cas. 1059 (C.C.S.D. N.Y. 1858).

Roy Export Co. Establishment v. Trs. of Columbia Univ., 344 F. Supp. 1350 (S.D.N.Y. 1972).

Rylands v. Fletcher, 3 H. & C. 744, 159 Eng. Rep. 737, *rev'd,* L.R. 1 (Ex. 265), *aff'd,* L.R. 3 H.L. 330 (1868) (English & Irish Appeals).

Screen Gems-Columbia Music, Inc. v. Mark-Fi Records, Inc., 256 F. Supp. 399 (S.D.N.Y. 1966).

Shapiro, Bernstein & Co. v. H.L. Green Co., 316 F.2d 304 (1963).

Sony Corp. of Am. v. Universal City Studios, Inc., 464 U.S. 417 (1984).

Southwestern Tool Co. v. Hughes Tool Co., 98 F.2d 42 (10th Cir. 1938).

Strang v. Hollowell, 387 S.E.2d 664 (N.C. Ct. App. 1990).

Ted Browne Music Co. v. Fowler, 290 F. 751 (2d Cir. 1923).

Telling v. Bellows-Claude Neon Co., 77 F.2d 584 (6th Cir. 1935).

Walker v. Anderson, 232 S.W.3d 899 (Tex. App. 2007).

Wechsler v. Macke Int'l Trade, Inc., 486 F.3d 1286 (Fed. Cir. 2007), *appeal withdrawn,* 274 Fed. Appx. 870 (Fed. Cir. 2008).

Weller Mfg. Co. v. Wen Prods. Inc., 231 F.2d 795 (7th Cir. 1956).

White v. Mar-Bel, Inc., 509 F.2d 287 (5th Cir. 1975).

White v. Marshall, 693 F. Supp. 2d 873 (E.D. Wis. 2009).

Word Music, LLC v. Lynns Corp. of Am., 2010 U.S. Dist. LEXIS 95559 (M.D. Tenn. Sept. 13, 2010).

Wordtech Systems, Inc. v. Integrated Networks Solutions, Inc., 609 F.3d 1308 (Fed. Cir. 2010).

Secondary Sources

Calabresi, Guido, *Some Thoughts on Risk Distribution and the Law of Torts,* 70 YALE L. J. 499 (1961).

Calabresi, Guido and Jon T. Hirschoff, *Toward a Test for Strict Liability in Torts,* 81 YALE L. J. 1055 (1972).

CHISUM, DONALD S., CHISUM ON PATENTS (2012).

Coolley, Ronald B., *Personal Liability of Corporate Officers and Directors for Infringement of Intellectual* Property, 68 J. PAT. & TM. OFF. SOC'Y 228 (1986).

EPSTEIN, RICHARD A., MODERN PRODUCTS LIABILITY Law (1980).

Glynn, Timothy P., *Beyond "Unlimiting" Shareholder Liability: Vicarious Tort Liability for Corporate Officers,* 57 VAND. L. REV. 329 (2004).

Grossman, Craig A., *The Evolutionary Drift of Vicarious Liability and Contributory Infringement: From Interstitial Gap Filler to Arbiter of the Content Wars,* 58 SMU L. REV. 357 (2005).

Gugliuzza, Paul R., *Rethinking Federal Circuit Jurisdiction*, 100 GEO. L.J. 1437 (2012).

KEETON, W. PAGE ET AL., PROSSER & KEETON ON THE LAW OF TORTS (5th ed. 1984).

Lowenstein, Mark J., *Veil Piercing to Non-owners: A Practical and Theoretical Inquiry*, 41 SETON HALL L. REV. 839 (2011).

Oh, Peter B., *Veil-Piercing*, 89 TEX. L. REV. 81 (2010).

Oswald, Lynda J., *The Personal Liability of Corporate Officers for Patent Infringement*, 44 IDEA 115 (2003).

Oswald, Lynda J., *Strict Liability of Individuals Under CERCLA: A Normative Analysis*, 20 B.C. ENVT'AL AFF. L. REV. 579 (1993).

POSNER, RICHARD A., ECONOMIC ANALYSIS OF LAW (8th ed. 2011).

RESTATEMENT (SECOND) OF AGENCY (1958).

RESTATEMENT (SECOND) OF TORTS (1977).

RESTATEMENT (THIRD) OF TORTS: PRODUCTS LIABILITY (1998).

Statistics, Caseload by Category, Appeals Filed, 2013, U.S. COURT OF APPEALS FOR THE FEDERAL CIRCUIT (2012), at www.cafc.uscourts.gov/the-court/statistics.html (accessed Sept. 8, 2014).

Thompson, Robert B., *Piercing the Veil within Corporate Groups: Corporate Shareholders as Mere Investors*, 13 CONN. J. INT'L L. 379 (1999).

Thompson, Robert B., *Piercing the Corporate Veil: An Empirical Study*, 76 CORNELL L. REV. 1036 (1991).

White, Barbara Ann, *Economizing on the Sins of our Past: Cleaning up Our Hazardous Wastes*, 25 HOUS. L. REV. 899 (1988).

Wietjes, Jason A. and Michael D. Pegues, *Director and Officer Liability for Inducement of Patent Infringement*, 21 INTELLECTUAL PROPERTY LITIGATION, no. 2, at p. 3 (Winter 2010) (published by ABA Section of Litigation, Intellectual Property Litigation Committee).

www.uscourts.gov/FederalCourts.aspx.

2. Employee-created health care innovation at a crossroads

Julie Manning Magid

Innovation has nothing to do with how many R&D dollars you have … .
It's not about money. It's about the people you have,
how you're led, and how much you get it.[1]

In early 2012, Dr. Joseph Grocela, an urologist employed by Massachusetts General Hospital (MGH), invented a device for voice training that helps a musician harmonize and a singer to sing notes with more tonal precision.[2] Another use of the same device is to enable mute patients, such as people who have had a laryngectomy (a surgical removal of the larynx or voice box) to phonate. Dr. Grocela conceived of the "voice box invention" outside the hospital, on his own time, at his own expense, and the device is unrelated to the practice of urology.[3] However, MGH and its corporate parent, Partners HealthCare System, claimed ownership over the invention because Dr. Grocela signed an intellectual property agreement with the hospital that included an assignment of future inventions.[4]

The court ruled the intellectual property agreement valid as to Dr. Grocela's voice box invention despite the lack of connection between the invention and Dr. Grocela's specialty or the use of any hospital resources.[5] The court reasoned that the free sharing of staff inventions

---

[1] David Kirkpatrick, *The Second Coming of Apple,* FORTUNE, Nov. 9, 1998, *available at* http://money.cnn.com/magazines/fortune/fortune_archive/1998/11/09/250834 (quoting Steve Jobs describing how to innovate).

[2] Grocela v. Gen. Hosp. Corp., No. 120459, 2012 Mass. Super. LEXIS 206, at *5, (Mass. Super. July 12, 2012).

[3] *Ibid.* at *5–6.

[4] *Ibid.* However, Dr. Grocela conceded that the invention "utilizes or incorporates knowledge that [he] generated or acquired in the course of his clinical, research, educational, or other activities as a member of the professional staff at MGH." *Id.* at *6.

[5] *Ibid.* at *5.

benefited the patient population served by MGH and that Dr. Grocela received adequate compensation from the hospital and reaped the rewards of clinical resources, office space, access to patients and "professional prestige."[6]

Understanding innovation and, in particular, what motivates innovation in health care is increasingly important. Companies in the United States employing engineers and scientists require them, nearly universally, to assign their inventions to their employer.[7] Such assignments reflect a trend in many organizations that innovation should come from all employees at all times and that the organization "owns" any such innovation.[8] Now, that same phenomenon is occurring in the medical field as the proportion of physicians being employed by hospital systems increases to respond to the difficult provider market. For example, a 2012 survey by the American College of Cardiology showed that the percent of cardiologists employed by hospitals rose from 11 percent in 2007 to 35 percent in 2012.[9]

Will the new employment relationship between doctors and hospitals impact health care innovation? A key question for hospitals in remaining competitive in an increasingly challenging market is how to maximize intellectual property, an issue that combines patent law, the Bayh-Dole Act,[10] common law, and contract law with some important underlying employment considerations. Finally, policy consideration of maximizing innovation should examine global views on restrictive covenants, such as invention assignment agreements.

This chapter examines the changing landscape of health care in the context of employment and innovation. Part I of the chapter surveys the health care industry and the changes in incentives for innovation,

---

[6]   *Ibid.*

[7]   Parker Howell, *Whose Invention Is It Anyway? Employee Invention-Assignment Agreements and Their Limits*, 8 WASH J.L. TECH. & ARTS 79, 80 (2012).

[8]   Julian Birkinshaw, Cyril Bouquet and J.L. Barsoux, *The 5 Myths of Innovation*, 52 MIT SLOAN MGMT. REV. 43, 43 (2011) ("the new imperative is to view innovation as an "all the time, everywhere capability").

[9]   Press Release, Am. Coll. of Cardiology, New American College of Cardiology Practice Census Shows Continued Trend Towards Hospital Integration (September 10, 2012), *available at* www.cardiosource.org/News-Media/Media-Center/News-Releases/2012/09/Leg-Conf.aspx.

[10]   Pub. L. No. 96-517, 94 Stat. 3015 (1980) (codified as amended at 35 U.S.C. §§200-212 (2012)).

including the Affordable Care Act.[11] Part II then explores intellectual property created by agents and employees, and changes in patent law with the passage of the Leahy-Smith America Invents Act.[12] This part highlights the Bayh-Dole Act's crucial role in transforming innovation in research and teaching hospitals.

The final part of the chapter discusses the renewed importance of invention assignment agreements and contract law following the U.S. Supreme Court's decision in *Stanford v. Roche*.[13] Are effective assignment agreements vital in protecting innovation and containing health care costs? Do such agreements strike the best balance in motivating innovation or does the current trend value short-term monetization of intellectual property over long-term innovation? A brief discussion of the global perspective on invention assignment agreements and the legal avenues pursued in the global context to incentivize innovation is provided in Part III.

I. IMPLICATIONS OF A CHANGING HEALTH CARE LANDSCAPE

The impact of the health care industry on the economy of the United States is impressive. In 2012, aggregate spending on health care in the country represented 2.9 trillion dollars, or 17.9 percent of gross domestic product (GDP).[14] This is the highest percentage of GDP health care spending in the world.[15] The Health and Human Services Department expects that the health care share of GDP will continue its growth and reach 19.5 percent by 2021.[16] The spending is distributed 31 percent to

---

[11] Patient Protection and Affordable Care Act, Pub. L. No. 111-148, 124 Stat. 119 (2010) (codified as amended in scattered sections of the U.S.C.).

[12] Pub. L. No. 112-29, 125 Stat. 284 (2011) (codified in scattered sections of 35 U.S.C.).

[13] Bd. of Trs. of the Leland Stanford Junior Univ. v. Roche Molecular Sys., 131 S. Ct. 2188 (2011).

[14] Centers for Medicare and Medicaid Services, *National Health Expenditure Data*, National Healthcare Expenditure Projections 2012-2022, Table 1, *available at* https://www.cms.gov/Research-Statistics-Data-and-Systems/Statistics-Trends-and-Reports/NationalHealthExpendData/Downloads/Proj2012.pdf.

[15] Amitabh Chandra, Jonathan Holmes, and Jonathan Skinner, *Is This Time Different? The Slowdown in Healthcare Spending*, BROOKINGS PAPERS ON ECON. ACTIVITY, 261–62 (2013), *available at* http://www.brookings.edu/~/media/Projects/BPEA/Fall% 202013/2013b_chandra_healthcare_spending.pdf.

[16] *National Health Expenditure Data, supra* note 14 at Table 1.

hospital care, 20 percent to physician/clinical services, 10 percent to pharmaceuticals, 23 percent to home health care, nursing care or other personal health care, and 16 percent to administrative and other health care spending.[17]

Although there was a slowdown in growth of health care spending attributed to the recession in 2007–2010,[18] health care spending grew from 13.8 percent of GDP in 2000 to 17.9 percent of GDP in 2010.[19] A major factor in long-term health care spending growth is innovation in technology for new treatments and procedures and diffusion of existing technology.[20]

The health care industry was not always such a robust and dominant part of the U.S. economy. In 1929, it was a mere 3.5 percent of GDP.[21] By 1960 it had risen to 5.1 percent, a third of which was primarily for treatment of World War II veterans.[22] A period of rapid growth began after 1966 with the introduction of Medicare and Medicaid.[23] Costs tripled between 1970 and 1997. In 1980, expenditures comprised 7.9 percent of GDP; by 1997, they were 13.5 percent.[24]

---

[17]   Kaiser Family Foundation, *Healthcare Costs: A Primer*, 10 (2012), *available at* http://kaiserfamilyfoundation.files.wordpress.com/2013/01/7670-03.pdf. Other personal health care includes, for example, dental and other professional health services, and durable medical equipment. Other health spending includes public health activity, research, and structures and equipment. *Ibid.*

[18]   *See* Chandra, *supra* note 15, at 271 (citing other factors contributing to the slowdown in health care spending, including the Affordable Care Act implementation).

[19]   *Healthcare Costs: A Primer, supra* note 17, at Figure 1.

[20]   *Ibid* at 25.

[21]   Theodore Caplow, Louis Hicks and Ben J. Wattenberg, THE FIRST MEASURED CENTURY: AN ILLUSTRATED GUIDE TO TRENDS IN AMERICA, 1900–2000, 152 (2000).

[22]   *Ibid.*

[23]   Nina J. Crimm, *Evolutionary Forces: Changes in For-Profit and Not-For-Profit Health Care Delivery Structures; A Regeneration of Tax Exemption Standards*, 37 B.C. L. REV. 1, 18 (1995). The Medicare Act provides hospital and medical insurance for the aged and is financed by federal payroll taxes. Social Security Amendments of 1965, Pub. L. No. 89-97, § 102, 79 Stat. 286, 291–332 (1965) (current version at 42 U.S.C. §§ 1395–1395yy (2012)). The Medicaid Act provides matching federal funds for state medical assistance to the indigent. Social Security Amendments of 1965, Pub. L. No. 89-97, § 121, 79 Stat. 286, 343–52 (1965) (current version at 42 U.S.C. §§ 1396–1396v (2012)).

[24]   Caplow, *supra* note 21, at 152.

Beginning in 1929, concurrent with the onset of the Great Depression, a combination of three factors created a powerful force in the American health care system: privatized health care insurance.[25] First, due to the lack of support of health insurance by the American Medical Association, many people, particularly the poor, had little to no access to care.[26] Second, hospitals faced financial peril as a result of the Great Depression and were forced to find new ways to finance their services.[27] Third, Baylor University Hospital in Dallas, in order to raise revenue, offered a single hospital health insurance plan to schoolteachers in the area.[28] The plan was quickly replicated throughout the struggling hospital industry in the United States and by 1933 a number of innovative plans were offered by hospitals and related organizations.[29]

Private health insurance expanded following World War II and throughout the Post-War period with accelerating cost increases.[30] Despite these increases, attempts in both the legislative and executive branches of government to pass major health care reform met with little success. The changes in Medicare, Medicaid, and the passage of the Health Insurance Portability and Accountability Act (HIPAA) during this time were measured responses to significant health care cost issues.[31] The

---

[25] *See generally* Charles D. Weller, *"Free Choice" as a Restraint of Trade in American Health Care Delivery and Insurance,* 69 IOWA L. REV. 1351, 1360–62 (1984).

[26] *Ibid.* at 1362. The American Medical Association's resistance to group health insurance eventually resulted in its conviction for violating the Sherman Antitrust Act, 15 U.S.C. § 3 (1982). *See* Am. Med. Ass'n v. United States, 317 U.S. 519 (1943).

[27] Weller, *supra* note 25, at 1361.

[28] *Ibid.* at 1361 and n. 48.

[29] *Ibid.* at 1363. Although not necessarily embraced by all. *See ibid.* at 1364 ("These developments, however, were understandably threatening to the hospital and medical professions. They were particularly threatening to a profession built on a model of the individual solo practitioner in a period of scientific, social, and economic dislocation.").

[30] Crimm, *supra* note 23, at 15 ("As hospital and health care insurance coverage reached more people, demand for health care accelerated.").

[31] Health Insurance Portability and Accountability Act of 1996, Pub. L. No. 104–191, 110 Stat. 1936 (1996) (codified in scattered sections of 26 U.S.C.A., 29 U.S.C.A., & 42 U.S.C.A.) (HIPAA). These were relatively modest changes compared to the earlier enactments of Medicaid and Medicare. The defeat of President Clinton's health reform plan is one of the notable failures of health care reform during this time. *See* Laura D. Hermer, *Private Health Insurance in the United States: A Proposal for a More Functional System,* 6 HOUS. J. HEALTH L. & POL'Y 1, 53 (2005).

Patient Protection and Affordable Care Act of 2010 (ACA)[32] is the most significant attempt at reforming the U.S. health care system since the passage of Social Security and Medicare.[33] Some of the key effects of this law are: (1) the primary individual mandate;[34] (2) fundamental changes to the employee and health benefit plan market; (3) establishment of state health insurance exchanges; and (4) extension of Medicaid coverage.[35]

Just as hospitals needed to transform their relationship to financing patient care during the Great Depression, now hospitals must adjust to the changing health care landscape and increased costs of providing care, particularly the costs associated with technology such as innovations in new treatments and procedures.[36] A number of researchers who have examined the growth in health care spending in the United States conclude that it is the increased use and diffusion of innovation in treatments and procedures that drive cost.[37] The rate of use of sophisticated medical procedures in the United States outpaces the rate of use in all other countries.[38]

---

[32]   Pub. L. No. 111–148, 124 Stat. 119, amended by Health Care and Education Reconciliation Act of 2010, Pub. L. No. 111–152, 124 Stat. 1029 (codified as amended in scattered sections of 42 U.S.C.).

[33]   *See* Sarah Rosenbaum, *Realigning the Social Order: The Patient Protection and Affordable Care Act and the U.S. Health Insurance System*, 7 J. HEALTH & BIOMED. L. 1, 4 (2011) (noting that "contentiousness seems to be a basic ingredient of social welfare legislation").

[34]   *Ibid.* at 11–16 ("[T]he heart of the law is an individual mandate that requires "applicable" individuals to maintain "minimum essential health coverage" or face certain financial penalties.").

[35]   *Ibid.* at 11–16 (referring to these provisions as the "four pillars" of the ACA). It is beyond the scope of this chapter to discuss the ACA in depth. Rather, this chapter adopts an agnostic approach to it, characterizing the major changes to health care law as part of the historical evolution of health care in the United States that offers opportunities as well as challenges for those in the health care industry. For a discussion of the "bitter reception" of the ACA and the political aspects of its passage and implementation, see *ibid.* at 4–10.

[36]   Chandra, *supra* note 15, at 284–85.

[37]   Joseph Newhouse, *Medical Care Costs: How Much Welfare Loss?* 6 J. ECON. PERSP. 3, 3–21 (1992). Chandra, *supra* note 15, at 285.

[38]   Uwe E. Reinhardt, Peter S. Hussey & Gerard F. Anderson, *Cross-National Comparisons of Health Systems Using OECD Data, 1999,* HEALTH AFF. 169–182 (2002); Richard Rettig, *Medical Innovation Duels Cost Containment,* HEALTH AFF. 7–28 (1994); Joseph Newhouse, *An Iconoclastic View of Health Cost Containment,* HEALTH AFF. 152–71 (1993).

Such pervasive use of innovation in health care is associated with procedures of all kinds. For example, proton beam accelerators are used to treat prostate cancer patients and were projected to double in number between 2010 and 2014.[39] The cost of installation for each accelerator is hundreds of millions of dollars.[40] Even for technology that costs less for each item, such as cardiac stents to treat heart disease, if the use of the technology becomes the norm for a large number of patients, the impact on the cost of health care spending is significant. In the 1990s, the typical treatment for blockage in arteries was angioplasty, a balloon threaded into the artery and then expanded at the site of the blockage.[41] Later, cardiologists routinely utilized stents or multiple stents to widen narrow arteries. During the mid-2000s, several research trials questioned the benefits of cardiac stents in treatment of the most common type of heart disease. This led to a decline in the use of cardiac stents that impacted health care spending in both Medicare and the private insurance market and contributed to an overall decline in health care spending around 2004.[42]

Innovation in treatment and procedures and, more generally, the use of technology and technical equipment impacts the cost of health care overall. In response to the increased costs of providing care, as well as the decline in hospital use, hospitals are consolidating at a rapid pace.[43] This consolidation, in turn, may result in increasing consumer health care costs all the more.[44] Therefore, innovation in health care has the potential for broad patient benefits but also negative cost impact. The implications for innovation in the changing health care landscape require the industry to pursue innovation not just with an eye toward monetizing intellectual property but also toward transforming the industry to improve each hospital's value chain.

---

[39]   Chandra, *supra* note 15, at 286.

[40]   *Ibid.*

[41]   *Ibid.* at 279.

[42]   *Ibid.*

[43]   David M. Cutler and Fiona Scott Morton, *Hospitals, Market Share and Consolidation*, 310 J. AM. MED. ASS'N 1964, 1964 (2013). The authors note that many factors contribute to the consolidation trend, including the decline in hospital use. Between 1981 and 2011, hospital use as measured by inpatient days at short term acute hospitals declined by 33 percent despite the increase in population overall and the aging of the population. Coincident with the decline in number of days in hospitals, 15 percent of hospitals closed. *Ibid.* at 1965.

[44]   *Ibid.*

The hospital mergers that have become commonplace over the past decade not only reflect trends in innovation[45] but, in an effort to improve value chains, the mergers establish new employment relationships between hospitals and the physicians and health care practitioners who work there. With the implementation of the ACA, industry experts anticipate consolidation will increase.[46] Because the industry is seeing both horizontal consolidation and vertical consolidation,[47] there are important consequences to employment relationships in the health care industry. Moreover, many health systems now engage hospital employees in the process of innovation through academic medical centers. Often, hospitals now consist of a system built around one or more academic medical centers with community or short term acute centers supporting the academic medical center.[48]

Horizontal consolidation, or hospitals merging or acquiring other hospitals, typically results in hospitals becoming part of a health system. From 2007 to 2012, 432 hospital mergers and acquisitions were announced involving 835 hospitals.[49] Sixty percent of hospitals are now part of health systems, which is an increase of 7 percent in a decade.[50] In theory, the consolidation should result in cost savings for a hospital, but empirical studies show mixed results.[51] Often times, a larger hospital system with a flagship academic medical center has the market power to increase prices for medical procedures and hospital stays and, thus, fails to incorporate the full integration of the system that would lead to lower health care costs for consumers.[52]

Vertical consolidation within the health care industry has led to a marked increase in hospital ownership of physician practices. Data from the Medical Group Management Association (MGMA) surveys showed that the percentage of physicians working in practices owned by a hospital or integrated delivery system increased from 24 percent in 2004

---

[45]   Birkinshaw, *supra* note 8, at 43.
[46]   Cutler, *supra* note 43, at 1965.
[47]   *Ibid.*
[48]   *Ibid.* at 1964.
[49]   Center for Healthcare Economics and Policy, *Hospital Mergers and Acquisitions: 2007–June 2013*, available at http://www.aha.org/research/policy/2013.shtml.
[50]   Cutler *supra* note 43, at 1965.
[51]   *Ibid.* at 1967.
[52]   *Ibid.* ("[F]lagship academic medical centers offering perceived higher quality care often wield enormous market power... a patient who has a serious illness and also is well insured will seek out these hospitals with little regard for price.").

to 49 percent in 2011.[53] Although the American Medical Association takes issue with data suggesting close to 60 percent of physicians are now employed by hospitals,[54] there is no dispute that the trend is toward fewer physician-owned practices and more physicians employed by hospitals than ever before.[55] Just as in other industries that adopt an "everybody innovates" approach,[56] many hospitals hope that their newly acquired physician employees are the source of future innovation in health care that will offset the decrease in government payments under ACA.[57]

II. PROTECTING THE INVESTMENT IN HEALTH CARE INNOVATION

A. Statutory Protections

The Bayh-Dole Act[58] is known as "innovation's golden goose."[59] Prior to the Act, the patent laws of the United States, designed with an individual

---

[53]   Carol K. Kane and David W. Emmons, *New Data on Physician Practice Arrangements: Private Practice Remains Strong Despite Shifts Toward Hospital Employment*, POL'Y RESEARCH PERSP. 1, 1 (2013), *available at* http://www.nmms. org/sites/default/files/images/2013_9_23_ama_survey_prp-physician-practice-arrangements.pdf.

[54]   Donna Marbury, *AMA Says the Physician Exodus to Hospitals Overrated*, MED. ECON. (Sept. 23, 2013), *available at* http://medicaleconomics.modern medicine.com/medical-economics/news/ama-says-physician-exodus-hospitals-overrated.

[55]   *Ibid.* (citing a report by the American Hospital Association stating that the number of physicians employed by community hospitals increased by 32 percent between 2000 and 2012 and a survey conducted by Accenture concluding that only 36 percent of physicians would work at independent practices by the end of 2013). *See also* Abby Goodnough, *New Law's Demands on Doctors Have Many Seeking a Network,* N.Y. TIMES, A1 (March 3, 2014) *available at* http://www. nytimes.com/2014/03/03/us/new-laws-demands-on-doctors-have-many-seeking-a-network.html?_r=0.

[56]   Birkinshaw, *supra* note 8, at 43.

[57]   Max Nisen, *Hospitals Could Create the Next Big Wave of Healthcare Tech and Startups*, BUS. INSIDER (Jan. 3, 2013), *available at* http://www. businessinsider.com/innovation-coming-from-hospitals-2013-1.

[58]   Pub. L. No. 96–517, 94 Stat. 3015 (1980) (codified as amended at 35 U.S.C. §§200–212 (2012)).

[59]   *Innovation's Golden Goose*, ECONOMIST, Dec. 12, 2002, *available at* www.economist.com/node/1476653.

inventor in mind,[60] did not address the issue of the ownership of inventions that were created as part of employment.[61] Indeed, it is spelled out in the U.S. Constitution that protecting inventors is the best way to promote progress in science and useful arts.[62] Despite changes in the patent laws over time, the individual inventor, whether Henry Ford or Bill Gates, remains an important part of the American identity.[63]

One of the most widely discussed provisions of the most significant patent law reform in more than 50 years,[64] the Leahy-Smith America Invents Act[65] (AIA) relates to the law's impact on the individual inventor. The AIA changed the United States from a "first-to-invent" country to a "first-to-file" country,[66] thereby aligning U.S. patent law with most other patent systems throughout the world.[67] This change aroused controversy in the intellectual property community because it is perceived to favor

---

[60]   Richard A. Kamprath, *Patent Reversion: An Employee-Inventor's Second Bite at the Apple*, 11 CHI-KENT J. INTELL. PROP. 186, 189 (2012).

[61]   Toshiko Takenaka, *Serious Flaw of Employee Invention Ownership Under the Bayh-Dole Act in* Stanford v. Roche: *Finding the Missing Piece of the Puzzle in the German Employee Invention Act*, 20 TEX. INTELL. PROP. L.J. 281, 284 (2012).

[62]   U.S. CONST. art. I § 8 ("Congress shall have power ... to promote the progress of science and useful arts, by securing for limited times to authors and inventors the exclusive right to their respective writings and discoveries").

[63]   Kamprath, *supra* note 60, at 190 ("Our society has long recognized the intensely personal nature of an invention and the importance of providing stimulation and encouragement to inventors.").

[64]   Alexa L. Ashworth, *Race to the Patent Office! How the New Patent Reform Act will Affect Technology Transfer at Universities*, 23 ALB. L.J. SCI. & TECH. 383, 385 (2013).

[65]   Pub. L. No. 112–29, 125 Stat 284 (2011) (codified at 35 U.S.C. §§ 1–375).

[66]   Pub. L. No. 112–29, § 3, 125 Stat 284 (2011) (codified at 35 U.S.C. §§ 102). The section provides, in relevant part:

A person shall be entitled to a patent unless – (1) the claimed invention was patented, described in a printed publication, or in public use, on sale, or otherwise available to the public before the effective filing date of the claimed invention; or

(2) the claimed invention was described ... under section 122(b), in which the patent or application, as the case may be, names another inventor and was effectively filed before the effective filing date of the claimed invention.

[67]   Ashworth, *supra* note 64, at 395.

larger corporations and well-financed entities over the individual inventor. The concern is that corporations will quickly file patent applications to out-race the individual inventor.[68]

The change to a first-to-file system, taken in context with reduced filing fees for small and micro entities,[69] represents Congress' attempt to strike a balance that would protect intellectual property assets that are increasingly important to the domestic economy while creating more opportunities in the global economy.[70] However, if Steve Jobs is correct that it is not money that is required for innovation but rather well-managed people "who get it,"[71] proper incentives and motivation to invent still might be lacking.

The Bayh-Dole Act is a prime example of statutory changes that can spark interest in the investment and commercialization of technology. In the 1970s, there was growing concern that the era of American inventiveness, propelled by necessity during World War II, was over.[72] Production and investment in technology by U.S. corporations fell behind other countries, most notably Japan.[73] In 1980, Senators Bob Dole and Birch Bayh drafted the University and Small Business Procedures Act (commonly known as the Bayh-Dole Act) to "promote the utilization of inventions arising from federally supported research," "promote collaboration between commercial and non-profit organizations," and "ensure that the Government maintains sufficient rights in any supported inventions."[74]

To achieve its goals, the Bayh-Dole Act focused on federal funding agreements and the patentable products derived from research conducted

---

[68] *See, e.g.,* Kamprath, *supra* note 60, at n.5 ("This system favors those entities that can dedicate fiscal resources and personnel solely to creating patent application as fast as possible. Competing against large corporations and universities, America may well see the death of the individual inventor."); *Will The New Patent Laws Help or Hurt Small Businesses?*, N.Y. TIMES BLOGS (Feb. 8, 2012), http://boss.blogs.nytimes.com/2012/02/08/will-the-new-patent-laws-help-or-hurt-small-businesses/.

[69] Pub. L. No. 112–29, § 10, 125 Stat. 284, 31620 (2011) (codified at 35 U.S.C. § 123).

[70] Ashworth, *supra* note 64, at 395.

[71] Kirkpatrick, *supra* note 1.

[72] Parker Tresemer, *Best Practices for Drafting University Technology Assignment Agreements After* Filmtec, Stanford v. Roche, *and Patent Reform*, 2012 U. ILL. J.L. TECH. & POL'Y 347, 349 (2012).

[73] *Ibid.*

[74] Bd. of Trs. of the Leland Stanford Junior Univ. v. Roche Molecular Sys., 131 S. Ct. 2188, 2193 (2011).

under those funding agreements.[75] Universities and academic medical centers that participate in federally funded research were given incentives to collaborate with businesses and become involved in monetizing intellectual property to the financial benefit of the institutions. The institutions retained royalties derived from federally-funded research as long as any royalties were "utilized for the support of scientific research or education."[76] The Act does not grant the research institution complete rights to patentable products but, instead, establishes a hierarchical system that determines what entity or person has the right to retain title in the inventions produced from federal funding.

The first opportunity to retain title to federally-funded inventions developed by small businesses or not-for-profits belongs to those federal contractor organizations themselves.[77] If the federal contractor chooses not to retain title to the inventions, the federal government is next in line to take title to the inventions.[78] If the federal government also passes on the opportunity to retain title to inventions produced from the federal funding agreement, the individual employee-inventor working for the federal contractor has the right to sole title.[79]

If the federal contractor retains the rights to an invention, it commits to several key obligations including: reporting all "subject inventions,"[80] taking reasonable efforts to commercialize the invention through patenting or licensing, and granting the federal government a license to the subject invention.[81]

Medical researchers and the biotech industry are among those that laud the Bayh-Dole Act for its achievements in advancing biomedical research. One National Institute of Health (NIH) Report from 2001 stated: "Federally funded biomedical research, aided by the economic incentives of Bayh-Dole, has created the scientific capital of knowledge that fuels medical and biotechnology development."[82] Indeed, federal

---

[75]   35 U.S.C. § 201(b) (2012).

[76]   37 C.F.R. § 401.14 (2013).

[77]   35 U.S.C. § 202 (2013).

[78]   *See ibid.*

[79]   *See ibid.* § 203.

[80]   *Ibid.* § 201(e) ("The term 'subject invention' means any invention of the contractor conceived or first actually reduced to practice in the performance of work under a funding agreement ...").

[81]   Tresemer, *supra* note 72, at 357–58.

[82]   NIH Report, *A Plan to Ensure Taxpayers' Interests are Protected* (2001), *available at* http://www.ott.nih.gov/sites/default/files/documents/policy/wyden rpt.pdf.

contractor start-up companies created the entire biotechnology industry.[83] Although there are a few notable exceptions,[84] monetizing the inventions has proven to be a bigger challenge for the federal contractors involved in the federally-funded research, including academic medical centers. Technology transfer activity, such as invention disclosures, patent applications, patent issuances, and licenses, increased steadily following passage of the Act; however, the activity, more often than not, is a financial drain on academic centers rather than income generating.[85] In 2006, 52 percent of U.S. institutions spent more on technology transfer than the income generated from the activity.[86]

The difficulty with bringing patentable products to market and monetizing research to the financial benefit of the institution is not a failure of academic medical centers or universities uniquely. Research studies reveal that the difficulty with innovation is not the "good idea" but moving the idea through the process to revenue generation.[87] Effective restrictive covenants in contracts that the health care industry now utilizes extensively to secure intellectual property may help protect that "good idea" but little else. These restrictive covenants alone cannot motivate innovation as a process.[88]

B. *Stanford v. Roche* Interprets the Bayh-Dole Act

A recent U.S. Supreme Court decision challenged long-held interpretations of the Bayh-Dole Act and federal contractors' ability to secure intellectual property. Many commentators view the decision as tipping the delicate balance in the system of incentives created by the Bayh-Dole

---

[83] Vicki Loise and Ashley J. Stevens, *The Bayh-Dole Act Turns 30*, 30 SCI. TRANSL. MED. 52, 52 (2010).

[84] Richard Perez-Pena, *Patenting Their Discoveries Does not Pay Off for Most Universities, a Study Says*, N.Y. TIMES, Nov. 20, 2013, at A18, *available at* http://www.nytimes.com/2013/11/21/education/patenting-their-discoveries-does-not-pay-off-for-most-universities-a-study-says.html (noting that Columbia University received $790 million in revenue from patents involving inserting DNA into cells and New York University received more than $1 billion for a patent that led to an autoimmune drug).

[85] Loise, *supra* note 83, at 52.

[86] *Ibid.*

[87] Birkinshaw, *supra* note 8, at 44 (referring to the "eureka myth" that a single moment of insight is required to create innovation).

[88] *Ibid.*

Act for federal contractors and private industry.[89] In *Stanford v. Roche*, the Court held that the Act does not automatically grant title in intellectual property to federal contractors nor does it give federal contractors the right to take title to such property unilaterally.[90] The invention at issue in the case was Roche's HIV test kits that are used widely in hospitals and medical clinics around the world.[91] The facts of the case provide an interesting example of the process of commercializing technology in the health care industry.

The HIV test kits marketed by Roche began development at a small California research company, Cetus. Previously, Cetus had developed a Nobel Prize winning technique, polymerase chain reaction, known as PCR.[92] Using this technique, Cetus sought methods for quantifying blood-borne levels of HIV, the virus that causes AIDS. In 1988, Cetus started collaborating with researchers at Stanford University to test the efficacy of new AIDS drugs.[93] Dr. Mark Holodniy worked as a researcher at Stanford. When he began working there he signed an employment contract that included a "Copyright and Patent Agreement." Under the terms of that agreement, Holodniy agreed to assign to Stanford his "right, title and interest in" inventions created while employed there.[94]

Holodniy became interested in using the PCR technique to quantify HIV levels in patient blood samples. To learn more about PCR, he was permitted to conduct research at Cetus after signing a "Visitor's Confidentiality Agreement."[95] The agreement stated that Holodniy "will assign and do[es] hereby assign" to Cetus his "right, title and interest in each of the ideas, inventions and improvements" made as a result of having access to Cetus.[96] Holodniy's work with Cetus is an example of the collaboration between business and academic medical center research that the Bayh-Dole Act encouraged.

---

[89]   *See, e.g.,* Ashworth, *supra* note 64, at 370-371 ("legal disposition of intellectual property rights in federally funded inventions is currently in muddy waters"); Takenaka, *supra* note 61, at 288 ("Even though basic policies and objectives were expressly set out in the Bayh-Dole Act, they played no role in [the Court's] interpretation.").

[90]   Bd. of Trs. of the Leland Stanford Junior Univ. v. Roche Molecular Sys., 131 S. Ct. 2188, 2190 (2011).

[91]   *Ibid.* at 2192.

[92]   *Ibid.*

[93]   *Ibid.*

[94]   *Ibid.*

[95]   *Ibid.*

[96]   *Ibid.*

Holodniy conducted research at Cetus for nine months and, during that time, devised a PCR-based procedure for quantifying the amount of HIV in a blood sample. He returned to Stanford to test the HIV measurement technique with his colleagues. Stanford eventually obtained three patents related to the HIV measurement process after securing written assignment of rights from all Stanford employees involved in the research, including Holodniy.[97] Holodniy's Copyright and Patent Agreement with Stanford signed at the time of his employment required that he assign his rights in any intellectual property to Stanford.

In 1991, Roche Molecular Systems purchased all of Cetus' PCR-related assets, including the intellectual property rights that Cetus obtained through agreements, such as the one signed by Holodniy. After testing, Roche commercialized the HIV quantification technique by selling HIV test kits.[98] In 2005, Stanford filed suit against Roche contending that the HIV test kits violated the patents Stanford had obtained on the HIV measurement process.[99] Roche responded that it was co-owner of the HIV measurement process because the Visitor Confidentiality Agreement signed by Holodniy assigned his rights to the process to Cetus and later Roche when it purchased the assignment of rights. Stanford, however, asserted that Holodniy had no rights to assign through the Visitor Confidentiality Agreement because Stanford had superior rights over Holodniy as a federal contractor. Stanford reasoned that, because Holodniy's research was, in part, federally funded through an NIH grant, it was subject to the Bayh-Dole Act. Under the Act, Stanford believed that it had superior ownership rights, as first in line to acquire title, over the inventor himself who is last in line under the Bayh-Dole Act. Justice Roberts, writing on behalf of the Court, took exception to the idea that the inventor was the last in line to claim any rights to his own invention, believing such an interpretation of the Bayh-Dole Act turned patent law on its head. The Court began its opinion by noting that, "[s]ince 1790, the patent law has operated on the premise that rights in an invention belong to the inventor."[100] The Bayh-Dole Act, the Court concluded, did not violate that basic premise of patent law.[101] Congress was obligated to state its intention to change the fundamental rights of the inventor under patent law expressly if that, indeed, was its intention

---

97   *Ibid.*
98   *Ibid.*
99   *Ibid.* at 2194.
100 *Ibid.* at 2192.
101 *Ibid.* at 2199.

when creating the Bayh-Dole Act.[102] Instead of moving the inventor to the back of the line in priority to rights in an invention,[103] the Bayh-Dole Act, the Court determined, focused on rights between the federal contractor and the federal government only after the federal contractor obtained sole rights to the invention from the inventor.[104]

The Copyright and Patent Agreement that Holodniy signed upon his employment with Stanford University provided that he would assign rights to Stanford for inventions created during his employment there.[105] Before Stanford filed patent applications for the HIV measurement technique, it had obtained Holodniy's assignment of rights as well as the assignment from others involved in the research.[106] However, the Visitor Confidentiality Agreement that Holodniy signed before beginning work at Cetus happened before Stanford obtained its assignment of rights. Therefore, the assignment of rights that Cetus obtained occurred while Holodniy retained full rights in his research.[107] In that way, Cetus received a full assignment of rights to the patentable technology while Stanford had a future promise to assign rights. The Court held that the Bayh-Dole Act did not change inventors' rights under patent law nor did it change principles of contract law. Stanford failed to obtain the proper

---

[102]   *Ibid.* at 2194 (In the past, Congress has excluded inventors from patent rights, including certain contracts dealing with nuclear material and atomic energy. Congress provided that title to such inventions "shall be vested in, and be the property of, the [Atomic Energy] Commission.").

[103]   The District Court held that the Bayh-Dole Act "provides that the individual inventor may obtain title" to a federally funded invention "only after the government and the contracting party have declined to do so." *Ibid.* at 2194.

[104]   *Ibid.* at 2198 ("The Bayh-Dole Act expressly confers on contractors the right to challenge a Government-imposed impediment to retaining title to a subject invention. ... [T]here is no need to protect inventor or third-party rights, because the only rights at issue are those of the contractor and the Government.").

[105]   *Ibid.* at 2192 (The Copyright and Patent Agreement provided that Holodniy agreed to assign "right, title and interest in" inventions created while employed there).

[106]   *Ibid.* at 2194.

[107]   *Ibid.* at 2192 (The Visitor Confidentiality Agreement provided that Holodniy "will assign and do[es] hereby assign" to Cetus his "right, title and interest in each of the ideas, inventions and improvements" made as a result of having access to Cetus).

assignment of rights and its status of a federal contractor did not provide superior rights in the research.[108]

Stanford v. Roche, in some respects, simply reinforced the importance of careful contracting to secure fully the employee assignment agreement in federally-funded research.[109] The Court noted that NIH guidelines made it clear to federal contractors that not all aspects of intellectual property are controlled under the Bayh-Dole Act.[110] In essence, federally-funded research is on an equal footing with innovation provided by employees to any organization and monetizing that innovation requires careful assignment agreements.[111]

Another perspective on *Stanford v. Roche* is one that goes well beyond contracts. The ruling underscores the law's recognition that innovation by employees is unique. The Court rejected the notion that employers treat innovation as just another duty of employment. The concept that employers own what employees produce is clear. The Court conceded that "[n]o one would claim that an autoworker who builds a car while working in a factory owns that car."[112] The Court saw an important distinction when the employee is creating a patentable invention for a federal contractor, however.[113] The right of inventors to their inventions is "one of the fundamental precepts of patent law," according to the Court, and the Bayh-Dole Act did not change that.[114] This perspective is important in

---

[108]   *Ibid.* at 2199 ("With an effective assignment, those inventions – if federally funded – become 'subject inventions' under the Act, and the statute as a practical matter works pretty much the way Stanford says it should.").

[109]   Ashworth, *supra* note 64, at 348 ("Although much remains unclear in the wake of ... Stanford v. Roche, the need for airtight employee assignment agreements has become glaringly apparent.").

[110]   *Stanford*, 131 S. Ct. at 2199 (In guidance documents made available to contractors, NIH has made clear that "[b]y law, an inventor has initial ownership of an invention" and that contractors should therefore "have in place employee agreements requiring an inventor to 'assign' or give ownership of an invention to the organization upon acceptance of Federal funds.").

[111]   Takenaka, *supra* note 61, at 285 ("many federal funded inventions will fall outside of the Bayh-Dole Act if contractors fail to execute written assignments with inventors").

[112]   *Stanford*, 131 S. Ct. at 2196.

[113]   *Ibid.* ("But, as noted, patent law has always been different: We have rejected the idea that mere employment is sufficient to vest title to an employee's invention in the employer.").

[114]   *Ibid.* at 2198 ("It would be noteworthy enough for Congress to supplant one of the fundamental precepts of patent law and deprive inventors of rights in their own inventions. To do so under such unusual terms would be truly surprising.").

the context of innovation in healthcare through intellectual assignment agreements.

III. INNOVATION THROUGH CONTRACT LAW

Although common law default rules permit, in some cases, an employer to obtain a "shop right" or a non-exclusive license to use the inventions of an employee, these common law rules are state-law based and are poorly defined generally.[115] This uncertainty underscores the value to employers of assignment contracts. As the facts of *Stanford v. Roche* illuminate, however, pre-invention agreements do not guarantee employer ownership of an invention given the fundamental precepts of patent law granting unique status to inventors. To date, few cases address the enforceability of these agreements. However, as invention assignment agreements become more ubiquitous in organizations, particularly as hospitals consolidate to form large health care systems with a focus on innovation,[116] these assignment agreements will receive closer scrutiny.

In a recent case, *Grocela v. General Hospital Corp.*,[117] Dr. Grocela challenged the Intellectual Property Policy (Policy) of his employer, Massachusetts General Hospital (MGH) as "an unreasonable, oppressive and unduly harsh restraint on trade."[118] Under the Policy, and as a condition of his biennial application for reappointment as a clinical staff physician with a surgical specialty in urology, Grocela, and all staff physicians, certified that the ownership and disposition of inventions and other intellectual property created during the time of appointment to the professional staff were determined by the Policy.[119] The Policy granted ownership rights to MGH of all staff inventions "that arise out of or

---

[115]   Howell, *supra* note 7, at 86 (characterizing the doctrine of "shop right" as "disorderly").

[116]   *See* Bob Herman, *Public-Private Enterprise: Why Intellectual Property is a Mainstay of Academic Hospitals*, BECKER'S HOSP. REV. (June 28, 2013), http://www.beckershospitalreview.com/finance/a-public-private-enterprise-why-intellectual-property-is-a-mainstay-at-academic-hospitals.html ("Most medical centers that are affiliated with universities have a technology transfer or commercialization office, and according to the Association of University Technology Managers, there are several dozen academic medical centers and health systems with such an office.")

[117]   Grocela v. Gen. Hosp. Corp., No. 120459, 2012 Mass. Super. LEXIS 206 (Mass. Super. July 12, 2012).

[118]   *Ibid.* at *3.

[119]   *Ibid.* at *1.

relate to the clinical, research, educational or other activities of the Inventor."[120]

The Research Ventures and Licensing Department at MGH administered the Policy concerning invention ownership. This department received disclosures about inventions created by staff physicians and, after determining ownership of the invention, decided whether to pursue patents or partners to market the invention. The department could decide to return ownership rights to the inventor and forego the opportunity to patent or market the invention.[121] Grocela participated in this process during his employment with MGH, disclosing at least nine inventions.[122] Three of the inventions disclosed by Grocela to MGH later reverted back to ownership by Grocela when, at his request, MGH assigned its interests back to him.[123]

In 2011, Grocela entered into an agreement to partner with Grindstone Medical to raise investment capital to develop and market his inventions and any future inventions not owned by MGH.[124] In 2012, Grocela created the "voice box invention" outside of the hospital, on his own time and at his own expense.[125] Although the voice box invention "utilizes or incorporates knowledge" that he gained as a physician at MGH, as stated in the Policy, Grocela objected to being restricted from creating his own business competition by virtue of his work as a surgeon.[126]

Grocela argued before the Massachusetts court that MGH's ownership of inventions under its Policy should be limited to inventions related to his specialty of urology. To read the Policy broadly to extend to all inventions whether connected to the work he is employed to perform or not, he reasoned, "bars [him] from ordinary competition and thus is contrary to public interest, which favors a person's right to carry on a trade freely."[127]

The court rejected Grocela's claim, finding, instead, that he was aware that his employer contemplated the discovery of inventions as part of his employment. Therefore, even if the inventions were created outside of employment, they were within the scope of his employment.[128] The court

---

[120] *Ibid.*
[121] *Ibid.*
[122] *Ibid.*
[123] *Ibid.* at *2.
[124] *Ibid.*
[125] *Ibid.*
[126] *Ibid.*
[127] *Ibid.*
[128] *Ibid.* at *4 (citing National Dev. Co. v. Gray, 316 Mass. 240, 247 (1944)).

found that the hospital had a compelling interest in promoting the free sharing of staff inventions to benefit the patient population served by MGH.[129]

Grocela, the court reasoned, received adequate compensation for discoveries because "[a]s a member of the staff, he reaps the benefit of the clinical resources, office space, access to doctor-patient relationships and professional prestige available to a physician who practices at one of this country's major teaching hospitals."[130]

Courts generally interpret invention assignment agreement disputes in favor of employers.[131] State statutes carve out some exceptions to the enforcement of invention assignment agreements, particularly in instances, such as the case in *Grocela*, where the invention takes place outside the place of employment and without employer resources.[132] Statutes in seven states create limitations to invention assignment clauses.[133] These statutes are generally modeled after Minnesota's law.[134] They do not confer specific rights on employees but limit the enforcement of the contract if such a contract attempts to bind employees beyond statute limitations.[135] Generally, statutes modeled after Minnesota's law prohibit employers from requiring invention assignment agreements unrelated to the employee's work or the employer's business.[136]

Statutes in two states–Utah and Nevada–take the pro-employer approach.[137] In Utah, the statute permits employers to acquire rights to employees' later inventions through invention assignment agreements, even if the invention is created outside of work on the employee's own time.[138] Nevada, however, eliminates the need for assignment agreements

---

[129]   *Ibid.* at *5.

[130]   *Ibid.*

[131]   Robert P. Merges, *The Law and Economics of Employee Inventions*, 13 HARV. J. L. & TECH. 1, 8 (1999).

[132]   Howell, *supra* note 7, at 81.

[133]   *See* CAL. LAB. CODE §§ 2870–72 (West 2011); DEL. CODE ANN. 19 § 805 (West 2006); 765 ILL. COMP. STAT. ANN. 1060/2 (West 2001); KAN. STAT. ANN. § 44–130 (West 2008); MINN. STAT. ANN. § 181.78 (West 2006); N.C. GEN. STAT. ANN. §§ 66–57.1, 66–57.2

(West 2012); WASH. REV. CODE §§ 49.44.140–150 (West 2008).

[134]   Howell, *supra* note 7, at 89.

[135]   *See* Evelyn D. Pisegna-Cook, *Ownership Rights of Employee Inventions: The Role of Preinvention Assignment Agreements and State Statutes*, 2 U. BALT. INTELL. PROP. L.J. 163, 178 (1994).

[136]   Howell, *supra* note 7, at 89.

[137]   *Ibid.*

[138]   UTAH CODE ANN. § 34-39-3(6) (West 2011).

altogether. Employer ownership of inventions created while employed is the default status. The statute, passed by the state legislature in 2001, provides: "Except as otherwise provided by express written agreement, an employer is the sole owner of any patentable invention or trade secret developed by his employee during the course of the employment that relates directly to work performed during the course of the employment."[139]

Nevada's approach is controversial.[140] It represents the opposite of the basic premise of patent law that the *Stanford v. Roche* Court found so compelling: "rights to an invention belong to the inventor."[141] Undoubtedly, Nevada's approach eases employers' transaction costs of securing rights in employees' inventions, but to what extent does it incentivize employees, the individuals employers rely on to create?

The facts of the *Grocela* case suggest that Grocela was more motivated to market and distribute his inventions than MGH. MGH assigned rights to him of earlier disclosed inventions and he created a partnership to further the inventions to market.[142] Although MGH's Policy adequately protected its rights in employees' inventions, the system may not adequately promote innovation and provide incentives to physicians to innovate.

This lack of clear incentive to innovate when the need for innovation is so great, particularly in the health care industry, should prompt legislatures to explore other approaches. In the same way that the AIA changed United States patent law from a "first to invent" country to a "first to file" country in order to align with most other patent systems around the world,[143] it is important to consider how other industrialized countries approach the issue of the ownership of intellectual property created by employees. Japan and Germany provide two examples of legal

---

[139] NEV. REV. STAT. ANN. § 600.500 (West 2000).

[140] *See* Mary LaFrance, *Nevada's Employee Inventions Statute: Novel, Nonobvious, and Patently Wrong*, 3 NEV. L.J. 88, 88 (2002) ("Nevada has become the only state that allows ownership of patentable inventions to be transferred from one party to another in the complete absence of an assignment agreement, and without any form of actual notice to the transferor.").

[141] Bd. of Trs. of the Leland Stanford Junior Univ. v. Roche Molecular Sys., 131 S. Ct. 2188, 2192 (2011).

[142] Grocela v. Gen. Hosp. Corp., No. 120459, 2012 Mass. Super. LEXIS 206, *2 (Mass. Super. July 12, 2012).

[143] *See supra* notes 66–69 and text accompanying.

approaches to invention assignment agreements that differ from the United States' state-based contract law system.[144]

Japan, unlike the United States, has a uniform approach to assignment agreements through a law that covers both private and public employers.[145] Japan's law restricts pre-invention assignment agreements so that they only apply to inventions that result from the employee's duties and relate to the employer's business.[146] Furthermore, the employer only obtains a non-exclusive license on the patent.[147] The employee may elect to assign the rights to obtain the patent to an employer and may choose to grant an employer an exclusive license to the invention, but the employer must pay reasonable compensation to receive this assignment of rights.[148] Reasonable compensation is based on two factors: the profit the employer will derive from the invention and the contribution the employee has made to completion of the invention.[149]

German patent law includes fundamental ownership rules that are substantially similar to the ownership rules in U.S. patent law.[150] The major difference, however, is that Germany supplemented its patent law with the Employee Invention Act (EIA) to balance the tension between patent law and labor and employment law.[151] Pursuant to the EIA, employers obtain ownership in inventions made by employee-inventors, but protect the employees' rights to reasonable compensation.[152] The compensation is a share of the value of the invention in addition to salary.[153] In practice, some commentators note, due to the lack of

---

[144] A thorough comparison of Japanese and German law regarding invention assignment agreements is beyond the scope of this chapter but a brief overview offers a perspective on the issue of motivating innovation.

[145] Vai Io Lo, *Employee Inventions and Works for Hire in Japan: A Comparative Study Against the U.S., Chinese and German Systems*, 16 TEMP. INT'L & COMP. L.J. 279, 291 (2002).

[146] Henrik D. Parker, *Reform for Rights of Employed Inventors*, 57 S. CAL. L. REV. 603, 608 n.35 (1984).

[147] Lo, *supra* note 145, at 282.

[148] *Ibid.*

[149] *Ibid.* Japan's Article 35 of the patent law grants the right to "reasonable remuneration for employed-inventors when the employee transfers the property right of the patent ... based on the profits of the employer and the proportionate contribution of the employee to the invention itself." Japanese Patent Act, Act No. 121 of 1959, art. 35.

[150] Takenaka, *supra* note 61, at 310.

[151] *Ibid.* at 284.

[152] *Ibid.*

[153] Merges, *supra* note 131, at 43.

definition or agreement to "reasonable compensation," many employee-inventors are left without a clear avenue for enforcing their rights.[154] Also, this compulsory license mechanism of the EIA eliminates freedom of contract between the employee and employer with regard to invention assignments.[155] Nonetheless, it is useful to consider the role of compensation related to the value of the invention, or the profit the employer could earn from the invention, to motivate employees to innovate.

If *Stanford v. Roche* created uncertainty related to the Bayh-Dole Act's role in intellectual property development and ownership, it also created an opportunity to consider what legislative changes could better motivate innovation, particularly in the healthcare industry. One global perspective is that innovation may require a compensation system for employee-inventors as is common for employee-inventors in Japan and Germany. Of course, there are examples of U.S. employers that have instituted a compensation incentive to innovation. The University of California system and other academic systems offer employee-inventors royalty-sharing plans.[156] A system that extends the royalty sharing with other employee incentives could offer the motivation necessary to advance innovation, particularly for the new health care environment of major hospital systems built around an academic medical center. But not all innovation experts agree.[157]

Research in behavioral economics suggests that motivation for innovation decreases if large incentives are offered.[158] Rather than focus on external rewards such as compensation to motivate innovation, the better motivator is recognition.[159] However, invention assignment agreements do not permit innovators to "participate in the process" of developing intellectual property.[160] The facts of *Grocela* documented that Dr. Grocela turned over inventions only to wait to see if the hospital system developed them in any way. On three different instances, he requested the

---

[154]   *Ibid.* at 43–44.

[155]   *Ibid.*

[156]   Kamprath, *supra* note 60, at 196 (but noting that "[c]ompulsory royalty sharing plans may appear to be fairer to the employee-inventor, but they suffer from some of the same problems as other employer-defined compensation systems: the employer totally controls the system and the employee-inventor has no recourse if left out in the cold").

[157]   Birkinshaw, *supra* note 8, at 48 ("Myth # 4. Pay is Paramount").

[158]   *Ibid.*

[159]   *Ibid.* (noting recognition and engagement such as participating in presenting ideas to senior management).

[160]   *See supra* notes 122–123 and text accompanying.

hospital return his rights to allow further development.[161] Innovation is a process that does not end with the "good idea."

IV. CONCLUSION

The health care industry is undergoing major changes as concern about increasing costs drives hospital consolidation into major academic medical center systems that employ a significant percentage of physicians in the United States. Innovation to both control the cost of health care and improve patient outcomes is necessary, but the incentive to achieve the innovation has faltered. The Bayh-Dole Act does not offer guarantees for federal contractors to monetize innovation and the disparity of state contract law brings more uncertainty to the industry.

The present crossroads in the health care industry is the ideal time to seize the opportunity to revitalize the Bayh-Dole Act in accordance with *Stanford v. Roche* to make inventors part of the innovative process. If the healthcare industry creates opportunities to balance its interests in inventions made by physicians and other health care practitioners while incentivizing innovation through a collaborative process rather than restrictive covenants in contracts, it would result in benefits of innovation to health care costs and patient outcomes.

BIBLIOGRAPHY

Constitution, Statutes and Codes

United States Constitution, U.S. Const. art. I § 8.
Bayh-Dole Act, Pub. L. No. 96-517, 94 Stat. 3015 (1980) (codified as amended at 35 U.S.C. §§ 200-212 (2012)).
Health Insurance Portability and Accountability Act of 1996, Pub. L. No. 104-191, 110 Stat. 1936 (1996) (codified in scattered sections of 26 U.S.C.A., 29 U.S.C.A., & 42 U.S.C.A.).
Leahy-Smith America Invents Act, Pub. L. No. 112-29, 125 Stat. 284 (2011) (codified in scattered sections of 35 U.S.C.).
Patient Protection and Affordable Care Act, Pub. L. No. 111-148, 124 Stat. 119 (2010) (codified as amended in scattered sections of the U.S.C.).
United States Code, 42 U.S.C. §§ 1395-1395yy (2012).
United States Code, 42 U.S.C. §§ 1396-1396v (2012).
United States Code, 15 U.S.C. § 3 (2012).

---

[161]   Grocela v. Gen. Hosp. Corp., No. 120459, 2012 Mass. Super. LEXIS 206, *2 (Mass. Super. July 12, 2012).

United States Code, 35 U.S.C. § 201(b) (2012).
United States Code, 35 U.S.C. § 202 (2012).
Code of Federal Regulations, 37 C.F.R. § 401.14 (2013).
California Labor Code, Cal. Lab. Code §§ 2870-72 (West 2011).
DELAWARE CODE, DEL. CODE ANN. 19 § 805 (West 2006).
Illinois Compiled Statutes, 765 ILL. COMP. STAT. ANN. 1060/2 (West 2001).
KANSAS STATUTES, KAN. STAT. ANN. § 44-130 (West 2008).
MINNESOTA STATUTES, MINN. STAT. ANN. § 181.78 (West 2006).
NEVADA REVISED STATUTES, NEV. REV. STAT. ANN. § 600.500 (West 2000).
NORTH CAROLINA GENERAL STATUTES, N.C. GEN. STAT. ANN. §§ 66-57.1, 66-57.2 (West 2012).
UTAH CODE, UTAH CODE ANN. § 34-39-3(6) (West 2011).
WASHINGTON REVISED CODE, WASH. REV. CODE §§ 49.44.140-150 (West 2008).
Japanese Patent Act, Act No. 121 of 1959, art. 35.

Cases

Am. Med. Ass'n v. United States, 317 U.S. 519 (1943).
Bd. of Trs. of the Leland Stanford Junior Univ. v. Roche Molecular Sys., 131 S. Ct. 2188 (2011).
Grocela v. Gen. Hosp. Corp., No. 120459, 2012 Mass. Super. LEXIS 206 (Mass. Super. July 12, 2012).

Secondary Sources

Ashworth, Alexa L., *Race to the Patent Office! How the New Patent Reform Act will Affect Technology Transfer at Universities*, 23 ALB. L.J. SCI. & TECH. 383 (2013).
Birkinshaw, Julian, Cyril Bouquet and J.L. Barsoux, *The 5 Myths of Innovation*, 52 MIT SLOAN MGMT. REV. 43 (2011).
Caplow, Theodore, Louis Hicks and Ben J. Wattenberg, THE FIRST MEASURED CENTURY: AN ILLUSTRATED GUIDE TO TRENDS IN AMERICA, 1900–2000 (2000).
Center for Healthcare Economics and Policy, Hospital Mergers and Acquisitions: 2007–June 2013, available at http://www.aha.org/research/policy/2013.shtml.
Centers for Medicare and Medicaid Services, *National Health Expenditure Data*, National Healthcare Expenditure Projections 2012-2022, Table 1, available at https://www.cms.gov/Research-Statistics-Data-and-Systems/Statistics-Trends-and-Reports/NationalHealthExpendData/Downloads/Proj2012.pdf.
Chandra, Amitabh, Jonathan Holmes and Jonathan Skinner, Is This Time Different? *The Slowdown in Healthcare Spending*, BROOKINGS PAPERS ON ECON. ACTIVITY (2013), available at http://www.brookings.edu/~/media/Projects/BPEA/Fall%20 2013/2013b_chandra_healthcare_spending.pdf.
Crimm, Nina J., *Evolutionary Forces: Changes in For-Profit and Not-For-Profit Health Care Delivery Structures; A Regeneration of Tax Exemption Standards*, 37 B.C. L. REV. 1 (1995).
Cutler, David M. and Fiona Scott Morton, *Hospitals, Market Share and Consolidation*, 310 J. AM. MED. ASS'N 1964 (2013).
Goodnough, Abby, *New Law's Demands on Doctors Have Many Seeking a Network*, N.Y. TIMES, A1 (March 3, 2014) available at http://www.nytimes.com/2014/03/03/us/new-laws-demands-on-doctors-have-many-seeking-a-network.html?_r=0.

Herman, Bob, *Public-Private Enterprise: Why Intellectual Property is a Mainstay of Academic HospitaLS*, BECKER'S HOSP. REV. (June 28, 2013), *available at* http://www.beckershospitalreview.com/finance/a-public-private-enterprise-why-intellectual-property-is-a-mainstay-at-academic-hospitals.html.

Hermer, Laura D., *Private Health Insurance in the United States: A Proposal for a More Functional System*, 6 HOUS. J. HEALTH L. & POL'Y 1 (2005).

Howell, Parker, *Whose Invention Is It Anyway? Employee Invention-Assignment Agreements and Their Limits*, 8 WASH J.L. TECH. & ARTS 79 (2012).

Innovation's Golden Goose, ECONOMIST, Dec. 12, 2002, available at www.economist.com/node/1476653.

Kamprath, Richard A., *Patent Reversion: An Employee-Inventor's Second Bite at the Apple*, 11 CHI-KENT J. INTELL. PROP. 186 (2012).

Kaiser Family Foundation, *Healthcare Costs: A Primer* (2012), available at http://kaiserfamilyfoundation.files.wordpress.com/2013/01/7670-03.pdf.

Kane, Carol K. & David W. Emmons, *New Data on Physician Practice Arrangements: Private Practice Remains Strong Despite Shifts Toward Hospital Employment*, POL'Y RESEARCH PERSP. 1 (2013), available at http://www.nmms.org/sites/default/files/images/2013_9_23_ama_survey_prp-physician-practice-arrangements.pdf.

Kirkpatrick, David, *The Second Coming of Apple*, FORTUNE, Nov. 9, 1998, available at http://money.cnn.com/magazines/fortune/fortune_archive/1998/11/09/250834.

LaFrance, Mary, Nevada's Employee Inventions Statute: Novel, Nonobvious, and Patently Wrong, 3 NEV. L.J. 88 (2002).

Lo, Vai Io, *Employee Inventions and Works for Hire in Japan: A Comparative Study Against the U.S., Chinese and German Systems*, 16 TEMP. INT'L & COMP. L.J. 279 (2002).

Loise, Vicki & Ashley J. Stevens, *The Bayh-Dole Act Turns 30*, 30 SCI. TRANSL. MED. 52 (2010).

Marbury, Donna, *AMA Says the Physician Exodus to Hospitals Overrated*, MED. ECON. (Sept. 23, 2013), available at http://medicaleconomics.modernmedicine.com/medical-economics/news/ama-says-physician-exodus-hospitals-overrated.

Merges, Robert P., *The Law and Economics of Employee Inventions*, 13 HARV. J. L. & TECH. 1 (1999).

Newhouse, Joseph, *Medical Care Costs: How Much Welfare Loss?* 6 J. ECON. PERSP. 3, 3–21 (1992).

Joseph Newhouse, *An Iconoclastic View of Health Cost Containment*, HEALTH AFF. 152 (1993).

NIH Report, *A Plan to Ensure Taxpayers' Interests are Protected* (2001), available at http://www.ott.nih.gov/sites/default/files/documents/policy/wydenrpt.pdf.

Nisen, Max, *Hospitals Could Create the Next Big Wave of Healthcare Tech and Startups*, BUS. INSIDER (Jan. 3, 2013), available at http://www.businessinsider.com/innovation-coming-from-hospitals-2013-1.

Parker, Henrik D., *Reform for Rights of Employed Inventors*, 57 S. CAL. L. REV. 603 (1984).

Perez-Pena, Richard, *Patenting Their Discoveries Does not Pay Off for Most Universities, a Study Says*, N.Y. TIMES, Nov. 20, 2013, available at http://www.nytimes.com/2013/11/21/education/patenting-their-discoveries-does-not-pay-off-for-most-universities-a-study-says.html.

Pisegna-Cook, Evelyn D., *Ownership Rights of Employee Inventions: The Role of Preinvention Assignment Agreements and State Statutes*, 2 U. BALT. INTELL. PROP. L.J. 163 (1994).

Press Release, Am. Coll. of Cardiology, New American College of Cardiology Practice Census Shows Continued Trend Towards Hospital Integration (September 10, 2012), available at www.cardiosource.org/News-Media/Media-Center/News-Releases/2012/09/Leg-Conf.aspx.

Reinhardt, Uwe E., Peter S. Hussey & Gerard F. Anderson, *Cross-National Comparisons of Health Systems Using OECD Data*, 1999, HEALTH AFF. 169 (2002).

Rettig, Richard, *Medical Innovation Duels Cost Containment*, HEALTH AFF. 7 (1994).

Rosenbaum, Sarah, *Realigning the Social Order: The Patient Protection and Affordable Care Act and the U.S. Health Insurance System*, 7 J. HEALTH & BIOMED. L. 1 (2011).

Takenaka, Toshiko, *Serious Flaw of Employee Invention Ownership Under the Bayh-Dole Act in Stanford v. Roche: Finding the Missing Piece of the Puzzle in the German Employee Invention Act*, 20 TEX. INTELL. PROP. L.J. 281 (2012).

Tresemer, Parker, *Best Practices for Drafting University Technology Assignment Agreements After* Filmtec, Stanford v. Roche, *and Patent Reform*, 2012 U. ILL. J.L. TECH. & POL'Y 347 (2012).

Will The New Patent Laws Help or Hurt Small Businesses? N.Y. TIMES BLOGS (Feb. 8, 2012), http://boss.blogs.nytimes.com/2012/02/08/will-the-new-patent-laws-help-or-hurt-small-businesses/.

Weller, Charles D., *"Free Choice" as a Restraint of Trade in American Health Care Delivery and Insurance*, 69 IOWA L. REV. 1351 (1984).

3. Contracts for knowledge protection across a global workforce

Norman D. Bishara

The complications and opportunities for firms operating in a globalized economy have been exhaustively catalogued in the last few decades. Increasingly there has been scholarly discussion of the complex issues surrounding the unwanted transfer of proprietary knowledge and trade secrets across borders that provides an unfair advantage to one firm at the expense of another.[1] The harm caused by these transfers has drawn the attention of U.S. government policy-makers,[2] scholars,[3] and commentators alike.[4] The headline-making cases tend to focus on the taking of technical commercially valuable knowledge developed from a firm's research and development or information with national defense implications, which are essentially trade-secret misappropriation situations.[5] While these cases may involve employees or former employees of a U.S.

---

[1] *See, e.g.*, Marisa A. Pagnattaro, *The Google Challenge: Enforcement of Non-Compete and Trade Secret Agreements in China*, 44 AM. BUS. L.J. 603, 604 (2007) ("In many cases, the success of a company competing on an international level depends upon its ability to preserve its proprietary information.") (citation omitted).

[2] *See* EXECUTIVE OFFICE OF THE PRESIDENT, *Administration Strategy on Mitigating the Theft of US Trade Secrets* (Feb. 2013), available at http://www.whitehouse.gov/sites/default/files/omb/IPEC/admin_strategy_on_mitigating_the_theft_of_US_trade_secrets.pdf (a policy statement form the U.S. White House, Office of the National Counterintelligence Executive, and the Defense Security Service).

[3] Pagnattaro, *supra* note 1.

[4] NATIONAL BUREAU OF ASIAN RESEARCH, *The Report of the Commission on the Theft of American Intellectual Property* (May 2013).

[5] For example, it has been reported that U.S. Companies are having "very frank conversations with the Chinese, (saying) 'You know it's one thing to accept a certain level of copyright knock-offs, but if you're going to take our core technology, then we're better off being in our home country.'" Doug Palmer, *U.S. Seeks to Tackle Trade-Secret Theft by China, Others*, REUTERS (Feb 20, 2013),

firm who take a company's proprietary information while on U.S. soil,[6] it is also the case that technology has made remote and anonymous thefts possible.[7]

However, as the misappropriation of intellectual property rights remains a crucial business and security issue, there has been less consistent focus on an important underlying transfer mechanism of that commercial knowledge, which companies can exert some influence over.[8] Specifically, the movement of knowledge across borders as a result of human capital movements has business implications on a par with the often-discussed theft of trade secrets. There is, in other words, a need to more closely examine the transfer of important commercial knowledge through the mobility of employees from one firm to an overseas competitor. Moreover, it is important to also identify a portfolio of legal options for businesses facing the dilemma of how to not only share business secrets with employees and to cultivate employee skills for the benefit of both parties, but also how to protect those investments in human capital when there is an increased risk of the employee leaving for an overseas competitor.

This chapter provides both a blueprint for U.S. businesses and an agenda for U.S. policy-makers interested in balancing issues of competitive advantage, innovation, and employee rights when it comes to using contractual and other means to manage key employees. The touchstone for these critiques and suggestions is the goal of improving human

---

available at http://www.reuters.com/article/2013/02/21/us-usa-trade-secrets-idUS BRE91J0T220130221 (quoting US Trade Representative Ron Kirk, commenting on US companies frustration with trade secret theft-related losses potentially adding up to $300 billion worldwide in 2012).

  [6] *Ibid.*

  [7] *See, e.g.*, Palmer, *supra* note 5 ("A hacker in China can acquire source code from a software company in Virginia without leaving his or her desk" and "[a]s new technology has torn down traditional barriers to international business and global commerce, they also make it easier for criminals to steal secrets and to do so from anywhere, anywhere in the world.") (Citing then U.S. Attorney General Eric Holder.)

  [8] One important exception is Marisa Pagnattaro's work on employee mobility in the Chinese context. *See, e.g.*, Pagnattaro *supra* note 1, at 604 ("[I]f a valuable employee who is privy to important business secrets is lured away by a competitor, the former employer may be at a significant competitive disadvantage."); and Marisa A. Pagnattaro, *Protecting Trade Secrets in China: Update on Employee Disclosures and the Limitations of the Law*, 45 AM. BUS. L.J. (2008) (discussing China Labor Contract Law of 2008 and China's arbitration court as a noncompete enforcement mechanism).

capital law and policy in a globalized economy that is related to these issues of cross-border knowledge transfer. Thus, this inquiry is not primarily concerned with trade secret misappropriation situations, which are more classically the result of intentional misdeeds that may even be criminal in nature. Those instances are in the realm of more traditional risk management concerns rather than human capital management, which is the focus of this chapter.

To begin, Section I briefly reviews the current state of the law and practice when it comes to using contractual tools, as well as non-contractual methods, to manage human capital mobility issues related to knowledge transfer across international borders. Admittedly, issues of jurisdictional variance in enforcement, choice of law, and the transaction costs of overseas enforcement, and even identifying the career path of former employees, can cause major complications to utilizing contractual approaches alone. Next, Section II introduces the legal and policy issues arising within the context of regulating knowledge dispersion across international borders through human capital contracts or with the possible non-contractual means. I argue that many of the traditional concerns about restricting post-employment mobility and information flow are absent with these sorts of key employees, who are likely to have international career mobility to a foreign competitor.

Section III presents suggestions for a business and policy agenda related to better management of the international employee mobility and knowledge interface. In that section, I argue that, from a U.S. business-centric perspective, many of the concerns about the use of restrictive covenants in employee contracts that were identified in Section II are less relevant in an international context. Moreover, I find that there is not a simple, "one size fits all" approach to limiting the dispersion of commercial knowledge through international human capital movements. A brief conclusion follows.

It is also important to note that this chapter is not a comparative study of restrictive covenants focusing on the differences across jurisdictions, although such studies are important and are starting to emerge in the legal literature.[9] Rather, my goal is to provide a useful picture of the current business and legal issues surrounding cross border knowledge transfer issues and a roadmap for how to proceed, from both a policy and business perspective, to address a growing business concern.

---

[9]   *See, e.g.*, Grant R. Garber, Note, *Intellectual Property: Noncompete Clauses: Employee Mobility, Innovation Ecosystems, and Multinational R&D Offshoring*, BERKELEY TECH. L.J. 28 (2013) (comparing CNCs in Brazil, China, and India).

I. THE STATE OF THE LAW AND PRACTICE

To begin, it is useful to explain some of the concepts inherent in this discussion, such as employee mobility, restrictive covenants in their various forms, and knowledge transfer. The concept of knowledge and the transfer of that knowledge are related to the idea of business advantage tied to information ownership. For example, in terms of the resource-based theory of the firm, which first emerged in the management and strategy literature,[10] a knowledge asset is information that is valuable, rare, inimitable, and non-substitutable, "such as trade secrets, processes, capabilities, and legal strategies."[11]

As the U.S. economy has moved from manufacturing (goods-producing) to a more service-oriented economy, the commercialization and portability of knowledge and innovation has become increasing important.[12] This change has created "a shift in business focus to information and knowledge creation and protection as a source of competitive advantage in a knowledge-based economy."[13] The rest of this section first discusses the contractual limitations on employees' post-employment mobility and then provides an overview of several non-contractual methods that may be used to discourage employee mobility. The various options, which include contract-based restrictions and non-contractual methods discussed here, should not be seen as in any way exclusive of other options. Rather, the options described in this chapter can form the basis of a flexible portfolio approach to managing knowledge and human capital issues.[14]

---

[10]   Norman D. Bishara and David Orozco, *Using the Resource-Based Theory to Determine Covenant Not to Compete Legitimacy*, 87 IND. L.J. 979, 1003 (2012).

[11]   *Ibid.* at 1009 (citations omitted).

[12]   *Ibid.* at 1003.

[13]   *Ibid.*

[14]   For example, in addition to the options mentioned in this chapter, there are always post-employment relationship options (i.e., *ex post* approaches) for renegotiation and even collaboration among current and former employers to modify a restrictive covenant. *See* Eric A. Posner and George G. Triantis, *Covenants Not to Compete from an Incomplete Contracts Perspective* 2-3 (UNIV. OF CHI. LAW & ECON., Working Paper No. 137, 2001), *available at* http://papers.ssrn.com/paper.taf?abstract_id=285805.

A.   Contractual Limitations on Mobility and Knowledge Transfer

As the global labor market evolves, employers seek to manage the negative spillovers from employee mobility between firms.[15] Employee mobility refers to an individual employee's ability to move from one job to another at a different employer and not within a firm. In particular, in the context of restrictive covenants, employee mobility is viewed vis-à-vis as a post-employment transfer of the individual worker (and their skills and knowledge) to a competitor entity or to a new entity, like a start-up or other entrepreneurial endeavor. The movement is from a current employer to another business, as opposed to the general phenomena of workers' upward career mobility. In this context, the concern is over shifting business interests and competitive advantage, thus the focus is on for-profit entities and not an employee's movement to or from a non-profit or government entity. This focus assumes that these new entities are not in competition with the business that is a party to the restrictive agreement, as could be the case with a state-owned enterprise operating as more of a business than a public entity.

Strictly defined, restrictive covenants are contracts that specify an action or actions that one party agrees to refrain from taking.[16] These contracts can be signed by the employee before or at the start of employment, but can also be signed during employment or even at the end of employment. Because the restrained party is otherwise lawfully allowed to take the actions covered by the covenant, these restrictions have sometimes become controversial and are constrained within the bounds of allowable public policy. In the employment context, the most common restrictive covenants are covenants not to compete (often called noncompetes or CNCs),[17] confidentiality or nondisclosure agreements

---

[15]   *See* Richard L. Hannah, *Post-Employment Covenants in the United States: Legal Framework and Market Behaviours*, 149 INT'L LAB. REV. 107, 116 (2010) (comment that restrictive employment covenants "are indicative of the institutional forces that are emerging in the twenty-first century" and that firm and employee behavior in this regard "remains highly uncertain because it is dynamic and evolving").

[16]   Terry M. Dworkin and Elletta S. Callahan, *Buying Silence*, 36 AM. BUS. L.J. 151 (1998).

[17]   Another form of noncompete relates to the sale of a business, whereby the seller of a business and the associated goodwill agrees to not, for a reasonable time and within a reasonable scope, compete against the business now owned by the purchaser. These CNCs are far less controversial than the employee noncompetes discussed, *infra*.

(NDAs), and various kinds of nonsolicitation agreements (NSAs).[18] Employers can generally rely on their employee's duty of loyalty during employment to protect against employees sharing knowledge with competitors.[19] However, employers will use these covenants to expand this duty to refrain from competing with the employer into the post-employment period.[20]

Employee noncompetes directly restrict an employee's post-employment mobility because these agreements disallow an employee from leaving the employer who is a party to the agreement and going to work for a competitor or to start a competing business.[21] Courts disfavor these agreements because they are, on their face, designed to limit competition.[22] However, these agreements have traditionally been allowed in the post-employment situations where the restrictions are reasonable in time and geographic scope, protect a legitimate business interest, are not unduly burdensome to the employee, and not injurious to the public interest.[23] Employers use noncompetes to protect the transfer of knowledge to competitors, at least within the bounds of the traditional reasonableness analysis.[24]

---

[18] *See* Norman Bishara, Kenneth Martin and Randall Thomas, *An Empirical Analysis of Noncompetition Clauses and other Restrictive Post-Employment Covenants*, 68 VAND. L. REV. 1, 3 (2015).

[19] *Ibid.*

[20] *Ibid.*

[21] For a general overview of noncompetes, see BRIAN M. MALSBERGER, ED., COVENANTS NOT TO COMPETE, A STATE-BY-STATE SURVEY (2011 and Cum. Supp. 2012) (an extensive treatise cataloging covenants not to compete across the U.S., jurisdiction by jurisdiction). *See also* Norman D. Bishara, *Fifty Ways to Leave Your Employer: Relative Enforcement of Covenant Not to Compete Agreements, Trends, and Implications for Employee Mobility Policy*, 13 U. PENN. J. BUS. L. 753 (2011).

[22] *See* Michael J. Garrison and John T. Wendt, *The Evolving Law of Employee Noncompete Agreements: Recent Trends and an Alternative Policy Approach*, 45 AM. BUS. L.J. 107 (2008).

[23] *See, e.g.,* CORBIN ON CONTRACTS, § 80.15 (2013) ("Post-Employment Restraint of Employees From Competition – Generally").

[24] *See* Bishara and Orozco's discussion of the resource-based theory of the firm and business knowledge, where they argue that:

the economic value of the individual worker's human capital, particularly in sectors such as high-tech where these workers develop and utilize knowledge in the production process, is an obvious source of competitive advantage for firms. Therefore, legal mechanisms such as covenants not to compete, which aid employers in retaining control over knowledge assets, are increasingly important to modern business activity. Moreover, the fact that employee-based

Employee nonsolicitation agreements generally come in two forms and, like noncompetes, are triggered in a post-employment situation (i.e., they are triggered after the employment is terminated, possibly for any reason). The first type is a restrictive covenant that prohibits the former employee from soliciting clients or customers of the employer, again for a reasonable time and within a reasonable geographic scope.[25] The second type, sometimes colloquially referred to as a restriction on "poaching," prohibits the former employee from soliciting other employees of the former employer to leave (and presumably join the first departing employee in a competing endeavor).[26]

Confidentiality agreements or so-called nondisclosure agreements (NDAs) are, as the name suggests, contracts that require the employee to refrain from disclosing the employer's information to any person or entity outside of the employer's entity.[27] These agreements often state that the employer's information must be kept confidential during employment as well as after the employment relationship has been terminated.[28] Theoretically, the contract extends the existing employee duty of confidentiality and can be open-ended, with the premise that the confidences are indefinitely protectable.[29] These agreements can provide additional support for the usual during-employment confidentiality and may serve as a reminder of that duty, as well as a post-employment mechanism to restrict competition.

NDAs tend to be less controversial than other restrictive covenants, perhaps because these agreements serve as a compliment to the default trade secret protections present across the states. The agreements may cover information that is protectable as a trade secret, but NDAs often cover broader information such as customer lists or employee training techniques. With a nondisclosure agreement alone, as with trade secret

---

knowledge can "walk out the door" and move to a competitor is particularly a concern for businesses. Subsequently, employee noncompete agreements have become highly attractive, low-cost ways for employers to restrict harmful knowledge spillovers that benefit rivals *(supra* note 10, at 1004 (citations omitted)).

[25]   *See, e.g.*, Revere Transducers, Inc. v. Deere & Co., 595 N.W.2d 751 (Iowa 1999).

[26]   *See, e.g.*, Bessemer Trust Co. v. Branin, 16 N.Y.3d 549 (2011).

[27]   For an overview of confidentiality and nondisclosure agreements, see generally Terry M. Dworkin and Elletta S. Callahan, *supra* note 16.

[28]   *Ibid.* at 169–71.

[29]   Norman D. Bishara and Michelle Westermann-Behaylo, *The Law and Ethics of Restrictions on an Employee's Post-Employment Mobility*, 49 AM. BUS. L.J. 1, 22–25 (2012).

misappropriation laws, the employee is not restricted from post-employment competition, but rather is prohibited from using the confidential or trade secret-covered information during that competition.

Garden leave is a more recent and likely less utilized type of restrictive covenant.[30] In this instance, the contract terms state that the employee must provide a long period of notice of termination prior to leaving the employer.[31] In effect, the employee still has duties of loyalty and confidentially to the existing employer that come with employment. However, the employee is not required to go to work and can be prohibited from accessing any new information or client contact.[32] This arrangement means that the employee is compensated during this furlough period, which arises at the end of the employment relationship.[33]

Thus from the employee's perspective garden leave is a relatively fair restrictive covenant as compared to a noncompete.[34] In addition, because the employer has to pay for the leave these arrangements are less likely to involve overreaching and would be limited to "high-value" employees whose departure could cause the most business damage when they leave and compete.[35] A related, yet not much-discussed option, could be a "sitting out the game" agreement.[36] Like garden leave, the employee is paid for the time away from competing, but this payment is made post-employment and is akin to a noncompete that is negotiated at the end of the relationship, which prohibits competition, but does not preclude other employment in some other field.[37]

---

[30] A recent March, 2014 search using the legal database Lexis-Nexis for U.S. litigated cases involving garden leave revealed only twelve cases mentioning the concept in a substantive way, with only a few with garden leave being a central issue for the court's consideration.

[31] *See* Bishara and Westermann-Behaylo, *supra* note 29 at 2–3.

[32] *Ibid.*

[33] *Ibid. See also* Bob Hepple, *The Duty of Employee Loyalty in English Law,* 20 COMP. LAB. L. & POL'Y J. 205, 214 (1999) (discussing the mechanics of the garden leave provision).

[34] Bishara and Westermann-Behaylo, *supra* note 29.

[35] *Ibid.*

[36] Donald Dowling, *Global HR Hot Topic-July 2012: Non-Competes and Other Restrictive Covenants in the Cross Border Context,* White & Case LLP (July 2012), *available at* http://www.whitecase.com/files/Publication/ee2b37a7-7021-41f0-be7a-eab9d4cc68d4/Presentation/PublicationAttachment/fc8bb6a9-9d91-4051-8840-eef31a073277/Global-HR-Hot-Topic-06-12.pdf.

[37] *Ibid.*

B. Non-Contractual Limitations on Mobility and Knowledge Transfer

Beyond the restrictive covenants discussed above in Section I.A., businesses have other possible levers with which to curtail or discourage the transfer of knowledge when an employee departs for a competitor. Some of these options function like restrictive covenants to hinder an employee's post-employment mobility, while others can function to retain the knowledge and the employee's loyalty (i.e., to keep them working exclusively with that employer) through incentives.

When restrictive covenants are absent, some firms will turn to a related and much-discussed, but apparently little-used, legal argument called the doctrine of inevitable disclosure.[38] Under this concept, even in the absence of a valid noncompete, an employee could be enjoined from moving to a competitor when there is threatened, albeit, not actual misappropriation of a trade secret.[39] The premise of an inevitable disclosure justification for enjoining an employee from moving to a competitor is that the individual is simply unable to refrain from using the protected knowledge in their new role.[40] This doctrine has proved controversial because in practice it would restrict employees from their choice of employment and use of their skills, even when there is no evidence of misappropriation and when they never agreed to, or were compensated for, a CNC.[41]

Another non-contractual, knowledge-retention mechanism, but not necessarily employee retention, would be simply not investing in the human capital development of the employee. Simply put, the employer who is concerned with the prospect of employees taking valuable knowledge and moving to a competitor in the U.S. or internationally could refrain from sharing the knowledge with its employees. This strategy reduces the risk of a knowledge-asset being transferred when an employee leaves, but it also may serve to harm the efficiency and effectiveness of the employees, or even profits. It could also harm the company's ability to recruit the most promising employees.

---

[38]   *See, e.g.*, Alan Hyde, *Should Noncompetes Be Enforced?: New Empirical Evidence Reveals the Economic Harm of Non-compete Covenants*, *in* REGULATION 6 (Winter 2010) (adapted from a chapter in RESEARCH HANDBOOK ON THE LAW AND ECONOMICS OF LABOR AND EMPLOYMENT LAW (Michael Wachter and Cynthia Estlund eds., 2012, Edward Elgar Publishing)).

[39]   *Ibid.*

[40]   Bishara and Westermann-Behaylo, *supra* note 29.

[41]   *Ibid.*

This type of intra-firm secrecy, however, may not even be practical for some industries or activities. For instance, restricting information access in a high-tech firm where the engineers must work with proprietary computer code and algorithms, or restricting access to customer lists and curtailing client contact for salespeople in any industry may be impossible. Moreover, this sort of antagonistic relationship ignores the benefits of a firm's collaboration with its employees, which is perhaps why it seems like an odd and counterproductive approach to human capital management.

Worse, avoiding hiring the best and brightest employees because they are not U.S. citizens, or have strong ties internationally, and may have a higher chance of leaving to work for a foreign competitor could surely backfire. This is the "head in the sand" approach to operating with knowledge-specific assets, which also seems nearly impossible to execute in an interconnected world where top employees inevitably have other employment prospects abroad. This approach may appeal in the short term to protect a trade secret or confidential information, but it is a potentially growth-stunting strategy because valuable knowledge changes quickly and new derivative uses may be harder to develop. Ultimately, this style of knowledge management would also be likely off-putting to the most valuable and ambitious employees who have market power to work for more flexible and collaborative employers.

There are even behind-the-scenes and anti-competitive methods that some firms have used to hinder employee mobility to competitors. In these instances, the competitors collude to limit employee mobility. For instance, there have been allegations of so-called "do not hire" or "non-poaching" agreements among large competitors in the high-tech sector, such as Apple, Google, Adobe, and Intel.[42] In this case, workers, many of them non-U.S. engineers, sued these firms for damages related to the suppression of their wages because of these informal agreements.[43] In effect, these arrangements work like under-the-table and illegal noncompetes where employees must shoulder the burden of being excluded from a truly free labor market among competitors.

An offshoot of this sort of improper behavior by employers could also occur in cases where the threat of a restrictive covenant or a case for trade secret misappropriation is actually exaggerated in part or in full.

---

[42] Bill Singer, *After Apple, Google, Adobe, Intel, Pixar, and Intuit, Antitrust Employment Charges Hit eBay*, Forbes.com (Nov. 19, 2012), *available at* http://www.forbes.com/sites/billsinger/2012/11/19/after-apple-google-adobe-pixar-google-and-intuit-antitrust-employment-charges-hit-ebay/.

[43] *Ibid.*

For instance, even in California where many restrictions such as non-competes are illegal,[44] these covenants are still requested by employers.[45] The threat to enforce the mobility restriction when it is overly broad or even completely unenforceable is the type of abusive overreaching discussed in Section II. This so-called chilling or *in terrorem* effect can be used as a scare tactic to retain an employee or to discourage them from going to a competitor. Interestingly, where international mobility is an option for an employee, the scare tactics may actually backfire and give an incentive for a former employee to avoid the threat of legal action by departing for a foreign jurisdiction where enforcement is far less likely.

There are also more market-based retention strategies that are proactive in nature. Rather than looking for ways to corral information by restricting employee mobility or curtailing knowledge sharing with employees, a firm could focus on winning employee loyalty. For instance, a firm could focus on both monetary and intangible incentives to retain the best workers and lower the risk that they would want to leave for a competitor.

General incentives for employee retention range from the intangible cachet of working for a leading U.S. firm and higher salaries and opportunities for bonus payments, excellent retirement benefits, internal promotions and increased management roles, and even workplace perks such as complimentary food, transportation, and fitness options.[46] Other incentives to stay with a current employer could also include a positive work environment, retention pay, and deferred compensation, such as stock options that vest over the long term and are tied to continued employment.

Admittedly, some of these incentives would be formally memorialized with employment contracts, as in the case of deferred compensation plans or retirement incentives. However, they fall into the category of non-contractual strategies to gain employee loyalty and, thus, stem the risk of

---

[44]   *See* California Business & Professional Code 16000 (2013) (prohibiting restrictive covenants in employment).

[45]   For example, in a recent study, the rate of CEOs with noncompete clauses across the U.S. was 80 percent. California-based CEO contracts was still approximately 65 percent, even when the clauses would not be enforceable. Bishara, Martin and Thomas, *supra* note 18, at 48, footnote 182

[46]   *See, e.g.*, Norman D. and Cindy A. Schipani, *Complementary Alternative Benefits to Promote Peace*, 89 J. Bus. ETHICS 539, 547–48 (2010) (discussing case studies of companies that provide non-traditional benefits to their workers).

employees departing for an overseas opportunity with a competitor.[47] The next section discusses some of the legal and policy issues related to the contractual and non-contractual options for curtailing the knowledge transfers that may come with those employee departures.

II. LEGAL AND POLICY ISSUES OF RESTRICTIVE COVENANTS IN AN INTERNATIONAL CONTEXT

The business concern about the unwanted dispersion of business knowledge to a competitor by a former employee raises well-known legal and policy issues in a purely domestic context. However, this concern is even more complicated in a cross-border situation where the laws and policies of the country governing the former employee's new firm may differ greatly from the U.S. This section first examines some of the legal complications of enforcing human capital contracts or implementing non-contractual solutions internationally and then discusses the related policy implications.

A. Legal Issues Involved

The challenges of enforcing any agreement across international boundaries can be complicated. Most obviously, the logistics of having a foreign court enforce a contract written in the U.S. can be daunting. Jurisdictional issues are the first to come to mind. A U.S. firm whose employment contracts are standard in the U.S. may be forced to hire local counsel and re-justify the contract terms, on their merits, to foreign courts when attempting to enforce an agreement abroad. Even with a favorable choice of law and venue being spelled out in a U.S. agreement, there is certainly no guarantee a former employee will return to the U.S. if sued or that a foreign court will enforce a judgment, especially when a mobility restriction may contravene local policies.

Insight into the complications of enforcing contracts across borders can be gleaned from the literature that addresses the variance in the U.S. states' restrictive covenant enforcement regimes. Even where the parties have expressed a choice of law and venue, the courts of a state where an employee moves to start new employment will first ask if that state's

---

[47] Nonetheless, despite these attempts to promote employee loyalty through financial incentives and even a high quality of life, a rogue employee set on stealing trade secrets and transporting them abroad is unlikely to be deterred.

public policy is consistent with the covenant.[48] Noncompetes, for instance, remain controversial across jurisdictions while confidentiality agreements are much more likely to withstand scrutiny across a variety of U.S. states.[49] The resulting uncertainty over whether the covenant is enforceable is less than ideal for the former employer seeking enforcement.[50] It also creates a situation where an employee who leaves a firm and moves to a new state is unsure of their contractual obligations.[51]

An illustrative example of the difficulties for U.S. employers when enforcing restrictive employment covenants if an employee moves abroad is the well-known case of Kai-Fu Lee. In that case, Dr. Lee, a prominent Taiwanese computer scientist who was working for Microsoft in Washington State, left to head Google's new operations in mainland China in July 2005.[52] Initially, Microsoft filed suit in Washington to enforce Dr. Lee's covenant not to compete, but obvious jurisdictional issues with enforcing the agreement soon arose.[53]

Eventually, Microsoft and Google reached an undisclosed settlement of the lawsuit and Dr. Lee continued to work for Google in China. Presumably Microsoft had a slim chance of obtaining enforcement of the restrictive covenant in Washington to enjoin Mr. Lee from working for a competitor in China, and then actually securing enforcement of the judgment in China through the Chinese courts. The fact that a settlement was reached, on one hand, seems like a promising model for allocating the rights of the parties. However, this case involved two U.S. tech giants with an incentive to compete fairly and Google possessed the credibility to keep any promises to segregate Dr. Lee's knowledge of Microsoft's proprietary information from his new position.[54] The prospects of such

---

[48]   *See, e.g.*, Gillian Lester and Elizabeth Ryan, *Choice of Law and Employee Restrictive Covenants: An American Perspective*, 31 COMP. LAB. L. & POL'Y J. 389 (2009).

[49]   *See, e.g.*, Geoffrey P. Miller, *Bargains Bicoastal: New Light on Contract Theory*, 31 CARDOZO L. REV. 1475, 1499–1500 (2010) (discussing New York and California policy on non-compete agreements and explaining that both "place limits on covenants not to compete and related clauses, but California is significantly more willing to reject agreements[on public policy] ground[s]").

[50]   *See* Bishara, *Fifty Ways to Leave Your Employer, supra* note 21.

[51]   *Ibid.*

[52]   For a thorough discussion of the facts and implications of this situation, including the negotiated outcome, see Pagnattaro, *supra* note 1, at 606–14.

[53]   *Ibid.*

[54]   There is some recent anecdotal evidence that firms in the U.S. are being more collaborative when it comes to post-employment renegotiation of restrictive

amiable resolution and assurance of knowledge protection when an employee moves from a large U.S. firm to a Chinese start-up is much less certain.

Some evidence of an increased awareness of the issues related to multi-jurisdictional workforces and employee mobility across borders is the number of recent legal treatises and online legal resources that collect information across jurisdictions. These are often prepared by law firms as client alerts or other marketing resources to attract clients who are encountering the issue of cross-border restrictive covenant enforcement.[55] Global consortiums of legal service providers also produce international legal handbooks and guides, often focused on employee noncompetes.[56]

In addition, several practitioner treatises are designed to identify and address the complications and uncertainty of drafting[57] and enforcing restrictive covenants across a global workforce.[58] These tend to be comparative in nature and focus on the enforcement regimes, if any, in specific countries as a means of estimating the likelihood that restrictive employment covenants would be enforced in that jurisdiction. However, there is much less academic writing on the subject to date, or discussion

---

covenants. *See* Joann S. Lublin, *Companies Loosen the Handcuffs on Non-Competes*, WALL ST. J. (Aug. 12, 2013) (providing examples of negotiations between former and prospective or new employers to release an employee from a non-compete agreement).

[55]   *See, e.g.*, John P. Barry, et al, *Tying and Untying the Knot: Non-Compete Agreements in the UK, EU and Latin America – How to Write Them; How to Fight Them* (June 17, 2010), *available at* http://www.internationallaborlaw.com/files/2012/10/Tying-and-Untying-the-Knot.pdf (from various attorneys at the Proskauer Rose law firm); and FENWICK & WEST LLP, *Summary of Covenants Not To Compete: A Global Perspective* (Aug. 2009), *available at* http://www.fenwick.com/fenwickdocuments/rs_summary-of-covenants.pdf   (Covering the U.S. states and sixteen countries).

[56]   *See, e.g.*, IUS LABORIS, *Non-Compete Clauses: An International Guide* (May 2010), *available at* http://www.globalhrlaw.com/international-hr-law-guides?guideid=33 (covering 25 countries); and LEX MUNDI, *Global Practice Guide: Non-Competition* (2012), *available at* www.lexmundi.com/Document.asp?DocID=3904 (covering 31 countries or territories and 11 U.S. states and territories).

[57]   *See* M. Scott McDonald and Jacqueline Johnson, *Drafting and Enforcing Covenants Not to Compete*, w/ 2013 Cum. Supp. (2013).

[58]   *See* Wendi S. Lazar and Gary R. Siniscalco, *Confidentiality, Trade Secrets, and Other Duties and Restrictive Covenants in a Global Economy*, in RESTRICT-IVE COVENANTS AND TRADE SECRETS IN EMPLOYMENT LAW, AN INTERNATIONAL SURVEY (Wendi S. Lazar and Gary R. Siniscalco eds., 2010).

of what other options businesses have to protect their valuable commercial knowledge in this situation. Next, I present some of the public policy issues at stake for the parties.

B.   Policy Issues Involved

Restrictive covenants have been critiqued since their inception.[59] In recent years, noncompetes, in particular, have again garnered harsh criticism[60] as have other restrictive covenants in the United States.[61] These critiques go to the nature of restrictive covenants' and come from two general perspectives. The first argues that business and innovation suffer when noncompetes curtail the information flows associated with unfettered employee mobility and the second takes a justice and fairness approach.

From a promotion of business activity perspective, the prohibitions on employee mobility have been judged to be shortsighted and harmful to innovation,[62] or even detrimental to economic development.[63] A few empirical studies of the impact of restrictive covenants, particularly noncompetes, have emerged in the last few years and provide some evidence that CNCs impact high-tech worker mobility,[64] new venture creation,[65] and investment.[66] While it has been assumed that U.S. firms

---

[59]   For example, noncompetes have been critiqued from the first recorded instances of these restrictive covenants in the common law. *See* Harlan M. Blake, *Employee Agreements Not to Compete*, 73 HARV. L. REV. 625 (1960).

[60]   *See, e.g.*, Alan Hyde, *supra* note 38.

[61]   *See generally* ORLY LOBEL, TALENT WANTS TO BE FREE: WHY WE SHOULD LEARN TO LOVE LEAKS, RAIDS, AND FREE RIDING, Yale Univ. Press (2013).

[62]   *Ibid.*

[63]   KAUFMANN FOUNDATION, *A Start-Up Act for the States* (2010).

[64]   Bruce Fallick, Charles A. Fleischman and James B. Rebitzer, *Job Hopping in Silicon Valley: Some Evidence Concerning the Micro-Foundations of a High Technology Cluster*, 88 REV. ECON. & STAT. 472 (2006).

[65]   Matt Marx, *The Firm Strikes Back: Non-Compete Agreements and the Mobility of Technical Professionals*, 76 AM. SOC. REV. 695 (2011).

[66]   Mark J. Garmaise, *Ties That Truly Bind: Non-competition Agreements, Executive Compensation, and Firm Investment*, 27 J.L. ECON. & ORG. 376 (2009).

increasingly use restrictive covenants, one recent study of public-company CEO contracts finds that those key employees regularly agree to a variety of restrictive covenants in their employment contracts.[67]

The second general critique of restrictive covenants is directed at the potential unfairness of the employer overreaching any legal enforcement or ethical bounds by exerting its superior bargaining position and specifying how restrictive covenants are formed and enforced to the employee's detriment. At the start of the employment relationship, the typical employee has less bargaining power than the employer. Thus, there is a risk that restrictive covenants are essentially contracts of adhesion where the employee is in an unenviable "take it or leave it" position.[68]

At the end of the employment relationship, there is a risk that an employer will overreach and use a CNC signed at the start of employment as a means of restricting the employee's choice beyond what is needed to protect a legitimate business interest.[69] Scholars have also found that confidentiality agreements may also unfairly restrict employee choice in pursuing opportunities by empowering employers to over-reach.[70] Advocates for this pro-employee approach argue that noncompetes and other restrictive covenants should be limited or even banned.[71] Similarly, in some countries restrictive covenants such as noncompetes are prohibited to preserve a person's right of dignity and a fundamental right to work.[72]

In contrast, well-designed and fairly enforced restrictive covenants can create the correct mix of incentives for both parties. For example, some have argued that using a resource-based theory analysis to evaluate noncompete enforcement would allow courts to fairly adjudicate disputes over knowledge ownership.[73] Balancing the rights of the parties and

---

[67]   Bishara, Martin and Thomas, *supra* note 18 (finding an increase in CEO noncompetes over several decades).

[68]   *See* Rachel S. Arnow-Richman, *Bargaining for Loyalty in the Information Age: A Reconsideration of the Role of Substantive Fairness in Enforcing Employee Noncompetes*, 80 OR. L. REV. 1163, 1214–15 (2001) (discussing the disadvantageous position of a new employee faced with a request to sign a noncompete and the risk of having the employment offer revoked).

[69]   *Ibid.*

[70]   *See* Dworkin and Callahan, *supra* note 16.

[71]   *See, e.g.*, Arnow-Richman, *supra* note 68. *See also* Katherine V.W. Stone, *The New Psychological Contract: Implications for the Changing Workplace for Labor and Employment Law*, 48 UCLA L. REV. 519 (2001).

[72]   Dowling, *supra* note 36.

[73]   Bishara and Orozco, *supra* note 10.

maximizing noncompete enforcement for certain types of works may also yield fair results.[74] In addition, a restriction on mobility like garden leave is consistently more fair for employees than other restrictive covenants because the arrangement compensates the worker for the more limited period of employment immobility.[75]

The non-contractual options for managing human capital-based knowledge flows discussed in Section I can be, on balance, more equitable to employees than, for instance a noncompete, and address the potential employer-overreaching problem. This is because approaches like using a deferred compensation scheme or positive workplace incentives reward the employee for the choice to stay at the firm and continue to use the firm's knowledge, to both parties' benefit. These sorts of arrangement force the employer to properly value the employee's contribution to the firm, and thus they help avoid the overreaching problem associated with restrictive covenants like noncompetes.

Next, in Section III, these various contractual and noncontractual options are evaluated in the context of international employee mobility. Following that discussion, I propose some approaches to how business can use these methods to address the potential harm of an employee taking business knowledge with them to an overseas competitor.

III.   A BUSINESS AND POLICY AGENDA FOR CROSS BORDER KNOWLEDGE TRANSFER

This section aims to provide an overview of the current business and legal issues with respect to cross-border knowledge transfer issues. In addition, it begins to develop a roadmap for how to proceed, from both a policy and business perspective.

The assumption of much of the anti-restrictive covenant argument is that there are inherent meta-business benefits – particularly innovation – from unfettered human capital movement; and knowledge dispersion is, a priori, a positive thing. This is a relatively safe assumption when it comes

---

[74] *See, e.g.*, Norman D. Bishara, *Balancing Innovation from Employee Mobility with Legal Protection for Human Capital Investment: 50 States, Public Policy, and Covenants Not to Compete in an Information Economy*, 27 BERKELEY J. EMP. & LAB. L. 287 (2006).

[75] *See* Bishara and Westermann-Behaylo, *supra* note 29, at 55 ("In our assessment, garden leave, which seems to be relatively new to the United States, generally provides an improvement over the existing structure of judicial enforcement of noncompete clauses or the inevitable disclosure doctrine.").

to economic growth within the borders of a country and that specific country's firm's interests are being considered. However, when knowledge transfers to overseas firms harm a domestic firm's competitiveness, the mobility stunting spillover of restrictive covenants can actually offer some protection.

In other words, the first set of policy problems identified above – that restrictive covenants may harm innovation and business growth – is not a concern if the unit of analysis is the U.S. domestic market for knowledge-based labor. For businesses, using restrictive covenants or non-contractual incentives to maintain loyalty at the expense of overseas mobility could be a net positive for profits. Purely as a business issue, the risk of allowing these options does not rise to the level of trade protectionism if the safeguards are seen as legitimate and necessary protections, much like the widely accepted norm of global trade-secret protections laws. Nonetheless, the difficult logistics of implementing contractual restrictions against a former employee who now resides in a foreign jurisdiction remain.

However, the employee fairness critiques of restrictive covenants remain whether it is a domestic or foreign mobility discussion. Some of these concerns might even be heightened with employees such as foreign nationals working in the U.S. because employer overreaching could be more rampant.[76] On the other hand, the non-contractual incentives for loyalty, such as more positive workplaces, benefits, and financial incentives, still remain promising options for a fair way to discourage knowledge transfers through mobility, be it domestic or foreign moves.

Yet, once a piece of valuable commercial knowledge is transferred to a competitor overseas it is gone forever from the exclusive control and use of the U.S. employer. Again, there may be important trade-secret protections that are part of international treaties that should, in theory, address the misappropriation of information. However, while some firms have resorted to extraordinary measures to protect their intellectual property, the knowledge that is embedded in a departing employee's head is nearly impossible to control.[77] With that in mind, which of the

---

[76] To address the problem of employers overreaching by securing harsh or overly one-sided terms related to a specific special class of employees in this situation, in this case J1 visa-holding foreign doctors, who are hired from overseas to work in rural communities as a prerequisite to enhanced immigration status in the U.S., some states have legislation prohibiting noncompetes for these employees. *See, e.g.*, NEV. ST. ANN. § 439A.175 (2012).

[77] In addition, the transfer of business knowledge that is valuable in the United States to commercial entities in other countries has potential national

restrictive covenants and non-contractual options should a U.S.-based employer utilize to protect against the loss of valuable knowledge to an overseas competitor?

A more difficult, and perhaps longer-term, solution to the issue of knowledge transfer to foreign competitors through employee mobility would be to have reciprocal covenant enforcement across countries. To accomplish this in a meaningful way these protections could be attached to a bi-lateral trade agreement. Essentially, the agreement would allow for the courts of each country to enforce the restrictive covenant policy of the other to the benefit of businesses facing knowledge outflows. This approach may also appeal to U.S. policy-makers who are already concerned with knowledge outflows.[78] Admittedly, this approach poses challenges to implementation and could still conflict with existing restrictive covenant policies in some nations.

If this level of bi-lateral reciprocity in enforcing restrictive covenants were possible, then both countries could benefit. Still, the country whose firms have the most valuable knowledge to protect will have the most to lose by lenient foreign enforcement of the covenants. Most likely the U.S. employer would also have to go to the trouble and expense of retaining local counsel in the foreign jurisdiction. Nonetheless, this option would at least partially remove the incentive for firms to keep foreign employees insulated from key intellectual property and other trade secrets, which could lead to economic inefficiencies and under utilization of these employees' valuable skills.

Beyond the challenges with enforcing contracts overseas against a former employee, there may also be a moral signaling effect in including restrictive covenants in employee contracts. Even when these agreements are not ultimately enforceable overseas, having the contract clauses as a statement of the importance of the knowledge, and that it belongs to the firm, can be useful. This is because the clauses can set the tone for the relationship and at a minimum place the issue of knowledge transfers at the forefront of the employment relationship should the employee take the knowledge to a competitor. Currently most U.S. employment contracts do not seem to contemplate the issues of international job-hopping by key employees, even though including such clauses is essentially costless at the start of employment.

---

security and competitiveness issues that are absent with restrictive covenants in a domestic context.

[78]　*See, e.g.*, EXECUTIVE OFFICE OF THE PRESIDENT, *Administration Strategy on Mitigating the Theft of U.S. Trade Secrets, supra* note 2.

Finally, the possible non-contractual methods of retaining key employees should remain in a business toolkit for knowledge management in the human capital context. These methods may have many positive impacts on profitability by attracting and retaining the best workers. By conceiving of these methods as a knowledge protection strategy as well, firms can better understand the portfolio of proactive policies they have for discouraging key employees from departing for a foreign competitor.

IV. CONCLUSION

The transfer of business knowledge across borders through employee mobility is a significant concern to both U.S. businesses and policymakers. This chapter has analyzed the restrictive covenant (contractual) as well as several non-contractual approaches to addressing this issue. The suggestions on how to deploy a comprehensive knowledge protection strategy for business are imperfect solutions. However, the first step is to conceive of the problem of knowledge outflows as both a business decision as well as a potential legal problem and to admit that legal solutions alone are unlikely, since cross-border contract enforcement will remain unpredictable and costly.

One possible approach, however difficult and potentially complicated to execute, is to have the enforcement of restrictive covenants in employment contracts become an explicit part of international trade treaties. Nonetheless business-centric options are already available, such as including choice of venue and choice of law clauses in the usual restrictive covenants that address the international scope component in key employee's employment agreements. The other proactive method that holds some promise is to retain the loyalty, and thus knowledge and skills, of key employees by providing the best incentive packages possible.

BIBLIOGRAPHY

Statutes and Codes

CALIFORNIA BUSINESS & PROFESSIONAL CODE § 16000 (2013). NEVADA ST. ANN. § 439A.175 (2012).

Cases

Bessemer Trust Co. v. Branin, 16 N.Y.3d 549 (2011).
Revere Transducers, Inc. v. Deere & Co., 595 N.W.2d 751 (Iowa 1999).

Secondary Sources

Arnow-Richman, Rachel S., *Bargaining for Loyalty in the Information Age: A Reconsideration of the Role of Substantive Fairness in Enforcing Employee Noncompetes*, 80 OR. L. REV. 1163 (2001).
Barry, John P., Daniel Ornstein, Yasmine Tarasewicz, and Bettina B. Plevan, *Tying and Untying the Knot: Non-Compete Agreements in the UK, EU and Latin America – How to Write Them; How to Fight Them* (June 17, 2010), *available at* http://www.internationallaborlaw.com/files/2012/10/Tying-and-Untying-the-Knot.pdf.
Bishara, Norman D., *Balancing Innovation from Employee Mobility with Legal Protection for Human Capital Investment: 50 States, Public Policy, and Covenants Not to Compete in an Information Economy*, 27 BERKELEY J. EMP. & LAB. L. 287 (2006).
Bishara, Norman D., *Fifty Ways to Leave Your Employer: Relative Enforcement of Covenant Not to Compete Agreements, Trends, and Implications for Employee Mobility Policy*, 13 U. PENN. J. BUS. L. 753 (2011).
Bishara, Norman D. and David Orozco, *Using the Resource-Based Theory to Determine Covenant Not to Compete Legitimacy*, 87 IND. L.J. 979 (2012).
Bishara, Norman D., Kenneth Martin and Randall Thomas, *An Empirical Analysis of Noncompetition Clauses and other Restrictive Post-Employment Covenants*, 68 VAND. L.REV. 1(2015).
Bishara, Norman D. and Cindy A. Schipani, *Complementary Alternative Benefits to Promote Peace*, 89 J. BUS. ETHICS 539 (2010).
Bishara, Norman D. and Michelle Westermann-Behaylo, *The Law and Ethics of Restrictions on an Employee's Post-Employment Mobility*, 49 AM. BUS. L.J. 1 (2012).
Blake, Harlan M., *Employee Agreements Not to Compete*, 73 HARV. L. REV. 625 (1960).
CORBIN ON CONTRACTS, § 80.15 (2013) ("Post-Employment Restraint of Employees From Competition – Generally").
Dowling, Donald, *Global HR Hot Topic-July 2012: Non-Competes and Other Restrictive Covenants in the Cross Border Context,* White & Case LLP (July 2012), *available at* http://www.whitecase.com/files/Publication/ee2b37a7-7021-41f0-be7a-eab9d4cc68d4/Presentation/PublicationAttachment/fc8bb6a9-9d91-4051-8840-eef31a073277/Global-HR-Hot-Topic-06-12.pdf.
Dworkin, Terry M. and Elletta S. Callahan, *Buying Silence*, 36 AM. BUS. L.J. 151 (1998).
EXECUTIVE OFFICE OF THE PRESIDENT, *Administration Strategy on Mitigating the Theft of US Trade Secrets* (Feb. 2013), available at http://www.whitehouse.gov/sites/default/files/omb/IPEC/admin_strategy_on_mitigating_the_theft_of_US_trade_secrets.pdf.

Fallick, Bruce, Charles A. Fleischman and James B. Rebitzer, *Job Hopping in Silicon Valley: Some Evidence Concerning the Micro-Foundations of a High Technology Cluster*, 88 REV. ECON. & STAT. 472 (2006).

FENWICK & WEST LLP, *Summary of Covenants Not To Compete: A Global Perspective* (Aug. 2009), *available at* http://www.fenwick.com/fenwickdocuments/rs_summary-of-covenants.pdf.

Garber, Grant R., *Note, Intellectual Property: Noncompete Clauses: Employee Mobility, Innovation Ecosystems, and Multinational R&D Offshoring*, BERKELEY TECH. L.J. 28 (2013).

Garmaise, Mark J., *Ties That Truly Bind: Non-competition Agreements, Executive Compensation, and Firm Investment*, 27 J.L. ECON. & ORG. 376 (2009).

Garrison, Michael J. and John T. Wendt, *The Evolving Law of Employee Noncompete Agreements: Recent Trends and an Alternative Policy Approach*, 45 AM. BUS. L.J. 107 (2008).

Hannah, Richard L., *Post-Employment Covenants in the United States: Legal Framework and Market Behaviours*, 149 Int'l Lab. Rev. 107 (2010).

Hepple, Bob, *The Duty of Employee Loyalty in English Law*, 20 COMP. LAB. L. & POL'Y J. 205 (1999).

Hyde, Alan, *Should Noncompetes Be Enforced? New Empirical Evidence Reveals the Economic Harm of Non-compete Covenants*, *in* REGULATION 6 (Winter 2010) (adapted from a chapter in RESEARCH HANDBOOK ON THE LAW AND ECONOMICS OF LABOR AND EMPLOYMENT LAW (Michael Wachter & Cynthia Estlund eds., 2012)).

IUS LABORIS, *Non-Compete Clauses: An International Guide* (May 2010); *available at* http://www.globalhrlaw.com/international-hr-law-guides?guideid=33.

KAUFMANN FOUNDATION, *A Start-Up Act for the States* (2010).

Lazar, Wendi S. and Gary R. Siniscalco, *Confidentiality, Trade Secrets, and Other Duties and Restrictive Covenants in a Global Economy*, *in* RESTRICTIVE COVENANTS AND TRADE SECRETS IN EMPLOYMENT LAW, AN INTERNATIONAL SURVEY (Wendi S. Lazar & Gary R. Siniscalco eds., 2010).

Lester, Gillian and Elizabeth Ryan, *Choice of Law and Employee Restrictive Covenants: An American Perspective*, 31 COMP. LAB. L. & POL'Y J. 389 (2009).

LEX MUNDI, *Global Practice Guide: Non-Competition* (2012), *available at* www.lexmundi.com/Document.asp?DocID=3904.

LOBEL, ORLY, TALENT WANTS TO BE FREE: WHY WE SHOULD LEARN TO LOVE LEAKS, RAIDS, AND FREE RIDING, Yale Univ. Press (2013).

Lublin, Joann S., *Companies Loosen the Handcuffs on Non-Competes*, WALL ST. J. (Aug. 12, 2013).

MALSBERGER, BRIAN M., ED., COVENANTS NOT TO COMPETE, A STATE-BY-STATE SURVEY (2011 and Cum. Cupp. 2012).

Marx, Matt, *The Firm Strikes Back: Non-Compete Agreements and the Mobility of Technical Professionals*, 76 AM. SOC. REV. 695 (2011).

McDonald, M. Scott and Jacqueline Johnson, *Drafting and Enforcing Covenants Not to Compete*, w/ 2013 Cum. Supp. (2013).

Miller, Geoffrey P., *Bargains Bicoastal: New Light on Contract Theory*, 31 CARDOZO L. REV. 1475 (2010).

NATIONAL BUREAU OF ASIAN RESEARCH, *The Report of the Commission on the Theft of American Intellectual Property* (May 2013).

Pagnattaro, Marisa A., *Protecting Trade Secrets in China: Update on Employee Disclosures and the Limitations of the Law*, 45 AM. BUS. L.J. 399 (2008).

Pagnattaro, Marisa A., *The Google Challenge: Enforcement of Non-Compete and Trade Secret Agreements in China*, 44 AM. BUS. L.J. 603 (2007).

Palmer, Doug, *U.S. Seeks to Tackle Trade-Secret Theft by China, Others*, REUTERS (Feb 20, 2013), *available at* http://www.reuters.com/article/2013/02/21/us-usa-trade-secrets-idUSBRE91J0T220130221.

Posner, Eric A. and George G. Triantis, *Covenants Not to Compete from an Incomplete Contracts Perspective* 2-3 (Univ. of Chi. Law & Econ., Working Paper No. 137, 2001), *available at* http://papers.ssrn.com/paper.taf?abstract_id=285805.

Singer, Bill, *After Apple, Google, Adobe, Intel, Pixar, and Intuit, Antitrust Employment Charges Hit eBay*, Forbes.com (Nov. 19, 2012), *available at* http://www.forbes.com/sites/billsinger/2012/11/19/after-apple-google-adobe-pixar-google-and-intuit-antitrust-employment-charges-hit-ebay/.

Stone, Katherine V.W., *The New Psychological Contract: Implications for the Changing Workplace for Labor and Employment Law*, 48 UCLA L. REV. 519 (2001).

PART II

Workplace ramifications

4. Certification marks as private employment regulation

Jamie Darin Prenkert

This chapter will address a mechanism through which private ordering occurs, such that intellectual property can be used to create private employment and labor regulations. Certification marks can be used as the bases for certification and labeling systems that require adopters/licensees to commit to particular processes, practices, or behaviors that are intended to benefit workers. These can range from the prohibition of child labor to nondiscrimination commitments, and from wage and hour protections to health and safety standards, to name just a few. The chapter first provides the background on what certification marks are and how they undergird many certification systems, particularly those focused on social goals like the protection and ethical treatment of workers. It then provides a rough taxonomy of certification systems as they relate to employment and labor regulation, providing examples of five such approaches. Finally, the chapter identifies four characteristics – embodied in four questions – that inform how likely it is that the use of certification marks would effect change for workers, the intended beneficiaries of these private regulatory systems.

I. BACKGROUND

Prior to examining current examples of certification and evaluating how they might affect employment and labor conditions, this part provides an explanation of certification marks and a brief description of the history of certification.

A.   The Legal Status of Certification Marks

McCarthy describes certification marks as "special creatures" of trade-mark law.[1] They are used to indicate that the product or service that bears the mark has been certified as meeting a particular standard required by the licensor, the owner of the mark. In the United States, the Lanham Act defines "certification mark" as follows:

> any word, name, symbol or device, or any combination thereof (1) used by a person other than its owner, or (2) which its owner has a bona fide intention to permit a person other than the owner to use in commerce and files an application to register on the principal register established by this chapter, to certify regional or other origin, material, mode of manufacture, quality, accuracy, or other characteristics of such person's goods or services or that the work or labor on the goods or services was performed by members of a union or other organization.[2]

As such, certification marks serve a different purpose from traditional trademarks. In fact, the two are mutually exclusive to the extent that a mark used as a symbol of certification cannot be registered as a trademark.[3] A trademark identifies and distinguishes goods or services bearing the mark as coming from the owner of the mark. A certification mark, by contrast, provides an identifiable guarantee that the goods or services bearing the mark meet the standards set forth by the mark's owner, which has licensed the mark's use in relation to that good or service. Thus, unlike trademarks, which require the owner to be involved in the production of the product or the provision of the service bearing the mark – or risk loss of trademark rights as a result of abandonment[4] – certification mark owners are prohibited from using or displaying their marks on their own products or services.[5] Stated more directly, "[t]he owner of the mark is prohibited by law from practicing a self-produced mark, because self-certification is inherently self-interested."[6]

---

[1]   3 J. Thomas McCarthy, McCarthy on Trademarks and Unfair Competition § 19:91 (4th ed. 2005).

[2]   Lanham Act § 45, 15 U.S.C. § 1127 (2006).

[3]   *See* McCarthy, *supra* note 1, § 19:94.

[4]   *See* 15 U.S.C. § 1064.

[5]   *See ibid.* § 1054.

[6]   Ian Ayres and Jennifer Gerada Brown, *Mark(et)ing Nondiscrimination: Privatizing ENDA with a Certification Mark*, 104 Mich. L. Rev. 1639, 1643 (2006).

Owners of certification marks are expected to adhere to high standards of conduct regarding their licensing and enforcement of the mark. Decisions to certify a product can be based only on the standards the owner has promulgated for use of the mark. For instance, a mark owner cannot base the certification decision on whether the user/licensee is willing to pay the owner for using the mark (with the exception of fees to cover the cost of administering the certification mark).[7] Failure to conform to the standards of conduct expected of a certification mark owner can ultimately undermine the registration process and/or the rights the owner has in the mark.[8]

Internationally, certification marks have long been recognized and resemble the approach outlined in the Lanham Act. In fact, the United States was somewhat tardy in providing official recognition to certification marks in 1946. A number of the states had already provided such recognition and protection, following the lead of foreign countries.[9] For example, Britain provided legislative recognition of certification marks in 1905.[10]

Today, certification marks are recognized throughout much of the world, though not always under the "certification mark" appellation. They are protected due in part to the fact that the Paris Convention's reference to collective marks is generally understood to include certification marks as well.[11] That reference has led to the protection of certification marks under the TRIPS Agreement, at least to the extent that a certification mark is an indication of geographical origin.[12]

---

[7] *See Ibid.* ("In effect, the certifying entity must operate as a nonprofit.").

[8] *See* Mark R. Barron, Comment, *Creating Consumer Confidence or Confusion? The Role of Product Certification marks in the Market Today*, 11 MARQ. INTELL. PROP. L. REV. 413, 416 (2007) (citing Terry E. Holtzman, *Tips from the Trademark Examining Operation*, 81 TRADEMARK REP. 180 (1991)).

[9] *See* Paul Duguid, *A Case of Prejudice? The Uncertain Development of Collective and Certification Marks*, 86 BUS. HIST. REV. 311, 312 (2012) ("These [collective and certification] marks had been widely protected, not only outside the United States, but also within individual U.S. states, for more than fifty years.").

[10] *Ibid.* (noting that a revision to U.S. trademark law in that same year ignored collective and certification marks).

[11] Daphne Zografos Johnson, *International Intellectual Property Scholars series: Using Intellectual Property Rights to Create Value in the Coffee Industry*, 16 MARQ. INTELL. PROP. L. REV. 283, 305 (2012) (citing NORMA DAWSON, CERTIFICATION TRADE MARKS, LAW AND PRACTICE 13 (1988)).

[12] *Ibid.*

In some instances and some jurisdictions, certification marks are registered by the government. "Actual control of the use of [certification] marks may be vested in private bodies, or public bodies, such as government agencies or departments."[13] This chapter, however, focuses on the use of certification marks by private entities (perhaps in relationship with a public entity, in a public-private partnership) to accomplish or to supplement public goals. In other words, it explores certification marks' role as private regulation.

B. The History of Certification Marks as Regulation

Even before the Lanham Act provided formal recognition for certification marks, U.S. activists, union leaders, politicians, and bureaucrats recognized the potential power in certification labeling. The National Consumers' League certified garments as "made under clean and healthful conditions" with its "White Label," which was in use for roughly twenty years around the turn of the twentieth century.[14] The "White Label" was a progressive era response to deplorable working conditions in tenement sweatshops in the United States. Likewise, throughout the late nineteenth century and well into the middle of the twentieth century, trade unions used labels to promote the fact that products had been made by unionized workforces. At the height of the "union label" movement, more than sixty unions in the United States used labels to denote the source of a product's labor, and most of the states recognized the legal authority of unions to do so.[15] For instance, lumber mills used a stamp created by the Carpenter's Eight-Hour League of San Francisco to show that they ran on a more humanitarian eight-hour schedule than the otherwise prevailing ten-hour schedule.[16] Paul Duguid conjectures that courts' and Congress' antipathy to union activity at the turn of the twentieth century may

---

[13] JEFFREY BELSON, CERTIFICATION MARKS 26 (2002).

[14] Katheryn Kish Sklar, *The Consumers' White Label Campaign of the National Consumers' League, 1898–1918*, in GETTING AND SPENDING: EUROPEAN AND AMERICAN CONSUMER SOCIETIES IN THE TWENTIETH CENTURY 17, 18 (Susan Strasser et al., eds., 1998).

[15] *See* Duguid, *supra* note 9, at 317–18 (noting that, 'in 1900, the Cigar Makers' International Union (CMIU) gave out more than one billion [labels] and spend over thirty million dollars on 'label agitation,'" making it the most widespread and well supported of the union labels).

[16] *See* Ayres and Brown, *supra* note 6, at 1643 (citing ERNEST R. SPEDDEN, THE TRADE-UNION LABEL 10 n.2 (1910)).

explain why the United States was slow in recognizing certification marks in federal law.[17]

In a fascinating attempt to capitalize on the power of symbols and labeling that was a precursor to today's regulation by certification, the Roosevelt administration developed the "Blue Eagle" in 1933, in conjunction with the National Industrial Recovery Act (NIRA) and the National Recovery Administration (NRA).[18] As part of the "First New Deal," the NIRA tried to empower the president to address the market instability that was seen as the cause of the Great Depression by authorizing the Administration, through the NRA, to develop codes of fair competition through public hearings and to negotiate voluntary agreements with industries to address work hours, rates of pay, and price fixing.[19] The first director of the NRA was Hugh Samuel Johnson, who called on every business in every industry to agree to a "blanket code," which included a minimum wage of between twenty and forty-five cents per hour, a maximum work week of 35 to 45 hours, and an end to child labor.[20] Johnson utilized the Blue Eagle symbol,[21] depicted in Figure 4.1, to indicate those businesses that voluntarily accepted the blanket code. In turn, consumers were encouraged to give preference only to those businesses displaying the Blue Eagle. Johnson said, "when every American housewife understands that the Blue Eagle on everything that she permits into her home is a symbol of its restoration to security, may God have mercy on the man or group of men who attempt to trifle with this bird."[22]

---

[17] *See* Duguid, *supra* note 9, at 313. See *supra* text accompanying notes 9–10 for a discussion of the United States' tardiness in recognizing certification marks until the passage of the Lanham Act in 1946.

[18] *National Industrial Recovery Act*, U.S. HIST., http://www.u-s-history.com/ pages/h1663.html (last visited Aug. 25, 2014).

[19] *Ibid.*

[20] *The New Deal*, AM. HIST. SCRAPBOOK, http://mfaewillard.weebly.com/ the-new-deal.html (last visited Aug. 25, 2014).

[21] Many sources credit Charles T. Coiner, a noted advertising art director, with the design of the Blue Eagle logo. *See, e.g., Charles T. Coiner, 91, Ex-Art Chief at Ayer*, N.Y. TIMES, Aug. 16, 1989; *Charles Coiner Papers: An Inventory of His Papers at Syracuse University*, SYRACUSE UNIV. LIBR., http:// library.syr.edu/digital/guides/c/coiner_c.htm (last visited Aug. 25, 2014). Others credit Johnson with conceiving and initially sketching it. *See* ROBERT HIMMEL-BERG, THE ORIGINS OF THE NATIONAL RECOVERY ADMINISTRATION (2d ed., 1993).

[22] ALONZO L. HAMBY, FOR THE SURVIVAL OF DEMOCRACY 164 (1994).

Figure 4.1   NRA "Blue Eagle" poster (public domain)

The Blue Eagle never had the opportunity to reach the level of domin-
ance envisioned by Johnson because the U.S. Supreme Court declared
relevant portions of the NIRA unconstitutional. In *Schechter Poultry
Corp. v. United States*,[23] the Court held that the mandatory codes sections
of the NIRA were an unconstitutional delegation of power to the
executive and exceeded Congress' commerce clause power.[24] As a

---

[23]   295 U.S. 495 (1935).
[24]   *Ibid.* Note that this decision preceded the "switch in time that saved nine,"
in *West Coast Hotel v. Parrish*, 300 U.S. 379 (1937), which headed off President
Roosevelt's court-packing plan and heralded the end of the Lochner Era.

result, the Blue Eagle emblem was discontinued and its use as a symbol prohibited by law.[25]

Following the enactment of the Lanham Act, certification marks were largely used for the balance of the twentieth century in the United States as indictors of product quality. The most famous certification marks included the Underwriters Laboratories (UL) label, which originally signified electrical safety for the U.S. market (and has since branched out to multiple other areas of certification);[26] the Orthodox Union mark, which serves as a kosher certification;[27] and the Good Housekeeping Seal of Approval, which serves as an endorsement by the Good Housekeeping Research Institute that the product to which it is affixed will perform as intended and as a limited warranty by Good Housekeeping if a labeled product is defective.[28]

C. The Impetus and Goals of Modern Social Certification Systems

A number of recent certification mark labeling initiatives have returned to the original focus on the conditions under which products are manufactured, including the employment and labor conditions in a business' facilities and along its supply chain. Due to globalization, consumers are confronted with products that are manufactured all over the world, particularly in countries and regions with underdeveloped labor and employment protections or limited capacity to enforce those protections.[29] Moreover, no national legal authority has sufficient reach to comprehensively regulate them. UN Special Representative of the Secretary-General on the Issue of Human Rights and Transnational Corporations and Other Business Enterprises, John Ruggie, called these

---

[25]   Jennifer Bair et al., *To Label or Not to Label, Is That the Question? in* WORKER'S RIGHTS AND LABOR COMPLIANCE IN GLOBAL SUPPLY CHAINS: IS A SOCIAL LABEL THE ANSWER?, at 3, 9 (Jennifer Bair et al. 2013).

[26]   *See Marks and Labels*, UNDERWRITERS LAB., http://ul.com/corporate/marks/ (last visited Mar. 18, 2015) ("UL is a global leader in testing, inspection, certification, auditing and validation. The UL Mark is the single most accepted Certification Mark in the United States, appearing on 22 billion products annually.").

[27]   *Kosher Certification Policy*, OU KOSHER, http://oukosher.org/kosher-certification-policy/ (last visited Aug. 25, 2014).

[28]   *About the GH Limited Warranty Seal*, GOOD HOUSEKEEPING (Mar. 31, 2014, 6:00 AM), http://www.goodhousekeeping.com/product-reviews/history/about-good-housekeeping-seal.

[29]   Ayres and Brown, *supra* note 6, at 1441.

limitations "governance gaps."[30] While he was focused more broadly on businesses' responsibilities related to human rights, those concerns encompass the labor and employment conditions under which many products and services are manufactured and provided. Governance gaps result from inadequate national regulatory reach, a nonexistent international regulatory framework, and/or insufficiently organized and empowered non-state market and social actors. Governance gaps manifest in a variety of forms. Structurally, public governance is fragmented along national territorial lines, while the global economy transcends such territorial boundaries.[31] Even within and among those national jurisdictions, governments often lack both vertical and horizontal policy coherence.[32] Finally, states often lack the ability or desire to develop or enforce regulatory measures, because they fear either a lack of capacity to enforce them or a litany of negative market-based consequences for regulating in a way that is interpreted as hostile to business interests.[33] Thus, certification schemes have been rolled out as one way to bridge the governance gaps that have resulted.

Certification systems can serve as a form of private, market-based regulation. Generally a certification system works through an association that develops standards, accredits auditors, and provides some sort of certification for organizations that meet the standards as determined by

---

[30] *See* Jamie Darin Prenkert, *Conflict Minerals and Polycentric Governance of Business and Human Rights*, *in* LAW, BUSINESS AND HUMAN RIGHTS: BRIDGING THE GAP 203, 207 (Bird et al., eds., 2014) (describing governance gaps).

[31] Report of the Special Representative of the Secretary-General on Human Rights, Transnational Corporations, and Other Business Enterprises, Protect, Respect and Remedy: A Framework for Business and Human Rights, Hum. Rts. Council, U.N. Doc. A/HRC/8/5 (April 7, 2008), *available at* http://198.170.85.29/Ruggie-report-7-Apr-2008.pdf.

[32] *Ibid.* Vertical incoherence occurs when a state adopts an obligation – for instance through legislation – but fails to give sufficient regard or effort to its implementation. Horizontal incoherence occurs when states regulate in one area in isolation (e.g., child labor in a particular industry) with little regard for how that interacts with or affects regulatory efforts elsewhere in the government. *See also* John Gerard Ruggie, Special Representative of the Secretary-General on the Issue of Human Rights and Transnational Corporations and Other Business Enterprises, Keynote Address at the 3rd Annual Responsible Investment Forum, New York, NY (Jan. 12, 2009), *available at* http://www.reports-and-materials.org/sites/default/files/reports-and-materials/Ruggie-address-to-Responsible-Invest-Forum-12-Jan-2009.pdf.

[33] Ruggie, *supra* note 32.

the accredited auditors. One way, though not the only way,[34] of providing and communicating the certification is for the certifying organization to authorize the use of a certification mark. This process is regulatory in a couple of senses. First, though it is voluntary and does not have the full legitimacy and coercive power that accompanies state regulation, a certification system incorporates more aspects of a hard law system than some other soft law approaches, like corporate codes of conduct or international guidance instruments.[35] Certification systems usually involve "standards that are often precise and prescriptive, plus rationalized procedures for assessing compliance, and adjudicating disputes."[36] Nonetheless, the "'price' of non-compliance is set by market forces, not by administrative authority."[37] Whether the standards imposed by the certification system confer benefits on the populations the standards are promulgated to support depends on what that price is and how it is imposed. In public-private certification systems, that cost might be debarment or disqualification from selling products in a particular market. If the focus of the certification system is the granting of a license to use a certification mark in relation to a product, the price will be loss of the privilege to use the mark and any other damages that might come from violating the license.

Second, certification systems are, at least in part, regulation by information disclosure. That information disclosure is available not only to consumers but also to other stakeholders, such as suppliers and buyers, investors, employees, advocacy organizations, the general citizenry, and lawmakers.[38] Therefore, the regulatory nature of certification systems is not solely marked-based, but it can also come about "through political and legal mobilization."[39] Nonetheless, the amount and type of information that is produced through certification systems is often less

---

[34]   Some certification systems do not utilize certification marks, but will allow certified organizations to make limited use of the certifying organization's trademark in their own marketing materials or on their Web sites to indicate or report on the certification, but not to affix it to any particular product.

[35]   Tim Bartley, *Certification as a Mode of Social Regulation*, in HANDBOOK ON THE POLITICS OF REGULATION 441, 444 (David Levi-Faur ed., 2011).

[36]   *Ibid.* at 442.

[37]   *Ibid.*

[38]   *Cf.* Stephen Kim Park, *Human Rights Reporting as Self-Interest: The Integrative and Expressive Dimensions of Corporate Disclosure*, in LAW, BUSINESS AND HUMAN RIGHTS: BRIDGING THE GAP, *supra* note 30, at 48 (arguing that disclosure serves an internal educative and expressive purpose, as well as an external informational purpose).

[39]   Bartley, *supra* note 36, at 443.

extensive than other types of mandatory disclosures.[40] Certification only provides positive information about businesses that voluntarily choose to submit to the certification and satisfy the certification standards.[41] The usefulness of the certification mark is dependent on the various stakeholders' understanding of the contours and implications of those standards. In a system that focuses primarily on granting a license to use a certification mark, the access to what the mark means will depend largely on the fame and exposure of the mark and the standards it represents.

In the context of certification systems focused on labor and employment standards, there are several ways that certification marks have been used to accomplish these regulatory goals. The following section addresses five different approaches to the use of certification marks in certification systems. In discussing these approaches, I offer a taxonomy of sorts to describe a continuum of reliance on marks in various contexts.

II. APPROACHES TO THE USE OF CERTIFICATION MARKS FOR LABOR AND EMPLOYMENT REGULATION

This section provides an overview of five uses of certification marks. The five certifications differ along several variables. First, the centrality of the mark to the system varies. Second, there are significant differences in the breadth of the conduct sought to be regulated, ranging from issues that are unrelated to the workplace in addition to general labor and employment conditions to limited and specific such conditions. Third, they differ on whether the certification is limited to a particular product or service or rather certifies the organization as a whole. Finally they may supplement existing regulation that for whatever reason is perceived as lax or underenforced, or they may fill a regulatory void. The following section provides examples that cross-cut each of these variables.

---

[40] *See, e.g.*, Conflict Minerals, 77 Fed. Reg. 56,274 (Sept. 12, 2012) (to be codified at 17 C.F.R. pts. 240 and 249b) (describing disclosure requirements for public reporting companies for whom certain minerals that have been connected with conflict in the Democratic Republic of the Congo and its neighboring states are necessary for the functionality or production of a product they manufacture).

[41] Bartley, *supra* note 36, at 443.

A. Multi-Stakeholder Codes and Ancillary Use of Certification Marks

Two major standard-setting organizations offer certifications that address workplace conditions to varying degrees. Each sets standards for processes and workplace conditions rather than for products and, thus, does not allow the use of the organization's associated marks on individual products. In other words, these certifications say nothing about the quality of a product, so the standard-settings organizations refuse to allow labeling of products out of fear that marketing the products as certified would be false and misleading. The approach used by these groups most resembles the prototype of certification described in the previous section.[42] The two organizations will be discussed in turn: the International Organization for Standardization (ISO) and Social Accountability International (SAI).

1. ISO

No discussion of certification would be complete without describing ISO. It is the world's largest organization dedicated to the development of voluntary international standards for products, services, and practices or processes.[43] ISO is a nongovernmental, independent organization headquartered in Geneva, Switzerland, consisting of the national standards bodies of more than 160 countries.[44] Its goal in doing so is to help make industry more effective and efficient.[45] The standards developed by ISO are used in conformity assessments, which can take the form of certification, inspection, and testing. While testing is the most common, certification is the most well-known and relevant to this discussion.[46] ISO does not provide conformity assessment or certification on its own; rather, certification bodies provide auditing and certification consistent with the ISO standards.[47] Thus, a company or organization cannot be certified *by* ISO; it can only be certified *to* an ISO standard and will receive a certificate from the certification body verifying that fact.[48]

---

[42] *See supra* text preceding note 34.

[43] *About ISO*, ISO, http://www.iso.org/iso/home/about.htm (last visited Aug. 25, 2014).

[44] *Ibid.*

[45] *Ibid.*

[46] *What Is Conformity Assessment?*, ISO, http://www.iso.org/iso/home/about/conformity-assessment.htm (last visited Aug. 25, 2014).

[47] *Certification*, ISO, http://www.iso.org/iso/home/standards/certification.htm (last visited Aug. 25, 2014).

[48] *Ibid.*

Though most of ISO's wide-ranging standards have little or nothing to do with labor or employment conditions, the ISO 9000 Quality Management family of standards has some relevance to the workplace experience of employees. In particular, Principle 2 (Leadership) of the Quality Management Principles will lead to "[c]reating and sustaining shared values, fairness and ethical role models at all levels of the organization" and "providing people with the required resources, training and freedom to act with responsibility and accountability."[49] However, unlike the other standards and certifications discussed below, none of the ISO standards directly address issues like child labor, workplace health and safety, nondiscrimination, employees' freedom of association, or wage and hour requirements.

Once a company or organization obtains certification to an ISO standard by a certification body, ISO has strict rules about the usage of ISO marks and logos. Certified organizations are prohibited from using the ISO logo or adapting or modifying the logo for their own use.[50] Individual certification bodies sometimes provide their own certification marks, but ISO does not control, monitor, or regulate their use.[51] For example, BSI, a certification body in the United Kingdom, provides ISO 9001 conformity assessment and certification.[52] Once certified, BSI provides a certification mark that organizations can use in their advertising and informational materials. However, consistent with an ISO mandate, Quality Management standards certify processes, not products, so certification marks may not be displayed on products, product labels, or product packaging.[53]

In general, consumers are not the target audience for ISO 9001 certification, because information about the standards has not sufficiently saturated the consciousness of the general public to provide much in the way of marketing leverage. Rather, other external audiences are more likely the targets, including suppliers, buyers, and contracting parties.

---

[49] ISO, QUALITY MANAGEMENT PRINCIPLES (2012), *available at* http://www.iso.org/iso/qmp_2012.pdf.

[50] ISO, PUBLICIZING YOUR ISO 9001:2008 OR ISO 14001:2004 CERTIFICATION 2 (2010), *available at* http://www.iso.org/iso/publicizing_iso9001_iso14001_certification_2010.pdf.

[51] *Ibid.*

[52] *Certification to ISO 9001 Quality Management*, BSI, http://www.bsigroup.com/en-GB/iso-9001-quality-management/Certification-for-ISO-9001/ (last visited Apr. 20, 2014).

[53] *See* ISO, *supra* note 50, at 2.

The labeling of individual products would not likely be particularly meaningful.

2. SAI

SAI is a multi-stakeholder, nongovernmental organization that seeks to advance the human rights of workers around the world.[54] Thus, unlike ISO, SAI is uniquely focused on the experience of workers and the workplace. The centerpiece of SAI's work in this regard is the SA8000 Standard. The SA8000 is "one of the world's first auditable certification standards for decent workplaces, across all industrial sectors."[55] Companies that comply with SA8000 standards adopt policies and procedures that address the nine elements of the standard: child labor, forced and compulsory labor, health and safety, freedom of association and right to collective bargaining, discrimination, disciplinary practices, working hours, remuneration, and management systems.[56] These elements are drawn from International Labour Organization (ILO) conventions, United Nations declarations and conventions, and prevailing national laws.[57] SA8000 certification signifies that a company's codes of conduct and similar policies are sufficiently well-drafted and implemented to ensure the protection of the nine elements of workers' human rights. Whereas codes of conduct are voluntarily adopted and are not generally accompanied by any legal or regulatory compulsion,[58] the SA8000 provides some accountability for those codes and policies through auditing and complaint processes.[59]

---

[54] *About SAI*, Soc. Accountability Int'l, http://www.sa-intl.org/index.cfm?fuseaction=Page.ViewPage&pageId=472 (last visited Aug. 25, 2014) ("SAI works to protect the integrity of workers around the world by building local capacity and developing systems of accountability through socially responsible standards.").

[55] *SA8000® Standard*, Soc. Accountability Int'l, http://www.sa-intl.org/index.cfm?fuseaction=Page.ViewPage&pageId=937 (last visited Aug. 25, 2014).

[56] *Ibid.*

[57] *Ibid.*

[58] *See* Michael Urminsky, *Self-Regulation in the Workplace: Codes of Conduct, Social Labeling and Socially Responsible Investment* 13 (ILO, MCC Working Paper No. 1) ("The International Organization of Employers (IOE) estimates that 80 per cent of codes of conduct fall into the category of general business ethics with no implementation methods.").

[59] For a description of the complaint resolution program related to SA8000 and administered by the SAAS complaint management system, see *Complaint Resolution Program*, Soc. Accountability Int'l, http://www.sa-intl.org/index.cfm?fuseaction=Page.ViewPage&pageId=1460 (last visited Apr. 20, 2014).

Like the ISO, SAI is the standard-setting organization, while Social Accountability Accreditation Services (SAAS) evaluates and accredits auditing organizations that provide SA8000 certification.[60] For example, Bureau Veritas provides certification services worldwide, including SA8000 certification.[61] In addition to certification marks licensed by accredited certification bodies like Bureau Veritas,[62] SAI allows the use of the SA8000 logo[63] by certified companies or facilities "on promotional material, websites, and other print or online materials."[64] Moreover, SAI provides guidelines for the use of hangtags to advertise a consumer-level product as having been produced in an SA8000-certified facility.[65] However, a certified organization or retailer must do so in a way that does not suggest product certification, because "the marketing of a product as being 'SA8000-certified' is false and misleading."[66] While, like the ISO certification, SA8000 certification relates to the company's or facility's policies and processes, SAI apparently sees greater utility in allowing some consumer-oriented use of logos and hangtags to indicate that products were manufactured in SA8000-certified facilities, even if the products themselves are not specifically certified. As I suggest in the Part III below, the worker-focused human rights that are the subject of SA8000 certification have more salience and are more easily valued and understood by consumers than the more abstract ISO 9001 Quality Management standards. Though a detailed appreciation of the nuances of the SA8000 standards is still likely beyond the average informed consumer, the notion of a clear and unambiguous commitment to worker's rights can be communicated through the use of the logo in association with consumer-level products.

---

[60] Soc. Accountability Accreditation Servs., http://www.saasaccreditation. org/ (last visited Aug. 25, 2014).

[61] Bureau Veritas Certification Servs., *SA8000 Certification*, Bureau Veritas, http://www.bureauveritas.com/wps/wcm/connect/3494830047e94ad7af7aafafdca0d0a3/SA8000.pdf?MOD=AJPERES&CACHEID=3494830047e94ad7af7aafafdca0d0a3 (last visited Aug. 25, 2014).

[62] See *Ibid.* for a representation of the Bureau Veritas Certification Mark, modified for SA8000 certification purposes. "The Bureau Veritas Certification Mark is a globally recognized symbol of your organization's ongoing commitment to excellence, sustainability and reliability." *Ibid.*

[63] For a representation of the SA8000 logo, see Soc. Accountability Int'l, Guidelines for Corporate Communication and Graphic Standards 9 (2012).

[64] *Ibid.* at 6.

[65] *Ibid.* at 5.

[66] *Ibid.* at 6.

B. Product-Level Certification Mark with Ancillary Impact on Labor Standards

Among the most famous social labels is the FAIRTRADE Mark, owned by Fairtrade International (FLO).[67] In stark contrast to the ISO and SAI approaches, which prohibit use of marks to signify product certification, the FAIRTRADE Mark is a "product label[] primarily intended for use on product packaging."[68] It is found on a range of products, from foods and drinks to cotton, clothing, and jewelry. The use of the FAIRTRADE Mark signifies that all the ingredients or component parts of the labeled product are sourced from Fairtrade certified producers.

The Fairtrade certification system is administered by FLO-CERT, a separate entity from FLO. Like other certification systems, FLO-CERT engages in auditing and inspection to ensure that products bearing the FAIRTRADE Mark come from producers who meet Fairtrade Standards promulgated by FLO.[69] Although a long list of standards applies to specific products, there are generic standards, which include the Standard

---

[67]   There are actually a series of FAIRTRADE Marks, including the FAIR-TRADE Mark and FAIRTRADE Program Marks, which deal with sourcing certification for cocoa, sugar, and cotton. *See The FAIRTRADE Program Marks*, FAIRTRADE INT'L, http://www.fairtrade.net/fairtrade-program-mark.html. For ease of reference and because the labor standards are more specifically implicated under the FAIRTRADE Mark, I refer only to it here.

In September 2011, Fair Trade USA, the leading third-party certifier of U.S. Fair Trade products, resigned its membership in the international Fairtrade system. *Q&A on Fairtrade International and Fair Trade USA*, FAIRTRADE INT'L, http://www.fairtrade.net/897.html (last visited Aug. 25, 2014). Fair Trade USA runs its own independent certification system and licenses the Fair Trade Certified label. *Certification Mark: Frequently Asked Questions*, FAIR TRADE USA, http://fairtradeusa.org/sites/all/files/wysiwyg/filemanager/label/Fair-Trade-USA-FAQ-newcertificationmark.pdf (last visited Aug. 25, 2014). Similar to Fairtrade International, Fair Trade USA has a Farm Workers Standard as part of its certification standards, which closely resembles the principles and requirements under the International Hired Labor Standard. *See* FAIR TRADE USA, FAIR TRADE USA COMPLIANCE CRITERIA FOR THE FARM WORKERS STANDARD 1.1 (2014), *available at* http://fairtradeusa.org/sites/all/files/wysiwyg/filemanager/FT USA_FWS_CC_1.1v3_EN_040214.pdf.

[68]   *The Fairtrade Marks*, FAIRTRADE INT'L, http://www.fairtrade.net/the-fair trade-marks.html (last visited Aug. 25, 2014).

[69]   *FAQs: Frequently Asked Questions*, FAIRTRADE INT'L, http://www. fairtrade.net/faqs.html (last visited Aug. 25, 2014) ("For a product to display the FAIRTRADE Certification Mark it must meet international Fairtrade Standards. These standards are established by Fairtrade International and … are the result of broad consultations of different stakeholders and external experts.").

for Hired Labor.[70] The Standard for Hired Labor is based on principles related to the management of the Fairtrade Premium, which is a premium payment over and above the minimum Fairtrade Price and is reinvested to build long-term sustainability for the producers and the community;[71] freedom of association and collective bargaining; safe working conditions, including standards on child labor and health and safety; nondiscrimination; and equitable pay.[72] Certification by FLO-CERT includes an initial audit and evaluation. If certification is reached following that, FLO-CERT will carry out at least two additional audits[73] during the ensuing three-year "certification cycle." At the end of that cycle, FLO-CERT will issue a renewed certification if the interim audits are successfully completed.[74]

Manufacturers, producers, retailers, and other organizations can make use of the FAIRTRADE Mark on a product to signify that all ingredients or components in the product that can be sourced from a Fairtrade certified producer have been.[75] Use of the Mark requires a license from Fairtrade International, a national Fairtrade organization,[76] or a Fairtrade marketing organization.[77]

As product-level certification marks the FAIRTRADE Mark and the Fair Trade Certified mark both put a premium on direct-to-consumer information sharing regarding the certification standards. Though the

---

[70] *List of Fairtrade International Standards Available on Website*, FAIRTRADE INT'L, http://www.fairtrade.net/fileadmin/user_upload/content/2009/standards/documents/2012-08-03_LIST_OF_FLO_Standards.pdf (last visited Aug. 25, 2014).

[71] Caspar van Vark, *Q&A: Fair Trade for All*, THEGUARDIAN (Feb. 27, 2008, 8:13 AM), http://www.theguardian.com/environment/2008/feb/27/qa.fairtrade.

[72] FAIRTRADE INT'L, FAIRTRADE STD. FOR HIRED LABOUR (Jan. 1, 2014), *available at* http://www.fairtrade.net/fileadmin/user_upload/content/2009/standards/documents/generic-standards/2014-03-14_HL_EN.pdf.

[73] *How It Works*, FLOCERT, http://www.flo-cert.net/fairtrade-services/fairtrade-certification/how-it-works/ (last visited Aug. 25, 2014) ("If we classify an organization as 'high risk' – perhaps because of the complexity of its trade chains or high volume of trade – more audits may be needed. We also widely carry out unannounced audits.").

[74] *Ibid.*

[75] *Using the FAIRTRADE Marks*, FAIRTRADE INT'L, http://www.fairtrade.net/using-the-fairtrade-mark.html (last visited Aug. 25, 2014).

[76] In the United States, the national Fairtrade organization is Fairtrade America. *See* FAIRTRADE AMERICA, http://fairtradeamerica.org/ (last visited Apr. 21, 2014).

[77] *Using FAIRTRADE Marks*, *supra* note 75.

standards deal with trade, pricing, sourcing, and specific product attributes in addition to labor conditions, the latter are an important part of what the certification standards communicate to the consumers. And the marks have developed a general aura of social consciousness that likely aids in their effectiveness at encouraging adherence to those standards through market pressure.

C. Limited Product/Broad Labor Standard Certification

In May 2008, the largest ever single-site immigration raid occurred at the Agriprocessors plant in Postville, Iowa. U.S. Immigration and Customs Enforcement officials arrested and handcuffed nearly 400 immigrant workers who were unauthorized to work in the United States.[78] Many of them served jail time for identity theft before being deported.[79] The Agriprocessors plant workforce was devastated. As the nation's largest supplier of kosher beef, the disruption at the Postville plant affected or at least caught the attention of Jewish communities in the United States.[80]

Certification marks play a central role in assisting consumers to identify kosher products. The Orthodox Union's mark, a *U* inside of an *O*, appears on more than 400,000 products from Oreo cookies to Land O' Lakes butter.[81] A number of other smaller, state- and local-level kosher certifying agencies also exist.[82] They are all focused, though, on the requirements of the *kashrut*, the Jewish dietary laws. Agriprocessors' products were certified as kosher by the Orthodox Union and others, but a constituency of Orthodox and Conservative Jewish leaders were concerned that no certification process looked at the social and ethical standards under which kosher products were produced. Thus, the Magen Tzedek was born.

---

[78] Spencer S. Hsu, *Immigration Raid Jars Small Town*, WASH. POST (May 18, 2008), http://www.washingtonpost.com/wp-dyn/content/article/2008/05/17/AR2008051702474.html.

[79] Harvey Popolaw, *Recalling the Postville Tragedy: Impetus for Comprehensive Immigration Reform Bill*, JEWISH SOC. JUST. ROUNDTABLE (May 10, 2013, 10:44 AM), http://jewishsocialjustice.org/blog/recalling-postville-tragedy-impetus-comprehensive-immigration-reform-bill.

[80] *See* Hsu, *supra* note 78.

[81] Louis Nayman, *Kosher Gets Ethical*, IN THESE TIMES (Jan. 7, 2011), http://inthesetimes.com/article/6743/kosher_gets_ethical.

[82] *Directory of Kosher Certifying Agencies*, CHICAGO RABBINICAL COUNCIL, http://www.crcweb.org/agency_list.php (last updated Aug. 18, 2014).

Magen Tzedek means "star of justice" and was founded to bring the "Jewish commitment to ethics and social justice directly into the market-place ... and the home."[83] The Magen Tzedek Commission has created a certification mark that it will license to kosher product producers that meet a series of standards related to labor practices, animal welfare, consumer protection, corporate integrity, environmental impacts, and traceability, which the Commission developed in consultation with SAAS.[84] The labor standards deal with living wages and benefits (including maternity and parent care leave, bereavement leave, child care, and other benefits), freedom of association and the right to collective bargaining, health and safety, antidiscrimination, and child and forced labor.[85] SAAS will accredit auditing and certification bodies that will, in turn, certify kosher products that are produced in accordance with the Magen Tzedek standards.

Only otherwise certified kosher products are eligible for Magen Tzedek certification.[86] Thus, the audience for the Magen Tzedek mark is an already well-informed consumer (i.e., the kosher buyer). As a result, it may be more likely that this specialized consumer will be attuned to the addition of the Magen Tzedek mark to a kosher product (or lack thereof). Thus, the price of noncompliance may be greater than in the foregoing examples of certification. Nonetheless, Magen Tzedek has been met with some resistance, because it supplements what some Jewish leaders see as sufficient existing legal requirements. Rabbi Avi Shafran, who is the spokesperson for one of the leading fundamentalist Orthodox religious, educational, and advocacy organizations, Agudath Israel of America, stated: "I think that many consumers have no reason to distrust the government agencies and law enforcement agencies as adequate safe-guards for all those areas... I know of no *halachic* [Jewish law] opinion requiring a kosher consumer to try to ensure that companies go beyond what governmental rules require of them."[87] So the supplemental charac-ter of the certification regulatory scheme represented by Magen Tzedek may or may not work in its favor.

---

[83] *Mission Statement*, MAGEN TZEDEK, http://www.magentzedek.org/about-us/mission-statement/ (last visited Apr. 21, 2014).

[84] *See* MAGEN TZEDEK COMMISSION, CERTIFICATION STANDARDS FOR THE MAGEN TZEDEK SERVICE MARK (2012).

[85] *Ibid* at 8–13.

[86] *Ibid.* at 5.

[87] Nayman, *supra* note 81.

D. Limited Product/Limited Standard Certification Filling a Traditional Governance Gap

In response to reports of widespread use of child labor in the hand-knotted rug producing industry, particularly in India, a demand for a certification standard to eradicate child labor from it arose. Originally entitled "Rugmark," the Goodweave certification system and certification mark is intended to prohibit the export of rugs made with child labor, and it is guided by ILO Conventions 138, regarding minimum age for work, and 182, regarding the eradication of the worst forms of child labor.[88] Goodweave inspectors and auditors not only look for compliance, but if they find noncompliant employment of child labor, they are empowered by the standards to remedy the situation by removing the child from the workplace, returning him or her home, and ensuring his or her enrollment in school.[89] The Goodweave mark seeks to fill a governance gap created by states that lack the capacity or will to monitor, enforce, and remedy child labor violations.

The Goodweave International Certification Division administers the Goodweave International Generic International Standard for Rug Producers. The standard requires compliance with the following commitments:

- A ban on the use of labor by children younger than 14;
- cooperation with Goodweave remediation efforts;
- recordkeeping on wage and benefits paid;
- disclosure and traceability of supply chain and production processes; and
- providing Goodweave inspectors and auditors access to production facilities.[90]

Noncompliance with these requirements, if not corrected, will result in revocation of the license to use the Goodweave label.[91]

Because the Goodweave mark represents a specific and limited labor standard within a circumscribed industry, its salience to consumers will

---

[88] GOODWEAVE INT'L, GENERIC INTERNATIONAL STANDARD FOR RUG PRODUCERS 2 (2012), *available at* https://www.goodweave.org/uploads/GWI-Generic-Intl-Standard-v2-3.pdf.

[89] *Ibid.* at 5.

[90] *Ibid.* at 3–4.

[91] *Ibid.* at 2. For a visual representation of the Goodweave label, see GOODWEAVE INT'L, GOODWEAVE INTERNATIONAL (GWI) TRADEMARK POLICY 2 (2013).

likely be high. Moreover, because it seeks to regulate an area in which states have traditionally failed to sufficiently fulfill their responsibilities, consumer demand, as well as consumer and producer efficacy, are likely to be high. Because producers understand that they are under an international human rights obligation not to use child labor, even if state efforts are lax, producers are unlikely to seek to avoid private regulation efforts.

E. Product Labeling/Certification in an Area of Otherwise Absent Regulation

The Employment Nondiscrimination Act (ENDA) has been introduced in Congress every term since 1993, yet it has never been enacted.[92] Nonetheless, public opinion is strongly in favor of protecting LGBT employees from discrimination in employment.[93] Given that these facts exist in some tension, law professors Ian Ayres and Jennifer Gerada Brown conceived of a certification scheme to allow employers to commit to nondiscrimination on the basis of sexual orientation and gender identity. Ayres and Brown registered the Fair Employment Mark with the U.S. Patent and Trademark Office as a certification mark.[94] They offered to license the Fair Employment Mark free of charge to any employer who will make two promises:

1. Not to discriminate in employment on the basis of sexual orientation or gender identity; and
2. To grant all of its employees and applicants the right to sue the employer directly for a remedy of any breach of the nondiscrimination promise.[95]

The first promise is represented in the Fair Employment Mark license agreement by the licensee agreeing to adhere to the dictates of ENDA as though it were duly enacted by Congress. The second promise is included

---

[92] Examples of failed versions of ENDA are S. 2056, 104th Cong. (1996); H.R. 1863, 104th Cong. (1995); and H.R. 4636, 103d Cong. (1994).

[93] *See* Ian Ayres and Jennifer Gerada Brown, *Privatizing Employment Protections*, 49 ARIZ. L. REV. 587, 587 (2007).

[94] *See* Ayres and Brown, *supra* note 6, at 1641 & n.6.

[95] *Ibid.* at 1644; *see also* Ayres and Brown, *supra* note 93, at 596–97 (describing a revision to the original license agreement for the Fair Employment Mark to include a prohibition against gender identity discrimination, in line with the evolution of ENDA).

in the license agreement through an express grant to the licensee's employees and applicants of third-party beneficiary status under the agreement.[96]

Because of the nature of these commitments, Ayres and Brown, as owners of the Fair Employment Mark, do not face the daunting task of developing standards, accrediting certifying agencies, and/or engaging in extensive and repeated auditing and certification reviews. Rather, the signing the license agreement is coextensive with the required promises from the owners' standpoint.[97] The provision of third-party beneficiary status to employees and applicants supplies the enforcement mechanism, in contrast to other certification marks that require the owner to police compliance through complaint procedures and repeated inspections.[98] From the perspective of the owners, the process is nearly costless.

Ayres and Brown explain that signing the license agreement allows, but does not require, a licensee to affix the Fair Employment Mark to its marketing materials, product packaging, and any other medium it desires to signal its commitment to nondiscrimination on the basis of sexual orientation and gender identity.[99] However, in signing the license, the employer takes on contractual liability under a legal standard (i.e., ENDA) that it would not otherwise face. Presumably, a licensee would do so to win market share from LGBT consumers and allies, to recruit and retain LGBT and ally employees, and to simply signal an ethical commitment to equality.[100]

In reality, though, there has been little to no uptake of the Fair Employment Mark. This could be due to the lack of general knowledge of the consuming public about the details of ENDA, despite the support for LGBT nondiscrimination in employment. Moreover, unlike the foregoing schemes, where the mark supplements or reinforces existing legal and regulatory duties of the licensee, the Fair Employment Mark would require the licensee to adopt a legally binding obligation to third parties where one otherwise does not exist. That likely appears to be a substantial cost in the cost-benefit analysis any potential licensee would go through, especially when some of the assumed signaling benefit – to consumers, employees, and the general public – of the Fair Employment

---

[96]   Ayres and Brown, *supra* note 6, at 1644.

[97]   *Ibid.* at 1644 ("Because the licensing agreement expressly includes both of these elements [i.e., the promises], we can truthfully certify these matters merely by certifying that the licensee has signed the license.").

[98]   *Ibid.* at 1641.

[99]   *Ibid.*

[100]   *Ibid.* at 1679–88.

Mark could be captured by voluntary policies and codes of conduct that profess a commitment to equal treatment and nondiscrimination on the basis of sexual orientation and gender identity.

III. IMPLICATIONS AND REFLECTIONS

Certification systems have become an increasingly utilized mechanism with which to impose private ordering in a number of institutions, particularly the workplace. Certification is often focused on issues of importance to the human rights of employees. Yet, as the examples above indicate, not all certification systems have equal likelihood of success in bringing about the hoped-for changes in workplace conditions. This part identifies four characteristics – embodied in four questions – that inform how likely it is for the use of certification marks to effect change for workers, the intended beneficiaries of these private regulatory systems.

A. Does it Focus on Standards that are Otherwise Obligatory on the Licensee?

Whether a regulatory system based on certification is likely to make a difference in the labor and employment environment of the average worker depends at least in part on whether the standards and commitments under the system or license actually impose upon the adopting organization an obligation to which it is not otherwise subject via domestic law or regulatory system. The more the obligation fills a governance gap the more likely it is to have a true effect on the workplace. The Goodweave and Fair Employment marks fit the bill best in this regard. And yet, the more the certification imposes on the adopter or licensee an obligation that is unique and that opens it to a new or expanded risk of liability, the greater the disincentive for potential participants to commit to it. The Fair Employment Mark suffers from this drawback. Thus, one might expect to see the greatest impact under this consideration when the standards of conduct or commitments under the certification system supplement an existing and highly valued – but under-enforced – obligation, like the Goodweave system dealing with child labor or Magen Tzedek's commitment to ethical labor standards (like the above-minimum-wage/living-wage requirement).

B. Does it Incorporate an Effective Complaint and Enforcement Mechanism?

Each of the examples described in Part II incorporates some sort of complaint and enforcement system. How much that system empowers the stakeholders who are the intended beneficiaries of the certification will determine whether it has an impact on them. Clearly, the Fair Employment Mark's full empowerment of employees and applicants by making them express third-party beneficiaries of the licensee's promises empowers them to the greatest degree. Most certification systems do not go that far. For the more typical system, the access the intended beneficiaries have to file simple complaints and the certifier's mechanism to respond will have a significant impact on its effectiveness. Probably the least likely to effect change in the lives of the intended beneficiaries (all else being equal) are those systems wherein the only hammer is the revocation of the use of a certification mark and that only after the lapse of a certification cycle. This approach most resembles the FAIRTRADE Mark. Goodweave International, in contrast, explicitly reserves the right to revoke the license to use the Goodweave mark whenever a licensee is noncompliant.[101]

C. Does it Focus on Issues of Salience to External Markets?

To the extent that a certification, particularly one that is based on product labeling with a certification mark, relies on market pressure to effect change for the benefit of workers, it is more likely to be successful if it focuses on issues that are of high regard and salience to those external markets. To create sufficient market response and pressure, the information-disclosure nature of a certification has to be able to command the attention of the external audiences with enough strength and urgency to affect their behaviors as a result of the information it provides.[102] Magen Tzedek may be more effective here because the

---

[101] *See Child-Labor-Free Certification*, GOODWEAVE INT'L, http://goodweave.org/about/child_labor_free_rugs (last visited Aug. 25, 2014) (describing the certification program, including penalties for noncompliance).

[102] Generalized appeals to consumers' empathetic reactions to poor conditions is unlikely to work. Consumers are so easily influenced by small differences in costs that they are unlikely to be motivated by simple appeals to conscience. *See* Jesse J. Prinz, *Is Empathy Necessary for Morality?, in* EMPATHY: PHILOSOPHICAL AND PSYCHOLOGICAL PERSPECTIVES 211, 211 (Amy Coplan & Peter Goldie eds., 2011) ("[S]tudies suggest that empathy is not a major player

audience for the Magen Tzedek mark is an already well-informed consumer (i.e., the kosher buyer) who is more likely primed to be sensitive to the addition of the Magen Tzedek mark to a kosher product (or lack thereof).

D. Does it Provide a Signal that is Clear and Simple Enough for External Audiences to Make an Informed Associative Choice as a Result?

Related to the prior question, the information disclosed by a certification must be clear and simple enough for the target external audience(s) to understand and make informed choices about whether to associate with the certified (or noncertified) organization as a result. This is particularly true when the associative choice involves consumption, as with product labeling. Consumers will not be moved to purchase labeled products or avoid non-labeled products unless they understand the information the label is intended to convey. The more a mark focuses on a single issue, the greater the likelihood that external audiences will exert a market reward or price for having or not having the label. The Goodweave Mark is probably the best example of this. Child labor problems are well-known in the rug-weaving industry, and a commitment to combat it is well-understood. The Fair Employment Mark likely falls short. Though a commitment to nondiscrimination may be compelling to some consumers, it is unclear that the specific commitment to follow the dictates of an unenacted statute provides sufficiently greater clarity and simplicity of information to mobilize the intended audience to push for the greater commitment of the Fair Employment Mark. Similarly, the more complex the certification standards and the more diverse the subjects of the standards, like the ISO standards, the less likely it will result in clear associative choices by consumers or other stakeholders, unless and until the mark itself develops an aura of quality or importance despite that complexity. The FAIRTRADE Mark likely embodies that level of reputation and recognition most closely among the examples in Part II.

IV. CONCLUSION

Approaches to regulating the workplace through certification schemes, and the prominence of certification marks in those schemes, vary widely.

---

when it comes to moral motivation. Its contribution is negligible in children, modest in adults, and non-existent when costs are significant.").

This chapter has provided examples of five different approaches, which varied on whether processes or products were the subject of certification and labeling, how broad the focus of the regulation is, and the extent to which the certification is a supplement to existing state-based regulation or fills a gap states have failed to address. Having identified the important role certification marks sometimes play in this private ordering, this chapter identifies four characteristics – embodied in four questions – that inform how likely it is for the use of certification marks to effect change for workers, the intended beneficiaries of these private regulatory systems.

BIBLIOGRAPHY

Statutes and Codes

Conflict Minerals, 77 Fed. Reg. 56,274 (Sept. 12, 2012) (to be codified at 17 C.F.R. pts. 240 and 249b).
H.R. 1863, 104th Cong. (1995).
H.R. 4636, 103d Cong. (1994).
Lanham Act, 15 U.S.C. §§ 1054, 1064, 1127 (2006).
S. 2056, 104th Cong. (1996).

Cases

Schechter Poultry Corp. v. United States, 295 U.S. 495 (1935).
West Coast Hotel v. Parrish, 300 U.S. 379 (1937).

Secondary Sources

About the GH Limited Warranty Seal, GOOD HOUSEKEEPING (Mar. 31, 2014, 6:00 AM), http://www.goodhousekeeping.com/product-reviews/history/about-good-housekeeping-seal.
About ISO, ISO, http://www.iso.org/iso/home/about.htm (last visited Aug. 25, 2014).
About SAI, SOC. ACCOUNTABILITY INT'L, http://www.sa-intl.org/index.cfm?fuseaction=Page.ViewPage&pageId=472 (last visited Aug. 25, 2014).
Ayres, Ian and Jennifer Gerada Brown, *Mark(et)ing Nondiscrimination: Privatizing ENDA with a Certification Mark*, 104 MICH. L. REV. 1639 (2006).
Ayres, Ian and Jennifer Gerada Brown, *Privatizing Employment Protections*, 49 ARIZ. L. REV. 587 (2007).
Bair, Jennifer et al., *To Label or Not to Label, Is That the Question?* in WORKER'S RIGHTS AND LABOR COMPLIANCE IN GLOBAL SUPPLY CHAINS: IS A SOCIAL LABEL THE ANSWER? (Jennifer Bair et al. 2013).
Barron, Mark R., Comment, *Creating Consumer Confidence or Confusion? The Role of Product Certification marks in the Market Today*, 11 MARQ. INTELL. PROP. L. REV. 413 (2007).

Bartley, Tim, *Certification as a Mode of Social Regulation*, *in* HANDBOOK ON THE POLITICS OF REGULATION 441 (David Levi-Faur ed., 2011).

BELSON, JEFFREY, CERTIFICATION MARKS (2002).

Bureau Veritas Certification Servs., *SA8000 Certification*, BUREAU VERITAS, http://www.bureauveritas.com/wps/wcm/connect/3494830047e94ad7af7aafafdca0d0a3/SA8000.pdf?MOD=AJPERES&CACHEID=3494830047e94ad7af7aafafdca0d0a3 (last visited Aug. 25, 2014).

Certification, ISO, http://www.iso.org/iso/home/standards/certification.htm (last visited Aug. 25, 2014).

Certification Mark: Frequently Asked Questions, FAIR TRADE USA, http://fairtradeusa.org/sites/all/files/wysiwyg/filemanager/label/Fair-Trade-USA-FAQ-new certificationmark.pdf (last visited Aug. 25, 2014).

Certification to ISO 9001 Quality Management, BSI, http://www.bsigroup.com/en-GB/iso-9001-quality-management/Certification-for-ISO-9001/ (last visited Apr. 20, 2014).

Charles Coiner Papers: An Inventory of His Papers at Syracuse University, SYRACUSE UNIV. LIBR., http://library.syr.edu/digital/guides/c/coiner_c.htm (last visited Aug. 25, 2014).

Charles T. Coiner, 91, Ex-Art Chief at Ayer, N.Y. TIMES, Aug. 16, 1989.

Child-Labor-Free Certification, GOODWEAVE INT'L, http://goodweave.org/about/child_labor_free_rugs (last visited Aug. 25, 2014).

Complaint Resolution Program, SOC. ACCOUNTABILITY INT'L, http://www.sa-intl.org/index.cfm?fuseaction=Page.ViewPage&pageId=1460 (last visited Apr. 20, 2014).

Directory of Kosher Certifying Agencies, CHICAGO RABBINICAL COUNCIL, http://www.crcweb.org/agency_list.php (last updated Aug. 18, 2014).

Duguid, Paul, *A Case of Prejudice? The Uncertain Development of Collective and Certification Marks*, 86 BUS. HIST. REV. 311 (2012).

FAIRTRADE AMERICA, http://fairtradeamerica.org/ (last visited Apr. 21, 2014).

FAIRTRADE INT'L, FAIRTRADE STD. FOR HIRED LABOUR (Jan. 1, 2014), *available at* http://www.fairtrade.net/fileadmin/user_upload/content/2009/standards/documents/generic-standards/2014-03-14_HL_EN.pdf.

The Fairtrade Marks, FAIRTRADE INT'L, http://www.fairtrade.net/the-fairtrade-marks.html (last visited Aug. 25, 2014).

The FAIRTRADE Program Marks, FAIRTRADE INT'L, http://www.fairtrade.net/fairtrade-program-mark.html.

FAIR TRADE USA, FAIR TRADE USA COMPLIANCE CRITERIA FOR THE FARM WORKERS STANDARD 1.1 (2014), *available at* http://fairtradeusa.org/sites/all/files/wysiwyg/filemanager/FTUSA_FWS_CC_1.1v3_EN_040214.pdf.

FAQs: Frequently Asked Questions, FAIRTRADE INT'L, http://www.fairtrade.net/faqs.html (last visited Aug. 25, 2014).

GOODWEAVE INT'L, GENERIC INTERNATIONAL STANDARD FOR RUG PRODUCERS 2 (2012), *available at* https://www.goodweave.org/uploads/GWI-Generic-Intl-Standard-v2-3.pdf.

GOODWEAVE INT'L, GOODWEAVE INTERNATIONAL (GWI) TRADEMARK POLICY (2013).

HAMBY, ALONZO L., FOR THE SURVIVAL OF DEMOCRACY (1994).

HIMMELBERG, ROBERT, THE ORIGINS OF THE NATIONAL RECOVERY ADMINISTRATION (2d ed., 1993).

How It Works, FLOCERT, http://www.flo-cert.net/fairtrade-services/fairtrade-certification/how-it-works/ (last visited Aug. 25, 2014).

Hsu, Spencer S., *Immigration Raid Jars Small Town*, WASH. POST (May 18, 2008), http://www.washingtonpost.com/wp-dyn/content/article/2008/05/17/ AR2008051702474.html.

ISO, PUBLICIZING YOUR ISO 9001:2008 OR ISO 14001:2004 CERTIFICATION 2 (2010), *available at* http://www.iso.org/iso/publicizing_iso9001_iso14001_ certification_2010.pdf.

ISO, QUALITY MANAGEMENT PRINCIPLES (2012), *available at* http://www.iso.org/iso/ qmp_2012.pdf.

Johnson, Daphne Zografos, *International Intellectual Property Scholars series: Using Intellectual Property Rights to Create Value in the Coffee Industry*, 16 MARQ. INTELL. PROP. L. REV. 283 (2012).

Kosher Certification Policy, OU KOSHER, http://oukosher.org/kosher-certification-policy/ (last visited Aug. 25, 2014).

List of Fairtrade International Standards Available on Website, FAIRTRADE INT'L, http://www.fairtrade.net/fileadmin/user_upload/content/2009/standards/documents/ 2012-08-03_LIST_OF_FLO_Standards.pdf (last visited Aug. 25, 2014).

McCARTHY, J. THOMAS, McCARTHY ON TRADEMARKS AND UNFAIR COMPETITION (4th ed. 2005).

MAGEN TZEDEK COMMISSION, CERTIFICATION STANDARDS FOR THE MAGEN TZEDEK SERVICE MARK (2012).

Mission Statement, MAGEN TZEDEK, http://www.magentzedek.org/about-us/mission-statement/ (last visited Apr. 21, 2014).

National Industrial Recovery Act, U.S. HIST., http://www.u-s-history.com/pages/ h1663.html (last visited Aug. 25, 2014).

Nayman, Louis, *Kosher Gets Ethical*, IN THESE TIMES (Jan. 7, 2011), http:// inthesetimes.com/article/6743/kosher_gets_ethical.

The New Deal, AM. HIST. SCRAPBOOK, http://mfaewillard.weebly.com/the-new-deal.html (last visited Aug. 25, 2014).

Park, Stephen Kim, *Human Rights Reporting as Self-Interest: The Integrative and Expressive Dimensions of Corporate Disclosure*, in LAW, BUSINESS AND HUMAN RIGHTS: BRIDGING THE GAP 48 (Bird et al., eds., 2014).

Popolaw, Harvey, *Recalling the Postville Tragedy: Impetus for Comprehensive Immigration Reform Bill*, JEWISH SOC. JUST. ROUNDTABLE (May 10, 2013, 10:44 AM), http://jewishsocialjustice.org/blog/recalling-postville-tragedy-impetus-comprehensive-immigration-reform-bill.

Prenkert, Jamie Darin, *Conflict Minerals and Polycentric Governance of Business and Human Rights*, in LAW, BUSINESS AND HUMAN RIGHTS: BRIDGING THE GAP 203 (Bird et al., eds., 2014).

Prinz, Jesse J., *Is Empathy Necessary for Morality?*, in EMPATHY: PHILOSOPHICAL AND PSYCHOLOGICAL PERSPECTIVES 211 (Amy Coplan and Peter Goldie eds., 2011).

Q&A on Fairtrade International and Fair Trade USA, FAIRTRADE INT'L, http:// www.fairtrade.net/897.html (last visited Aug. 25, 2014).

Report of the Special Representative of the Secretary-General on Human Rights, Transnational Corporations, and Other Business Enterprises, Protect, Respect and Remedy: A Framework for Business and Human Rights, Hum. Rts. Council, U.N. Doc. A/HRC/8/5 (April 7, 2008), *available at* http://198.170.85.29/Ruggie-report-7-Apr-2008.pdf.

Ruggie, John Gerard, Special Representative of the Secretary-General on the Issue of Human Rights and Transnational Corporations and Other Business Enterprises,

Keynote Address at the 3rd Annual Responsible Investment Forum, New York, NY (Jan. 12, 2009), *available at* http://www.reports-and-materials.org/sites/default/files/reports-and-materials/Ruggie-address-to-Responsible-Invest-Forum-12-Jan-2009.pdf.

SA8000® Standard, SOC. ACCOUNTABILITY INT'L, http://www.sa-intl.org/index.cfm?fuseaction=Page.ViewPage&pageId=937 (last visited Aug. 25, 2014).

Sklar, Katheryn Kish, *The Consumers' White Label Campaign of the National Consumers' League, 1898-1918*, *in* GETTING AND SPENDING: EUROPEAN AND AMERICAN CONSUMER SOCIETIES IN THE TWENTIETH CENTURY 17 (Susan Strasser et al., eds., 1998).

SOC. ACCOUNTABILITY ACCREDITATION SERVS., http://www.saasaccreditation.org/ (last visited Aug. 25, 2014).

SOC. ACCOUNTABILITY INT'L, GUIDELINES FOR CORPORATE COMMUNICATION AND GRAPHIC STANDARDS (2012).

Urminsky, Michael, *Self-Regulation in the Workplace: Codes of Conduct, Social Labeling and Socially Responsible Investment* (ILO, MCC Working Paper No. 1).

Using the FAIRTRADE Marks, FAIRTRADE INT'L, http://www.fairtrade.net/using-the-fairtrade-mark.html (last visited Aug. 25, 2014).

Vark, Caspar van, *Q&A: Fair Trade for All*, THEGUARDIAN (Feb. 27, 2008, 8:13 AM), http://www.theguardian.com/environment/2008/feb/27/qa.fairtrade.

Marks and Labels, UNDERWRITERS LAB., http://ul.com/corporate/marks/ (last visited Mar. 18, 2015).

What Is Conformity Assessment?, ISO, http://www.iso.org/iso/home/about/conformity-assessment.htm (last visited Aug. 25, 2014).

5. The intersection of smartphone technology and fair labor standards

Robert C. Bird

As the multi-billion dollar smartphone patent wars continue unabated,[1] one fact remains certain: the smartphone will remain an omnipresent technology. Smartphones transform how we receive information, dictate our personal lives, and influence interactions with our world.[2] One of the venues in which the smartphone will predominate is the modern workplace. Smartphones at work enable employees to multitask, communicate more readily, and gather information instantaneously. Employers can enjoy productivity benefits from their workforce as employees react to challenges and opportunities with minimal delay.

The introduction of smartphones, however, is not entirely cost free. The presence of this technology means that employers can reach virtually any employee at any time. A smartphone can transform the employee's location into a virtual office with more than sufficient information available and ready to execute the employer's wishes.[3] This ability to communicate through voice, text, or data at any moment exerts a new power over employees that has never been fully exerted until the advent of such technology. The use of communicative technology can in essence create a twenty-four-hour workplace, with all its associated demands and responsibilities, whether employees like it or not.

---

[1] See Thomas A. Chia, Note, *Fighting the Smartphone Patent War with Rand-Encumbered Patents*, 27 BERKELEY TECH. L.J. 209, 209 (2012) ("The smartphone patent war refers to the multitude of patent infringement suits currently taking place against competing companies in the increasingly competitive and litigious smartphone industry.").

[2] See, e.g., *Smartphones Will Transform Our Lives in Ways we cannot Even Imagine Today*, THE MIRROR (Aug. 5, 2011), http://www.mirror.co.uk/uk-news/smartphones-will-transform-our-lives-in-ways-we-cannot-145919.

[3] See Marian K. Reidy, Suman Beros and H. Joseph Wen, *Managing Business Smartphone Data*, 14 J. INTERNET L. 3, 8 n.66 (2011).

As with the introduction of many new technologies, legal questions follow in their wake. Employers are increasingly using smartphone and other technology to reach employees outside of working hours and not compensate them for their working time. The Fair Labor Standards Act of 1938 (FLSA) requires that employees be compensated for all hours worked, and employers must pay covered employees an overtime premium for hours worked exceeding forty hours in a workweek.[4] While "exempt" employees working in an executive, administrative, or professional capacity are not covered under the FLSA,[5] millions of "non-exempt" employees not falling within these criteria are entitled to the FLSA's protections. This results in potential liability for employers utilizing smartphone technology in the workplace with non-exempt employees.

This chapter explores the intersection of two important factors: the new and increasing use of smartphones and technology to reach employees outside of working hours; and the venerable regulation of the Fair Labor Standards Act (FLSA), designed in part to protect covered workers from employer abuses of working time. Part I of this chapter chronicles the rise of fair labor standards and the evolution of boundaries between work and personal time. Part II reviews leading cases related to the use of portable technology like smartphones and the compensation of off-shift working time. Part III proposes a reform to the FLSA to alleviate misuses of off-shift time and offers strategies for employers to minimize administrative costs. Part IV concludes.

I. THE RISE OF THE FAIR LABOR STANDARDS ACT AND PROTECTABLE PERSONAL TIME

The concept of reasonable hours worked and associated legislation protective of personal time in the United States was far from inevitable. Rather, such standards arose from evolving economic necessity and social changes in what are acceptable as humane hours of work and rest. During the colonial period, work arrangements through apprenticeships could last for years at a time and apprentices were "bound body and

---

[4] Fair Labor Standards Act of 1938, Pub. L. No. 75–718, 52 Stat. 1060 (codified as amended at 29 U.S.C. §§ 201–219 (2012)) [hereinafter FLSA].
[5] 29 U.S.C. § 213(a)(1) (2012).

soul" to their masters.[6] In these relationships, every moment of the worker's time was subject to the discretion of the employer. During the nineteenth century, coordinated labor movements fought for a reduction in, and regulation of, working hours.[7] This created an established and protectable separation between work and personal time. Contracts for wages were viewed differently from other agreements because they were based on an individual's personal labor.[8]

During the early twentieth century, sporadic gains were made in various industries until 1938, when the landmark FLSA was enacted.[9] The FLSA profoundly changed the American workplace by creating a minimum wage, imposing limits on the use of child labor, and requiring employers to pay a minimum wage and an overtime rate for work exceeding forty hours a week.[10] The FLSA represented one of the most important advancements in the protection of employee working time in the past century and the forty-hour work week remained the standard for decades afterward.[11]

The FLSA has been in existence for over seventy-five years,[12] and its core principle remains a simple one.[13] Employers must pay employees for "all hours worked," including overtime.[14] Unfortunately, the FLSA does not fully define the boundaries of the term "work," leaving it up to the courts to fill the statutory gap.[15]

---

[6] WASHINGTON STATE DEPT. OF LABOR & INDUSTRIES, HISTORY OF APPRENTICESHIP, http://www.lni.wa.gov/TradesLicensing/Apprenticeship/About/History/ (last visited Dec. 14, 2013).

[7] Scott D. Miller, *Revitalizing the FLSA*, 19 HOFSTRA LAB. & EMP. L.J. 1, 10 (2001).

[8] *Ibid.*

[9] FLSA, *supra* note 4.

[10] Jennifer Clemons, *FLSA Retaliation: A Continuum of Employee Protection*, 53 BAYLOR L. REV. 535, 535 (2001).

[11] *Ibid.* at 535–36.

[12] *See, e.g.,* Jefferson Cowie, *The Future of Fair Labor*, N.Y. TIMES (Jun. 24, 2013), http://www.nytimes.com/2013/06/25/opinion/the-future-of-fair-labor.html (looking back on the seventy-fifth anniversary of the FLSA); Seth Harris, *75 Years of Rewarding Work and Responsibility*, U.S. DEP'T OF LABOR: WORK IN PROGRESS (Jun. 24, 2013) (similar).

[13] FLSA, *supra* note 4.

[14] *E.g.,* Perez v. Mountaire Farms, Inc., 650 F.3d 350, 363 (4th Cir. 2011) (citing 29 U.S.C. §§ 206, 207 (2006)).

[15] *See, e.g.,* IBP, Inc. v. Alvarez, 546 U.S. 21, 25 (2005) ("Neither 'work' nor 'workweek' is defined in the statute."). The Court noted: "The most pertinent definition provides: '"Employ" includes to suffer or permit to work.'" *Ibid.* at 25 n.1 (quoting 29 U.S.C. § 203(g)).

Initial court cases interpreted the concept of paid working time with some breadth. In *Tennessee Coal, Iron & Ry. Co. v. Muscoda Local No. 13*,[16] the U.S. Supreme Court ruled that miners were entitled to compensation for time spent before each shift making the compulsory and hazardous trip to the employer's underground iron mines.[17] The Court reasoned that such travel was essential to the employer's production, and although it was non-productive, it was a necessary pre-condition activity for the job.[18] The Court also constructed working time from the perspective of exertion, that of engaging in some activity that is required by the employer over a certain period. This view of working time includes any time spent in "physical or mental exertion (whether burdensome or not) controlled or required by the employer and pursued necessarily and primarily for the benefit of the employer and his business."[19] This definition focuses on the act of work rather than its location and also incorporates the idea that the employer benefits in some way from the worker's actions.

The Supreme Court during this time also examined working time from the notion of availability. In *Armour & Co. v. Wantock*,[20] the Court remarked that, "an employer, if he chooses, may hire a man to do nothing, or to do nothing but wait for something to happen. Refraining from other activity often is a factor of instant readiness to serve, and idleness plays a part in all employments in a stand-by capacity."[21] This implies that time spent monitoring employer interests, even though that monitoring many not necessitate actual worker action, also falls within the ambit of compensable time.

A subsequent Supreme Court decision expanded FLSA coverage to "all time during which an employee [was] necessarily required to be on the employer's premises, on duty or at a prescribed workplace."[22] That triggered a flood of litigation in federal courts by workers seeking

---

[16]   321 U.S. 590 (1944), *superseded on other grounds by statute*, 29 U.S.C. § 254 (2012).

[17]   *Ibid.* at 599–600.

[18]   *Ibid.* at 599. The court cited watching and "guarding a building, waiting for work, and standing by on call" as work necessary for production. *Ibid.* (citations omitted). Thus, the miners performed "a fossorial activity bearing all the indicia of hard labor." *Ibid.*

[19]   *Ibid.* at 598.

[20]   323 U.S. 126, 168 (1944).

[21]   *Ibid.* at 133.

[22]   Anderson v. Mt. Clemens Pottery, 328 U.S. 680, 690-91 (1946), *superseded by statute*, 29 U.S.C. §§ 251–62 (2012).

compensation for work time previously accepted as non-compensable.[23] In response, in 1947, Congress amended the FLSA by passing the Portal-to-Portal Act, which narrowed the FLSA by exempting "preliminary or postliminary" activities surrounding the compensable "principal activity" of working time.[24] This important language has left courts today with the challenge of interpreting what tasks are compensable as principal activities and what tasks are merely non-compensatory preliminary or postliminary actions.

In the twenty-first century, the FLSA remains the statutory authority most relevant to regulation of hours worked. The purpose of the FLSA continues to be to prohibit labor conditions that erode the minimum standard of living necessary for the health, efficiency, and well-being of workers.[25] President Franklin Roosevelt perceived the FLSA as a centerpiece of the New Deal that would "end starvation wages and intolerable hours."[26] Implicit in that purpose may also be the intent to ensure a reasonable quality of life outside the workplace.[27] However, according to the Department of Labor, the FLSA does not speak directly to schedule

---

[23] Marc Linder, *Class Struggle at the Door: The Origins of the Portal-to-Portal Act of 1947*, 39 BUFF. L. REV. 53, 133 (1991) ("Workers had filed 727 portal suits in federal courts during the last six months of 1946, but in January 1947 alone an additional 1,186 were recorded.").

[24] 29 U.S.C. §§ 251-262 (2012). Congress explicitly stated that: "The Congress finds that the Fair Labor Standards Act of 1938 ... has been interpreted judicially in disregard of long-established customs, practices, and contracts between employers and employees, thereby creating wholly unexpected liabilities, immense in amount and retroactive in operation, upon employers with the results." *Ibid.* at § 251(a).

[25] 29 U.S.C. § 202(a)–(b) (2012). *See also* Tennessee Coal, Iron & R. Co. v. Muscoda Local No. 123, 321 U.S. 590, 592 (1944) (explaining that FLSA protects "the rights of those who toil, of those who sacrifice a full measure of their freedom and talents to the use and profit of others"), *superseded on other grounds by statute*, 29 U.S.C. § 254 (2012). The Court emphasized that workers are not "mere chattels or articles of trade." *Ibid.* at 597.

[26] President Franklin D. Roosevelt, Annual Message to the Congress, Jan. 3, 1938, *available at* http://www.presidency.ucsb.edu/ws/?pid=15517.

[27] *See, e.g.,* Kathryn S. Crouss, Note, *Employment Law – Welcome to the Jungle: Salespeople and the Administrative Exemption to the Fair Labor Standards Act*, 34 W. NEW ENG. L. REV. 205, 209 (2012); Craig A. Cunningham, Note, *Mind the Gap: A Legal and Economic Analysis of Stockbroker Overtime Eligibility Under the Fair Labor Standards Act*, 2009 U. ILL. L. REV. 1243, 1246.

construction, leaving that to private agreement between the employer and the employee.[28]

II.　TECHNOLOGY AND WORKING TIME IN CONFLICT

In spite of the FLSA, conflicts have arisen related to whether use of portable technologies for work beyond standard work hours constitutes FLSA-protectable working time. Before the era of advanced technology, working time and personal time remained largely separate. Workers could not easily bring their jobs home with them, as the equipment and material necessary for production remained with the employer. Today, that work/ home division is blurring. Employees are carrying employer-provided smartphones home, and are being required by their employer to access their smartphone for work reasons during personal time. The result is that an employer can request work from the employee at any time without consequence, or in some cases, compensation.

As a result, non-exempt workers have filed lawsuits against their employers for compensated recovery for hours worked. One dispute starkly highlights how differently employers and employees can perceive the imposition of technology on working time. In *West v. Verizon Services Corp.*,[29] Delia West worked mostly from home via her Blackberry phone as a personal account manager for Verizon customers.[30] West was required to answer customer calls between 9:00am and 9:00pm, Monday through Saturday, "without fail."[31] At least 90 percent of such calls had to be answered live, without voicemail, and had to be followed up on to ensure customer satisfaction.[32] Each call and the interaction also had to be documented on Verizon's website.[33] Each personal account manager was paid $400 per week with opportunities to receive additional commissions for sales and bonuses based on customer satisfaction scores.[34] West sued, claiming that she was entitled to unpaid overtime compensation

---

[28]　U.S DEP'T OF LABOR, FLEXIBLE SCHEDULES, http://www.dol.gov/compliance/topics/wages-other-flex.htm (last visited Aug. 19, 2014).

[29]　2011 WL 208314 (M.D. Fla.).

[30]　*Ibid.* at *1, *2.

[31]　*Ibid.* at *1.

[32]　*Ibid.*

[33]　*Ibid.*

[34]　*Ibid.* at *2.

under the FLSA.[35] West sought $9,600 in overtime compensation, liquidated damages, and attorney's fees and costs.[36]

Verizon's apparent perception of the job was that only time spent actually completing calls and interacting with the website constituted compensable work. In support of Verizon's belief that personal account managers should work less than 40 hours weekly, Verizon surveyed similarly situated employees and found that personal account managers reported on average working 36.5 hours per week.[37] Verizon produced West's call records and log entry time and showed West worked hours well under 40 hours per week.[38] Verizon reported that most weeks resulted in under 12 hours of phone time for West and in one week phone records reported less than one hour of communication.[39] Therefore, according to Verizon, West was not entitled to any overtime.[40]

West's understanding of her employment, and the attendant obligations associated with it, shows a different construction of working time. West was mostly able to work at home or from any convenient location.[41] Yet, West's testimony reveals that, through the ever-present Blackberry technology provided by her employer, her freedom to engage in personal activities was significantly restricted throughout her working period.[42] West was responsible for over 1,000 customers and her work involved "answering incoming customer calls, making outbound calls, calling technical support and the billing department for customers, reading and responding to emails (from Verizon clients and from Verizon employees), upgrading and selling Verizon products, and logging everything on the Verizon website."[43] West reported that she was "pretty much trapped at

---

[35]   *Ibid.* at *4. West sued both Verizon, for whose customers she was responsible to respond, as well as PDS Technical Services, a staffing company that Verizon contracted with to recruit and manage personal account managers like West. *Ibid.* at *1.

[36]   *Ibid.* at *4.

[37]   *Ibid.* at *2.

[38]   *Ibid.* at *5.

[39]   *Ibid.* at *4.

[40]   *Ibid.* at *6.

[41]   *Ibid.* at *2. West was required to work from a Verizon location during weekly meetings with supervisors and during the initial training process. *Ibid.*

[42]   *See, e.g.,* Owens v. Local No. 169, 971 F.3d 347, 350 (9th Cir. 1992) (noting that determining compensability of on-call work cases relies on the parties' agreements and "the degree to which the employee is free to engage in personal activities").

[43]   2011 WL 208314 at *3.

my computer" due to the volume of work and painfully slow speed of Verizon's computer system.[44] West reported that she was so busy that:

> There were times I didn't even get to go to the bathroom during the day because I would have those incoming e-mails. And not only would it be customers, but [supervisors] … would send out stuff. So the time we weren't making phone calls, we were reading those, and a lot of times, there were policy changes during the middle of the day.[45]

According to West, her phone "started ringing at 7:00 in the morning and many times it didn't stop ringing until after midnight."[46]

As noted earlier,[47] the standard for determining whether waiting for work is compensable is whether the waiting time is "primarily for the benefit of the employer and his business."[48] Not only was West constantly engaged with her employer during scheduled working time, but her personal freedom during the work period was substantially restricted. She could not leave her home to attend to personal matters during call times.[49] West could not drive her children to school, attend church, complete housework, socialize with friends, take her children outside the home, or provide meals during these on-call hours.[50] She did not read, did not watch television, never took a vacation, and did not take time off due to illness.[51] Personal activities were simply suspended for twelve hours each day, and other activities outside the 72-hour window-of-work were also impaired.

---

[44]   *Ibid.* West described the laboriously sluggish system:

[Y]ou had to log everything. And anytime that we needed to talk to the billing department, we couldn't e-mail them through the Web mail. We had to notify them through the [personal account manager] Web site, which was extremely slow. I mean, you could type a line and sit there for a minute, type a line and sit there for a minute.

Ibid. at *3.

[45]   *Ibid.*

[46]   *Ibid.*

[47]   *See supra* text accompanying note 19.

[48]   Armour & Co. v. Wantock, 323 U.S. 126, 132 (1944).

[49]   Plaintiff's Memorandum of Law in Opposition to PDS Technical Services Inc.'s Motion for Partial Summary Judgment, West v. Verizon Services Corp. at 9, No. 8:08-cv-01325-VMC-MAP, 2010 WL 5808203 (M.D. Fla. Nov. 29, 2010).

[50]   *Ibid.* at 9.

[51]   *Ibid.* at 6.

West characterized her relationship with Verizon as not merely an "on-call" job, but a complete employment relationship equivalent to standard physically-present work:

> What Defendants have done here is set up a virtual call center. Instead of employing people to sit in a call center and take calls, Defendants required [personal account managers] to sit at home (or wherever they happened to be) and take calls. The time [personal account managers] were required to be available should be considered similar to time spent in a call center.[52]

West thus argued in her motion opposing summary judgment that her time was so restricted by her employer that it should constitute compensable time.[53] Citing disputed issues of material fact, the trial court denied the defendants' motion for summary judgment.[54]

The *West* case is not an isolated incident. In *Agui v. T-Mobile, Inc.*,[55] employees claimed that they were required to review and respond to communications from employer-issued smartphones.[56] Their tasks included receiving and placing calls to co-workers and customers and participating in frequent conference calls.[57] These communications would occur at all hours and often without compensation for overtime.[58]

Employees sued under the FLSA, claiming that they were entitled to overtime wages for the ten to fifteen hours per week spent dealing with employer emails, texts, and phone calls.[59] The lawsuit grew from a three-worker action to a pleading on behalf of all similarly-situated current and former employees, raising the real possibility of a costly class action.[60] The employer likely felt the threat of substantial liability, and entered into a confidential settlement agreement less than one year after the lawsuit's filing.[61]

---

[52]   *Ibid.* at 8.

[53]   *Ibid.* at 9 (citing Birdwell v. City of Gadsden, 970 F.2d 802 (11th Cir. 1992)).

[54]   2011 WL 208314 at *12.

[55]   No. 09-2955 (E.D.N.Y. July 10, 2009).

[56]   Maria L. Barbu, *The Ubiquitous Blackberry: The New Overtime Liability*, 5 LIBERTY U. L. REV. 47, 62 n.95 (2010).

[57]   Class and Collective Action Complaint, Agui v. T-Mobile USA Inc. at 9–10, No. 09-2955, 2009 WL 2251810 (E.D.N.Y. Jul. 10, 2009).

[58]   Barbu, *supra* note 56, at 62 n.95.

[59]   Steven M. Guiterrez and Joseph Neguse, *Emerging Technologies and the FLSA*, 39 COLO. LAW. 49, 51 (2010). A manager allegedly stated that such activities were "standard business practices." *Ibid.*

[60]   *Ibid.*

[61]   *Ibid.*

Employees feeling similarly mistreated filed an action in *Rulli v. CB Richard Ellis, Inc.*[62] In this case, employees were given smartphones and other devices and were required to use them beyond normal working hours and without compensation in violation of the FLSA.[63] Responses were required within fifteen minutes of receipt regardless of time of day or location of the employee.[64] According to plaintiff's counsel, workers were receiving text messages from supervisors while watching a movie or eating dinner at home, and were obliged to respond with no expectation of compensation.[65] Similar to *Agui*, the employee filed a "collective action" claim,[66] implying that the lawsuit would attempt to represent all employees similarly-situated in the firm. The case was believed to have the potential to provide "important guidance" because it was one of the first that focused on the technology-FLSA intersection.[67] Perhaps also sensing potential exposure, the employer settled the claims prior to a published opinion in the case.[68]

When a case generated a published opinion on this issue, the results were satisfying for employees, but only on the surface. In *Rutti v. Lojack Corp., Inc.*,[69] the employee filed a putative class action claiming that time spent commuting to worksites in company vehicles and time spent uploading data about his work to the company after he returned home constituted FLSA-compensable time.[70] The appellate court found that the employee's commuting time was not compensable even if it was a condition of employment and involved a work vehicle.[71] However, the court did find that certain off-clock activities might be compensable, specifically the requirement to upload transmissions to the employer after the workday was finished.[72] These transmissions appeared to be "part of the regular work of the employees in the ordinary course of business,"

---

[62] No. 2009cv00289 (E.D.Wis. March 13, 2009).

[63] Guiterrez and Neguse, *supra* note 59, at 51.

[64] *Ibid.*

[65] *Ibid.* (quoting Plaintiff's attorney, Nola Hitchcock).

[66] Anna M. Pepelnjak, *Employee Use of Smartphones: FLSA Implications*, WEISS BERZOWSKI BRADY LLP (Sep. 14, 2011), http://www.wbb-law.com/multimedia/blog/employee-use-smartphones-flsa-implications.

[67] Guiterrez and Neguse, *supra* note 59, at 51.

[68] Pepelnjak, *supra* note 66.

[69] 596 F.3d 1046 (9th Cir. 2010).

[70] *Ibid.* at 1048–50.

[71] *Ibid.* at 1052–53.

[72] *Ibid.* at 1058–59. This finding would be conditioned on determining whether such activities were so brief as to be considered non-compensable *de minimis* time. *Ibid. See* Amanda M. Riley, *The De Minimis Rule: Trifles of Time*,

and were "necessary to the business and [were] performed by the employees, primarily for the benefit of the employer, in the ordinary course of that business."[73] The court, though choosing to remand for further factual development, did remark that such transmissions, according to the plaintiff:

> take about 15 minutes a day. This is over an hour a week. For many employees, this is a significant amount of time and money. Also, the transmissions must be made at the end of every work day, and appear to be a requirement of a technician's employment. This suggests that the transmission[s] are performed as part of the regular work of the employees in the ordinary course of business ...[74]

While the court's finding that certain off-clock activities may be compensable should be encouraging for employees, the quotation above reveals that the court left open a gap in protection. The court qualified that "split second absurdities" or "trifles" in time beyond scheduled working hours should not be compensable.[75] This is a gap that, under certain circumstances, should be narrowed under the FLSA, as it enables employers to continue using employee's personal time.

The "split-second absurdities" phrase originates from a Supreme Court decision in 1946.[76] During that industrial era, split seconds were perhaps indeed absurdities. The pace of work and the division of time was substantially less precise. Workers had no access to immediately-responding technology, and the Internet did not exist. The Supreme Court could not have anticipated rapid advances in information technology. Today, small fractions of time substantially matter, as since an email or a data upload that can take mere seconds can transfer hundreds or thousands of gigabytes of data. Technology enables us to measure that time in increasingly small amounts.

---

45 ORANGE CTY. LAW. 18 (2003). *See generally* Jeff Nemerofsky, *What is a "Trifle" Anyway?*, 37 GONZ. L. REV. 315 (2001–02).

[73]   *Rutti*, 596 F.3d at 1058 (quoting Dunlop v. City Electric, Inc., 527 F.2d 394, 401 (5th Cir. 1976)).

[74]   *Ibid.* at 1059 (citation omitted).

[75]   *Ibid.* at 1056–57.

[76]   Anderson v. Mt. Clemens Pottery Co., 328 U.S. 680, 692 (1946) ("When the matter in issue concerns only a few seconds or minutes of work beyond the scheduled working hours, such trifles may be disregarded. Split-second absurdities are not justified by the actualities of working conditions or by the policy of the Fair Labor Standards Act.").

Yet, the *Rutti* court was comfortable with imposing upwards of ten minutes of working time daily on employees without compensation. This was not a discussion of split seconds, but rather of a number of minutes each day. The court noted that most other courts have readily found such a daily time erosion to be *de minimis*.[77] The court reasoned that there was "practical administrative difficulty" with recording such small amounts of time.[78]

However, this statement conflicts with technological reality. Smartphone applications and other devices can easily record the time used and data spent on using applications or completing tasks. It is notable that the *Rutti* court primarily relied on *Lindow v. United States* for its reasoning for *de minimis* time.[79] The *Lindow* case was decided in 1984, in an era when employee time, especially mobile employees, could not be as easily or as cheaply tracked.[80] There is no need for courts to live in an era, or for employers to be shielded by a view, that incremental periods of time that cumulate to an hour a week, or more, are outside the bounds of permissible compensation. Where technology makes it feasible to track working time with precision, the FLSA *de minimis* exception should not be used as a weapon to unnecessarily infringe on employees' personal time.

III. RECOMMENDATIONS FOR REFORM AND EMPLOYER STRATEGIES

In light of the incongruence between the time-sensitive use of modern technology such as smartphones and the outdated language of the FLSA, this section proposes a reform to the FLSA that better reflects modern realities of working time. This section also reflects on the administrative burdens any reform might impose, and offers recommendations for employers to minimize the compliance and related costs of such reforms.

---

[77] *Rutti*, 596 F.3d at 1056.
[78] *Ibid.* at 1056–57.
[79] *See* Lindow v. United States, 738 F.2d 1057 (9th Cir. 1984).
[80] *Ibid.*

A. The FLSA Working Time Rules Should Better Reflect Modern Uses of Technology at Work

The FLSA should be amended to better protect the personal time of employees in an age of portable technology. The FLSA permits employers to not compensate work by employees when the work is thought to be *de minimis*. Regulations define *de minimis* time as "uncertain and indefinite periods of time involved of a few seconds or minutes duration, and where the failure to count such time is due to considerations justified by industrial realities."[81] The regulations further explain that "holding that working time amounting to $1 of additional compensation a week is 'not a trivial matter to a workingman' and was not *de minimis* ... [t]o disregard workweeks for which less than a dollar is due will produce capricious and unfair results."[82] One dollar of additional working time in 1952 is equivalent to $8.79 in 2014.[83] The rationale behind this exception is that tracking such time is too difficult or time-consuming for employers to capture.[84]

The *de minimis* exception should be narrowed to permit compensation of more precise accounts of working time where it is feasible for the employer to do so. The *de minimis* exception as currently interpreted does not match the capabilities of today's modern workforce. Time tethered to an electronic device is no longer uncertain. Small blocks of time can be easily tracked. It is interesting to note that the most recent court case cited by the regulation to justify this construction of the *de minimis* rule is from 1955.[85]

If today's technologies can track slivers of time that courts once dismissed as trifles,[86] then such technology can be implemented to give employees their full compensation for time worked outside normal hours. Such technology need not be complicated. Employer-provided and personal smartphones can be equipped with time-tracking technology that employees can turn on and off to monitor fractional work outside of

---

[81] 29 C.F.R. § 785.47 (2014).

[82] *Ibid.* (citing Glenn L. Martin Nebraska Co. v. Culkin, 197 F. 2d 981, 987 (8th Cir. 1952) and Addison v. Huron Stevedoring Corp., 204 F.2d 88, 95 (2d Cir. 1953)).

[83] *See* Inflation Calculator, http://www.dollartimes.com/calculators/inflation.htm (last visited Aug. 14, 2014).

[84] *See, e.g.,* Hesseltine v. Goodyear Tire & Rubber Co., 391 F. Supp.2d 509, 519 (E.D. Tex. 2005) (noting this administrative difficulty).

[85] *Ibid.*

[86] *See generally* Riley, *supra* note 72; Nemerofsky, *supra* note 72.

normal working hours. Once those factional time periods reach a certain threshold, the employee can be compensated for additional time. Supervisors would likely be more careful to avoid abuse of workers' personal time if they knew that such time would come at the same compensatory cost as working time obligations. Employees would be more aware that when outside work time contact is initiated, it is indeed significant enough to warrant giving their attention to this problem.

Even if employers are required to compensate employees for small fractions of time, they may still take advantage of employees' personal time. A problem may arise when the employer still deems the cost of the fractional time to be worth the employees' attention while off work. For the employer, the cost is simply the fractional additional cost of the working time. A quick email or text to an employee on the weekend may mean a problem resolved before the following week begins. The ten minutes, thirty minutes, or hour where the employee must drop everything to resolve the off-shift problem may be worth the cost for the employer.

For the employee, however, such off-shift interruptions come at a substantially greater cost. A substantial benefit of personal time for employees is that it relaxes and rejuvenates employees through separation from work obligations. Constant interruptions, even if the employee is paid, can be unpleasant. Even brief off-shift work tasks interrupt the relaxation and recovery process. Employer requests interrupt meals and disrupt social outings, especially if the employer demands immediate action. The inability of employees to entirely switch off from work during their leisure time is not only stressful, but has been associated with a number of health ailments such as fatigue, sleeping problems, and cardiovascular disease.[87] Such interruptions to personal time, however brief, are no mere inconveniences, but can impair workers' health in no less concrete ways than an unsafe on-site work environment.

The FLSA could further help protect employees' personal time from technological intrusion. Non-exempt employees could be given the right to refuse work outside of established working hours. Such a right would also protect employees from retaliation should the employer wish to

---

[87]　*See, e.g.,* Marc Cropley and Lynne J. Millward, *How Do Individuals "Switch-Off" From Work During Leisure? A Qualitative Description of the Unwinding Process in High and Low Ruminators,* 28 LEISURE STUDIES 333 (2009); Torbjörn Akerstedt et al., *Mental Fatigue, Work, and Sleep,* 57 J. PSYCHOSOMATIC RES. 427 (2004); Poul Suadicani et al., *Are Social Inequalities Associated with the Risk of Ischemic Heart Diseases as a Result of Psychological Working Conditions,* 101 ATHEROSCLEROSIS 165 (1993).

penalize the employee for defending her personal time. This would give employees the opportunity to receive the full uninterrupted leisure and rest periods necessary to recover from work and avoid unnecessary health-related stresses. If exceptions were to be made, they would only be allowed in the event of an established business necessity. If a necessity existed, the off-shift obligation could be separately negotiated or it might command an overtime premium with a minimum payment of fractional time for any interruption. There is no need for employers to acquire free labor from their workforce. If technology can enable the performance of work, then technology can also track the time for payment.

Finally, any FLSA-tracking legislation can offer exceptions to protect employers from the most burdensome obligations. Such exceptions can be based on limitations from well-established statutes. For example, the Family and Medical Leave Act (FMLA) grants to covered employees the right to use up to twelve weeks of unpaid leave in one year to provide care for a child, spouse, parent, or oneself arising from a serious medical condition.[88] FMLA regulations specifically address leave in small increments, and require employers to grant time increments as leave that are no greater than the smallest increment used for other types of leave.[89] An FLSA exception to tracking can be based on such an increment, or be affixed to standards relevant to current practice in the industry. If a particular job commonly means carrying out work in small increments, and the technology to track is readily available, then imposing such a requirement on employers through reform would be a relatively small burden. Conversely, a tracking standard which is unusual in an industry, or highly burdensome due to the nature of the job, might be exempted. This would create a standard that could adjust with changes in technology and industry practice regarding employee tracking over time. This standard would be analogous to the familiar "justified by industrial realities" language that courts use to determine whether time should be compensated.[90] Such limitations would relieve employers from being forced to account for very small deviations in working time while also

---

[88]   29 U.S.C. § 2612(a)(1) (2012).

[89]   29 C.F.R. § 825.205(a) (2014).

[90]   *See, e.g.,* Hiner v. Penn-Harris-Madison School Corp., 256 F. Supp.2d 854, 861 (N.D. Ind. 2003) (stating that "[t]he *de minimis* rule applies only where there are uncertain and indefinite periods of time involved of a few seconds or minutes [in] duration, and where the failure to count such time is due to considerations justified by industrial realities.") (citing 29 C.F.R. § 785.47 (2014)).

ensuring that meaningful blocks of time remain protected and compensable under the FLSA.

B. The Protections and Opportunities of Precise Tracking of Work Time

A potential concern is that precise tracking will generate administrative costs in managing FLSA reforms. Employers may cite monetary cost and concerns about hassle regarding such tracking. Fortunately, there is both flexibility and opportunities in closely tracking employees' working time that can mitigate employer costs.

First, firms have substantial flexibility in how they track and manage the time of their employees. No legal requirements exist regarding the form or type of timekeeping records to be collected or retained. As the Department of Labor states, "[e]mployers may use any timekeeping method they choose. For example, they may use a time clock, have a timekeeper keep track of employee's work hours, or tell their workers to write their own times on the records. Any time management plan is acceptable as long as it is complete and accurate."[91] The Department of Labor offers a free app, for example, called Timesheet that allows employees to manage their own working time records.[92] Such an app can not only reduce employer tracking costs, but also provide helpful evidence during an investigation by the Department of Labor if an employer has failed to keep accurate or complete records. If an employer wants to comprehensively track employee time through technology, a number of software systems exist that can contemporaneously track and record hours worked by employees at little cost.[93]

Second, firms can leverage the information generated by recording small increments of time into a competitive advantage for the enterprise, making such a requirement a benefit rather than a cost. For example, UPS uses a host of sensors on its delivery trucks that monitor its

---

[91] U.S. Dep't of Labor, *Fact Sheet # 21: Recordkeeping Requirements under the Fair Labor Standards Act* (Jul. 2008) *available at* http://www. dol.gov/whd/regs/compliance/whdfs21.htm. *See also* 29 C.F.R. § 516.1(a) (2014).

[92] *See* U.S. Dep't of Labor, *Mobile Applications*, http://www.dol.gov/dol/apps/ (last visited July 16, 2014).

[93] *See, e.g,* TimeForce, http://www.mytimeforce.com (last visited July 14, 2014); TimeStation, http://www.mytimestation.com (last visited July 14, 2014); TSheets, http://www.tsheets.com (last visited July 14, 2014).

workers' actions.[94] These sensors can monitor to the second when an employee opens a door, closes it, buckles a seatbelt, and starts the truck.[95] Just one minute of productivity improvement per driver per day increases UPS annual financial results by $14.5 million.[96] Time tracking software can also be used to streamline internal processes, maximize efforts on important projects, monitor quality, and assign employees to tasks at which they are most effective.[97]

Third, these reforms will encourage the use of timekeeping software, the absence of which, unbeknownst to some employers, can be a substantial source of vulnerability in FLSA-related disputes. In *West v. Verizon Services Corp.*,[98] discussed earlier, a source of weakness in the employers' case was the absence of formal timekeeping systems. Neither Verizon nor the contracted staffing company tracked West's hours or expected West to track her own time.[99] West simply assumed she worked 72 hours a week, every week, and would be compensated for that time.[100] The court cited this lack of tracking data as the primary reason for denying the employers' summary judgment motion, concluding:

> the Court cannot grant summary judgment as to the number of hours that West worked per week. This is because neither Verizon nor [the staffing firm] kept track of West's hours worked. They required her to be available to answer customer calls from 9:00 a.m. to 9:00 p.m. six days per week.[101]

Furthermore, the employers' alleged ignorance that West was working overtime did not shield the defendants from liability. After noting that an employer can have "constructive knowledge" of an employee's overtime work when it has reason to know an employee is working overtime

---

[94] Jacob Goldstein, *To Increase Productivity, UPS Monitors Drivers' Every Move*, NPR (Apr. 17, 2014), *available at* http://www.npr.org/blogs/money/2014/04/17/303770907/to-increase-productivity-ups-monitors-drivers-every-move.

[95] *Ibid.*

[96] *Ibid.*

[97] *E.g.,* Andre Smith, *Improve Profits and Productivity with Time Tracking Software*, Decoded, http://www.decoded.com/view-post/How-Small-Businesses-Can-Improve-Profits-and-Productivity-With-Time-and-Attendance-Trackin-1 (last visited July 16, 2014); Cathedral Consulting Group, *Time Tracking to Improve Productivity*, http://cathedralconsulting.com/files/April%202014%20TOPIC%20Financial%20Systems.pdf (last visited July 16, 2014).

[98] 2011 WL 208314 (M.D. Fla.).

[99] *Ibid.* at *3.

[100] *Ibid.*

[101] *Ibid.* at *8.

hours,[102] the court stated that the employer had a duty to investigate overtime issues.[103] These facts, plus Verizon's awareness that a significant number of employees like West worked over 40 hours per week, created a genuine issue of material fact whether West's employers knew or should have known about West's overtime.[104]

Finally, when firms do utilize timekeeping software to track employees, it is not likely that courts will rigidly use such software against the employer when an employee sues for unpaid working time. For example, in *Zivali v. AT&T Mobility Inc.*,[105] plaintiffs challenged the use of MyTime, "a 'punch in,' 'punch out' system that ... contemporaneously record[ed] hours worked only when employees are physically present at the retail store or otherwise logged in to MyTime."[106] The plaintiffs argued that MyTime failed to capture time sending certain emails, opening and closing retail stores, lunch breaks, and other tasks.[107] The court gave the employer substantial deference regarding the method by which it recorded employee hours worked.[108] The court also noted that the software contained an adjustment feature that employees could utilize by contacting a manager and requesting a change in hours recorded.[109] As long as the firm's timekeeping system was ultimately a "complete and accurate recording" the court would not render the system impermissible under the FLSA.[110]

IV. CONCLUSION

The intersection of technology and working time has much promise, but can also create conflict. The advent of the smartphone and related technology has given employees the opportunity to access and respond to information at a nearly instantaneous pace. That same technology,

---

[102]   *Ibid.* at *9.
[103]   *Ibid.* at *10 (citing Brock v. Norman's Country Market, Inc., 835 F.2d 823, 828 (11th Cir.1988) ("It is firmly established where an employer has not kept adequate records of their employee's wages and hours as required by the FLSA, the employees will not be denied a recovery of back wages on the ground that their uncompensated work cannot be precisely determined.")).
[104]   *Ibid.*
[105]   784 F. Supp.2d 456 (E.D.N.Y. 2013).
[106]   *Ibid.* at 460.
[107]   *Ibid.*
[108]   *Ibid.*
[109]   *Ibid.* at 461.
[110]   *Ibid.*

however, has also granted employers nearly unfettered access to their employees regardless of the time of day, location, or personal circumstances.

The result of this access has been unjustified infringements upon an employee's personal time. Such infringements interrupt the relaxation and recovery process employees need to sustainably and healthily participate in long-term employment. These infringements also frequently occur in smaller increments that encourage employers to ignore or deny appropriate compensation.

The FLSA is the statute most relevant to working time, and one that mandates that employees must be paid for hours worked. However, the FLSA and its *de minimis* exception remain poorly equipped to manage the tiny increments of working time that technology has enabled to occur on a regular basis. The result is the FLSA, which has served many employees well for over 75 years, is in need of reform.

This chapter proposes a modest reform to the FLSA that requires employers to more precisely track employees' working time and compensate accordingly. Technology is readily available to track such time in small increments; without such reform, employees will be increasingly subject to abuse. The proposed reform also includes exceptions to alleviate any unusual burdens that may arise from precise tracking requirements in certain situations.

Close tracking of working time protects employees from abuse, but also creates opportunities and reduces liability for the employer, even under current rules. Tracking software can increase productivity and streamline production processes. Such software can also clarify evidence in a legal dispute that can help otherwise-compliant employers to reduce legal costs. Thus, narrowing the *de minimis* exception, and its associated obligations, can protect employers from future liability.

As technology advances, changes in working time practices will inevitably follow. This chapter represents a modest step towards updating industrial-era regulation and making it relevant to the modern age. Without such attention to the impact of technology on working time, misuse of such time against the workforce's most vulnerable populations may increase in the future.

BIBLIOGRAPHY

Statutes and Codes

Code of Federal Regulations, 29 C.F.R. § 516.1(a) (2014).
Code of Federal Regulations, 29 C.F.R. § 785.47 (2014).
Code of Federal Regulations, 29 C.F.R. § 825.205(a) (2014).
Fair Labor Standards Act of 1938, Pub. L. No. 75-718, 52 Stat. 1060 (codified as amended at 29 U.S.C. §§ 201–219 (2012)).
United States Code, 29 U.S.C. § 202(a)–(b) (2012).
United States Code, 29 U.S.C. § 213(a)(1) (2012).
United States Code, 29 U.S.C. §§ 251–262 (2012).
United States Code, 29 U.S.C. § 2612(a)(1) (2012).

Cases

Agui v. T-Mobile, Inc., No. 09-2955 (E.D.N.Y. 2009).
Anderson v. Mt. Clemens Pottery, 328 U.S. 680 (1946).
Armour & Co. v. Wantock, 323 U.S. 126 (1944).
Hesseltine v. Goodyear Tire & Rubber Co., 391 F. Supp.2d 509 (E.D. Tex. 2005).
Hiner v. Penn-Harris-Madison School Corp., 256 F. Supp.2d 854 (N.D. Ind. 2003).
IBP, Inc. v. Alvarez, 546 U.S. 21 (2005).
Lindow v. United States, 738 F.2d 1057 (9th Cir. 1984).
Owens v. Local No. 169, 971 F.3d 347, (9th Cir. 1992).
Perez v. Mountaire Farms, Inc., 650 F.3d 350 (4th Cir. 2011).
Rulli v. CB Richard Ellis, Inc., No. 2009cv00289 (E.D. Wis. 2009).
Rutti v. Lojack Corp., Inc., 596 F.3d 1046 (9th Cir. 2010).
Tennessee Coal, Iron & Ry. Co. v. Muscoda Local No. 13, 321 U.S. 590 (1944).
West v. Verizon Services Corp., 2011 WL 208314 (W.D. Fla.).
Zivali v. AT&T Mobility Inc., 784 F. Supp.2d 456 (E.D.N.Y. 2013).

Secondary Sources

Akerstedt, Torbjörn, et al., *Mental Fatigue, Work, and Sleep*, 57 J. PSYCHOSOMATIC RES. 427 (2004).
Barbu, Maria L., *The Ubiquitous Blackberry: The New Overtime Liability*, 5 LIBERTY U. L. REV. 47 (2010).
Cathedral Consulting Group, *Time Tracking to Improve Productivity*, http://cathedral consulting.com/files/April%202014%20TOPIC%20Financial%20Systems.pdf.
Chia, Thomas A., Note, *Fighting the Smartphone Patent War with Rand-Encumbered Patents*, 27 BERKELEY TECH. L.J. 209 (2012).
Clemons, Jennifer, *FLSA Retaliation: A Continuum of Employee Protection*, 53 BAYLOR L. REV. 535 (2001).
Class and Collective Action Complaint, Agui v. T-Mobile USA Inc., No. 09-2955, 2009 WL 2251810 (E.D.N.Y. 2009).
Cowie, Jefferson, *The Future of Fair Labor*, N.Y. TIMES (Jun. 24, 2013), http://www.nytimes.com/2013/06/25/opinion/the-future-of-fair-labor.html.

Cropley, Marc and Lynne J. Millward, *How Do Individuals "Switch-Off" From Work During Leisure? A Qualitative Description of the Unwinding Process in High and Low Ruminators*, 28 LEISURE STUDIES 333 (2009)

Cunningham, Craig A., Note, *Mind the Gap: A Legal and Economic Analysis of Stockbroker Overtime Eligibility Under the Fair Labor Standards Act*, 2009 U. ILL. L. REV. 1243.

Crouss, Kathryn S., Note, *Employment Law – Welcome to the Jungle: Salespeople and the Administrative Exemption to the Fair Labor Standards Act*, 34 W. NEW ENG. L. REV. 205 (2012).

Goldstein, Jacob, *To Increase Productivity, UPS Monitors Drivers' Every Move*, NPR (Apr. 17, 2014), *available at* http://www.npr.org/blogs/money/2014/04/17/ 303770907/to-increase-productivity-ups-monitors-drivers-every-move.

Guiterrez, Steven M. and Joseph Neguse, *Emerging Technologies and the FLSA*, 39 COLO. LAW. 49 (2010).

Harris, Seths, *75 Years of Rewarding Work and Responsibility*, U.S. DEP'T OF LABOR: WORK IN PROGRESS (Jun. 24, 2013).

Inflation Calculator, http://www.dollartimes.com/calculators/inflation.htm.

Linder, Marc, *Class Struggle at the Door: The Origins of the Portal-to-Portal Act of 1947*, 39 BUFF. L. REV. 53 (1991).

Miller, Scott D., *Revitalizing the FLSA*, 19 HOFSTRA LAB. & EMP. L.J. 1 (2001).

Nemerofsky, Jeff, *What is a "Trifle" Anyway?*, 37 GONZ. L. REV. 315 (2001–02).

Pepelnjak, Anna M., *Employee Use of Smartphones: FLSA Implications*, WEISS BERZOWSKI BRADY LLP (Sep. 14, 2011), http://www.wbb-law.com/multimedia/ blog/employee-use-smartphones-flsa-implications.

Plaintiff's Memorandum of Law in Opposition to PDS Technical Services Inc.'s Motion for Partial Summary Judgment, West v. Verizon Services Corp. at 9, No. 8:08-cv-01325-VMC-MAP, 2010 WL 5808203 (M.D. Fla. Nov. 29, 2010).

President Franklin D. Roosevelt, Annual Message to the Congress, Jan. 3, 1938, *available at* http://www.presidency.ucsb.edu/ws/?pid=15517.

Reidy, Marian K., Suman Beros and H. Joseph Wen, *Managing Business Smartphone Data*, 14 J. INTERNET L. 3, 8 n.66 (2011).

Riley, Amanda M., *The De Minimis Rule: Trifles of Time*, 45 ORANGE CTY. LAW. 18 (2003).

Smartphones Will Transform Our Lives in Ways we Cannot Even Imagine Today, THE MIRROR (Aug. 5, 2011), http://www.mirror.co.uk/news/uk-news/smartphones-will-transform-our-lives-in-ways-we-cannot-145919.

Smith, Andre, *Improve Profits and Productivity with Time Tracking Software*, DECODED, http://www.decoded.com/view-post/How-Small-Businesses-Can-Improve-Profits-and-Productivity-With-Time-and-Attendance-Trackin-1.

Suadicani, Poul et al., *Are Social Inequalities Associated with the Risk of Ischemic Heart Diseases as a Result of Psychological Working Conditions*, 101 ATHERO-SCLEROSIS 165 (1993).

Timeforce, http://www.mytimeforce.com.

Timestation, http://www.mytimestation.com.

TSheets, http://www.tsheets.com.

U.S. Dep't of Labor, *Fact Sheet # 21: Recordkeeping Requirements under the Fair Labor Standards Act* (Jul. 2008) available at http://www. dol.gov/whd/regs/ compliance/whdfs21.htm.

U.S. Dep't of Labor, *Flexible Schedules*, http://www.dol.gov/compliance/topics/ wages-other-flex.htm.

146 Managing the legal nexus between intellectual property and employees

U.S. Dep't of Labor, *Mobile Applications*, http://www.dol.gov/dol/apps.
Washington State Dept. of Labor & Industries, *History of Apprenticeship*, http://www.lni.wa.gov/TradesLicensing/Apprenticeship/About/History/.

PART III

Global intersections

6. Employee misappropriation: using Section 337 to combat trade secret theft

Marisa Anne Pagnattaro and Stephen Kim Park

The protection of trade secrets continues to be a vexing global challenge. Although it is difficult to quantify the value of intangible intellectual property assets, including trade secrets, they can represent as much as 85 percent of a corporation's value.[1] Preventing disclosures of trade secrets is of critical importance in the maintenance of corporate value. In fact, the number of U.S. companies doing business in China reporting that intellectual property theft causes "material damage to China operations rose by 12 percentage points, to 34 percent. The percentage of those who reported material damage to global operations also rose by 4 percent, to 14 percent."[2] According to the House of Representatives Intelligence Committee, U.S. companies suffered estimated losses of over $300 billion in 2012, due to the theft of trade secrets, with a large share of those losses being due to Chinese cyber espionage.[3] A wide range of companies, including General Motors, Dow Chemical, Cargill, Boeing, and DuPont,[4] are all significantly affected by the loss of trade secrets in the global context.

---

[1]   PriceWaterhouseCoopers, *Redefining Intellectual Property Value: The Case of China* 2 (2005), http://www.pwc.com/en_us/us/technology-innovation-center/assets/ipr-web_x.pdf.

[2]   AmCham China, *Business Climate Survey Report* (2013), http://www.amchamchina.org/businessclimate2013.

[3]   Doug Palmer, *U.S. Seeks to Tackle Trade-Secret Theft by China, Others*, REUTERS, (Feb. 20, 2013), http://www.reuters.com/article/2013/02/21/us-usa-trade-secrets-idUSBRE91J0T220130221; Siobahn Gorman and Jared A. Favole, *U.S. Ups Ante for Spying on Firms: China, Others are Threatened with New Penalties,* WALL ST. J., Feb. 21, 2013, at A1.

[4]   *Ibid.*

For global employers, protecting trade secrets from employee disclosure is a common problem.[5] Many times, rogue employees play a crucial role in the misappropriation of trade secrets. This was particularly evident in the recent prosecutions of former DuPont employees who were convicted for selling trade secrets to a Chinese competitor.[6] In another landmark case, preliminary injunction and asset preservation orders were issued in China against a former employee of a U.S.-based pharmaceutical company who improperly downloaded documents containing trade secrets from the company's database.[7] Despite the fact that he signed a confidentiality agreement, the former employee admitted downloading highly confidential information to his personal USB drive and computer.[8]

There are a number of reasons why current and former employees are the groups most often responsible for trade secret misappropriation.[9] One important reason is the reality that many workers are increasingly mobile and very unlikely to spend their career with the same employer.[10] Top talent employees increasingly see themselves as global and are likely to move repeatedly for better opportunities.[11] This movement, however, comes at a peril for employers who are at risk of losing trade secrets. The portability of work further compounds this risk in a number of ways, such as employees routinely saving work on portable devices, checking e-mail from non-work locations, and working from remote locations.[12] The expansion of global supply chains, cross-border joint ventures, and

---

[5] WENDY S. LAZAR AND GARY R. SINISCALO, RESTRICTIVE COVENANTS AND TRADE SECRETS IN EMPLOYMENT LAW: AN INTERNATIONAL SURVEY, Vol. 1 Preface i. (2010).

[6] Karen Gullo, *DuPont Trade Secret Theft for China Leads to Conviction*, BLOOMBERGBUSINESSWEEK, (Mar. 5, 2014), http://www.businessweek.com/news/2014-03-05/california-man-convicted-of-stealing-dupont-trade-secrets-1.

[7] Andreas Lauffs and Jonathan Isaacs, *First Ever Preliminary Injunction and Asset Preservation Orders in Trade Secrets Case Issued by Court*, ABA INT'L LABOR & EMPLOYMENT L. COMMITTEE NEWSLETTER (Sept. 2013), http://www.americanbar.org/content/newsletter/groups/labor_law/int_newsletter/2013/sept2013/china9-13.html.

[8] *Ibid.*

[9] David S. Almeling, et al., *A Statistical Analysis of Trade Secret Litigation in Federal Courts*, 45 GONZ. L. REV. 291, 302-04 (2010).

[10] David S. Almeling, *Seven Reasons Why Trade Secrets are Increasingly Important*, 27 BERKELEY TECH. L.J. 1091, 1101 (2012).

[11] PriceWaterhouseCoopers, *Talent Mobility 2020: The Next Generation of International Assignments* (2010), http://www.pwc.com/gx/en/managing-tomorrows-people/future-of-work/pdf/talent-mobility-2020.pdf.

[12] Almeling, *supra* note 10, at 1103.

foreign affiliate relationships provide more opportunities for employees to misappropriate information while making it more challenging for companies to monitor, deter, and combat such behavior. Lastly, in a world filled with file sharing and social media, there is an evolving perception of the importance of secrecy, which may make it more difficult to impress on employees the value of keeping proprietary material secret.[13]

Where misappropriation occurs abroad, U.S. companies may find that it is difficult to obtain adequate redress. Section 337 of the Tariff Act of 1930 (Section 337) offers an avenue of redress, as it can be used to block goods produced with misappropriated trade secrets from being imported into the United States.[14] Despite criticism, Section 337 is emerging as an important tool with which to protect the rights of U.S. trade secret owners.

Section I details the background of Section 337 and its use in the trade secret context. Section II discusses several early cases, and then focuses on the *TianRui* case,[15] which significantly expanded the potential use of Section 337. This section then reviews a number of recent post-*TianRui* cases brought under Section 337 to demonstrate the growing jurisprudence in this area. Section III identifies ongoing trends in trade secret enforcement actions under Section 337 and addresses criticism about the use of Section 337 to address unfair acts occurring entirely outside of the United States. Section IV then analyzes how this relatively new use of Section 337 can be used strategically to help trade secret owners protect their valuable assets.

I. BACKGROUND: "UNFAIR PRACTICES" AND SECTION 337 OF THE TARIFF ACT OF 1930

Pursuant to Section 337, the U.S. International Trade Commission (ITC or Commission) has the authority to review unfair trade practices involving imported goods.[16] There are two distinct kinds of claims that may be brought under Section 337. The first involves the part of Section 337 that specifically prevents the importation and sale in the United States of goods that infringe on a valid and enforceable patent, copyright,

---

[13] *Ibid.*
[14] 19 U.S.C. § 1337 (2012).
[15] TianRui Group Co. Ltd. v. Int'l Trade Comm., 661 F.3d 1322 (2011).
[16] 19 U.S.C. § 1332(a)-(c) (2012).

or trademark.[17] A claim for statutory intellectual property misappropriation must show that an industry related to the protected articles "exists or is in the process of being established."[18] The use of Section 337 is well established to protect against these kinds of statutory intellectual property misappropriation. These claims, particularly patent-related claims, comprise a significant portion of Section 337 claims.[19]

The second kind of claim that may be asserted under the more generic rubric of "unfair practices," includes misappropriation of trade secrets as well as a list of other possibilities, such as trade dress infringement and false advertising.[20] For such claims, it must be shown that "in the sale of such articles by the owner, importer, or consignee, the threat or effect of is

1. to destroy or substantially injure an industry in the United States;
2. to prevent the establishment of such an industry; or
3. to restrain or monopolize trade and commerce in the United States.[21]

To determine whether there is injury, the Commission may consider a number of factors, including loss of customers, declining sales, decreased production and profitability, the volume of imports, the level of market penetration, and the capacity of the foreign entity to increase imports.[22] This relatively new application of Section 337[23] is important for domestic

---

[17] *Ibid.* at § 1337(a)(1)(B)-(E) (2012).

[18] *Ibid.* at § 1337(a)(2) (2012).

[19] U.S. International Trade Commission, *FY 2012 At a Glance* (2013), http://www.usitc.gov/press_room/documents/YIR_OP2_final.pdf. *See generally* Thomas Yeh, *The International Trade Commission and the Nonpracticing Entity: Reviving the Industry Requirement for Domestic Industries Based on Licensing,* 80 GEO. WASH. L. REV. 1574 (2012) (discussing patent cases brought under Section 337).

[20] 19 U.S.C. § 1337 (a)(1)(A) (2012).

[21] *Ibid. See generally* Andrew F. Popper, *Beneficiaries of Misconduct: A Direct Approach to IT Theft,* 17 MARQ. INTELL. PROP. L.J. 27, 42 (2013) (discussing the drawbacks of seeking Section 337 enforcement).

[22] Gary M. Hnath, *Section 337 Investigations at the US International Trade Commission Provide a Powerful Remedy Against Misappropriation of Trade Secrets,* 22 INTELL. PROP. & TECH. L. J., 1, 3 (2010).

[23] *See ibid.* at 3 (noting that while "more than 90 percent of cases under § 337 involve allegations of patent infringement, the statute is not limited to patent cases").

industries to consider as they endeavor to protect their trade secrets from misappropriation in the international context.[24]

A private party, including a U.S. company, may initiate a request for an investigation.[25] The Commission is then required to investigate any alleged violation of Section 337 and determine whether or not there is a violation.[26] Notice of the commencement of an investigation is published in the Federal Register and the Commission is charged with concluding its investigation and making a determination at "the earliest practicable time after the date" of the notice.[27] Because expeditious adjudication is a priority, in all cases, within 45 days after the investigation is initiated, the Commission must establish a target date for its final determination.[28]

After an investigation, if the Commission determines that there is a violation, it may direct that the articles at issue "be excluded from entry into the United States."[29] Generally, the Commission's authority to order exclusion of articles is limited to persons it determines are violating Section 337, unless "a general exclusion from entry of articles is necessary to prevent circumvention of an exclusion order limited to products of named persons" or "there is a pattern" violating Section 337 and "it is difficult to identify the source of the infringing products."[30]

In addition to, or in lieu of excluding articles from entry, the Commission may issue a cease-and-desist order preventing the party at issue "from engaging in the unfair methods or acts involved."[31] All remedial orders are sent to the President, who has 60 days to disapprove an order.[32] If the President does not disapprove the Commission's order during the review period, infringing articles may no longer be imported

---

[24] Unlike some other jurisdictions with laws similar to Section 337, the United States limits such actions to complainants that have a domestic industry. *See* Thomas A. Broughan III, *Modernizing §337's Domestic Industry Requirement for the Global Economy*, 19 FED. CIR. B.J. 41, 59-60 (2009) (noting that the European Union and Japan have similar processes, but do not have a domestic industry requirement).

[25] 19 C.F.R. § 201.7 (1998).

[26] 19 U.S.C. § 1337(b)–(c) (2012).

[27] *Ibid.* at § 1337(b)(1) (2012).

[28] *Ibid.*

[29] *Ibid.* at § 1337(e) (2012).

[30] *Ibid.* at § 1337 (d)(2) (2012).

[31] *Ibid.* at § 1337(f) (2012).

[32] *Ibid.* at § 1337(j) (2012).

into the United States. Although the Commission may order civil penalties for violations,[33] it cannot award damages to the complaining party.

On its face, Section 337 offers companies a number of legal advantages in combating the theft of trade secrets occurring outside of the United States. The first advantage is that the Commission may have broader jurisdiction over foreign parties than U.S. federal courts, as it has national *in rem* jurisdiction over the articles at issue in the complaint.[34] Moreover, if the respondent does not respond to the complaint or otherwise fails to appear to answer, and does not show good cause why he should not be held in default, the Commission may "presume the facts alleged in the complaint to be true" and it has the power to issue an exclusion from entry, a cease and desist order, or both.[35]

A second factor is that there may be expanded opportunities for discovery, as the evidentiary standards are more liberal than in federal courts.[36] A third major advantage is the speed of resolution. Section 337 investigations are typically resolved by the Commission within 16 months,[37] which is much quicker than cases brought in other venues, such as federal district courts. The Commission has also launched a pilot program aimed at early disposition of Section 337 issues, such as rendering a determination about the "domestic industry" issue to adjudicate crucial threshold issues early in the proceedings.[38]

Lastly, perhaps the most substantial factor is the power of the Commission to prevent the alleged infringing party from profiting from the goods in the United States. The Commission has the power to exclude infringing goods from being imported into the United States, as well as

---

[33] *Ibid.* at § 1337(f) (2012).

[34] Daniel D. Quick and H. Jonathan Redway, *Barring the Door: The International Trade Commission As a Means to Prevent Importation of Goods Utilizing Misappropriated Trade Secrets*, 32 MICH. BUS. L.J. 39 (2012).

[35] 19 U.S.C. § 1337(g) (2012).

[36] *See* P. Andrew Riley and Jonathan R.K. Stroud, *A Survey of Trade Secret Investigations at the International Trade Commission: A Model for Future Litigants*, 15 COLUM. SCI. & TECH. L. REV. 41, 45 (2013) (noting that "the ITC allows for broader discovery, as it must fully address each claim raised").

[37] U.S. International Trade Commission, *FY 2011 Highlights: USITC Sees Record Number of Intellectual Property Infringement Cases Filed*, http://www. usitc.gov/press_room/documents/featured_news/337_timeframes_article.htm (noting that cases were resolved in 13.7 months on average).

[38] U.S. International Trade Commission, *Pilot Program Will Test Early Disposition of Certain Section 337 Investigations,* http://www.usitc.gov/press_room/documents/featured_news/337pilot_article.htm.

issue cease and desist orders that prohibit the person found in violation of Section 337 from selling, marketing, distributing, offering for sale, selling or otherwise transferring the articles concerned in the United States. Although the Commission does not award damages, these trade remedies are powerful tools to protect the rightful owners of the trade secrets from unfair competition. The threat or actual entry of an exclusion order provides trade secret owners with powerful leverage against alleged violators. Taken together, these factors make Section 337 actions attractive to companies that are seeking a relatively speedy way to stop infringing goods from entering the U.S. market.

II. CASES APPLYING SECTION 337 IN THE TRADE SECRET CONTEXT

There were a limited number of cases brought under Section 337 for trade secret misappropriation prior to the *TianRui* decision. After that important case, however, there has been a surge in cases, as Section 337 is evolving as an important tool to combat trade secret theft in the international context. The following discussion of these cases demonstrates the developing jurisprudence in this area, and how this trade provision can be an effective remedy. As is demonstrated by a number of the cases, disclosures by former employees are often times the source of the misappropriation.

A. Early Cases

Prior to the *TianRui* decision, several cases stand out as significant in the development of the law.[39] The first investigation in which the ITC issued a remedy in a case involving trade secret misappropriation was in 1979.[40] In that case, *Certain Apparatus for the Continuous Production of Copper Rod (Copper Rod)*, the complainant, Southwire Company, alleged that Fried, Krupp GmbH, and Krupp International, Inc. (collectively "Krupp") misappropriated fourteen trade secrets.[41] At one time, Southwire and Krupp established a contractual confidential business relationship in

---

[39] *See* Riley and Stroud, *supra* note 36, at 66–67 (providing a survey of early Section 337 trade secret cases).

[40] Certain Apparatus for the Continuous Production of Copper Rod, Inv. No. 337-TA-52, USITC Pub. 1017 (Nov. 23, 1979), *available at* http://www.usitc.gov/publications/337/pub1017.pdf.

[41] USITC Pub. 1017, Commission Memorandum Opinion at 38.

connection with a project, in which Krupp had access to ten of Southwire's trade secrets.[42] Southwire alleged that the other four trade secrets were "misappropriated by Krupp through third parties by unfair means."[43] According to the Commission, "to prove misappropriation of a trade secret for purposes of establishing an unfair act within the purview of section 337, four elements must be proven:

1. the existence of a trade secret which is not in the public domain,
2. that the complainant is the owner of the trade secret or possesses a proprietary interest therein,
3. that the complainant disclosed the trade secret to respondent while in a confidential relationship or that the respondent wrongfully took the trade secret by unfair means, and
4. that the respondent has used or disclosed the trade secret causing injury to the complainant.[44]

The Commission modeled these criteria on the *Restatement of Torts.*[45]

After a hearing on the evidence, the ITC found that two of the respondents misappropriated trade secrets for the continuous production of copper rods.[46] Accordingly, although the ITC issued cease and desist orders to remedy the violations, it did not issue an exclusion order, stating that such a remedy would be "inappropriate" for a Section 337 trade secret violation.[47] The use of Section 337 in the trade secret context was significantly less attractive without the exclusion remedy.

Five years after *Copper Rod*, however, in *Certain Processes for the Manufacture of Skinless Sausage Casings and Resulting Product* (*Sausage Casings*) the ITC considered another case involving alleged misappropriation of trade secrets.[48] In *Sausage Casings,* the ITC re-iterated the four elements articulated in *Copper Rod* necessary to prove

---

42 *Ibid.* at 39.
43 *Ibid.*
44 *Ibid.* at 38.
45 *Ibid.* (citing the Restatement (Third) of Torts § 757 (2010)).
46 USITC Pub. 1017, Commission Determination and Order at 2
47 *Ibid.* at 3–5 and Commission Memorandum Opinion at 67.
48 Certain Processes for the Manufacture of Skinless Sausage Casings and Resulting Product, Inv. (hereinafter "Sausage Casings") No. 337-TA-148 and 337-TA-169, USITC Pub. 1624 (July 31, 1984), *available at* http://www.usitc. gov/publications/337/pub1624.pdf. Similar to the Copper Rod case, this proceeding involved both patent and trade secret claims.

trade secret misappropriation.[49] After finding that the respondent misappropriated trade secrets owned by the complainant, in a sharp departure from *Copper Rod*, the ITC issued a limited exclusion order prohibiting all infringing products from entry into the United States (except under a license from the complainant) for ten years.[50] Respondent Viscofan, S.A. appealed to the Federal Circuit, seeking review of the ten-year exclusion order, which applied to specified "'sausage casings manufactured by Viscofan' or any affiliated company or related business entity."[51] In reaching its decision, the Federal Circuit stated, "the Commission has broad discretion in selecting the form, scope and extent of the remedy, and judicial review of its choice of remedy is necessarily limited."[52]

The Federal Circuit agreed with the ITC that a cease and desist order "would not effectively correct the violations found."[53] Moreover, the Federal Circuit found that the ITC "correctly recognized that 'the duration of relief in a case of misappropriation of trade secrets should be the period of time it would have taken respondent independently to develop the technology using lawful means.'"[54] Establishing the availability of such a broad exclusion order as a remedy was an important development in protecting owners of trade secrets from unlawful infringement, establishing an important foundation for subsequent cases.[55]

In another case important to this early development of Section 337, the ITC considered whether the hangers produced and imported by the respondents infringed on the complainants' trade secrets. In *Garment Hangers*, the action was dismissed because the complainants were not able to demonstrate that the hangers were produced using their misappropriated trade secrets.[56] An important aspect of this case was the emphasis on the "nexus" requirement necessary to prove misappropriation of trade

---

[49] USITC Pub. 1624, Commission Opinion at 38.

[50] *Ibid.* at Commission Action and Order at 5.

[51] Viscofan, S.A. v. U.S. Int'l Trade Comm'n, 787 F.2d 544, 546 (Fed. Cir. 1986).

[52] *Viscofan*, 787 F.2d at 548.

[53] *Ibid.* at 549.

[54] *Ibid.* at 550.

[55] *See* Riley and Stroud, *supra* note 36, at 67-68 (observing that this "remedy for trade secret violations is potentially broad and open-ended and can include an exclusion order").

[56] Garment Hangers, Inv. No. 337-TA-255, Initial Determination, at 107-11, (June 17, 1987), *available at* http://info.usitc.gov/ouii/public/337inv.nsf/56ff5 fbca63b069e852565460078c0ae/a30523307fc9a34c85256613007253b7?Open Document&Highlight=0,hangers.

secrets.[57] From these early cases, it became clear that Section 337 could be an effective way to combat theft of trade secrets outside of the United States.[58]

B. TianRui Group Co. Ltd. v. U.S. International Trade Commission

Copper Rod, *Sausage Casings*, and *Garment Hangers* were important in laying the groundwork for trade secret cases under Section 337, yet it was a Federal Circuit decision[59] affirming an ITC determination[60] that reinvigorated such claims. The *TianRui* case is important because it established that Section 337 could be used to prohibit the importation of articles in cases in which the acts of misappropriation occurred outside of the United States.[61] The importance of former employees in the misappropriation of trade secrets in *TianRui* cannot be overstated. The facts showed that complainant Amsted Industries Inc. (Amsted) owned two secret processes for manufacturing steel railway wheels.[62] One of those was the "ABC process," which Amsted used at one time at its foundry in Alabama.[63] Many steps were taken to keep the ABC process confidential, including informing employees with access to the information that it was to be kept confidential, sharing the information in process manuals with a limited number of named individuals, keeping the manuals out of the general file system at the research center, and limiting access to visitors at the foundry.[64]

TianRui Group Company Limited and TianRui Group Foundry Company Limited (collectively "TianRui") sought to license Amsted's wheel technology, but were unable to reach an agreement with the company.[65] TianRui then hired nine employees from one of Amsted's Chinese licensees, including employees who were trained at Amsted's foundry in Alabama.[66] Pursuant to its contractual obligations, this Amsted licensee

---

57 *Ibid.*

58 *See* Riley and Stroud, *supra* note 36, at 69–74 (discussing other early Section 337 investigations and appellate decisions).

59 *TianRui*, 661 F.3d at 1322.

60 In the matter of Certain Cast Steel Railway Wheels, Certain Processes for Manufacturing the Same and Certain Products Containing Same, ITC Initial Determination (hereinafter "Certain Cast Steel"), 2009 WL 4261206.

61 *TianRui*, 661 F.3d at 1335.

62 *Ibid.* at 1324.

63 *Ibid.* at 1324.

64 *Certain Cast Steel,* 2009 WL 4261206 at 13–14.

65 *TianRui*, 661 F.3d at 1324.

66 *Ibid.*

took a number of reasonable steps to keep the information secret, including informing employees through a written code of conduct that the information was proprietary and must be kept confidential, notifying employees that they had a duty not to disclose the information, keeping the facility secure and gated, maintaining password-protected computers, and not connecting computers with key documents to the company intranet or Internet.[67] The ITC found that at the time TianRui started hiring employees familiar with the ABC process, there were reasonable measures in place to protect the trade secrets.[68] Although the employees were notified that the ABC process was proprietary and confidential in accordance with the written employee code of conduct and eight out of the nine employees had signed confidentiality agreements, they apparently revealed the details of the ABC process to TianRui, who then "exploited that information in producing" the goods at issue.[69]

Acknowledging that misappropriated trade secrets may be used in the manufacture of goods abroad, the Federal Circuit stated that barring the Commission from considering this activity because it occurs outside of the United States would be "inconsistent with the congressional purpose of protecting domestic commerce from unfair methods of competition in importation such as trade secret misappropriation."[70] In reaching this conclusion, the Federal Circuit agreed with the Commission's interpretation of Section 337, noting that this position is consistent with previous cases, including *Sausage Casings*, and that the interpretation is also "consistent with the purpose and legislative background of the statute."[71] Moreover, the Federal Circuit stated that a determination of whether or not this kind of trade secret misappropriation constitutes "unfair methods of competition" or "unfair acts" under Section 337 should be "one of federal law ... decided under a uniform federal standard, rather than by reference to a particular state's tort law."[72] Although the decision does not articulate the actual standard, it cites the Restatement of Unfair Competition and the Uniform Trade Secrets Act, as well as the federal criminal statute governing theft of trade secrets as establishing the general standard.[73] Additionally, the court points to the salient facts in the case that are sufficient to establish misappropriation of trade secrets:

---

67 *Certain Cast Steel,* 2009 WL 4261206 at 15.
68 *Ibid.*
69 *TianRui,* 661 F.3d at 1324, 1328.
70 *Ibid.* at 1335.
71 *Ibid.* at 1332.
72 *Ibid.* at 1327.
73 *TianRui,* 661 F.3d at 1328.

obtaining access to confidential information through former employees who were charged with keeping the information confidential and exploiting that confidential information in producing the goods at issue.[74]

Another important aspect of *TianRui* is the Federal Circuit's holding that the complainant could obtain relief under Section 337, even if it is not currently engaged in manufacturing that uses the trade secrets.[75] TianRui contended that in order for the Commission to grant relief, "the domestic industry must practice the misappropriated trade secret."[76] Because evidence was submitted indicating that "the imported TianRui wheels could directly compete with wheels domestically produced by the trade secret owner," this was deemed sufficient to "constitute an injury to an 'industry'" under Section 337.[77] Central to the lasting importance of the *TianRui* decision is that the Commission has the authority to use a federal standard to investigate and grant relief based on extraterritorial conduct if it is necessary to protect domestic industries from injuries arising out of unfair competition.[78]

The *TianRui* case is particularly important because a similar case in China, *Siwei Industries (Shenzhen) Co. Ltd. v. Avery Dennison Corp.*,[79] stands for the proposition that liability under China's Unfair Competition Law does not encompass the sale of the products.[80] As such, Section 337 can help to offset the limiting effect of the decision by allowing legal recourse in the United States for infringing products.[81] Moreover, it was unclear if there was any adequate relief in China for Amsted even though Amsted took steps to protect its trade secrets.

---

[74] *Ibid.*

[75] *Ibid.* at 1336–37.

[76] *Ibid.* at 1335.

[77] *Ibid.* at 1337.

[78] *See* Natalie Flechsig, *Trade Secret Enforcement After TianRui: Fighting Misappropriation Through the ITC*, 28 BERKELEY TECH. L.J. 449, 450 (2013) (suggesting that trade secret filings will increase after *TianRui* due to the ITC's liberal interpretation of the domestic industry requirement); Stephen McJohn, *Top Tens in 2011: Copyright and Trade Secrets*, 10 NW. J. TECH. & INTELL. PROP. 331 (2012) (reviewing top copyright and trade secret cases from 2011).

[79] *See* J. Benjamin Bai and Guoping Da, *Strategies for Trade Secrets Protection in China*, 9 N.W. J. TECH. & INTELL. PROP. 351, 371–72 (2011) (describing the complicated procedural history of *Siewei*).

[80] *Ibid.*

[81] Marisa Anne Pagnattaro, *Preventing Know-How From Walking Out the Door in China: Protection of Trade Secrets*, 55 BUS. HORIZONS 329, 333 (2012).

C. Post-*TianRui* Cases

Following the initial ITC determination in *TianRui*, a number of cases have been filed with the Commission seeking relief for misappropriation of trade secrets. In each of these cases, the complainant asked the Commission to find that trade secret infringement occurred, resulting in unfair trade practices, which should result in blocking the entry and sale of the infringing products in the United States. In each of these cases, despite steps taken by each company to safeguard its trade secrets, the alleged misappropriation occurred as the result of disclosure by former employees.

1. DC-DC controllers and products containing the same

In December 2009, after the ITC's initial determination in *TianRui*, complainants Richtek Technology Corp. and Richtek USA, Inc. (collectively "Richtek") filed a complaint with the ITC alleging patent infringement and unfair acts arising from misappropriating Richtek's proprietary and trade secret information "used to develop, market, and manufacture DC-to-DC controllers for customers in the United States."[82] Richtek brought the action against a number of entities, including uPI Semiconductor Corp. of Taiwan ("uPI") and several downstream manufacturers.[83] With regard to trade secrets, Richtek accused uPI of misappropriating seventeen trade secrets, consisting of both business trade secrets and technical trade secrets.[84]

After full discovery and filing pretrial briefs, in August 2010, uPI agreed to a unilateral Consent Order in which the Commission ordered uPI not to import, sell or offer to sell or knowingly aid, abet, encourage, participate in, or induce importation into the United States of articles produced using, or which contain, Richtek's trade secrets.[85] Accordingly, the investigation was terminated. In September 2011, however, the Commission instituted a formal enforcement proceeding to determine if there was a violation of that consent order and if any enforcement measures were appropriate.[86]

---

[82] In the Matter of Certain DC-DC Controllers and Products Containing Same (hereinafter DC Controllers), Inv. No. 337-TA-698, Enforcement Initial Determination at 86 (June 8, 2012). On November 30, 2012, ALJ David P. Shaw issued the public version of the Enforcement Initial Determination.

[83] *DC Controllers* at 1.

[84] *Ibid.* at 86.

[85] *Ibid.* at 2 (referring to the August 13, 2010 consent order).

[86] *Ibid.* at 3.

In the Enforcement Initial Determination, Administrative Law Judge ("ALJ") David Shaw found that uPI had violated the consent order.[87] Relying on *TianRui*, ALJ Shaw found that federal common law governed the trade secret allegations.[88] As such, he applied the standard articulated in *Garment Hangers* and *Sausage Casings*, stating that Richtek must prove, by a preponderance of the evidence, that "(1) one or more trade secrets exist and are not within the public domain; (2) Richtek is the owner of the trade secret(s) or possesses a proprietary interest therein; (3) either Richtek disclosed the trade secret to uPI personnel while in a confidential relationship, or uPI wrongfully took the trade secret from Richtek by unfair means, and (4) uPI used or disclosed the trade secret, causing injury to Richtek."[89]

Although evidence was presented that Richtek "took steps to train its employees to identify confidential trade secret information" and "made reasonable efforts to preserve the secrecy of its trade secrets," former Richtek employees did not maintain that confidentiality.[90] Employees, including those at issue, were trained to "identify confidential and trade secret information."[91] In fact, thirteen of uPI's employees, including its founders and management team, were former Richtek employees who were "key participants in the design" of Richtek's product lines at issue.[92] Importantly, these employees had "access to Richtek's most sensitive and confidential technical trade secrets and could not have been unaware of the importance of those secrets to Richtek's business."[93] These allegations were supported by expert testimony stating, "uPI acquired 'vast quantities of Richtek proprietary, trade secret information without authorization from Richtek' through former Richtek employees."[94]

Based on this evidence, ALJ Shaw concluded that "any importation, sale for importation, or sale after importation" of accused products after August 13, 2010, "constitutes a violation of the uPI consent order," but the evidence did not establish that uPI products developed after the consent order contain any misappropriated trade secrets.[95] Accordingly,

---

87   *Ibid.* at 99–100.
88   *Ibid.* at 41.
89   *Ibid.* at 42.
90   *Ibid.* at 93.
91   *Ibid.* at 92.
92   *Ibid.* at 93–94.
93   *Ibid.* at 94.
94   *Ibid.* at 94–95.
95   *Ibid.* at 99–100 and 109.

he recommended that, if a violation is found, the civil penalty "should equal $10,000 times the number of days on which an importation or sale occurred in violation of the consent order."[96] Inasmuch as Richtek did not allege circumstances warranting a general exclusion order, he recommended retaining the existing consent order (with a modification to include uPI's affiliated companies) and not replacing it with a limited exclusion order.[97]

2. Electric fireplaces, components thereof

This case is a consolidated action based on two complaints filed by Twin-Star International, Inc. ("Twin Star") and TS Investment Holding Corp. (collectively referred to as "Twin Star") alleging a violation of Section 337 by Yue Qui Sheng ("Yue") and his company Shenzhen Reliap Industrial Co. ("Reliap") of China.[98] Yue was an employee of Twin Star's wholly-owned subsidiary in China.[99] In connection with his employment, Yue signed a Subscription and Stockholders' Agreement ("SSA") that included a nondisclosure clause and a noncompetition clause.[100] This agreement was important to the employment relationship as Yue had access to Twin-Star's confidential information related to the manufacture of kinetic sculptures for electric fireplaces, as well as access to confidential retail customer lists, product manufacturing specifications, component suppliers, and specific cost information provided to Twin-Star's customers.[101] Less than three years after he started working for Twin-Star, Yue left that employment to work for a new company he formed, Reliap, to compete directly with Twin-Star manufacturing, distributing, selling, and marketing electric fireplace products to Twin-Star's retail customers and exporting the fireplaces to the United

---

[96] *Ibid.* at 111 (citing 19 U.S.C. § 1337(f)(2) that the maximum daily penalty is US $100,000 per day, with the alternative penalty of twice the domestic value of the articles entered or sold on such day in violation of the order).

[97] *Ibid.* at 110 and 123.

[98] In the Matter of Certain Electric Fireplaces, Inv. Nos. 337-TA-826/791.

[99] In the Matter of Certain Electric Fireplaces, Complaint, 337-TA-791 at ¶ 24 (hereinafter "In the Matter of Certain Electric Fireplaces June 2011 Complaint") (June 17, 2011), *available at* http://www.itcblog.com/wp-content/uploads/2011/06/twinstarcomplaint17jun11.pdf.

[100] *Ibid.* at ¶ 27.

[101] *Ibid.* at ¶ 28.

States.[102] Twin-Start claimed that Reliap wrongfully acquired its trade secrets through Yue.[103]

In support of its assertions, Twin-Star articulated a number of steps it took to maintain the secrecy and confidentiality of its trade secrets, Component Supplier List, and Customer Lists, including maintaining manufacturing operations and production drawings in secured and access-controlled facilities; adopting and publishing its employees confidentiality and non-disclosure obligations; limiting the number of manufacturing facilities used and keeping 24-hour security on those facilities; restricting the personnel who had access to the trade secrets; and using password-protected computers that were not publicly accessible.[104]

Later, Twin-Star brought a second complaint against Reliap and Yue, as well as Whalen Furniture Manufacturing, Inc. ("Whalen"), a company doing business in California.[105] Twin-Star alleged additional misappropriation of its trade secrets learned by Yue while he was employed by Twin-Star.[106] In both complaints, Twin-Star alleged that Yue breached his Stockholder Agreement.[107] In the second complaint, Twin-Star also alleged trade secret misappropriation and copyright infringement by Yue, Reliap, and Whalen, as well as tortious interference with contract by Reliap and Whalen.[108] Because Yue and Reliap failed to participate in the investigation, and also did not appear at the pretrial conference, both parties were found to be in default and in violation of Section 337.[109] The

---

[102]   *Ibid.* at ¶¶ 32, 36 and 114.

[103]   *Ibid.* at ¶¶ 108–16.

[104]   *Ibid.* at ¶¶ 85–93.

[105]   Certain Electric Fireplaces, Complaint, 337-TA-826 24 (hereinafter "In the Matter of Certain Electric Fireplaces Dec. 2011 Complaint") (Dec. 13, 2011), *available at* http://www.itcblog.com/wp-content/uploads/2011/12/twinstar complaint.pdf. In addition to trade secret misappropriation, Twin-Star also alleged copyright infringement. Twin-Star also brought the following related actions for copyright infringement: Twin-Star International, Inc. and TS Investment Holding Corp. v. Whalen Furniture Manufacturing, Inc., 3:2011cv1984 (S.D. Cal. 2011) and Twin-Star International, Inc. and TS Investment Holding Corp. v. Yue Qui Sheng, Elements International LLC and Elements International Group LLC 1:2011cv00919 (D. Del. 2011).

[106]   In the Matter of Certain Electric Fireplaces Dec. 2011 Complaint, at ¶¶ 116–150.

[107]   *Ibid.* at ¶¶ 162–182 and In the Matter of Certain Electric Fireplaces June 2011 Complaint, at ¶¶ 150–70.

[108]   In the Matter of Certain Electric Fireplaces June 2011 Complaint, at ¶¶ 116–203.

[109]   In the Matter of Certain Electric Fireplaces, Commission Opinion (hereinafter "Twin-Star Commission Opinion"), Inv. No. 337-TA-791/826 at 1 and 5

Commission determined that the appropriate form of relief should be a "limited exclusion order prohibiting the entry of unlicensed" products made using Twin-Star trade secrets.[110]

There was an open question, however, as to whether a breach of contract claim can give rise to a Section 337 claim.[111] The Commission requested that the parties brief the following question:

> whether a breach of contract claim can give rise to a violation of 19 U.S.C. § 1337(a)(1)(A), and discuss any relevant statutory language, legislative history, and legal precedent.[112]

Twin-Star claimed a Section 337 violation based on allegations that there was a breach of or tortious interference with four provisions of the SSA: (1) disclosing confidential information; (2) competing with Twin-Star in the United States during Yue's employment and during the two-year period after he terminated employment, which was a "Restricted Period" pursuant to the SSA; (3) soliciting Twin-Star customers during the Restricted Period; and (4) soliciting Twin-Star's distributors, suppliers, vendors, and agents during the "Restricted Period."[113] In reaching its decision, the Commission stated that because it "grants *prospective* relief only" it "cannot find a violation" of Section 337 based on a breach of three of the expired contract provisions.[114] With regard to the remaining claim for breach of the SSA based on disclosure of Twin-Star's confidential information, the Commission found that it was unclear what information was at issue.[115] As such, it reversed an earlier decision to the extent that it was based on a breach of, or tortious interference with, the SSA.[116] Thus, overall, the Commission found that the primary contract claims in the investigation were "mooted" and the remaining claim was

---

(May 29, 2013), *available at* http://www.kslaw.com/library/newsletters/ITC Section337Update/2013/June_3/I.nvNo791-826.pdf.

[110] In the Matter of Certain Electric Fireplaces, Limited Exclusion Order, Inv. No. 337-TA-791/826 at 2 (May 1, 2013), *available at* http://info.usitc.gov/sec/ exclusion.nsf/72b1a4074ed08da7852567fd0064ad21/960354157f5e151685257b6 30051dac3/$FILE/337-ta-826_791.pdf.

[111] In the Matter of Certain Electric Fireplaces, Notice of Commission Decision to Review-in-Part an Initial Determination at 3 (Sept. 14, 2012).

[112] Twin-Star Commission Opinion, *supra* note 109, at 6 (citing 77 Fed. Reg. 58407-09).

[113] *Ibid.* at 7.

[114] *Ibid.* at 9.

[115] *Ibid.* at 11–12.

[116] *Ibid.* at 12.

"presented on a record that is inadequate to entitle Twin-Star to relief."[117] The Commission "declined to rule on the broad question of whether any breach of contract claim could be cognizable" as an unfair act or unfair method of competition under Section 337.

Ultimately, the Commission determined that a limited exclusion order was an appropriate measure of relief for five years for the trade secret misappropriation.[118] The duration of this remedy is directly related to the minimum amount of time estimated to be "necessary to develop the trade secrets at issue."[119] In reaching its determination, the Commission also found that the issuance of the limited exclusion order "would have no adverse impact on the statutory public interest factors."[120]

3. Rubber resins and processes for manufacturing same

This case, involving trade secrets associated with the manufacture of rubber resins, is particularly interesting as it involves action taken both in China and the United States to address alleged misappropriation by a former employee, Xu Jie ("Xu").[121] Xu, who began working at a Shanghai facility owned by SI Group Inc. ("SI Group"), which is based in New York, was a member of SI Group's Manufacturing Integration Team, a select group of employees with access to the company's global processing technology resources.[122] Additionally, Xu was the only employee at SI Group's Shanghai plant with access to the entire trade secret processes for making two specific kinds of resin and tackifier, including the one at issue in the case.[123] When Xu resigned from SI Group, he denied that he was leaving to join a competitor, yet Sino Legend, a direct competitor, did employ Xu. Not long afterward, Sino Legend began to market a resin and tackifier product substantially the

---

[117] *Ibid.* at 14.

[118] *Ibid.* at 16. With regard to the copyright claims, the Commission also determined that the limited exclusion order should be in place for the remaining terms of the asserted copyrights.

[119] *Ibid.* at 16.

[120] *Ibid.* at 17.

[121] In the Matter of Certain Rubber Resins and Processes for Manufacturing Same, Complaint (hereinafter "Rubber Resins Complaint"), Inv. No. 337-TA-849, May 21, 2012, *available at* http://www.itcblog.com/wp-content/uploads/2012/05/SI-complaint.pdf. *See* Thomas Stiebel, *Defending Intellectual Property Rights in China: Leading Lawyers on Protecting Clients' Rights in China's Evolving IP Environment*, 2013 WL 4193290 at 9–10 (July 2013) (discussing the significance and history of the SI Group case).

[122] Rubber Resins Complaint, at ¶¶ 89 and 91.

[123] *Ibid.* at ¶ 92.

same as the one produced by SI Group, using the trade secrets which Xu had access to during his employment.[124] According to SI Group, Sino Legend now "has taken a large portion of SI Group's worldwide market share of tackifier sales."[125]

According to SI Group, it "took and continues to take strict and vigorous measures to maintain its trade secrets," including marking key documents "confidential"; keeping a confidential schedule for different types of documents, designating who in the company has permission to access both online and written documents based on the degree of confidentiality; logging in and out of documents; reclaiming and destroying old documents; and maintaining records of the foregoing measures.[126] SI Group also had multiple contracts with employees imposing confidentiality and non-disclosure requirements, and it also had employee policies, handbooks, and training for maintaining SI Group's trade secrets.[127] Pursuant to these policies, employee Xu signed a Labor Contract containing non-disclosure provisions, a separate Non-Disclosure Agreement, a Supplementary Agreement and another agreement affirming that he would abide by the terms in the SI Group China Employee Manual.[128] When employees left SI Group, it also conducted exit interviews reminding employees of their continuing obligations not to disclose any confidential information.[129]

Before filing a complaint with the ITC, SI Group initiated both criminal and civil legal actions in China.[130] In 2008, SI Group initiated a criminal investigation against Xu with the Shanghai Public Security Bureau ("PSB").[131] PSB officers encouraged SI Group to drop the criminal action, assuring SI Group that it had a "vast amount of evidence" that it would turn over if SI Group pursued a civil action.[132] Despite this claim, after determining that there was a "lack of evidence," the PSB terminated its investigation.[133] Thereafter, in February 2010, SI Group filed two civil actions against Sino Legend and Xu in the Shanghai No. 2 Intermediate People's Court for misappropriation of trade

---

[124]   *Ibid.* at ¶¶ 97–98.
[125]   *Ibid.* at ¶ 106.
[126]   *Ibid.* at ¶¶ 6 and 85.
[127]   *Ibid.* at ¶ 86.
[128]   *Ibid.* at ¶ 86.
[129]   *Ibid.* at ¶ 87.
[130]   *Ibid.* at ¶ 86 and Section IX.
[131]   *Ibid.* at ¶ 145.
[132]   *Ibid.* at ¶ 152.
[133]   *Ibid.* at ¶¶ 152–53.

secrets.[134] These claims, however, were to no avail,[135] which led to SI Group seeking remedies in the United States to prevent the importation of goods manufactured using its trade secrets.

Undoubtedly frustrated by the lack of action in China, SI Group filed a complaint under Section 337 alleging misappropriation of trade secrets and unlawful importation of the goods into the United States.[136] Just a little over a year later, the presiding ALJ issued a final initial determination in the investigation, finding a violation of Section 337.[137] Ultimately, the Commission also determined that there was a misappropriation of trade secrets, that there was actual injury and the threat of injury to a domestic industry, and that Sino Legend and Xu violated Section 337 in the importation or sale for importation of the rubber resins at issue.[138] In reaching its determination, the Commission cited *TianRui*, applying the law as it was developed in that case and also *Certain Sausage Casings*.[139]

A significant aspect to this case is the remedy. The ALJ recommended issuance of a ten-year general exclusion order.[140] In support of this remedy, SI Group argued that "there would be no practical way to prevent circumvention" of a limited exclusion order "because of the 'shifting sands'" of the respondents' corporate names and forms and because it is also difficult to identify the source of the goods.[141] Respondents argued that issuance of a general exclusion order would be contrary to precedent.[142] A general exclusion order is appropriate if it is "necessary to prevent circumvention of an exclusion order limited to products of named persons" or if "there is a pattern of violation" and it is "difficult to identify the source of infringing products."[143] The Commission disagreed with the ALJ finding that there was a "likelihood of circumvention based on the convoluted corporate structure" of the respondents.[144] Moreover, the Commission found that no pattern of

---

[134]   *Ibid.* at ¶ 154.
[135]   *Ibid.* at ¶ 144.
[136]   *Ibid.* at ¶ 1.
[137]   In the Matter of Certain Rubber Resins and Processes for Manufacturing Same, Initial Determination, Inv. No. 337-TA-849 (June 17, 2013).
[138]   In the Matter of Certain Rubber Resins and Processes for Manufacturing Same, Commission Opinion (hereinafter "Rubber Resins Commission Opinion") at 3 Inv. No. 337-TA-849 (Feb. 26, 2014).
[139]   Rubber Resins Commission Opinion at 9–10.
[140]   *Ibid.* at 75.
[141]   *Ibid.* at 76.
[142]   *Ibid.* at 79.
[143]   *Ibid.* at 81 (citing 19 U.S.C. § 1337(d)(2)(A) and (B)).
[144]   *Ibid.*

violations was established.[145] Accordingly, the Commission determined that the appropriate remedy would be the issuance of a limited exclusion order, which would also extend to those selling on behalf of the named respondents.[146] To determine the appropriate duration of the limited exclusion order, similar to *Sausage Casings*,[147] the Commission considered the amount of time it would have taken to independently develop the trade secrets.[148] There was wide disagreement on this point with testimony ranging from six months to at least ten years and perhaps even twenty years to develop the confidential material.[149] Stating that it did not find the six-month period credible, the Commission concluded, "the most reasonable duration of the exclusion order is a 10 year remedy."[150] Although the Commission stopped short of issuing a general exclusion order, its order represents a significant victory for SI Group.

4. Certain paper shredders, certain processes for manufacturing or relating to same

As with most of the other cases brought under Section 337 in connection with misappropriation of trade secrets, *Certain Paper Shredders, Certain Processes for Manufacturing or Relating to Same* involved allegations that the respondents "hired away employees" of the complainant, Fellowes, Inc. ("Fellowes") from an affiliated Chinese joint venture, Fellowes Manufacturing (Changzhou) Co. Ltd. ("Jinsen").[151] Following problematic attempts by an individual to gain access to Fellowes' trade secrets through Jinsen, respondents hired Jinsen's former operations manager, Randall Graves, as well as other Jinsen employees and engineers with knowledge of Fellowes' trade secrets.[152] Fellowes undertook a number of steps to protect its trade secrets: restricting access to Jinsen, a walled and guarded facility; requiring employees to sign confidentiality agreements; providing all employees with a written Code of Conduct, and advising them that they had a duty not to disclose Fellowes' trade

---

[145] *Ibid.* at 82.
[146] *Ibid.*
[147] *Viscofan*, 787 F.2d at 550.
[148] Rubber Resins Commission Opinion at 82.
[149] *Ibid.* at 82–83.
[150] *Ibid.* at 83.
[151] In the Matter of Certain Paper Shredders, Certain Processes for Manufacturing or Relating to Same, Complaint (hereinafter "Paper Shredders Complaint") at ¶¶ 3 and 9, Inv. No. 337-TA-863, (Dec. 2012), *available at* http://www.itcblog.com/wp-content/uploads/2012/12/felllowescomplaint.pdf.
[152] Paper Shredders Complaint at ¶¶ 9 and 10.

secrets; labeling and restricting access to confidential information stored on Fellowes' computers, including using a strict password policy; prohibiting "employees from downloading unauthorized and/or personal software on their company-issued laptops to avoid security breaches"; and requiring suppliers and vendors to enter into confidentiality agreements.[153]

Despite their duty not to disclose Fellowes' trade secrets, various employees and engineers allegedly divulged the information to the respondents, eight Chinese producers and one U.S. producer of paper shredders. In addition to the Section 337 complaint, Fellowes also sought relief in U.S. and Chinese courts. Fellowes filed an action in the Luwan District People's Court of Shanghai alleging that certain respondents were using its molds and tools.[154] Although the Luwan Court issued preservation orders prohibiting the use of the molds and tools, this was "willfully ignored."[155] After Jinsen filed an action in China seeking payment for goods, Fellowes filed an action in the United States District Court for the Northern District of Illinois, alleging that Jinsen breached Fellowes' purchase orders by refusing to ship the finished products.[156] After the ITC voted to institute a Section 337 investigation, the parties settled.[157]

5. Certain robotic toys and components thereof

Another case, *Certain Robotic Toys and Components Thereof*, also alleged misappropriation of trade secrets by a former engineer, yet the respondent in the case was not the competitor manufacturer.[158] This was an unusual case in which an action was filed against a retailer, not the party involved in the alleged misappropriation of trade secrets. The complaint, filed by three related entities collectively referred to as Innovation First, alleged that CVS Pharmacy, Inc. ("CVS"), a retailer, was importing and selling robotic toys that were manufactured in China

---

[153] *Ibid.* at ¶¶ 30 and 38.

[154] *Ibid.* at ¶ 158.

[155] *Ibid.* at ¶ 158.

[156] *Ibid.* at ¶¶ 155–58.

[157] In the Matter of Certain Paper Shredders, Certain Processes for Manufacturing or Relating to Same, Inv. No. 337-TA-863, http://info.usitc.gov/ouii/public/337inv.nsf/56ff5fbca63b069e852565460078c0ae/e5f7b90b9867f38885257afd00646881?OpenDocument&Highlight=0,863.

[158] In the Matter of Certain Robotic Toys and Components Thereof, Complaint (hereinafter "Robotic Toys Complaint"), Inv. No. 337-869, (Jan. 4, 2013), *available at* http://www.itcblog.com/wp-content/uploads/2013/01/IFIcomplaint.pdf.

by Zuru, Inc. using misappropriated trade secrets.[159] An Innovation First engineer, Xiaoping Lu ("Lu") developed HEXBUG® technologies for Innovation First in China, then provided Zuru with the trade secrets in violation of his separation agreement.[160] CVS then imported and sold the robotic toys, including Robe Fish, in the United States. This is an odd case, because Zuru was not a named respondent. Innovation First sought a limited exclusion order, a cease and desist order, an order destroying all robotic toys manufactured using the trade secrets, and an order requiring CVS to turn over all documents and things related to the trade secrets.[161] The ITC subsequently instituted an investigation, naming both CVS and Zuru as respondents.[162] A few months later, Chief ALJ Charles E. Bullock issued an order granting Innovation First's motion seeking issuance of a request for international judicial assistance pursuant to the Hague Convention.[163] Thereafter, the parties settled.[164]

6.   Certain crawler cranes and components thereof

In the most recent case to be filed for Section 337 relief in the trade secret context, *Certain Crawler Cranes and Components Thereof*, complainant Manitowoc Cranes, LLC ("Manitowoc Crane") alleged that respondents Sany Heavy Industry Co., Inc. and Sany America, Inc. (collectively "Sany") wrongfully designed and manufactured certain crawler cranes and components using Manitowoc Crane's trade secrets.[165] Manitowoc Crane alleged that one of its high-ranking

---

[159]   Robotic Toys Complaint at ¶ 6.

[160]   *Ibid.* at ¶ 7.

[161]   *Ibid.* at Relief Requested.

[162]   In the Matter of Certain Robotic Toys and Components Thereof, Notice of Institution of Investigation, Inv. No. 337-869, (Feb. 5, 2013), *available at* http://www.itcblog.com/wp-content/uploads/2013/02/noiin869.pdf.

[163]   In the Matter of Certain Robotic Toys and Components Thereof, Order No. 6: Granting Motion to Approve Request for International Judicial Assistance in Procuring Evidence from Xiaoping Lu, Inv. No. 337-869, (Apr. 10, 2013), *available at* http://www.itcblog.com/wp-content/uploads/2013/07/Robotic-Toys-Order-6-19Jul13.pdf.

[164]   In the Matter of Certain Robotic Toys and Components Thereof, Inv. No. 337–869, *available at* http://info.usitc.gov/ouii/public/337inv.nsf/56ff5fbca63b0 69e852565460078c0ae/bb7739b00196e9a585257b0b0075c881?OpenDocument &Highlight=0,869.

[165]   Certain Crawler Cranes and Components Thereof, Complaint ("Crane Complaint"), Inv. No. 337-TA-887, (June 12, 2013), *available at* http://www. itcblog.com/wp-content/uploads/2013/06/manitowoccomplaint.pdf (the complaint also alleges patent infringement and Manitowoc also filed an action in U.S.

engineers, John Lanning, was recruited by Sany.[166] Lanning was involved in the development of the trade secrets for Manitowoc Crane and allegedly provided Sany with the information, giving them "significant competitive advantages."[167] The relief requested includes a permanent exclusion order, as well as permanent cease and desist orders.[168]

The ITC voted to institute an investigation.[169] Sany filed a motion for a summary determination, arguing that Manitowoc's list of alleged trade secrets failed as a matter of law for three reasons: first, many of the alleged items did not qualify for legal protection as trade secrets; second, many of the alleged "trade secrets" were not "secret"; and third, even if the information was subject to trade secret protection, Manitowoc failed to "adduce any admissible evidence that would allow a fact finder to conclude that Sany misappropriated the alleged trade secrets.[170] The ITC disagreed, finding that genuine issues of material fact existed and, therefore, denied Sany's motion.[171] In a separate order, the ALJ granted Manitowoc's motion for summary determination, finding that it had satisfied the economic prong of the domestic injury requirement for trade misappropriation.[172] The ITC subsequently determined that a violation of Section 337 had occurred, which included the misappropriation of trade secrets.[173]

District Court for the Eastern Dist. of Wisconsin alleging patent infringement). *Ibid.* at ¶ 13.1.

[166] Crane Complaint at ¶ 1.8.

[167] *Ibid.* at ¶¶ 1.16–1.17.

[168] *Ibid.* at Relief Requested.

[169] USITC Institutes Section 337 Investigation of Certain Crawler Cranes and Components Thereof, Inv. No. 337-TA-887, (July 11, 2013), *available at* http://www.usitc.gov/press_room/news_release/2013/er0711ll3.htm.

[170] In the Matter of Certain Crawler Cranes and Components Thereof, Order No. 21 (hereinafter "Crawler Cranes Order No. 21"), at 2 and 5-6, (Feb. 20, 2014), *available at* http://www.itcblog.com/wp-content/uploads/2014/03/Crawler-Cranes-Order-21-25Feb14.pdf.

[171] Crawler Cranes Order No. 21 at 6–12.

[172] In the Matter of Certain Crawler Cranes and Components Thereof, Notice (July 11, 2014), *available at* http://www.itcblog.com/alj-shaw-issues-notice-of-initial-determination-finding-violation-of-section-337-in-certain-crawler-cranes-337-ta-887.

[173] In the Matter of Certain Crawler Cranes and Components Thereof, Notice of Commission Determination to Review in Part Determination Granting Summary Determination, (Mar. 19, 2014), *available at* http://www.itcblog.com/wp-content/uploads/2014/03/Crawler-Cranes-Notice-19Mar14.pdf.

III. IMPLICATIONS OF *TIANRUI* FOR SECTION 337 TRADE SECRET ENFORCEMENT

At this point, because Section 337 is a viable tool against foreign trade secret misappropriation, it is worthwhile considering trends, as well as critiques and questions, raised in connection with this rapidly evolving area of law.

A.   Trends in Section 337

Taken together, *TianRui* and its progeny illustrate the ways in which Section 337 can be used to address misappropriation in the global context. Although it is too early to predict the full impact of this remedy, it seems that the issuance of a general exclusion order will be reserved for the most extreme cases. The more narrowly tailored limited exclusion orders seem to be favored in the cases resolved to date. Moreover, it seems that the initiation of an investigation sometimes provides the incentive for the parties to settle.

With trade-related remedies gaining popularity, and a resulting increase in complainants seeking investigations of alleged unfair trade practices, the Commission announced in 2014 that it was launching a pilot program aimed at early disposition of Section 337 cases. This is a significant step to dispose of cases early in the process to reduce unnecessary litigation and reduce associated costs. As such, companies seeking Section 337 relief will need to be particularly diligent in establishing key issues such as standing and the economic prong of the domestic industry requirement.

B.   Critiques and Questions About the Extraterritorial Scope of Section 337

The extraterritorial application of Section 337 has sparked a far-reaching debate about the appropriateness of using international trade law to address business espionage. The following discussion describes the extraterritorial issues in *TianRui* and subsequent ITC cases, addresses criticisms of Section 337 extraterritoriality, and briefly explores potential means of addressing this issue.

Extraterritoriality involves the extension of domestic law to activity outside of the country's territory.[174] The use of Section 337 to address foreign trade secret misappropriation is an example of "direct" extraterritoriality, i.e., domestic regulation that applies directly to international actors and activities either through their effects on the regulating country or their contact with the regulating country.[175]

Critics of Section 337 extraterritoriality claim that *TianRui* failed to correctly apply the presumption against extraterritoriality, a judicial canon of interpretation that presumes, absent evidence of contrary Congressional intent, that a federal law is applicable only within the territory of the United States.[176] The Supreme Court's decision in *Morrison v. Nat'l Austl. Bank Ltd.* limited the scope of anti-fraud actions under U.S. federal securities law between foreign parties concerning foreign activities.[177] Citing *Morrison,* and echoing the dissent in *TianRui,* critics argue that there is insufficient evidence that Congress intended to regulate foreign business conduct through Section 337.[178] In addition, critics claim that the acts of misappropriation at issue in Section 337 cases lack sufficient contact with the United States due to the fact they took place in China.[179]

Notwithstanding these criticisms, Section 337 extraterritoriality can be justified on several interrelated legal, public policy, and normative

---

[174]   Stephen Kim Park, *Guarding the Guardians: The Case for Regulating State-Owned Financial Entities in Global Finance*, 16 U. PA. J. BUS. L. 739, 748 (2014).

[175]   *See* Chris Brummer, *Territoriality as a Regulatory Technique: Notes from the Financial Crisis*, 79 U. CIN. L. REV. 499, 506 (2010); *see also* Park, *supra* note 174, at 752–54 (describing effects and conduct-based extraterritorial regulation).

[176]   *See* EEOC v. Arabian Am. Oil. Co., 499 U.S. 244, 248 (1991).

[177]   Morrison v. Nat'l Austl. Bank Ltd., 130 S. Ct. 2869 (2010).

[178]   *See TianRui*, 661 F.3d at 1341 (Moore, J., dissenting) (stating that "[t]he legislative history, like the plain language of the statute, lacks a *clear* indication that Congress intended" Section 337 to apply extraterritorially); *see also* Viki Economides, *TianRui Group Co. v. International Trade Commission: The Dubious Status of Extraterritoriality and the Domestic Industry Requirement of Section 337*, 61 A.U. L. REV. 1235, 1244–45 (2012) (arguing that the text of Section 337 is too ambiguous to overcome the presumption against extraterritoriality); Kerrilyn Russ, *On the Wrong Side of the Tracks: An Analysis of the U.S. Court of Appeals for the Federal Circuit's Non-Application of the Presumption Against Extraterritoriality*, 52 WASHBURN L.J. 685, 707–08 (suggesting that Congress must amend Section 337 to add explicit language establishing that it applies to foreign conduct).

[179]   *See* Economides, *supra* note 178, at 1245; Russ, *supra* note 178, at 705.

grounds. First and foremost, while foreign trade secret theft occurs outside the borders of the United States, the act of importation is indisputably within the territorial jurisdiction of U.S. regulators. Section 337 jurisdiction is triggered upon importation, not upon the act of misappropriation itself.[180] The Federal Circuit in *TianRui* expressly embraced this principle by identifying a jurisdictional nexus with the United States upon importation of the infringing products.[181] Second, Section 337 should be viewed in the context of U.S. trade laws and its public policy rationales. The "border enforcement" purpose of Section 337 is similar to other "unfair" trade remedies for dumping or subsidies by foreign producers.[182] In its current form, Section 337 does not racially discriminate against foreigners.[183] Section 337 does not distinguish between domestic and foreign companies whose trade secrets have been misappropriated: a foreign-based trade secret owner may also seek a remedy from the ITC so long as it satisfies Section 337's domestic industry requirement.[184] Finally, Section 337 can be justified as a remedy of last resort. Section 337 may be the only feasible means for companies to combat foreign trade secret theft.[185] Although the WTO Agreement for Trade Related Aspects of Intellectual Property ("TRIPS") recognizes the

---

[180] *See* 19 U.S.C. § 1337(a)(1)(A) (referring to "[u]nfair methods of competition and unfair acts in the importation of articles … into the United States, or in the sale of such articles by the owner, importer, or consignee").

[181] *See TianRui*, 661 F.3d at 1332–33.

[182] *See* Joel W. Rogers and Joseph P. Whitlock, *Is Section 337 Consistent with the GATT and the TRIPs Agreement?* 17 AM. U. INT'L L. REV. 459, 470 (2002) (describing Section 337 as a "powerful border enforcement mechanism"); *see also* Elizabeth A. Rowe and Daniel M. Mahfood, *Trade Secrets, Trade, and Extraterritoriality*, 66 ALA. L. REV. 63, 95–96 (2014) (justifying the *TianRui* interpretation of Section 337 from a "border control" perspective). *But see* MICHAEL TREBILCOCK, ROBERT HOWSE AND ANTONIA ELIASON, THE REGULATION OF INTERNATIONAL TRADE 525 (4th ed. 2013) (contrasting Section 337 with other trade remedy laws).

[183] *See* Colleen V. Chien, *Patently Protectionist? An Empirical Analysis of Patent Cases at the International Trade Commission*, 50 WM. & MARY L. REV. 63, 76–78 (2008). *But see* Rogers and Whitlock, *supra* note 182, at 498–504 (arguing that Section 337 may be technically inconsistent with the national treatment provisions of the GATT).

[184] Ron Vogel, *The Great Brain Robbery: TianRui and the Treatment of Extraterritorial Unfair Trade Acts*, 22 FED. CIR. BAR J. 641, 672 (2013).

[185] *See* Jacob Mackler, *Intellectual Property Favoritism: Who Wins in the Globalized Economy, the Patent or the Trade Secret?*, 12 WAKE FOREST J. BUS. & INTELL. PROP. L. 263, 290-91 (2012); *see also* David Orozco, *Amending* the *Economic Espionage Act to Require the Disclosure of National Security-Related*

protection of trade secrets, global coordination on enforcement is inconsistent at best.[186]

A more trenchant criticism of Section 337 extraterritoriality suggests that it may open the floodgates to cases that seek to address a wide range of "unfair methods of competition."[187] To address concerns about regulatory overreach, applications of Section 337 could be subject to a conflict of laws test. The authority of the United States in regulating its internal markets and the interests of trade secret owners, on the one hand, would be balanced against the legal treatment of the offshore activity under local law. That is, the ITC could take into account whether the misappropriation was illegal in the jurisdiction in which it occurred. The amount of deference that should be given to foreign legal determinations could be developed through a canon of judicial interpretation or preferably by amendments to Section 337.[188]

IV. USING SECTION 337 FOR STRATEGIC ADVANTAGE

Companies can adopt a variety of measures to prevent trade secret misappropriation by foreign employees and business partners.[189] Towards that broad end, we suggest three specific ways that companies can use Section 337 strategically to protect their trade secrets.

Technology Thefts, 62 CATH. U. L. REV. 877, 884-87 (2014) (comparing Section 337 to state and other federal laws).

[186] Rowe and Mahfood, *supra* note 182, at 81–82.

[187] *See* Vogel, *supra* note 184, at 673–74 (observing that Section 337 creates a slippery slope that may permit actions against imported products made with foreign child labor or through locally polluting production).

[188] This issue is disputed among legal scholars. *See, e.g.*, Timothy R. Holbrook, *Extraterritoriality in U.S. Patent Law*, 49 WM. & MARY L. REV. 2119 (2008) (proposing that U.S. courts only be permitted to enforce a patent if there is infringement under foreign patent law); Rowe and Mahfood, *supra* note 182, at 93 (proposing that the presence or absence of a conflict of laws could serve as a discretionary consideration); Vogel, *supra* note 184, at 673 (suggesting that the ITC should consider, but not defer to, foreign findings of fact and conclusions of law).

[189] *See* Pagnattaro, *supra* note 81, at 334–36 (recommending steps that companies can take to prevent disclosure of trade secrets in China); *see also* Norman D. Bishara and David Orozco, *Using the Resource-Based Theory to Determine Covenant Not to Compete Legitimacy*, 87 IND. L.J. 979, 995–96 (2012) (describing the use of private legal mechanisms such as non-disclosure and confidentiality agreements).

Expressly stipulate Section 337 as a legal remedy and the ITC as the designated forum for trade secret disputes. Companies that enter into joint ventures, licensing agreements, and other foreign business relationships where trade secrets may be vulnerable should seek to ensure that Section 337 is available as a remedy in the event of employee misappropriation. In most instances, it is in the interest of a trade secret owner to seek redress from the ITC instead of a U.S. federal district court[190] or a local court.[191] While submission to jurisdiction is not necessary in order to initiate a Section 337 action, referencing Section 337 in the legal documentation may incentivize foreign business partners to take appropriate preventative and deterrence measures. A contractual term stipulating Section 337 as a mutually acceptable remedy, accompanied by a clause that indicates the basis for trade secret infringement under local law, might also be favorably viewed by the ITC and the Federal Circuit (if the ITC's determination is appealed).

In addition, companies can negotiate the inclusion of an express waiver of conflict of laws or *forum non conveniens* claims. While ITC jurisdiction is conferred over the imported goods rather than the producer, this clause may address any counterclaims brought against the company by foreign business partners in local courts and under local law.

Require the implementation of internal controls and reporting mechanisms. Companies should require their foreign business partners to implement internal controls and reporting mechanisms in order to facilitate discovery in any potential Section 337 action. While the ITC can compel discovery through nationwide service of subpoenas for deposition, testimony, and documents,[192] this investigative process may be costly and uncertain for petitioners. Internal controls and reporting mechanisms may even preclude the need for the trade secret owner to compel production from the foreign business partner if it decides to initiate a Section 337 action, i.e., the company might already have this information.[193] These operational measures complement various private mechanisms – such as,

---

[190]   *See* Section I, *supra* (describing the strategic legal advantages of Section 337 actions before the ITC); *see also* Orozco, *supra* note 185, at 885 (noting the consensus that the ITC is a "more attractive, expedient, and powerful regulator of foreign trade secret theft").

[191]   *See* Bai and Da, *supra* note 79, at 362–63 (describing procedural hurdles for civil actions enforcing trade secrets in China).

[192]   *See* Flechsig *supra* note 78, at 473–74.

[193]   Internal controls and reporting mechanisms may also help a trade secret owner to recognize and respond to potential or ongoing misappropriation without bringing a Section 337 claim.

human resource and compliance systems, physical and electronic access restrictions[194] – to prevent and deter trade secret theft.

Require arbitration that comports with Section 337 principles. In many instances, it may be desirable to agree to commercial arbitration in contracts with a foreign business partner.[195] Notwithstanding the fact that a Section 337 action may be brought whether or not the parties have agreed to international arbitration, there may be circumstances in which the trade secret owner might prefer arbitration over Section 337. The ITC does not award monetary damages for trade secret misappropriation, and a foreign jurisdiction may refuse to enforce a judgment for monetary damages issued by a federal district court in a Section 337 case.[196] Further, ITC exclusion orders do not prevent trade secret theft from continuing to occur.[197] By agreeing to apply Section 337 rules and standards as substantive law, arbitration permits the trade secret owner to obtain and enforce damage awards while maintaining confidentiality over the proceedings.

V. CONCLUSION

Despite criticism, the jurisprudence developing in connection with Section 337 cases supports an extraterritorial reach. As such, it can be a very effective tool to prevent the importation of goods manufactured using misappropriated trade secrets.

BIBLIOGRAPHY

Statutes and Codes

19 C.F.R. § 201.7 (1998).
19 U.S.C. § 1332(a)–(c) (2012).
19 U.S.C. § 1337 (2012).
19 U.S.C. § 1337 (a)(1)(A) (2012).
19 U.S.C. § 1337(b)–(c) (2012).

---

[194] *See* Pagnattaro, *supra* note 81, at 335.

[195] *Ibid.* at 336 (referring to arbitration using the Chinese International Economic and Trade Commission ("CIETAC")).

[196] *See* Riley and Stroud, *supra* note 36, at 83–84.

[197] *See* Steven E. Feldman and Sherry L. Rollo, *Extraterritorial Protection of Trade Secrets in China: Do Section 337 Actions at the ITC Really Prevent Trade Secret Theft Abroad?*, 11 J. MARSHALL REV. INTELL. PROP. L. 523, 542 (2012).

19 U.S.C. § 1337(g) (2012).

Cases

EEOC v. Arabian Am. Oil. Co. 499 U.S. 244 (1991).
Morrison v. Nat'l Austl. Bank Ltd., 130 S. Ct. 2869 (2010).
TianRui Group Co. Ltd. v. Int'l Trade Comm., 661 F.3d 1322 (2011).
Viscofan, S.A. v. U.S. Int'l Trade Comm'n, 787 F.2d 544 (Fed. Cir. 1986).

Administrative Proceeding Materials

In the matter of Certain Cast Steel Railway Wheels, Certain Processes for Manufacturing the Same and Certain Products Containing Same, ITC Initial Determination, 2009 WL 4261206.

In the Matter of Certain Crawler Cranes and Components Thereof, Notice (July 11, 2014), *available at* http://www.itcblog.com/alj-shaw-issues-notice-of-initial-determination-finding-violation-of-section-337-in-certain-crawler-cranes-337-ta-887.

In the Matter of Certain Crawler Cranes and Components Thereof, Notice of Commission Determination to Review in Part Determination Granting Summary Determination, (Mar. 19, 2014), *available at* http://www.itcblog.com/wp-content/uploads/2014/03/Crawler-Cranes-Notice-19Mar14.pdf.

In the Matter of Certain Crawler Cranes and Components Thereof, Order No. 21 (Feb. 20, 2014), *available at* http://www.itcblog.com/wp-content/uploads/2014/03/Crawler-Cranes-Order-21-25Feb14.pdf.

In the Matter of Certain DC-DC Controllers and Products Containing Same, Inv. No. 337-TA-698, Enforcement Initial Determination (June 8, 2012).

In the Matter of Certain Electric Fireplaces, Inv. Nos. 337-TA-826/791.

In the Matter of Certain Electric Fireplaces, Commission Opinion, Inv. No. 337-TA-791/826 (May 29, 2013), *available at* http://www.kslaw.com/library/newsletters/ITCSection337Update/2013/June_3/I.nvNo791-826.pdf.

In the Matter of Certain Electric Fireplaces, Complaint, 337-TA-791 (June 17, 2011), *available at* http://www.itcblog.com/wp-content/uploads/2011/06/twinstar complaint17jun11.pdf.

In the Matter of Certain Paper Shredders, Certain Processes for Manufacturing or Relating to Same, Complaint, Inv. No. 337-TA-863, (Dec. 2012), *available at* http://www.itcblog.com/wp-content/uploads/2012/12/felllowescomplaint.pdf.

In the Matter of Certain Paper Shredders, Certain Processes for Manufacturing or Relating to Same, Inv. No. 337-TA-863, http://info.usitc.gov/ouii/public/337inv.nsf/56ff5fbca63b069e852565460078c0ae/e5f7b90b9867f38885257afd00646881?OpenDocument&Highlight=0,863.

In the Matter of Certain Robotic Toys and Components Thereof, Complaint, Inv. No. 337-869, (Jan. 4, 2013), *available at* http://www.itcblog.com/wp-content/uploads/2013/01/IFIcomplaint.pdf.

In the Matter of Certain Robotic Toys and Components Thereof, Inv. No. 337-869, *available at* http://info.usitc.gov/ouii/public/337inv.nsf/56ff5fbca63b069e852565460078c0ae/bb7739b00196e9a585257b0b0075c881?OpenDocument&Highlight=0,869.

In the Matter of Certain Robotic Toys and Components Thereof, Notice of Institution of Investigation, Inv. No. 337-869, (Feb. 5, 2013), *available at* http://www.itcblog.com/wp-content/uploads/2013/02/noiin869.pdf.

In the Matter of Certain Robotic Toys and Components Thereof, Order No. 6: Granting Motion to Approve Request for International Judicial Assistance in Procuring Evidence from Xiaoping Lu, Inv. No. 337-869, (Apr. 10, 2013), *available at* http://www.itcblog.com/wp-content/uploads/2013/07/Robotic-Toys-Order-6-19Jul13.pdf.

In the Matter of Certain Rubber Resins and Processes for Manufacturing Same, Commission Opinion, Inv. No. 337-TA-849 (Feb. 26, 2014).

In the Matter of Certain Rubber Resins and Processes for Manufacturing Same, Complaint, Inv. No. 337-TA-849, May 21, 2012, *available at* http://www.itcblog.com/wp-content/uploads/2012/05/SI-complaint.pdf.

In the Matter of Certain Rubber Resins and Processes for Manufacturing Same, Initial Determination, Inv. No. 337-TA-849 (June 17, 2013).

Secondary Sources

Almeling, David S., *Seven Reasons Why Trade Secrets are Increasingly Important*, 27 BERKELEY TECH. L.J. 1091 (2012).

Almeling, David S., et al., *A Statistical Analysis of Trade Secret Litigation in Federal Courts*, 45 GONZ. L. REV. 291 (2010).

AmCham China, *Business Climate Survey Report* (2013), http://www.amchamchina.org/businessclimate2013.

Bai, J. Benjamin and Guoping Da, *Strategies for Trade Secrets Protection in China*, 9 N.W. J. TECH. & INTELL. PROP. 351 (2011).

Bishara, Norman D. and David Orozco, *Using the Resource-Based Theory to Determine Covenant Not to Compete Legitimacy*, 87 IND. L.J. 979 (2012).

Broughan III, Thomas A., *Modernizing §337's Domestic Industry Requirement for the Global Economy*, 19 FED. CIR. B.J. 41 (2009).

Brummer, Chris, *Territoriality as a Regulatory Technique: Notes from the Financial Crisis*, 79 U. CIN. L. REV. 499 (2010).

Chien, Colleen V., *Patently Protectionist? An Empirical Analysis of Patent Cases at the International Trade Commission*, 50 WM. & MARY L. REV. 63 (2008).

Economides, Viki, *TianRui Group Co. v. International Trade Commission: The Dubious Status of Extraterritoriality and the Domestic Industry Requirement of Section 337*, 61 A.U. L. REV. 1235 (2012).

Feldman, Steven E. and Sherry L. Rollo, *Extraterritorial Protection of Trade Secrets in China: Do Section 337 Actions at the ITC Really Prevent Trade Secret Theft Abroad?*, 11 J. MARSHALL REV. INTELL. PROP. L. 523 (2012).

Flechsig, Natalie, *Trade Secret Enforcement After TianRui: Fighting Misappropriation Through the ITC*, 28 BERKELEY TECH. L.J. 449 (2013).

Gorman, Siobahn and Jared A. Favole, *U.S. Ups Ante for Spying on Firms: China, Others are Threatened with New Penalties*, WALL ST. J., Feb. 21, 2013, at A1.

Gullo, Karen, *DuPont Trade Secret Theft for China Leads to Conviction*, BLOOMBERGBUSINESSWEEK (Mar. 5, 2014), http://www.businessweek.com/news/2014-03-05/california-man-convicted-of-stealing-dupont-trade-secrets-1.

Hnath, Gary M., *Section 337 Investigations at the US International Trade Commission Provide a Powerful Remedy Against Misappropriation of Trade Secrets*, 22 INTELL. PROP. & TECH. L. J. 1 (2010).

Holbrook, Timothy R., *Extraterritoriality in U.S. Patent Law*, 49 WM. & MARY L. REV. 2119 (2008).

Lauffs, Andreas and Jonathan Isaacs, *First Ever Preliminary Injunction and Asset Preservation Orders in Trade Secrets Case Issued by Court*, ABA INT'L LABOR & EMPLOYMENT L. COMMITTEE NEWSLETTER (Sept. 2013), http://www.american bar.org/content/newsletter/groups/labor_law/int_newsletter/2013/sept2013/china9-13.html.

LAZAR, WENDY S. AND GARY R. SINISCALO, RESTRICTIVE COVENANTS AND TRADE SECRETS IN EMPLOYMENT LAW: AN INTERNATIONAL SURVEY, Vol. 1 (2010).

Mackler, Jacob, *Intellectual Property Favoritism: Who Wins in the Globalized Economy, the Patent or the Trade Secret?*, 12 WAKE FOREST J. BUS. & INTELL. PROP. L. 263 (2012).

McJohn, Stephen, *Top Tens in 2011: Copyright and Trade Secrets*, 10 NW. J. TECH. & INTELL. PROP. 331 (2012).

Orozco, David, *Amending the Economic Espionage Act to Require the Disclosure of National Security-Related Technology Thefts*, 62 CATH. U. L. REV. 877 (2014).

Pagnattaro, Marisa Anne, *Preventing Know-How From Walking Out the Door in China: Protection of Trade Secrets*, 55 BUS. HORIZONS 329 (2012).

Palmer, Doug, *U.S. Seeks to Tackle Trade-Secret Theft by China, Others*, REUTERS (Feb. 20, 2013), http://www.reuters.com/article/2013/02/21/us-usa-trade-secrets-idUSBRE91J0T220130221.

Park, Stephen Kim, *Guarding the Guardians: The Case for Regulating State-Owned Financial Entities in Global Finance*, 16 U. PA. J. BUS. L. 739 (2014).

Popper, Andrew F., *Beneficiaries of Misconduct: A Direct Approach to IT Theft*, 17 MARQ. INTELL. PROP. L.J. 27 (2013).

PriceWaterhouseCoopers, *Redefining Intellectual Property Value: The Case of China* (2005), http://www.pwc.com/en_us/us/technology-innovation-center/assets/ipr-web_x.pdf.

PriceWaterhouseCoopers, *Talent Mobility 2020: The Next Generation of International Assignments* (2010), http://www.pwc.com/gx/en/managing-tomorrows-people/future-of-work/pdf/talent-mobility-2020.pdf.

Quick, Daniel D. and H. Jonathan Redway, *Barring the Door: The International Trade Commission As a Means to Prevent Importation of Goods Utilizing Misappropriated Trade Secrets*, 32 MICH. BUS. L.J. 39 (2012).

Riley, P. Andrew and Jonathan R.K. Stroud, *A Survey of Trade Secret Investigations at the International Trade Commission: A Model for Future Litigants*, 15 COLUM. SCI. & TECH. L. REV. 41 (2013).

Rogers, Joel W. and Joseph P. Whitlock, *Is Section 337 Consistent with the GATT and the TRIPs Agreement?*, 17 AM. U. INT'L L. REV. 459 (2002).

Rowe, Elizabeth A. and Daniel M. Mahfood, *Trade Secrets, Trade, and Extraterritoriality*, 66 ALA. L. REV. 63 (2014).

Russ, Kerrilyn, *On the Wrong Side of the Tracks: An Analysis of the U.S. Court of Appeals for the Federal Circuit's Non-Application of the Presumption Against Extraterritoriality*, 52 WASHBURN L.J. 685 (2013).

Stiebel, Thomas, *Defending Intellectual Property Rights in China: Leading Lawyers on Protecting Clients' Rights in China's Evolving IP Environment*, 2013 WL 4193290 (July 2013).

TREBILCOCK, MICHAEL, ROBERT HOWSE AND ANTONIA ELIASON, THE REGULATION OF INTERNATIONAL TRADE (4th ed. 2013).

U.S. International Trade Commission, *FY 2011 Highlights: USITC Sees Record Number of Intellectual Property Infringement Cases Filed*, http://www.usitc.gov/press_room/documents/featured_news/337_timeframes_article.htm.

U.S. International Trade Commission, *FY 2012 At a Glance* (2013), http://www.usitc.gov/press_room/documents/YIR_OP2_final.pdf.

U.S. International Trade Commission, *Pilot Program Will Test Early Disposition of Certain Section 337 Investigations*, http://www.usitc.gov/press_room/documents/featured_news/337pilot_article.htm.

USITC Institutes Section 337 Investigation of Certain Crawler Cranes and Components Thereof, Inv. No. 337-TA-887, (July 11, 2013), *available at* http://www.usitc.gov/press_room/news_release/2013/er0711ll3.htm.

Vogel, Ron, *The Great Brain Robbery: TianRui and the Treatment of Extraterritorial Unfair Trade Acts*, 22 FED. CIR. BAR J. 641 (2013).

Yeh, Thomas, *The International Trade Commission and the Nonpracticing Entity: Reviving the Industry Requirement for Domestic Industries Based on Licensing*, 80 GEO. WASH. L. REV. 1574 (2012).

7. Reducing the risk of cross-border trade secret misappropriation

Elizabeth A. Brown

Trade secrets are among the most valuable and vulnerable corporate assets. As a form of intellectual property, they can be used to protect confidential business information in a wide range of industries. Manufacturers often rely on them for protection of valuable information, as do service industries such as advertising, marketing, business consulting and financial services.[1] Falling outside the more clearly delineated areas of patent, copyright and trademark law, they may be the most challenging intangible property to protect from theft by foreign competitors.

Companies doing business across borders face at least two critical issues with regard to trade secrets. First, the growth of the global workforce and the increasing portability of technology make trade secret loss more likely and costly. Second, the fragmentary nature of international trade secret protection and the differences in protection regimes from country to country make it especially difficult to litigate cross-border claims once a loss occurs.

Trade secret misappropriation has an enormous financial impact. The director of the National Security Agency (NSA), General Keith Alexander, has characterized online espionage as the "greatest transfer of wealth in history."[2] In May 2013, the Commission on the Theft of American Intellectual Property, an independent and bipartisan initiative, estimated that the total revenue lost by U.S. companies alone as a result of intellectual property theft is approximately $300 billion, comparable to

---

[1] *See Study on Trade Secrets and Confidential Business Information in the Internal Market*, EUROPEAN COMMISSION 2 (Apr. 2013), http://ec.europa.eu/internal_market/iprenforcement/docs/trade-secrets/130711_final-study_en.pdf (hereinafter 2013 EC Trade Secrets Study).

[2] Emil Protalinski, *NSA: Cybercrime is 'The Greatest Transfer of Wealth in History'*, ZDNET (July 10, 2012, 12:13 PM), http://www.zdnet.com/nsa-cybercrime-is-the-greatest-transfer-of-wealth-in-history-7000000598/.

the total value of U.S. exports to all of Asia.[3] There is a more subtle cost as well. Trade secret misappropriation can also translate to a reduced incentive to innovate and the ever-increasing diversion of revenue to intellectual property protection rather than intellectual property generation.[4]

While trade secret misappropriation is a global problem, no consensus as to the best global solution has yet emerged. While the cost and incidence of cross-border trade secret misappropriation is rising, current international protection measures often fall short of companies' needs. Disparities among national and regional approaches to trade secret protection and the lack of a central global protection mechanism make it difficult for any company to ensure the confidentiality of its trade secrets. The diversity of legal definitions and protection mechanisms available to businesses overseas, combined with the practical difficulties of securing protection even when available in theory, make global trade secret protection a primary concern for any business that operates across borders.

This chapter examines the risks of cross-border trade secret misappropriation, the regional differences in approaches to trade secret protection, the range of public and private remedies for trade secret misappropriation, and the realistic strategies businesses can employ to protect their valuable trade secrets. It explores the differences among various countries' trade secret regimes, beginning with the United States' evolving approach to foreign trade secret misappropriation and continuing with Europe, China and India. It then assesses the next wave of potential solutions, including both suggested efforts within the U.S. and proposed multi-national measures to increase global trade secret protection.

---

[3]　The Commission on the Theft of American Intellectual Property, *The IP Commission Report: The Report of the Commission on the Theft of American Intellectual Property*, THE IP COMMISSION 26-27 (May 2013), http://www.ipcommission.org/report/IP_Commission_Report_052213.pdf (hereinafter IP Commission Report). This estimate has appeared in previous reports as well. *See, e.g.*, David S. Almeling et al., *A Statistical Analysis of Trade Secret Litigation in Federal Courts*, 45 GONZ. L. REV. 291, 292 (2009).

[4]　*See* IP Commission Report, *supra* note 3.

I. TRADE SECRET MISAPPROPRIATION IS INCREASINGLY EXPENSIVE

The incidence of trade secret misappropriation is rising around the world. In a survey conducted for the European Commission, almost 40 percent of respondents reported their belief that the risk of trade secret misappropriation increased between 2002 and 2012. In that decade, 20 percent of respondents experienced at least one attempted or actual trade secret misappropriation in the European Union (EU).[5] The rate was higher in certain industries. One in three firms in the chemical, motor vehicles, and pharmaceutical sectors reported at least one attempted or actual trade secret misappropriation during that ten-year period.[6]

The financial impact is staggering. In October 2013, a World Trade Organization (WTO) panel estimated that the global cost of such misappropriation, while impossible to calculate precisely, likely amounted to hundreds of billions of dollars.[7] The magnitude of the confidential information stolen, even within the United States alone, is staggering as well. The U.S. Department of Defense has noted that "[e]very year, an amount of intellectual property larger than that contained in the Library of Congress is stolen from networks maintained by U.S. businesses, universities, and government departments and agencies."[8] This loss is bound to increase unless more effective protections emerge.

A. The Role of Technology in Trade Secret Loss

The rapid pace of technological development has contributed to the new urgency of global trade secret protection. The flow of employees and contractors in and out of companies and across borders, often carrying trade secrets with them, creates risks of its own. In over 85 percent of trade secret misappropriation cases, the alleged misappropriator is known to the trade secret owner, and is usually either an employee or a business

---

[5]   2013 EC Trade Secrets Study, *supra* note 1, at 13.

[6]   *Ibid.* at 128.

[7]   Managing Knowhow and Trade Secrets in Global Value Chains and the International Transfer of Technology, Panel at the World Trade Organization Public Forum 2013 (Workshop 1) (Oct. 1, 2013), *available at* http://bit.ly/1y88wAA

[8]   *See* Dep't of Def., *Department of Defense Strategy for Operating in Cyberspace*, UNITED STATES DEPARTMENT OF DEFENSE 4 (July 2011), http://www.defense.gov/news/d20110714cyber.pdf.

partner.[9] In one survey, the alleged misappropriator was a current or former employee 59 percent of the time.[10] The laxity of employees, especially those between the ages of 20 and 30, in protecting data secrecy adds to the risk of trade secret misappropriation as well.[11]

As the transnational workforce grows, the technology it uses exacerbates the problems of keeping trade secrets confidential. Workforce mobility, the exponential growth of cloud-based computing, the ubiquity of the internet in business, and developments in hacking all contribute to this problem. The increasing use of personal technology at work, in the form of smartphones and "bring your own device" computer policies, combined with the transfer of data onto the internet and into the cloud, makes it easier than ever for businesses to lose their trade secrets. As one writer put it, "[a] disgruntled employee can literally walk out the door with the company in his pocket."[12]

Other trends, such as the use of social media accounts incorporating customer lists or other putative trade secrets, further increase the risks that those trade secrets will lose their protection.[13] While these practices may make it more efficient for employees to collaborate around the globe, they also increase the risk of online data theft exponentially.

B.   Examples of Cross-Border Trade Secret Misappropriation

Several of the high-stakes, high-profile cases that have captured national attention in the United States involve allegations of foreign companies

---

[9]   *See* Almeling, *supra* note 3, at 303.

[10]   *Ibid.* at 302.

[11]   *See, e.g.*, Laura DiDio, *Careless, Reckless Staff are Corporate Security's Biggest Threat*, E-COMMERCE TIMES (Feb. 7, 2014, 8:00 AM), http://www.ecommercetimes.com/story/79930.html; Sarah Green, *Do Millennials Believe in Data Security?* HARV. BUS. REV. BLOG (Feb. 18, 2014, 9:00 AM), http://blogs.hbr.org/2014/02/do-millennials-believe-in-data-security/ (noting that millennials are more likely to engage in behavior that threatens data security than older workers even though they are more knowledgeable about the risks of doing so).

[12]   R. Mark Halligan & Richard F. Weyand, *The Sorry State of Trade Secret Protection*, THE TRADE SECRET OFF., INC. (Aug. 2001), http://www.thetso.com/Info/sorry.html.

[13]   *See, e.g.*, Paul Cowie, Bram Hanono & Dorna Moini, *Social Media: Protecting Trade Secrets and Proprietary Information*, 12 EMPLOYMENT & LABOR RELATIONS LAW 1 (2014), *available at* http://www.jdsupra.com/legal news/social-media-protecting-trade-secrets-a-98388/.

working in concert with a trade secret owner's current or former employees. For example:

- In April 2011, a former Ford Motor Company executive who resigned to work at Beijing Automotive Company was sentenced to 70 months in federal prison for theft of trade secrets that Ford valued at $50 million. The former employee copied 4000 Ford documents on a hard drive and took them to China.[14]
- In March 2012, a former DuPont scientist pleaded guilty to conspiracy to commit economic espionage, admitting that he gave trade secrets about DuPont's proprietary titanium dioxide manufacturing process to companies controlled by the Chinese government. He was convicted of trade secret misappropriation in March 2014. The global titanium dioxide market has been valued at about $12 billion dollars, and DuPont has the lion's share of the market.[15]
- In August 2012, a former software engineer for Motorola was sentenced to four years in prison for theft of trade secrets that Motorola had spent more than $400 million dollars to develop. She was stopped at the airport as she tried to travel to China with more than 1000 electronic and paper Motorola proprietary documents.[16]

Many of these cases involve large companies, such as DuPont and Motorola, which are most likely to have the resources necessary to pursue civil lawsuits. Trade secrets are often even more valuable, relative to other assets, in small and mid-size companies, where innovation is critical to performance and valuation, and where the perceived high cost of patent prosecution encourages the use of secrecy as a protective measure. These smaller companies, however, have less time and capital to pursue trade secret claims, especially in an unfamiliar legal environment. Start-up companies therefore face a growing but unmet need for stronger protection of their trade secrets.

---

[14]   *See, e.g.*, Ben Klayman, Ex-Ford engineer sentenced for trade secrets theft, REUTERS.COM, April 13, 2011 9:39 am, *available at* http://reut.rs/ 1AQQA9v

[15]   *See, e.g.*, Karen Gullo, *California Man Guilty of Stealing DuPont Trade Secrets*, BLOOMBERG.COM, (March 5, 2014), http://www.bloomberg.com/news/ 2014-03-05/California-man-guilty-of-stealing-dupont-trade-secrets.html.

[16]   *See, e.g.*, Ameet Sachdev, *Former Motorola engineer sentenced to 4 years in trade-secret case*, CHICAGOTRIBUNE.COM, (August 31, 2012), http:// articles.chicagotribune.com/2012-08-31/business/ct-biz-0830-moto-theft–201208 31_1_trade-secret-case-hanjuan-jin-trade-secrets.

C.   The Potential Problem of Conflicting Rulings

Many newsworthy trade secret cases in the United States involve allegations of theft by Chinese companies, as the preceding examples illustrate.[17] In some cases, U.S. and Chinese courts have reached different legal conclusions about the same set of allegations, causing further complications. In one example, the U.S. International Trade Commission (ITC) affirmed part of an administrative law judge's ruling that Sino Legend, a Chinese company, misappropriated trade secrets from the competing New York-based SI Group.[18] In doing so, the ITC directly contradicted a Chinese court's finding. The same set of facts wound its way through the Chinese and U.S. courts simultaneously, with opposing results.

In 2007, Sino Legend hired a former SI Group plant manager who knew how to make certain compounds stickier. The following year, SI Group brought claims against Sino Legend for trade secret misappropriation in a Chinese court, but failed to get relief.

Apparently frustrated by its lack of progress in the Chinese courts, SI Group then filed claims in the ITC against Sino Legend in May 2012 while appealing its losses in China. In January 2014, the ITC affirmed an administrative law judge's decision to enjoin Sino Legend from importing products to the United States for ten years, but narrowed the original injunction from a general prohibition to a limited injunction of importing any rubber resins made using SI Group's trade secrets.[19] Unfortunately for SI Group, the injunction had no effect on Sino Legend's ability to sell products made using SI Group's trade secrets in the lucrative Chinese market, where it has become the dominant player.

Seven months earlier, however, a Chinese court reached the opposite conclusion about Sino Legend's actions.[20] In June 2013, the Shanghai No.2 Intermediate People's Court concluded that SI's trade secret claims

---

[17]   Some scholars have suggested that Chinese companies are responsible for most reported trade secret misappropriation. *See, e.g.,* IP Commission Report, *supra* note 3, at 2.

[18]   United States International Trade Commission, Investigative History of Investigation No. 337-TA-849, *available at* http://1.usa.gov/YMqQzA.

[19]   Interestingly, *China Daily* reported – inaccurately – that Sino Legend had been cleared of any wrongdoing by the U.S. Court. *See* Hao Nan, *U.S. Trade Commission: No infringement by Sino Legend,* CHINA DAILY (Feb. 19, 2014, 8:53 AM), http://www.chinadaily.com.cn/kindle/2014-02/19/content_17291668.htm.

[20]   *Sino Legend Prevails in Legal Challenge; Court Rejects SI Group Trade Secret Arguments,* SINO LEGEND (June 17, 2013, 9:24 AM), http://www.sinolegend.com/show.asp?articleid=269.

against Sino Legend were invalid because the information at issue was not "unknown to the public." The Court also ruled that the technology Sino Legend used was not "identical or materially identical to any SI trade secret."[21]

There are other examples of simultaneous and potentially conflicting proceedings. In June 2013, the Department of Justice indicted Sinovel, a Beijing-based wind turbine maker and two of its employees for trade secret misappropriation from American Superconductor Corp. (AMSC), a U.S. supplier. Sinovel was accused of inducing an AMSC employee to copy proprietary AMSC code and give it to Sinovel along with certain AMSC trade secrets.[22] Sinovel challenged the efficacy of the Department of Justice's summons, claiming that it tried to serve Sinovel's U.S. subsidiary rather than the Chinese corporation itself. The Department of Justice responded that the U.S. subsidiary, which it claims Sinovel closed shortly before the claims were brought to avoid service, was Sinovel's alter ego.[23]

Chinese courts are also considering AMSC's trade secret, and other claims against Sinovel. AMSC filed trade secret misappropriation and other claims against Sinovel in China in 2011, seeking over $1.2 billion in damages. There had been little progress on those claims by the time of the U.S. indictment. In February 2014, the Supreme People's Court of China announced that it would hear AMSC's two copyright cases, rejecting efforts to move them to arbitration instead.[24]

The problem of conflicting rulings occurs elsewhere too. In March 2014, for example, business partners SanDisk and Toshiba separately filed lawsuits in the United States and Japan respectively regarding the same alleged trade secret misappropriation by the South Korean company SK Hynix Inc.[25]

As courts in different countries evaluate the same basic claims according to different rules and procedures, there are bound to be more

---

[21]   *See Ibid.*

[22]   *See* Indictment, U.S. v. Sinovel Wind Group Co., Ltd., No. 13 CR 84 BBC (W.D. Wis. filed June 27, 2013).

[23]   *See* Justin K. Beyer, *AMSC/Sinovel Industrial Espionage Thriller Takes a Procedural Detour, Threatening U.S. Criminal Prosecution*, tradesecretslaw.com, Sept. 9, 2013.

[24]   Justin Doom, *China Supreme Court Ruling Favors AMSC in Two Sinovel Suits*, BLOOMBERG (Feb. 19, 2014, 4:09 PM), http://www.bloomberg.com/news/2014-02-19/china-supreme-court-ruling-favors-amsc-in-two-sinovel-suits-1-.html.

[25]   Chang-Ran Kim and Miyoung Kim, *Toshiba, SanDisk Sue Hynix Over Suspected Flash Memory Technology Leak*, REUTERS (Mar. 13, 2014, 10:40 PM), *available at* http://reut.rs/1oSjRLo.

conflicting rulings like those in Sinovel. These cases underscore the need for a more effective means of resolving trade secret misappropriation disputes at the global level.

II.   COMPARISON OF NATIONAL APPROACHES

Bringing trade secret misappropriators in other countries to justice can be enormously challenging. The problems involved in litigating trade secrets across borders stem in part from the different ways in which countries treat trade secrets as a matter of law. Trade secrets are protected everywhere to some extent, but the doctrinal approach and efficacy of those protections vary greatly. These differences depend in part on whether a private right of action exists, whether trade secrets are included within contract law, fiduciary obligations, intellectual property or other areas of law, and issues of personal jurisdiction.

Recent surveys underscore these differences. One conducted for the European Commission noted that the definition of trade secrets and the scope of their protection vary significantly among member countries.[26] A 2014 OECD study described the differences among trade secret protection regimes among various WTO members.[27] The surveyed countries shared basic definitions of trade secrets, due partly to their obligations under the Agreement on Trade-Related Aspects of Intellectual Property Rights (TRIPS).[28] Most countries surveyed, for example, recognized similar categories of trade secrets, including technical information, confidential business information and know-how.[29] Most also recognized both independent creation and reverse engineering as defenses to theft, and that knowledge or reason to know of trade secret misappropriation played a large role in determining the liability of a third party.[30]

---

[26]   Managing Knowhow and Trade Secrets in Global Value Chains and the International Transfer of Technology, *supra* note 7.

[27]   Mark F. Schultz and Douglas C. Lippoldt, *Approaches to Protection of Undisclosed Information (Trade Secrets)* (OECD Trade Policy Papers, No. 162, 2014), *available at* http://www.oecd.org/officialdocuments/publicdisplaydocument pdf/?cote=TAD/TC/WP(2013)21/FINAL&docLanguage=En- 22 Jan 2014. [hereinafter OECD Trade Policy Paper].

[28]   *Ibid.* at 16; *see also* Agreement on Trade-Related Aspects of Intellectual Property Rights, *available at,* http://bit.ly/1t1KeDP.

[29]   *Ibid.*

[30]   *Ibid.*

Yet the OECD report concluded that differences among the surveyed countries outweighed the similarities. Differences emerged in the following areas:

- whether trade secrets are protected primarily by civil law, criminal law, or both;
- whether a breach of duty is required for liability or whether trade secrets are protected as rights alone;
- the nature and extent of damages available, including injunctions and seizure and return;
- procedures available for gathering evidence of misappropriation, including whether emergency action may be ordered to preserve proof;
- the extent to which former employees are obligated to preserve confidentiality; and
- the protections available to preserve secrecy during litigation.[31]

In the following sections, this chapter provides an overview of the ways in which the United States, the European Union, China and India approach trade secret protection. While a comprehensive study of the trade secret protections available in each country is beyond its scope, a review of the basic principles and procedures used in each place can help illuminate the protections each affords.

A. The United States' Approach to Trade Secret Protection

The United States protects trade secrets through state law, federal law, and diplomatic efforts with varying levels of efficacy. A series of events in 2013 highlighted the need for a stronger U.S. protection regime. In late January 2013, the *New York Times* reported that Chinese hackers had infiltrated its computer system several times over a four-month period.[32] In February 2013, Mandiant, a cyber-security firm in Alexandria, Virginia claimed to have evidence linking the People's Liberation Army in Shanghai to a global cyber-espionage campaign against nearly 150

---

[31] *See Ibid.* at 18–19.
[32] Nicole Perlroth, *Hackers in China Attacked The Times for Last 4 Months*, N.Y. TIMES (Jan. 30, 2013), *available at* http://nyti.ms/Xs8pyZ.

companies from 20 economic sectors "designed to steal large volumes of valuable intellectual property."[33] Although the Chinese government denied these accusations, the Mandiant report received a great deal of attention.[34]

The Obama Administration then issued a substantive report (Report) on its trade secret strategy, highlighting the scope and urgency of the problem and underscoring its ongoing efforts to monitor online espionage.[35] The Report focused on five main "Action Items:" (1) focusing diplomatic efforts to protect trade secrets overseas; (2) promoting voluntary best practice by private industry to protect trade secrets; (3) enhancing domestic law enforcement operations, particularly by the Department of Justice, the FBI, and the Office of the Director of National Intelligence; (4) improving domestic legislation; and (5) enhancing public awareness and stakeholder outreach.

Although the Report serves as a useful summary of the Administration's efforts to protect trade secrets domestically and abroad, it announced little in the way of new measures. For example, the "action item" of improving domestic legislation focused on two laws that had already been enacted, the Theft of Trade Secrets Clarification Act and the Foreign and Economic Espionage Penalty Enhancement Act, rather than announcing future legislative goals. One critic noted that the word "continue" appears more than 20 times in it.[36] Other Administration efforts to coordinate intellectual property protection have also met with criticism. For example, scholars have noted that the Office of the Intellectual Property Enforcement Coordinator, whose mandate is to coordinate and manage intellectual property enforcement, has suffered from severe shortcomings since its inception.[37]

---

[33] *APT1: Exposing One of China's Cyber Espionage Units*, MANDIANT, http://intelreport.mandiant.com/Mandiant_APT1_Report.pdf (last visited Jul. 16, 2014).

[34] *See, e.g.,* Ellen Nakashima, *U.S. Launches Effort to Stem Trade-Secret Theft*, WASHINGTON POST (Feb. 20, 2013), *available at* http://wapo.st/1phlfq5.

[35] Defense Security Service, *Administration Strategy on Mitigating the Theft of U.S. Trade Secrets*, WHITE HOUSE (Feb. 2013), http://www.whitehouse.gov/sites/default/files/omb/IPEC/admin_strategy_on_mitigating_the_theft_of_u.s._trade_secrets.pdf.

[36] Ellen Nakashima, *Obama Orders Voluntary Security Standards for Critical Industries' Computer Networks*, WASHINGTON POST (Feb. 12, 2013), http://wapo.st/1oSnoJO.

[37] *See, e.g.,* David Orozco, *The Knowledge Police*, 43 HOFSTRA L. REV. 2 (2014).

Also in February 2013, President Obama issued an Executive Order calling for the creation of voluntary standards to increase the security of computer networks in industries such as banking and electric power and for greater sharing of cyber-threat information by the federal government with the private sector.[38] Although the Executive Order was announced around the same time as the Chinese cyber-hacking report, it reportedly had been in the works for several months.[39]

1. State and federal laws

In the United States, the number of trade secret litigation cases doubled in the seven years from 1988 to 1995, and doubled again in the nine years from 1995 to 2004.[40] Scholars predict that federal trade secret cases will double again by 2017.[41] Most of these cases interpret state statutes adopting the Uniform Trade Secrets Act (UTSA), a model law.[42]

The UTSA defines a trade secret as "information, including a formula, pattern, compilation, program, device, method, technique or process" that derives economic value from not being generally known to the public. The trade secret owner is required to take reasonable steps to maintain the secrecy of the information.[43] All but two states, New York and Massachusetts, have adopted versions of the UTSA, but pending bills in Massachusetts would adopt the UTSA there as well.

Recognizing the limits of state law to remedy cross-border misappropriation, the U.S. legislature passed a federal law designed to target foreign trade secret misappropriation. The Economic Espionage Act (EEA), which criminalizes certain thefts of trade secrets, came into effect in 1996.[44] While there is no federal civil remedy for trade secret

---

[38]   *See* http://www.whitehouse.gov/the-press-office/2013/02/12/executive-order-improving-critical-infrastructure-cybersecurity.

[39]   *See* Orozco, *supra* note 37.

[40]   Almeling et al., *supra* note 3, at 293.

[41]   *Ibid.*

[42]   Uniform Trade Secrets Act with 1985 Amendments, National Conference of Commissioners on Uniform State Laws, *available at* http://www.uniform laws.org/shared/docs/trade%20secrets/utsa_final_85.pdf.

[43]   *Ibid.* at 5.

[44]   Economic Espionage Act of 1996, 18 U.S.C. §1831–837 (2012). The Computer Fraud and Abuse Act, which creates liability when a party damages a computer in connection with the theft of trade secrets, is another potential resource. 18 U.S.C. § 1030 (2008); *see* Charles Doyle, STEALING TRADE SECRETS AND ECONOMIC ESPIONAGE: AN OVERVIEW OF 18 U.S.C. 1831 AND 1832 (2013), available at http://fas.org/sgp/crs/secrecy/R42681.pdf.

misappropriation, bills were introduced in Congress attempting to establish such laws in 2012 and 2013. Several other bills have been introduced to further expand the reach of federal trade secret law.

Since its passage, and often in the wake of specific court rulings, Congress has become aware of certain shortcomings in the EEA.[45] In 2012, Congress passed two amendments designed to enhance it. The Theft of Trade Secrets Clarification Act[46] softened the requirements of the EEA, in the wake of a court decision overturning the conviction of a former Goldman Sachs programmer. The Foreign and Economic Espionage Penalty Enhancement Act[47] radically increased the penalties available under the EEA.

a.   The Theft of Trade Secrets Clarification Act of 2012   The Theft of Trade Secrets Clarification Act, signed into law on December 28, 2012, expanded the scope of trade secrets protected by the EEA. It was enacted in response to a legal loophole exposed by *United States v. Aleynikov*, a widely criticized 2012 decision of the U.S. Court of Appeals for the Second Circuit.[48]

In *Aleynikov*, a computer programmer appealed his conviction for trade secret misappropriation. The programmer had helped Goldman Sachs develop the source code for its high frequency trading (HFT) system, used to make large volumes of securities and commodities trades within fractions of a second. On his last day at Goldman, he encrypted and uploaded more than 500,000 lines of source code for the HFT system to a server in Germany. He downloaded the source code when he got to his home, for use at his new job with a start-up that intended to create its own HFT system. He was arrested by the FBI the following month. After a jury convicted him of violating both the EEA and the National Stolen Property Act, he was sentenced to 97 months in addition to three years under a supervised release program.

---

[45]   Scholars have also proposed amendments to the EEA. *See, e.g.*, David Orozco, *Amending the Economic Espionage Act to Require the Disclosure of National Security-Related Technology Thefts*, 62 Cath. U.L. Rev. 877 (2013) (proposing amending the Economic Espionage Act to mandate suspected trade secret thefts related to any technology that is under export restriction).

[46]   Theft of Trade Secrets Clarification Act of 2012, Pub. L. No. 112-236, 126 Stat. 1627 (2012).

[47]   Foreign and Economic Espionage Penalty Enhancement Act of 2012, Pub. L. No. 112-269, 126 Stat. 2442 (2013).

[48]   676 F.3d 71 (2d. Cir. 2012).

On appeal, he argued that the trial court should have granted his motion to dismiss the EEA charges because the HFT system did not fall within the EEA's definition of a trade secret. The Second Circuit agreed. It narrowly construed the portion of section 1832 that required the trade secret at issue to be "related to or included in a product that is produced for or placed in interstate or foreign commerce." According to the Second Circuit, "Goldman's HFT system was neither 'produced for' nor 'placed in' interstate commerce or foreign commerce. Goldman had no intention of selling its HFT system or licensing it to anyone."[49] As a result, the Second Circuit overturned the criminal conviction, essentially because of a loophole in the law.[50]

In order to close that loophole, the Theft of Trade Secrets Clarification Act replaced the EEA's requirement that the trade secret be related to something "produced for or placed in interstate or foreign commerce," with the looser requirement that the trade secret be related to "a product or service used in or intended for use in" interstate or foreign commerce.[51]

This amendment expanded the EEA's reach in two ways. First, it made clear that services may be protectable under the EEA in addition to products. Second, it clarified that products and services are protectable even if they are not themselves placed in interstate commerce, but are intended for such use in the future.

b. Foreign and Economic Espionage Penalty Enhancement Act of 2012
Another 2012 law enhancing trade secret protection is the Foreign and Economic Espionage Penalty Enhancement Act of 2012.[52] This law increased the maximum fine for offenses committed by individuals from $500,000 to $5,000,000, and for offenses committed by organizations, the law increased the fine from "not more than $10,000,000" to "not more than the greater of $10,000,000 or three times the value of the stolen trade secret to the organization, including expenses for research and design and other costs of reproducing the trade secret that the organization has thereby avoided."[53]

---

[49] *Ibid.* at 82.

[50] Robert Damien Jurrons, *Fool Me Once: U.S. v. Aleynikov and the Theft of Trade Secrets Clarification Act of 2012*, 28 BERKELEY TECH. L.J. 833, 834 (2014).

[51] Theft of Trade Secrets Clarification Act of 2012, Pub. L. No. 112–236, 126 Stat. 1627, §2 (2012).

[52] *See supra* note 47.

[53] *Ibid.* at §2(b).

As some scholars have noted, increasing the penalties against individual actors is unlikely to prove an effective deterrent against the government and corporate actors who benefit from trade secret misappropriation. As a domestic law, the EEA cannot target foreign governments. Increasing punishment for the individuals who steal trade secrets targets instead the "lowest actors on the international espionage ladder."[54] As one writer observed, "it is unlikely that an increase in the maximum fine will deter foreign governments from committing economic espionage when those foreign governments feel few repercussions from the penalty."[55] Consequently, neither the EEA nor the Penalty Enhancement Act provides a means of redress against foreign governments that solicit and/or benefit from economic espionage.

c. Section 337 of the U.S. Tariff Act   Another option for U.S. companies alleging trade secret misappropriation overseas is enforcement under Section 337 of the U.S. Tariff Act,[56] which has been used most frequently in patent cases.[57] This option became more popular after the 2011 decision in *TianRui Group Co. Ltd. v. Int'l Trade Comm'n*.[58] In this landmark ruling, the U.S. Court of Appeals for the Federal Circuit held that when a respondent has misappropriated trade secrets to make goods, the U.S. can block the importation of those goods if the misappropriation

---

[54]   Nathaniel Minott, *The Economic Espionage Act: Is the Law All Bark and No Bite?* 20 INFO. & COMM. TECH. L. 201, 209 (2011).

[55]   Robin L. Kuntz, *How Not to Catch a Thief: Why the Economic Espionage Act Fails to Protect American Trade Secrets*, 28 BERKELEY TECH. L.J. 901, 931 (2013).

[56]   U.S Tariff Act of 1930, 19 U.S.C. §1337 (2004).

[57]   In order to prove trade secret misappropriation before the ITC, the complainant must show: (1) existence of a trade secret, (2) ownership of or a proprietary interest in the trade secret, (3) disclosure of the trade secret in confidence or its acquisition by unfair means, and (4) use or disclosure of the trade secret causing injury to the complainant. *See* In the Matter of Certain Processes for the Manufacture of Skinless Sausage Casings and Resulting Product, Inv. No. 337-TA-148/169 (1984), *available at* http://www.usitc.gov/publications/337/pub1624.pdf. To establish the first element, the ITC considers the six factors from § 757 of the First Restatement of Torts: (1) the extent to which the information is known outside the business, (2) the extent to which the information is known inside the business, (3) the extent of measures taken to protect the secrecy of the information, (4) the value of the information to competitors, (5) the amount of time and effort or money expended, and (6) the ease or difficulty in proper acquisition or duplication. RESTATEMENT (FIRST) OF TORTS § 757 (1939).

[58]   661 F.3d 1322, 1325 (Fed. Cir. 2011).

causes domestic injury even though the misappropriation occurred out-side of the U.S. and no U.S. entity is practicing the trade secrets at issue.[59] Here, the respondent's products made overseas with complain-ants' misappropriated trade secrets competed with complainants' domes-tically made products made by another process, thus reducing the complainants' profits in the U.S.[60]

TianRui expanded the options for domestic victims of foreign trade secret misappropriation because it effectively broadened the ITC's power to rule on such theft occurring entirely outside of the U.S. It also underscored the ITC's power to deprive foreign companies of a U.S. market for items made using misappropriated trade secrets. In doing so, it strengthened an option for trade secret owners who would otherwise face significant hurdles in bringing foreign respondents to justice.[61] Following *TianRui*, more companies began to seek trade secret protection from the ITC.[62] Legal scholars, however, question the efficacy of Section 337 in protecting U.S. trade secrets from exploitation overseas.[63]

2. Pending bills

The growing recognition in Congress of the importance of uniform trade secret protection has led to a spate of trade secret bills. In 2012 and 2013, lawmakers introduced several bills designed to create additional federal remedies for trade secret misappropriation.

In July 2012, three U.S. Senators introduced the "Protecting American Trade Secrets and Innovation Act of 2012" (PATSIA).[64] PATSIA would

---

[59]   *Ibid.* at 1324.

[60]   *Ibid.*

[61]   Natalie Flechsig, *Trade Secret Enforcement After TianRui: Fighting Misappropriation Through the ITC*, 28 BERKELEY TECH. L.J. 449, 462 (2013).

[62]   *See, e.g., Certain Paper Shredders, Processes for Manufacturing or Related to Same*, Inv. No. 337-TA-863 (2013), *noticed in* 78 Fed. Reg. 5496 (Jan. 25, 2013) (Pender, J.); *Certain Robotic Toys and Components Thereof*, Inv. No. 337-TA-869 (2013), *noticed in* 78 Fed. Reg. 9740 (Feb. 5, 2013) (Bullock, C.J.); *Certain Rubber Resins and Processes for Manufacturing Same*, Inv. No. 337-TA-849 (2012), *noticed in* 77 Fed. Reg. 38,083 (June 26, 2012) (Roger, J.); *Certain Electric Fireplaces, Components Thereof, Manuals for Same, Manufacturing or Relating to Same and Products Containing Same*, Inv. No. 337-TA-791 (2012), *noticed in* 77 Fed. Reg. 2757 (Jan. 19, 2012) (Shaw, J.).

[63]   *See, e.g.*, Steven E. Feldman and Sherry L. Rollo, *Extraterritorial Protection of Trade Secret Rights in China: Do Section 337 Actions at the ITC Really Prevent Trade secret misappropriation Abroad?*, 11 J. MARSHALL REV. INTELL. PROP. L. 523 (2012).

[64]   S. 3389, 112th Cong. (2012).

have amended Section 1836 of the EEA to create federal civil remedies for misappropriation of a trade secret. The bill died in committee, in part because its definition of "trade secret" mirrored old language in the EEA that had been expanded by the Theft of Trade Secrets Clarification Act of 2012 to include product and services explicitly. Although the Theft of Trade Secrets Clarification Act was introduced in November 2012, four months after PATSIA, it sped through Congress, making PATSIA's narrower trade secret definition obsolete.[65] PATSIA did not make it out of the Judiciary Committee in 2012, but one of its sponsors introduced a similar bill during the 2014 Congressional session.[66]

Representative Zoe Lofgren introduced a streamlined version of PATSIA in June 2013. This bill, the "Private Right of Action Against Theft of Trade Secrets Act of 2013" (PRATSA), would have amended Section 1832 (Theft of Trade Secrets) of the EEA to allow victims of trade secret misappropriation to seek both compensatory damages and injunctive relief through a federal civil action. PRATSA also clarified that discoveries made through reverse engineering do not constitute trade secret misappropriation, but left out certain additional provisions that stymied PATSIA's passage.[67] As of this writing, the bill is still in committee.[68]

In November 2013, Senator Jeff Flake introduced another bill seeking to establish a federal civil remedy for trade secret misappropriation overseas. "The Future of American Innovation and Research Act" targets trade secret misappropriation by foreign actors. Specifically, it would allow a domestic trade secret owner to file a federal civil case for trade secret misappropriation outside of the United States or "on behalf of, or for the benefit of, a person located outside the territorial jurisdiction of the United States."[69] In other words, it would allow domestic corporations to file the same kinds of trade secret misappropriation claims they can now file under state law, but with the benefit of reaching those overseas who might otherwise evade the reach of state law.

---

[65] *Trying Again! Bolstering Federal Protection of Trade Secrets: Enacting a Companion Civil Right of Action to the Economic Espionage Act*, THE KELLER LAW FIRM, LLC, http://thekellerlawfirm.com/trying-again-bolstering-federal-protection-of-trade-secrets-enacting-a-companion-civil-right-of-action-to-the-economic-espionage-act/.

[66] The Defend Trade Secrets Act, S. 2267, 113th Cong. (2014).

[67] Bill Donahue, *In New Year, Congress Has Full Plate of Trade Secret Bills*, LAW360 (Jan. 8, 2014, 6:56 PM), http://www.law360.com/articles/499735/in-new-year-congress-has-full-plate-of-trade-secret-bills.

[68] H.R. 2466, 113th Cong. (2013).

[69] S.1770, 113th Cong. § (3)(a) (2013).

Two additional bills focused on misappropriation by foreign governments rather than private actors. In May 2013, Senator Carl Levin introduced a bill that would have required the Director of National Intelligence to develop a watch list and a priority watch list of foreign countries that engage in economic or industrial espionage in cyberspace with respect to United States trade secrets or proprietary information, and for other purposes.[70] A month later, the "Cyber Economic Espionage Accountability Act" (CEEAA) was introduced. The CEEAA would allow federal agencies to identify foreign officials that commit economic espionage and trade secret misappropriation, and then penalize them through asset seizures, travel bans, and other punitive measures.[71]

3. Procedural issues

Any law's effectiveness is limited by the extent to which the putative defendants can be brought to court. Some foreign corporations accused of trade secret misappropriation have delayed U.S. court appearances or avoided them entirely because they cannot be served properly under current rules. Service of overseas defendants has been an especially difficult issue in federal cases, leading observers to worry that "complicated U.S. procedural rules are getting in the way of the government's efforts to protect the nation from cybertheft, and allowing foreign defendants to violate U.S. law with impunity."[72] As Sinovel noted in its motion to quash service, the United States has not had much, if any, success in properly serving foreign corporations in criminal cases.[73]

According to the rules of criminal procedure, defendants must be served by summons delivered to their last known U.S. addresses.[74] Although the Justice Department has recommended amending those rules to facilitate the service of summons outside the United States, no such

---

[70] Deter Cyber Theft Act, S. 884, 113th Cong. (2013). The bill, however, died in committee.

[71] H.R. 2281, 113th Cong. (2013); Donahue, *supra* note 67.

[72] Mark P. Wine and Christina Von der Ahe, *UPDATE: Sur-Sur-Sur Reply Highlights the Short Arm of U.S. Law in Trade Secret Misappropriation*, ORRICK TRADE SECRETS WATCH (Sept. 24, 2013), http://blogs.orrick.com/trade-secrets-watch/2013/09/24/update-sur-sur-sur-reply-highlights-the-short-arm-of-u-s-law-in-trade-secret-theft/#more-447.

[73] Mem. of Specially-Appearing Defendant Sinovel Wind Group Co., Ltd. in in Support of Mot. to Quash Service at 4, U.S. v. Sinovel Wind Group Co., Ltd. No. 3:13-cr-84-bbc (W. D. Wi. filed Aug. 16, 2013), *available at* http://s3.amazonaws.com/cdn.orrick.com/files/Trade-Secret-Blog-Sep25-Sinovel-Motion-to-Quash.pdf.

[74] *See* FED.R.CRIM.PRO. 4(C)(3)(c).

amendments have been made. The *Liew* and *Kolon* cases illustrate the impact of these procedural limitations. In *United States v. Liew*, the Department of Justice was unable to serve China's Pangang Group Co. for several months due to what one attorney called "a procedural glitch … that's not insignificant or easy to resolve."[75]

The Department of Justice had issued a subpoena to Pangang in connection with a case in which DuPont had accused Walter Liew, a California resident, of selling trade secrets to Pangang.[76] Federal prosecutors served the summons on a New Jersey company that they believed was owned by Pangang and mailed a summons to a California address where Pangang had registered as a foreign corporation.[77] In challenging the summons, however, Pangang argued that it had never employed anyone in the United States or had an office in the United States. The court ruled that service was improper because the United States had not proven that the entities served were Pangang's agents.[78]

Federal prosecutors can serve foreign corporations through the use of Mutual Legal Assistance Treaties (MLATs), but those agreements can be so slow to take effect as to be virtually useless. For example, the Justice Department used an MLAT in *United States v. Kolon Indus., Inc.* to serve the South Korean company Kolon Industries, Inc., which was charged with trade secret misappropriation in a claim seeking $225 million in alleged criminal proceeds.[79] The summons was delivered to Kolon in South Korea two days after Kolon was supposed to appear in court for arraignment. Although prosecutors had also served a summons on Kolon USA in New Jersey, the District Court for the Eastern District of Virginia ruled that that summons was insufficient because they had not established that Kolon USA was Kolon Industries' agent.[80]

---

[75] Karen Gullo and Tom Schoenberg, *Pangang and Kolon, Like Edward Snowden, Elude U.S. Charge*, BLOOMBERG (July 18, 2013, 2:20 PM), http://www.bloomberg.com/news/2013-07-18/old-mail-rule-helps-pangang-kolon-elude-u-s-charges.html.

[76] *Ibid.*

[77] *Ibid.*

[78] U.S. v. Pangang Group Co. et al., 879 F. Supp. 2d 1052 (N.D.Cal., Jul. 23, 2012).

[79] Gullo and Schoenberg, *supra* note 75.

[80] 926 F. Supp. 2d 794 (E.D. Va. Feb. 22, 2013)*; but see* E.I. DuPont De Nemours and Co. v Kolon Indus., Inc., 286 F.R.D. 288 (E.D. Va. Oct. 5, 2012) (granting in part motion to compel production from Kolon subsidiaries).

4. Diplomatic efforts to protect trade secrets from overseas theft

In addition to legislative remedies, the United States uses diplomatic channels to encourage other nations to better monitor and prevent data theft and economic espionage. One is the Special 301 Report, issued annually by the U.S. Trade Representative's office, which creates various watch lists for countries whose trade secret effectiveness particularly concerns the United States. One of these lists, the Priority Watch List, catalogues those countries where increased diplomatic efforts to improve trade secret protection may be warranted.

The United States also tries to increase its protection of its companies' trade secrets by negotiating new treaty provisions. For example, the Trans-Pacific Partnership Agreement (TPPA), currently being negotiated by twelve countries which collectively contribute 40 percent of the world's GDP, will likely incorporate some level of intellectual property protection.[81] The U.S. Chamber of Commerce issued a report urging all signatories to the TPPA to adopt stringent protections for trade secrets.[82]

B. The European Union's Approach to Trade Secret Protection

Trade secret misappropriation has long been a source of frustration for companies doing business in Europe. Although copyrights and trade-marks are protected by European law, there is no comparably uniform legal protection for trade secrets.[83] Some observers have suggested that the recent negotiation of the Trans-Atlantic Trade and Investment Partnership (T-TIP) trade pact with the United States has created a sense of urgency within the European Union (EU) for the development of a more effective approach to trade secret protection.[84]

---

[81] The countries are America, Canada, Chile, Mexico, Peru, Australia, Brunei, Japan, Malaysia, New Zealand, Singapore and Vietnam. *See No End In Sight*, ECONOMIST (Feb. 25, 2014, 2:43 PM), http://www.economist.com/blogs/banyan/2014/02/trans-pacific-partnership-0.

[82] U.S. CHAMBER OF COMMERCE, THE CASE FOR ENHANCED PROTECTION OF TRADE SECRETS IN THE TRANS-PACIFIC PARTNERSHIP AGREEMENT, *available at* https://www.uschamber.com/sites/default/files/legacy/international/files/Final%20TPP%20Trade%20Secrets%208_0.pdf (last visited Mar. 28, 2014). The scope of such protection, however, has been subject to intense debate, as discussed further in Section 4(c).

[83] Danny Hakim, *Europe Moves to Keep Its Corporate Trade Data Secret*, N.Y. TIMES (Nov, 14, 2013), http://www.nytimes.com/2013/11/15/business/international/europe-moves-to-keep-its-corporate-trade-data-secret.html.

[84] *Ibid.*

The differences in trade secret protection among EU member states take a number of forms. The most striking variable is that there is no uniform definition of a trade secret in the European Union.[85] What constitutes a trade secret in France may not be considered protectable in Austria. For companies doing business in several countries, the process of determining whether certain information can be protected as a trade secret, therefore may require a country-by-country examination of the relevant laws.

The 28 member states within the European Union also vary in their doctrinal approaches to trade secret law. Some countries, such as Germany and Spain, root trade secret protection in unfair competition law.[86] Others, including the Netherlands and Luxembourg, use tort law to protect trade secrets.[87] In common law countries such as England and Ireland, contract law and the common law of confidence protect trade secrets. France protects manufacturing trade secrets through its Code of Industrial Property.[88] Only Sweden treats trade secret law as *sui generis*.[89] The differences in legal mechanisms for protecting trade secrets correlate to differences in the evidence necessary to demonstrate wrongdoing, as well as the remedies available for trade secret misappropriation.[90]

A survey conducted for the European Union in late 2012 suggested the presence of widespread support for standardized trade secret enforcement provisions across the Union.[91] In November 2013, the European Commission issued a directive proposing rules aimed at creating the European Union's first broad protection of trade secrets.[92] The proposed rules would replace the current country-by-country approach with a uniform set of guidelines. Each member state would write its own regulations in accordance with these guidelines. The guidelines include a requirement that the member states adopt penalties for trade secret misappropriation, including a recall of the infringing goods from the market, destruction of

---

[85]   2013 EC Trade Secrets Study, *supra* note 1, at 4-5.
[86]   *Ibid.* at 4.
[87]   *Ibid.*
[88]   *Ibid.*
[89]   *Ibid.*
[90]   *Ibid.* at 5–6.
[91]   *See Ibid.*
[92]   European Commission, *Proposal for a Directive of the European Parliament and of the Council on the Protection of Undisclosed Know-how and Business Information (Trade Secrets) Against Their Unlawful Acquisition, Use and Disclosure* (Nov. 28, 2013), *available at* http://ec.europa.eu/internal_market/iprenforcement/docs/trade-secrets/131128_proposal_en.pdf.

the infringing goods, and the destruction or delivery to the trade secret holder of anything containing or implementing the trade secret.[93] The release of the proposed regulations heralds the start of a negotiating process that may span years before the final version comes into effect.

According to the initial draft, the directive would require member states to adopt a wide range of conforming trade secret protection measures.[94] These guidelines mirror the TRIPS requirements in many ways. They include a uniform definition of trade secrets that requires them to be: (1) not generally known; (2) commercially valuable; and (3) subject to "reasonable steps under the circumstances" to keep it secret.[95] The directive would also establish guidelines for when the acquisition of trade secrets should be considered lawful. For example, the reverse engineering or disassembly of a product that has been "made available to the public" or is "lawfully in the possession of the acquirer of the information" would not constitute misappropriation.[96] It also requires member states to provide remedial measures for trade secret misappropriation, including a two-year statute of limitations period and methods of preserving the confidentiality of trade secrets during legal proceedings by both parties and courts.[97]

The draft directive would require member states to ensure that trade secret misappropriation could be punished by prohibiting the use of the trade secrets, the production, storage, or trade of the infringing goods, or a range of other corrective measures. These measures include a declaration of infringement, recall, destruction, or withdrawal from the market of infringing goods, and the destruction of any "document, object, material, substance or electronic file containing or implementing the trade secret."[98] Where the person who unlawfully acquired the trade secrets acted in good faith, the draft directive allows for pecuniary compensation to the rightful owner.

---

[93]   *Ibid.* at Section 3, Article 11(2).

[94]   European Commission, *Proposal for a Directive of the European Parliament and of the Council on the Protection of Undisclosed Know-How and Business Information(Trade Secrets) Against Their Unlawful Acquisition, Use and Disclosure* (August 13, 2013), *available at* http://bit.ly/1uBUnrt.

[95]   *Ibid.*, Article 2(1).

[96]   *Ibid.*, Article 4(1).

[97]   *Ibid.*, Article 7.

[98]   *Ibid.*, Article 11(2).

C. China's Approach to Trade Secret Protection

While the European Union is considering a uniform set of legal requirements for trade secret protection, China takes a more decentralized approach to trade secret law. The effectiveness of its system has been subject to criticism on a global scale, as discussed further below.

1. Chinese trade secret laws

Under Chinese law, a fragmented series of rules and regulations define and protect trade secrets. Unlike the United States, where most states have adopted the UTSA, Chinese law does not have a singular definition of trade secrets. Trade secrets are not addressed by the General Principles of the Civil Law, but can be found in a number of other bodies of law, including the Contract Law, Labor Law, Labor Contract Law and Company Law.[99] The 1997 revision of China's Criminal Law also criminalizes the misappropriation of trade secrets when the owner's consequent damages are sufficiently serious, as described below.[100] Whether a trade secret owner pursues civil or criminal charges in trade secret cases determines the type and extent of remedies that may be awarded.

The Chinese legal system also limits the means by which companies can protect their trade secrets through non-compete agreements. Under Chinese law, contracts that purport to limit competition with the employer after the employment has ended must compensate the former employee on a monthly basis for the term of the non-compete.[101]

a. Criminal cases　Chinese courts will only hear criminal cases of trade secret misappropriation when the alleged losses are either "serious" or "exceptionally serious," with different potential penalties attaching in each category. According to a 2004 interpretation of China's intellectual property laws, losses of at least ¥500,000 ($82,000) qualify as "serious" and those of at least ¥2.5 million ($412,000) merit treatment as "exceptionally serious" losses.[102]

Lawyers practicing in China generally pursue criminal cases when the trade secret owner has suffered enough loss for it to qualify as "serious"

---

[99]　Library of Congress, *Protection of Trade Secrets: China*, LIBRARY OF CONGRESS (Feb. 28, 2014), www.loc.gov/law/help/tradesecrets/china.php.
[100]　*Ibid.*
[101]　OECD Trade Policy Papers, *supra* note 27, at 75.
[102]　*Ibid.*

or "exceptionally serious."[103] Criminal prosecution offers at least two advantages over civil cases. First, it can be an effective deterrent because the penalties are much greater than in civil cases. Criminal penalties may include prison sentences of up to three years for serious losses and between three and seven years for exceptionally serious losses, in addition to fines. Civil cases have usually led only to the imposition of fines.

There is also an evidentiary advantage. Chinese civil law provides no right of discovery comparable to that of the U.S. legal system. Police can gather evidence more easily in criminal cases than can private parties in civil cases because they have the power to seize any relevant evidence.[104] The evidence they seize can then be used in civil and administrative cases. That said, it may not be easy to convince local authorities to pursue criminal cases in the first place, especially if the police do not view the case as sufficiently lucrative.[105] Some advocates have suggested that there would be a stronger deterrent to the theft of all kinds of intellectual property if China were to adopt the international standard of allowing criminal penalties (not just civil) in all cases of commercial intellectual property theft.[106]

b. Civil cases The primary Chinese trade secret law is the PRC Anti-Unfair Competition Law (AUCL) of 1993. AUCL's Article 10 defines business secrets as "the utilized technical information and business information which is unknown by the public, which may create business interests or profit for its legal owners, and also is maintained secrecy [sic] by its legal owners."[107] This legal definition encompasses a broad array of types of information, including customer lists, blueprints, management strategies and product designs.

A January 2007 document released by the Supreme People's Court shed more light on Chinese trade secret law. The Interpretation of Certain

---

[103] *Ibid.*

[104] *Ibid.*

[105] Ryan Ong, *Trade Secret Enforcement in China: Options and Obstacles*, CHINA BUSINESS REVIEW (Jan. 1, 2013), http://www.chinabusinessreview.com/trade-secret-enforcement-in-china-options-and-obstacles/.

[106] US-China Business Council, *USCBC 2013 China Business Environment Survey Results: Tempered Optimism Continues amid Moderating Growth, Rising Costs, and Persistent Market Barriers* 16, *available at* http://www.uschina.org/sites/default/files/USCBC – 2013Member%20Survey_0.pdf (last visited Mar. 28, 2014).

[107] Anti Unfair Competition Law of the People's Republic of China, *available at* http://en.chinacourt.org/public/detail.php?id=3306.

Issues Related to the Application of Law in Trials of Civil Cases Involving Unfair Competition ("Interpretation") offered answers to some questions about trade secret enforcement, and raised others.[108] For example, the Interpretation specifically provides that trade secrets may be acquired legally through reverse engineering and independent creation, without violating the AUCL.[109]

To seek compensatory damages in China, the trade secret owner must file a civil lawsuit. It may also seek an injunction in a civil case. Although Chinese courts have been hesitant to order injunctions in past trade secret cases, a recent decision suggests that courts may now order them more frequently. In August 2013, a Shanghai court granted a preliminary injunction in a trade secret case brought by U.S. plaintiff Eli Lilly.[110] In doing so, the court cited to Article 100 of China's newly amended Civil Procedure Law, establishing for the first time that courts may use that article to authorize injunctions.[111] This decision was widely hailed as an important sign of progress in the modernization of China's trade secret protection regime.[112]

Proving trade secret misappropriation in civil cases is made more difficult by the requirement, set out in the Interpretation, that the plaintiff provide clear evidence of when and how the alleged trade secrets were illegally obtained. In practice, doing so may pose an insurmountable challenge. Because China does not have a discovery process comparable to that of the United States, plaintiff companies must rely on their own resources to develop their case. Proving their case is further complicated by the fact that Chinese courts strongly prefer documentary evidence to witness testimony.[113]

In addition to evidentiary issues, the perception that Chinese officials have limited expertise in trade secret cases can hamper civil proceedings. For example, there may be long expert panel reviews to determine if certain confidential material qualifies as a trade secret, further complicating the process and adding to delays in resolution.[114]

---

[108] Ong, *supra* note 105.

[109] Library of Congress, *Protection of Trade Secrets: China*, *supra* note 99.

[110] Hao Nan, *Court Hands Down Milestone Ruling on Trade Secrets*, CHINA DAILY (Aug. 14, 2013, 7:39 AM), http://usa.chinadaily.com.cn/epaper/2013-08/14/content_16893667.htm.

[111] Library of Congress, *Protection of Trade Secrets: China*, *supra* note 99.

[112] Nan, *supra* note 110.

[113] Ong, *supra* note 105.

[114] *Ibid.*

c. Administrative cases　　A lack of familiarity with trade secret cases may make it difficult to convince local officials to hear these cases in the first place. The AUCL authorizes officials in the administrations of industry and commerce (AICs) to evaluate claims of trade secret misappropriation. It also authorizes them to order an array of remedies, including fines, the return of trade secret materials to the claimant, and the destruction of product made using stolen trade secrets.[115] According to one scholar, however, AICs and public security bureaus (PSBs) may be reluctant to accept trade secret cases unless they appear simple or high-value.[116] If the amount at stake is high enough, however, the plaintiffs may prefer to seek a remedy under criminal law.

2. Perceptions of trade secret risk under Chinese law

The effectiveness of China's trade secret protection regime has been the subject of international debate. Government agencies, legal scholars and business leaders have expressed concerns about China's effectiveness in protecting intellectual property for many years.[117] One scholar noted recently that "concern about intellectual property enforcement remains a major factor shaping companies' plans in China."[118] Although China's enforcement mechanisms appear to be improving, many companies are understandably doubtful that the Chinese legal system offers them adequate protection for their intellectual property.[119]

Recent reports underscore concerns about international intellectual property theft in China. The IP Commission Report, an independent, bipartisan report, which issued in May 2013, estimated that China was responsible for between 50 percent and 80 percent of such theft. Because the Chinese government is said to have a financial interest in so many Chinese companies, it is hard to separate state-sponsored theft from "independent" corporate-sponsored theft in that country. "National industrial policy goals in China encourage IP theft, and an extraordinary number of Chinese in business and government entities are engaged in this practice," the Report noted.[120]

---

[115]　*Ibid.*

[116]　*Ibid.*

[117]　*See, e.g.*, U.S. DEP'T OF COMMERCE INT'L TRADE ADMIN., PROTECTING YOUR INTELLECTUAL PROPERTY RIGHTS (IPR) IN CHINA: A PRACTICAL GUIDE FOR U.S. COMPANIES (Jan. 2003).

[118]　VICTORIA F. MAROULIS, CHINA'S EVOLVING IP REGIME AND AVENUES OF ENFORCEMENT (2013), *available at* 2013 WL 4192387.

[119]　*Ibid.*

[120]　IP Commission Report, *supra* note 3, at 3; *see also Ibid.* at 14–19.

Concern about the protection of trade secrets and other intellectual property rights limits foreign companies' confidence about doing business in China. According to the US-China Business Council's 2013 member company survey, trade secret protection remains the top intellectual property concern, with a record high number of respondents – 40 percent – ranking trade secrets as the most difficult area of intellectual property to protect in China.[121] When asked to name their greatest specific concern regarding trade secret protection, 38 percent of members cited difficulties in enforcing non-compete agreements and 26 percent cited insufficiencies in the legal framework. One member's comment illuminates the complexity of enforcing trade secrets in China particularly well:

> It is impossible to pick one [top concern with trade secrets] ... There is an overall lack of acknowledgement of the value of trade secrets. The penalties associated with violations are minor slaps of the hand. If the entity that misappropriated the trade secret is a government entity or well-connected private entity, you have no chance at even minimal redress. With respect to cases specifically, the lack of discovery and the strict requirement that all evidence be notarized makes it very difficult to even bring a case.[122]

China's lack of effective trade secret protection, in particular, has become a hot-button issue for trade relations between China and the U.S. In December 2013, the Office of the United States Trade Representative announced that Chinese representatives had agreed to make trade secret protection a "priority item" in their Action Plan for 2014.[123] During the U.S.-China Joint Commission on Commerce and Trade's meeting that month, China had agreed to adopt and publish an "Action Program" including specific enforcement actions, plans for improving public awareness about the importance of trade secret protection and penalties for theft, and "requirements for strict compliance with all laws, regulations, rules and other measures on trade secrets protection and enforcement by all enterprises and individuals."[124]

---

[121] US-China Business Council, *supra* note 106.
[122] *Ibid.*
[123] OFFICE OF THE UNITED STATES TRADE REPRESENTATIVE, 24TH U.S.-CHINA JOINT COMMISSION ON COMMERCE AND TRADE FACT SHEET, *available at* http://www.ustr.gov/about-us/press-office/fact-sheets/2013/December/JCCT-outcomes.
[124] *Ibid.*

D. India's Approach to Trade Secret Protection

Although China receives the brunt of criticism when it comes to trade secret protection regimes, India is not far behind. According to a report by the U.S. Chamber of Commerce's Global Intellectual Property Center, India had the weakest intellectual property protections of any country studied in 2013.[125] India also received the lowest ranking in 2012, when the annual study was first conducted.

One reason for India's dismal ranking is that Indian law provides no statutory protection for trade secrets.[126] Companies rely on contracts and common law to protect trade secrets, which have limitations of their own.[127] Although trade secret owners may bring criminal complaints for trade secret misappropriation under Section 378 of the Penal Code 1860, they may only do so if the trade secrets are in a hard copy form (for example, client lists, formulae or blueprints) and if the owner can prove that they were actually stolen. This limitation excludes the possibility of a criminal case for trade secrets in the form of "show-how" or other confidential knowledge that has not been reduced to physical form.[128]

While India lacks specific trade secret protection laws, companies doing business in India can benefit from various remedies if they can prove trade secret misappropriation under civil or criminal law. In criminal cases, as in civil cases, Indian courts require proof of actual damage to sustain liability. The remedies available in Indian trade secret actions include various forms of injunctions, seizure orders, and compensatory damages.[129]

1. Common law protection
Despite the lack of statutory protection, Indian courts recognize trade secrets in certain circumstances. In doing so, they adopt the UTSA

---

[125] U.S. Chamber of Commerce, *Charting the Course–The GIPC International IP Index, 2nd Edition*, GLOBAL INTELLECTUAL PROPERTY CENTER (Jan. 28, 2014), http://www.theglobalipcenter.com/charting-the-course-the-gipc-international-ip-index-2nd-edition/.

[126] Poorvi Chothani and Vidhi Agarwal, *Intellectual Property and Outsourcing to India*, 29 GPSOLO 68 (2012), *available at* http://www.americanbar.org/publications/gp_solo/2012/july_august/international_law_intellectual_property_outsourcing_india.html.

[127] Larry R. Wood et al., *Trade Secret Law and Protection in India*, 20 INTELL. PROP. & TECH. L.J. 25 (2008).

[128] Sahil Taneja and Samridh Bhardwaj, *The Viability of Trade Secret Protection*, INDIA: MANAGING THE IP LIFECYCLE 2013 16 (2013).

[129] Wood, *supra* note 127.

definition of "trade secrets" and Article 39(2) of TRIPS' definition of "undisclosed information."[130] Without statutory guidelines, Indian courts refer to traditional notions of equity and fair play. Because India is a common law jurisdiction, parties sometimes refer to cases from other countries including the United Kingdom. Indian common law also recognizes a "breach of confidence" tort which may be used where contract law does not apply.

Indian courts hesitate, however, to impose a duty of confidentiality on employees accused of trade secret misappropriation. In *American Express Bank Ltd. v. Puri*, for example, the plaintiff accused its former employee of disclosing confidential business information to a third party, and sought a permanent injunction prohibiting her from using that information or disclosing information about its clients.[131] The court refused to infer that all information provided to an employee is subject to an implied duty of confidentiality. Whether any such duty existed, the court noted, depended on four factors: (1) the nature of the employment; (2) the nature of the information; (3) whether the employer emphasized its confidential nature to the employee; and (4) whether the confidential information could be easily isolated from other information.

The *Puri* court found that no such duty existed. The former employee was not bound to protect confidential information after her employment ended.[132]

Indian courts have also followed the "springboard doctrine" to determine fault in several trade secret cases. This doctrine, used extensively in the United Kingdom and stemming from principles of equity, holds that courts should restrain people who come to possess confidential information and unlawfully use it as a "springboard" for economic or commercial gain, to the rightful owner's detriment.[133] In such cases, the court may grant an injunction that deprives the wrongdoer of the benefits of such unlawful acts, a measure known as "springboard relief."[134]

Springboard relief is not confined to cases of breach of confidence, but can also apply in cases of breaches of contractual and fiduciary duty.[135] The doctrine "flows from a wider principle that the court may grant an injunction to deprive a wrongdoer of the unlawful advantage derived

---

[130]   Taneja and Bhardwaj, *supra* note 128, at 13.
[131]   (2006) III L.L.J. (Delhi H.C.) 540 (May 24, 2006).
[132]   *Ibid.*
[133]   Taneja and Bhardwaj, *supra* note 128, at 14.
[134]   QBE Management Services (UK) Ltd. v. Dymoke, [2012] EWHC 80 (QB) Case No. HQ11X03120, para. 240–241.
[135]   *Ibid.* at para. 241.

from his wrongdoing."[136] That said, springboard relief is limited to cases where monetary relief is inadequate to provide relief for the misappropriation.[137] It must also be sought when the wrongdoer is still enjoying an unlawful advantage, which may be difficult to prove in practice.[138]

2. Contract law protection

Indian courts also recognize the validity of explicit contractual provisions designed to protect trade secrets, subject to key limitations. In *V.V. Sivaram and Ors v. Foseco India Ltd.*, for example, a manufacturer accused two former employees of stealing trade secrets and leaving to form a competing company that designed and sold a product much like the manufacturer's own design.[139] An appellate court affirmed that the former employees were bound by confidentiality and non-compete provisions in their employment contracts.[140] In doing so, it rejected the argument that Indian contract law prohibited the manufacturer from imposing duties on them beyond the term of their employment.[141] The *Puri* court had explained that confidentiality provisions can be upheld past the term of employment if the employee's unauthorized disclosure during employment was "a clear breach of the duty of good faith."[142]

One drawback of using contract law to protect trade secrets is the limitation of privity. The protection only extends to the parties themselves and requires a relatively detailed description of the trade secrets at issue, a potential disclosure hazard that creates problems of its own. Nor does it necessarily provide a remedy before or after the term of the contract, absent the kind of good faith obligations described in *Puri*. The drawbacks of contract law are obvious from this hypothetical. Suppose a U.S. company hires an Indian company to manufacture a certain kind of product, and reduces its trade secrets to writing in the contract. If the Indian company uses a subcontractor, however, the U.S. company has no direct legal recourse if the subcontractor discloses the U.S. company's trade secrets. The U.S. entity can sue the original Indian company under

---

[136]   *Ibid.*
[137]   *Ibid.* at para. 245.
[138]   *Ibid.* at para. 243.
[139]   2006 (1) Kar. L.J. 386.
[140]   *Ibid.*
[141]   *Ibid. See also* Brahmaputra Tea Co. Ltd. v. Scarth, I.L.R. 11 Cal. 545 (upholding non-compete provision during term of employment); Niranjan Shankar Golikari v. Century Spinning & Mfg. Co. Ltd., A.I.R. 1967SC1098 (upholding non-compete provision during five-year contract term).
[142]   *See Puri*, 2006 (1) Kar. L.J. 386.

the terms of its contract, but that litigation does not stem the flow of confidential information from the subcontractor to the wider world.

Another limitation is that Indian courts enforce contracts on a case-by-case basis, and it can be hard even for Indian lawyers to predict which employment contracts will withstand judicial scrutiny. Under the Indian Contract Act, contracts are not enforceable to the extent that they restrain a person from exercising a "lawful profession, trade or business of any kind."[143] In *Sivaram* and related cases, the Indian court upheld certain contract terms despite challenges under the Indian Contract Law, but the terms upheld were relatively limited in time.

III. POTENTIAL IMPROVEMENTS TO GLOBAL TRADE SECRET PROTECTION

Scholars have suggested several approaches to improving the global protection of trade secrets. The best of these will change the cost-benefit analysis for any entity that is engaged in trade secret misappropriation. If such theft has strongly negative consequences, ones that are severe enough to outweigh the commercial advantage provided by stealing another firm's intellectual property, the behavior and attitudes that underlie that theft will change. The effectiveness of the chosen remedies therefore depends on how strong their deterrent effect is likely to be, rather than on the capacity to redress past theft.

The viability of some suggestions is limited by legal realities in the United States, including due process concerns. The IP Commission's recommendations, for example, include empowering the Secretary of Commerce to deny the use of the U.S. banking system to foreign companies that steal U.S. trade secrets.[144] Such a measure would likely raise concerns about the propriety of imposing such a restriction on foreign companies, and could result in a backlash against the flow of U.S. funds to overseas institutions. It may also be difficult to implement the Commission's recommendation that the Securities and Exchange Commission investigate whether listed companies should disclose the "knowing, systematic or widespread use" of stolen trade secrets in its financial statements. Such a requirement would raise a host of issues, including the extent to which theft by related entities must be disclosed.

---

[143] Indian Contract Act of 1872 § 27, No. 9 of 1872, *available at* http://districtcourtallahabad.up.nic.in/articles/ICAct.pdf.

[144] IP Commission Report, *supra* note 3, at 66.

Time will be of the essence in any remedy. No matter what improvements are made to legal scope and jurisdiction, the normal pace of U.S. litigation may be too slow to offer effective protection for companies suffering from trade secret loss.[145] This is especially so for start-up companies whose value often derives from the ownership of relatively little confidential business information. Once that information has been misappropriated, the company's viability is called into question.

A. Improve U.S. Legal Remedies

There are several concrete steps that the United States might take to bolster trade secret protection. For example, in the wake of the *Tian Rui* decision, some observers have recommended that Section 337 would be even more useful to U.S. companies if such actions could be brought and resolved more quickly. Another potential reform of Section 337 would be to increase the United States' ability to impound imports suspected of benefitting from stolen trade secrets. Under this scheme, the suspect goods could be held until the court could determine that the importing company did not misappropriate trade secrets.[146]

Another set of reforms stems from the passage of more extensive federal trade secret laws. While the Theft of Trade Secrets Clarification Act and the Penalty Enhancement Act extended federal protection beyond the EEA, the number of bills introduced in 2013 and 2014 underscores the recognition that there is still room for improvement. There is also widespread support for EEA amendments that would allow a private right of action for trade secret misappropriation.[147]

The effectiveness of any federal remedy will be limited, however, until the United States reforms its civil and criminal procedure laws. In many cases, hauling foreign entities accused of stealing U.S. trade secrets into U.S. courts has proven insurmountably difficult because of procedural rules. Amending civil and criminal procedure rules to make service on foreign entities more feasible should be high on the priority list of any coordinated effort to improve trade secret protection.

---

[145] *Ibid.* at 3.
[146] *Ibid.* at 65.
[147] *Ibid.* at 73.

B. Strengthen Diplomatic Efforts

Trade negotiations and diplomatic dialogues offer another way to strengthen transnational trade secret protection.[148] While the United States has influence with its trading partners, its ability to persuade other countries to respect national security may have waned. The recent disclosures that the NSA has conducted its own espionage program on certain foreign governments and leaders may hurt diplomatic efforts to persuade other countries to limit their economic espionage programs.[149] In any event, bolstering trade secret protection globally is a worthwhile objective for its diplomatic efforts.

1. Centralize coordination of administrative actions

One limitation of the U.S. strategy is that the responsibility for carrying out that strategy is not centralized effectively. While there is a U.S. Intellectual Property Coordinator, a position established in 2008, it is located in the Office of Management and Budget. Coordinating U.S. policy and enforcement of intellectual property rights, including trade secrets, requires collaboration with a wide range of government agencies, Congress and the private sector. The IP Commission Report recommended that a cabinet-level official, such as the Assistant to the President for National Security Affairs, take on this responsibility.[150]

2. Capitalize on Special 301 Report

The importance of the Special 301 Report in combating trade secret misappropriation may be growing, at least in the eyes of the Administration. In 2013, for the first time, the Office of the U.S. Trade Representative dedicated a special section of the Special 301 Report to trade secret misappropriation and noted that it "reflects increased emphasis on the need to protect trade secrets."[151]

---

[148] Covington and Burling, LLP, *Economic Espionage and Trade Secret Misappropriation: An Overview of the Legal Landscape and Policy Responses* 17 (2013), http://homelandsecurity.gwu.edu/sites/homelandsecurity.gwu.edu/files/downloads/Covington_SpecialIssueBrief.pdf.

[149] Ken Dilanian, *A Spy World Reshaped by Edward Snowden*, LOS ANGELES TIMES (Dec. 22, 2013), http://articles.latimes.com/2013/dec/22/world/la-fg-nsa-snowden-20131222.

[150] IP Commission Report, *supra* note 3, at 62–63.

[151] OFFICE OF THE UNITED STATES TRADE REPRESENTATIVE, 2013 SPECIAL 301 REPORT 13 (2013), *available at* http://www.ustr.gov/sites/default/files/05012013%202013%20Special%20301%20Report.pdf.

While the United States has highlighted trade secret misappropriation in the most recent Special 301 Report, some believe that calling out offenders in this way has had little real impact.[152] Although the Trade Act of 1974 allows the U.S. Trade Representative to designate countries with a particularly egregious record of disregard for intellectual property rights as Priority Foreign Countries (PFCs), which could ultimately lead to WTO litigation and the imposition of tariffs, no such WTO actions have been taken to date.[153] Even in the 2013 Special 301 Report, only Ukraine rose to the level of a PFC, while China and India were put in the lower "Priority Watch List" category.[154]

3. Increase penalties for foreign trade secret misappropriators

The Defense Secretary and Secretary of State have raised the issue of trade secret misappropriation repeatedly with their Chinese counterparts. These measures, however, have been criticized for their lack of force and specificity. The director of the Atlantic Council's Cyber Statecraft Initiative, for example, urged the government to take more concrete steps such as denying visas to officials from foreign companies that steal U.S. companies' trade secrets and making those companies ineligible for U.S. government contracts.[155]

C. Define More Specific Treaty-Based Solutions

One set of potential solutions focuses on bringing more clarity and specificity to the protection of trade secrets through bilateral and multilateral agreements, beginning with a possible amendment to the intellectual property treaty that already has the most signatories.

1. Amend the TRIPS agreement

Perhaps the most powerful international treaty on intellectual property is TRIPS. TRIPS operates within the framework of the WTO, and all WTO

---

[152] IP Commission Report, *supra* note 3, at 1 and 20–21 ("The American response to date of hectoring governments … has been utterly inadequate to deal with the problem.").

[153] David P. Fidler, *Economic Cyber Espionage and International Law: Controversies Involving Government Acquisition of Trade Secrets through Cyber Technologies*, 17 AM. SOC'Y OF INT'L LAW (Mar. 20, 2013), http://www.asil.org/insights/volume/17/issue/10/economic-cyber-espionage-and-international-law-controversies-involving-government-acquisition-of-trade-secrets-through-cyber-technologies.

[154] 2013 SPECIAL 301 REPORT, *supra* note 151, at 6.

[155] Nakashima, *supra* note 34.

members, of which there are currently over 150, must abide by it. The TRIPS agreement incorporates several previous international treaties on intellectual property such as the Berne Convention, Paris Convention, and Rome Convention, supplementing them with certain provisions designed to address technological advances such as computer programs.[156] It establishes a minimum level of protection for several types of intellectual property, including the categories, exceptions, and enforcement require-ments that all signatories must protect.[157] A key TRIPS provision is its requirement that signatories grant each other both "national treatment" (treating foreigners and nationals equally) and "most-favored-nation treatment" (treating nationals of all WTO trading partners equally) with regard to intellectual property protection.[158]

While Article 39 of TRIPS creates minimum standards for the protec-tion of "undisclosed information," it does not define trade secrets with the kind of specificity that appears in many other bodies of law.[159] Nor does it specifically address the issues of cyber-espionage and cloud-based computing that have become commonplace since its adoption in 1994, during the Internet's infancy. It also lacks specific requirements to punish the incentivizing of trade secret misappropriation, as opposed to the theft itself, which creates a significant liability gap for entities that sponsor or otherwise encourage theft by their affiliates. The OECD's 2014 report on the ways in which WTO members already protect trade secrets provides additional insight into how TRIPS could be amended successfully. If most countries already allow the defense of reverse engineering, as the report suggests, then writing that requirement into TRIPS should not cause concern for those already compliant. Non-compliant countries, however, would have additional incentive to reform their laws to incor-porate the additional terms.[160]

Amending TRIPS to include more specific and consistent definitions of what constitutes a trade secret, in line with proposed EU rules and US trade secret definitions, would reduce uncertainties and disparities among various legal regimes. Its potential effectiveness is limited, however, in at

---

[156] Agreement on Trade-Related Aspects of Intellectual Property Rights, Annex 1C of the Marrakesh Agreement Establishing the World Trade Organ-ization, Apr. 15, 1994, 1867 U.N.T.S. 154., art. 10, 25, 27 [hereinafter TRIPS].

[157] *Intellectual Property: Protection and Enforcement*, WORLD TRADE ORGANIZATION, *available at* http://bit.ly/1uPKDrC (last visited Jul. 16, 2014).

[158] *Ibid.*

[159] TRIPS, *supra* note 156, at Art. 39.

[160] Russian law, for example, does not recognize the defense of reverse engineering. OECD Trade Policy Paper, *supra* note 27, at 162.

least two significant ways. First, the remedies it seeks to ensure in theory do not always translate into effective protection in practice, due to procedural obstacles and other practical difficulties in other countries. For example, when China entered the WTO in 2001, it did so under the condition that it would bring its domestic laws in line with TRIPS.[161] China may have TRIPS-compliant laws on its books, but the lack of pre-trial discovery in civil cases combined with Chinese courts' strong preference for original documentary evidence makes the prosecution of civil trade secret cases very difficult.[162]

A second limitation in amending TRIPS is that it does not reach trade secret misappropriation by one member against another. TRIPS requires WTO members to establish certain minimum intellectual property protections within their borders, but does not require those members to observe the limitations with regard to other countries.

2. Improve usage of WTO resolution procedures

Whether any amendment to TRIPS is worth the effort depends largely on the extent to which noncompliance with its terms can be remedied. The WTO's dispute resolution process has been criticized for its lack of effectiveness in resolving trade secret misappropriation concerns. For example, the WTO offers no straightforward way of addressing one country's economic espionage against the private industry of another. No such claim has yet been brought through the WTO. Even if a WTO member could bring such a claim, it is not clear that evidence collected by a private-sector entity, such as Mandiant, would be sufficient to support it.[163]

The WTO resolution procedure has other limitations as well. One is the time required to reach a conclusion. As with any judicial system, as noted above, timeliness is a critical issue. The rapid pace of technological development, especially for early stage companies, may render any dispute resolution procedure that takes months or longer to conclude essentially useless in remedying trade secret misappropriation. Its efficacy as a means of discouraging future trade secret protection, however, has yet to be seen.

---

[161] *See WTO Successfully Concludes Negotiations on China's Entry* (Sept. 17, 2001), WORLD TRADE ORGANIZATION, *available at* http://bit.ly/X9HOWZ.

[162] *See, e.g.,* OECD Trade Policy Paper, *supra* note 27, at 21, 231.

[163] *See* Fidler, *supra* note 153.

3. Develop new treaties protecting trade secrets

Another means of strengthening global trade secret protection is the inclusion of minimum safeguards in future treaties. While some have suggested the adoption of a new international treaty specifically addressing trade secret protection, it is not clear that such an extreme undertaking is necessary to effect better trade secret security.[164] As noted above,[165] the United States is currently negotiating the T-TIP with the European Union. This treaty provides another opportunity for both the United States and the European Union to reaffirm the importance of protecting trade secrets as an integral aspect of their commitment to trade facilitation.

Similarly, the final terms of the TPPA will have a significant impact on trade in the Pacific Rim. Although the draft terms of the TPPA have not been disclosed to the public, the negotiations have been going on since 2010 and certain proposals have been leaked.[166] One leaked version of the Intellectual Property Chapter, however, contained terms that would strengthen protections for trade secrets. These terms, proposed by the United States, Mexico, Canada, New Zealand and Japan, would require signatories to criminalize the misappropriation or disclosure, "wilfully and without authority, of trade secrets relating to a product in national or international commerce for purposes of commercial advantage or financial gain, and with the intent to injure the owner of such trade secrets." These terms have been opposed by Australia, Singapore, Malaysia, Peru, Vietnam, Chile and Brunei.[167] Given the negotiation's secrecy and open-ended schedule, it is impossible to know how and when this dispute will be resolved.

Recent negotiations between China and the United States raise the issue of whether Bilateral Investment Treaties (BITs) might also be used

---

[164]   Covington and Burling, *supra* note 148, at 17.

[165]   *See* Hakim, *supra* note 83.

[166]   Joseph E. Stiglitz, *On the Wrong Side of Globalization*, N.Y. TIMES (Mar. 15, 2014, 5:06 PM), http://opinionator.blogs.nytimes.com/2014/03/15/on-the-wrong-side-of-globalization/. This lack of disclosure has, in some ways, intensified concerns about the likely impact of the TPP in some quarters. *See, e.g.*, *Trans-Pacific Partnership Agreement*, ELECTRONIC FRONTIER FOUNDATION, https://www.eff.org/issues/tpp (last visited Mar. 28, 2014).

[167]   Joel Smith & Kristin Stammer, I*ncreased Protection for Trade Secrets Under the Trans-Pacific Partnership and in Europe*, (Jan. 23, 2014), http://www.herbertsmithfreehills.com/insights/legal-briefings/increased-protection-for-trade-secrets-under-the-trans-pacific-partnership-and-in-europe.

to enhance the protection of trade secrets.[168] BITs give investors a mechanism to pursue international arbitration against a foreign government as well as improved market access and protections from arbitrary or discriminatory treatment. The U.S.-China negotiations present a unique opportunity for improving the protection of trade secrets, especially in light of U.S. companies' focus on China as a source of concern about data security.[169]

IV. CONCLUSION

Recent changes in how businesses operate, especially the increased global flow of employees, have made trade secret misappropriation easier and more profitable than ever. While companies benefit from many technological developments, including the inexorable shift of business from the internet to the cloud and the increasing mobility of employees along with their devices, they also suffer tremendous financial losses from the trade secret misappropriation that such developments facilitate. It is neither possible nor desirable to stop the movement of employees from one country to another, but it is vital to stop the problem of trade secret appropriation that so often accompanies that movement.

Although there is no quick fix to the problem of transnational trade secret loss, there is also no lack of attention to the problem. The wide range of diplomatic and treaty-based solutions emerging from political and scholarly discussions attests to the importance of this issue. In order to be effective, these solutions must take into account both the significant differences to trade secret protection from country to country, including differences in both the doctrinal and practical approaches to the issue, and the common need for protection of trade secrets as commonly defined. Adopting these solutions will be critical to strengthening and securing the global economy in coming decades.

---

[168] *See, e.g.,* Annie Lowrey, *U.S. and China to Discuss Investment Treaty, but Cybersecurity Is a Concern,* N.Y. TIMES (July 11, 2013), http://www.nytimes.com/2013/07/12/world/asia/us-and-china-to-discuss-investment-treaty-but-cybersecurity-is-a-concern.html; Chen Weihua, *US, China Hopeful of BIT After Talks Reignited,* CHINA DAILY (July 13, 2013), http://www.chinadaily.com.cn/cndy/2013-07/13/content_16770417.htm; *US Presses China to Stop Growing Trade secret misappropriation,* REUTERS (May 1, 2013), http://www.cnbc.com/id/100697434.

[169] Covington and Burling, *supra* note 148, at 18.

BIBLIOGRAPHY

Statutes and Codes

The Computer Fraud and Abuse Act, 18 U.S.C. § 1030 (2008).
The Defend Trade Secrets Act, S. 2267, 113th Cong. (2014).
Deter Cyber Theft Act, S. 884, 113th Cong. (2013).
Digital Millennium Copyright Act, H.R. 2281, 113th Cong. (2013).
Economic Espionage Act of 1996, 18 U.S.C. §1831-1837 (2012).
Foreign and Economic Espionage Penalty Enhancement Act of 2012, Pub. L. No. 112-269, 126 Stat. 2442 (2013).
Future of American Innovation and Research (FAIR) Act, S.1770, 113th Cong. § (3)(a) (2013).
Indian Contract Act of 1872 § 27, No. 9 of 1872, *available at* http://district courtallahabad.up.nic.in/articles/ICAct.pdf.
Private Right of Action Against Theft of Trade Secrets Act, H.R. 2466, 113th Cong. (2013).
Protecting American Trade Secrets and Innovation Act of 2012, S. 3389, 112th Cong. (2012).
Theft of Trade Secrets Clarification Act of 2012, Pub. L. No. 112-236, 126 Stat. 1627 (2012).
U.S Tariff Act of 1930, 19 U.S.C. §1337 (2004).

Cases

American Express Bank Ltd. v. Ms. Priya Puri (2006) III L.L.J. (Delhi H.C.) 540 (May 24, 2006).
Brahmaputra Tea Co. Ltd. v. Scarth, I.L.R. 11 Cal. 545.
E.I. DuPont De Nemours and Co. v Kolon Indus., Inc., 286 F.R.D. 288 (E.D. Va. Oct. 5, 2012).
Niranjan Shankar Golikari v. Century Spinning & Mfg. Co. Ltd., A.I.R. 1967SC1098.
Puri, 2006 (1) Kar. L.J. 386.
QBE Management Services (UK) Ltd. v. Dymoke, [2012] EWHC 80 (QB) Case No. HQ11X03120.
TianRui Group Co, Ltd. v. International Trade Commission, 661 F.3d 1322 (Fed. Cir. 2011).
United States v. Aleynikov, 676 F.3d 71 (2d. Cir. 2012).
United States v. Kolon Indus, Inc., 926 F. Supp. 2d 794 (E.D. Va. Feb. 22, 2013).
United States v. Pangang Group Co., 879 F. Supp. 2d 1052 (N.D.Cal., Jul. 23, 2012).
Indictment, United States v. Sinovel Wind Group Co., Ltd., No. 13 CR 84 BBC (W.D. Wis. filed June 27, 2013).
Mem. of Specially-Appearing Defendant Sinovel Wind Group Co., Ltd. in Support of Mot. to Quash Service at 4, United States. v. Sinovel Wind Group Co., Ltd. No. 3:13-cr-84-bbc (W. D. Wi. filed Aug. 16, 2013), *available at* http://s3.amazonaws. com/cdn.orrick.com/files/Trade-Secret-Blog-Sep25-Sinovel-Motion-to-Quash.pdf.

Secondary Sources

Agreement on Trade-Related Aspects of Intellectual Property Rights, *available at,* http://bit.ly/1t1KeDP.

Agreement on Trade-Related Aspects of Intellectual Property Rights, Annex 1C of the Marrakesh Agreement Establishing the World Trade Organization, Apr. 15, 1994, 1867 U.N.T.S. 154., art. 10, 25, 27 [hereinafter TRIPS].

Almeling , David S. et al., *A Statistical Analysis of Trade Secret Litigation in Federal Courts*, 45 GONZ. L. REV. 291 (2009).

Anti Unfair Competition Law of the People's Republic of China, *available at* http://en.chinacourt.org/public/detail.php?id=3306.

APT1: Exposing One of China's Cyber Espionage Units, MANDIANT, http://intelreport.mandiant.com/Mandiant_APT1_Report.pdf (last visited Jul. 16, 2014).

Beyer, Justin K., *AMSC/Sinovel Industrial Espionage Thriller Takes a Procedural Detour, Threatening U.S. Criminal Prosecution,* tradesecretslaw.com, Sept. 9, 2013.

Certain Electric Fireplaces, Components Thereof, Manuals for Same, Manufacturing or Relating to Same and Products Containing Same, Inv. No. 337-TA-791 (2012), *noticed in* 77 Fed. Reg. 2757 (Jan. 19, 2012) (Shaw, J.).

Certain Paper Shredders, Processes for Manufacturing or Related to Same, Inv. No. 337-TA-863 (2013), *noticed in* 78 Fed. Reg. 5496 (Jan. 25, 2013) (Pender, J.).

Certain Robotic Toys and Components Thereof, Inv. No. 337-TA-869 (2013), *noticed in* 78 Fed. Reg. 9740 (Feb. 5, 2013) (Bullock, C.J.)

Certain Rubber Resins and Processes for Manufacturing Same, Inv. No. 337-TA-849 (2012), *noticed in* 77 Fed. Reg. 38,083 (June 26, 2012) (Roger, J.).

Chothani, Poorvi and Vidhi Agarwal, *Intellectual Property and Outsourcing to India*, 29 GPSOLO 68 (2012), *available at* http://www.americanbar.org/publications/gp_solo/2012/july_august/international_law_intellectual_property_outsourcing_india.html.

The Commission on the Theft of American Intellectual Property, *The IP Commission Report: The Report of the Commission on the Theft of American Intellectual Property*, THE IP COMMISSION 26–27 (May 2013), http://www.ipcommission.org/report/IP_Commission_Report_052213.pdf.

Covington & Burling, LLP, *Economic Espionage and Trade secret misappropriation: An Overview of the Legal Landscape and Policy Responses* 17 (2013), http://home landsecurity.gwu.edu/sites/homelandsecurity.gwu.edu/files/downloads/Covington_SpecialIssueBrief.pdf.

Cowie, Paul, Bram Hanono and Dorna Moini, *Social Media: Protecting Trade Secrets and Proprietary Information*, 12 EMPLOYMENT & LABOR RELATIONS LAW 1 (2014), *available at* http://www.jdsupra.com/legalnews/social-media-protecting-trade-secrets-a-98388/.

Defense Security Service, *Administration Strategy on Mitigating the Theft of U.S. Trade Secrets*, WHITE HOUSE (Feb. 2013), http://www.whitehouse.gov/sites/default/files/omb/IPEC/admin_strategy_on_mitigating_the_theft_of_u.s._trade_secrets.pdf.

Dep't of Def., *Department of Defense Strategy for Operating in Cyberspace*, UNITED STATES DEPARTMENT OF DEFENSE 4 (July 2011), http://www.defense.gov/news/d20110714cyber.pdf.

DiDio, Laura, *Careless, Reckless Staff are Corporate Security's Biggest Threat*, E-COMMERCE TIMES (Feb. 7, 2014, 8:00 AM), http://www.ecommercetimes.com/story/79930.html.

Dilanian, Ken, *A Spy World Reshaped by Edward Snowden*, LOS ANGELES TIMES (Dec. 22, 2013), http://articles.latimes.com/2013/dec/22/world/la-fg-nsa-snowden-20131222.

Donahue, Bill, *In New Year, Congress Has Full Plate of Trade Secret Bills*, LAW360 (Jan. 8, 2014, 6:56 PM), http://www.law360.com/articles/499735/in-new-year-congress-has-full-plate-of-trade-secret-bills.

Doom, Justin, *China Supreme Court Ruling Favors AMSC in Two Sinovel Suits*, BLOOMBERG (Feb. 19, 2014, 4:09 PM), http://www.bloomberg.com/news/2014-02-19/china-supreme-court-ruling-favors-amsc-in-two-sinovel-suits-1-.html.

Doyle, Charles, STEALING TRADE SECRETS AND ECONOMIC ESPIONAGE: AN OVERVIEW OF 18 U.S.C. 1831 AND 1832 (2013), available at http://fas.org/sgp/crs/secrecy/R42681.pdf.

European Commission, *Proposal for a Directive of the European Parliament and of the Council on the Protection of Undisclosed Know-How and Business Information (Trade Secrets) Against Their Unlawful Acquisition, Use and Disclosure* (August 13, 2013), *available at* http://bit.ly/1uBUnrt.

European Commission, *Proposal for a Directive of the European Parliament and of the Council on the Protection of Undisclosed Know-how and Business Information (Trade Secrets) Against Their Unlawful Acquisition, Use and Disclosure* (Nov. 28, 2013), *available at* http://ec.europa.eu/internal_market/iprenforcement/docs/trade-secrets/131128_proposal_en.pdf.

FED.R.CRIM.PRO. 4(C)(3)(c).

Feldman, Steven E. and Sherry L. Rollo, *Extraterritorial Protection of Trade Secret Rights in China: Do Section 337 Actions at the ITC Really Prevent Trade secret misappropriation Abroad?*, 11 J. MARSHALL REV. INTELL. PROP. L. 523 (2012).

Fidler, David P., *Economic Cyber Espionage and International Law: Controversies Involving Government Acquisition of Trade Secrets through Cyber Technologies*, 17 AM. SOC'Y OF INT'L LAW (Mar. 20, 2013), http://www.asil.org/insights/volume/17/issue/10/economic-cyber-espionage-and-international-law-controversies-involving-government-acquisition-of-trade-secrets-through-cyber-technologies.

Flechsig, Natalie, *Trade Secret Enforcement After TianRui: Fighting Misappropriation Through the ITC*, 28 BERKELEY TECH. L.J. 449 (2013).

Green, Sarah, *Do Millennials Believe in Data Security?* HARV. BUS. REV. BLOG (Feb. 18, 2014, 9:00 AM), http://blogs.hbr.org/2014/02/do-millennials-believe-in-data-security/

Gullo, Karen, *California Man Guilty of Stealing DuPont Trade Secrets*, BLOOMBERG-.COM, (March 5, 2014), http://www.bloomberg.com/news/2014-03-05/California-man-guilty-of-stealing-dupont-trade-secrets.html.

Gullo, Karen and Tom Schoenberg, *Pangang and Kolon, Like Edward Snowden, Elude U.S. Charge*, BLOOMBERG (July 18, 2013, 2:20 PM), http://www.bloomberg.com/news/2013-07-18/old-mail-rule-helps-pangang-kolon-elude-u-s-charges.html.

Hakim, Danny, *Europe Moves to Keep Its Corporate Trade Data Secret*, N.Y. TIMES (Nov, 14, 2013), http://www.nytimes.com/2013/11/15/business/international/europe-moves-to-keep-its-corporate-trade-data-secret.html.

Halligan, R. Mark and Richard F. Weyand, *The Sorry State of Trade Secret Protection*, THE TRADE SECRET OFF., INC. (Aug. 2001), http://www.thetso.com/Info/sorry.html.

In the Matter of Certain Processes for the Manufacture of Skinless Sausage Casings and Resulting Product, Inv. No. 337-TA-148/169 (1984), *available at* http://www.usitc.gov/publications/337/pub1624.pdf.

Intellectual Property: Protection and Enforcement, WORLD TRADE ORGANIZATION, *available at* http://bit.ly/1uPKDrC (last visited Jul. 16, 2014).

Jurrons, Robert Damien, *Fool Me Once: U.S. v. Aleynikov and the Theft of Trade Secrets Clarification Act of 2012*, 28 BERKELEY TECH. L.J. 833 (2014).

Kim, Chang-Ran and Miyoung Kim, *Toshiba, SanDisk Sue Hynix Over Suspected Flash Memory Technology Leak*, REUTERS (Mar. 13, 2014, 10:40 PM), *available at* http://reut.rs/1oSjRLo

Klayman, Ben, Ex-Ford engineer sentenced for trade secrets theft, REUTERS.COM, April 13, 2011 9:39 am, *available at* http://reut.rs/1AQQA9v

Kuntz, Robin L., *How Not to Catch a Thief: Why the Economic Espionage Act Fails to Protect American Trade Secrets*, 28 BERKELEY TECH. L.J. 901 (2013).

Library of Congress, *Protection of Trade Secrets: China*, LIBRARY OF CONGRESS (Feb. 28, 2014), www.loc.gov/law/help/tradesecrets/china.php.

Lowrey, Annie, *U.S. and China to Discuss Investment Treaty, but Cybersecurity Is a Concern*, N.Y. TIMES (July 11, 2013), http://www.nytimes.com/2013/07/12/world/asia/us-and-china-to-discuss-investment-treaty-but-cybersecurity-is-a-concern.html

Managing Knowhow and Trade Secrets in Global Value Chains and the International Transfer of Technology, Panel at the World Trade Organization Public Forum 2013 (Workshop 1) (Oct. 1, 2013), *available at* http://bit.ly/1y88wAA

MAROULIS, VICTORIA F., CHINA'S EVOLVING IP REGIME AND AVENUES OF ENFORCE-MENT (2013), *available at* 2013 WL 4192387.

Minott, Nathaniel, *The Economic Espionage Act: Is the Law All Bark and No Bite?* 20 INFO. & COMM. TECH. L. 201 (2011).

Nakashima, Ellen, *Obama Orders Voluntary Security Standards for Critical Industries' Computer Networks*, WASHINGTON POST (Feb. 12, 2013), http://wapo.st/1oSnoJO.

Nakashima, Ellen, *U.S. Launches Effort to Stem Trade-Secret Theft*, WASHINGTON POST (Feb. 20, 2013), *available at* http://wapo.st/1phlfq5.

Nan, Hao, *Court Hands Down Milestone Ruling on Trade Secrets*, CHINA DAILY (Aug. 14, 2013, 7:39 AM), http://usa.chinadaily.com.cn/epaper/2013-08/14/content_16893667.htm.

Nan, Hao, *U.S. Trade Commission: No Infringement by Sino Legend*, CHINA DAILY (Feb. 19, 2014, 8:53 AM), http://www.chinadaily.com.cn/kindle/2014-02/19/content_17291668.htm.

No End In Sight, ECONOMIST (Feb. 25, 2014, 2:43 PM), http://www.economist.com/blogs/banyan/2014/02/trans-pacific-partnership-0.

OFFICE OF THE UNITED STATES TRADE REPRESENTATIVE, 24TH U.S.-CHINA JOINT COMMISSION ON COMMERCE AND TRADE FACT SHEET, *available at* http://www.ustr.gov/about-us/press-office/fact-sheets/2013/December/JCCT-outcomes.

OFFICE OF THE UNITED STATES TRADE REPRESENTATIVE, 2013 SPECIAL 301 REPORT 13 (2013), *available at* http://www.ustr.gov/sites/default/files/05012013%202013%20Special%20301%20Report.pdf.

Ong, Ryan, *Trade Secret Enforcement in China: Options and Obstacles*, CHINA BUSINESS REVIEW (Jan. 1, 2013), http://www.chinabusinessreview.com/trade-secret-enforcement-in-china-options-and-obstacles/.

Orozco, David, *Amending the Economic Espionage Act to Require the Disclosure of National Security-Related Technology Thefts*, 62 CATH. U.L. REV. 877 (2013).

Orozco, David, *The Knowledge Police*, 43 HOFSTRA L. REV. 2 (2014).

Perlroth, Nicole, *Hackers in China Attacked The Times for Last 4 Months*, N.Y. TIMES (Jan. 30, 2013), *available at* http://nyti.ms/Xs8pyZ.

Protalinski, Emil, *NSA: Cybercrime is 'The Greatest Transfer of Wealth in History'*, ZDNET (July 10, 2012, 12:13 PM), http://www.zdnet.com/nsa-cybercrime-is-the-greatest-transfer-of-wealth-in-history-7000000598/.

RESTATEMENT (FIRST) OF TORTS § 757 (1939).

Sachdev, Ameet, *Former Motorola engineer sentenced to 4 years in trade-secret case*, CHICAGOTRIBUNE.COM, (August 31, 2012), http://articles.chicagotribune.com/2012-08-31/business/ct-biz-0830-moto-theft–20120831_1_trade-secret-case-hanjuan-jin-trade-secrets.

Schultz, Mark F. and Douglas C. Lippoldt, *Approaches to Protection of Undisclosed Information (Trade Secrets)* (OECD Trade Policy Papers, No. 162, 2014), *available at* http://www.oecd.org/officialdocuments/publicdisplaydocumentpdf/?cote=TAD/TC/WP(2013)21/FINAL&docLanguage=En- 22 Jan 2014

Sino Legend Prevails in Legal Challenge; Court Rejects SI Group Trade Secret Arguments, SINO LEGEND (June 17, 2013, 9:24 AM), http://www.sinolegend.com/show.asp?articleid=269.

Smith, Joel and Kristin Stammer, *Increased Protection for Trade Secrets Under the Trans-Pacific Partnership and in Europe*, (Jan. 23, 2014), http://www.herbertsmithfreehills.com/insights/legal-briefings/increased-protection-for-trade-secrets-under-the-trans-pacific-partnership-and-in-europe.

Stiglitz, Joseph E., *On the Wrong Side of Globalization*, N.Y. TIMES (Mar. 15, 2014, 5:06 PM), http://opinionator.blogs.nytimes.com/2014/03/15/on-the-wrong-side-of-globalization/.

Study on Trade Secrets and Confidential Business Information in the Internal Market, EUROPEAN COMMISSION 2 (Apr. 2013), http://ec.europa.eu/internal_market/iprenforcement/docs/trade-secrets/130711_final-study_en.pdf (hereinafter 2013 EC Trade Secrets Study).

Taneja, Sahil and Samridh Bhardwaj, *The Viability of Trade Secret Protection,* INDIA: MANAGING THE IP LIFECYCLE 2013 16 (2013).

Trans-Pacific Partnership Agreement, ELECTRONIC FRONTIER FOUNDATION, https://www.eff.org/issues/tpp (last visited Mar. 28, 2014).

Trying Again! Bolstering Federal Protection of Trade Secrets: Enacting a Companion Civil Right of Action to the Economic Espionage Act, THE KELLER LAW FIRM, LLC, http://thekellerlawfirm.com/trying-again-bolstering-federal-protection-of-trade-secrets-enacting-a-companion-civil-right-of-action-to-the-economic-espionage-act/.

Uniform Trade Secrets Act with 1985 Amendments, National Conference of Commissioners on Uniform State Laws, *available at* http://www.uniformlaws.org/shared/docs/trade%20secrets/utsa_final_85.pdf.

U.S. Chamber of Commerce, *Charting the Course–The GIPC International IP Index, 2nd Edition*, GLOBAL INTELLECTUAL PROPERTY CENTER (Jan. 28, 2014), http://www.theglobalipcenter.com/charting-the-course-the-gipc-international-ip-index-2nd-edition/.

U.S. CHAMBER OF COMMERCE, THE CASE FOR ENHANCED PROTECTION OF TRADE SECRETS IN THE TRANS-PACIFIC PARTNERSHIP AGREEMENT, *available at* https://www.uschamber.com/sites/default/files/legacy/international/files/Final%20TPP%20Trade%20Secrets%208_0.pdf.

US-China Business Council, *USCBC 2013 China Business Environment Survey Results: Tempered Optimism Continues amid Moderating Growth, Rising Costs, and Persistent Market Barriers*, *available at* http://www.uschina.org/sites/default/files/USCBC – 2013Member%20Survey_0.pdf (last visited Mar. 28, 2014).

United States International Trade Commission, Unfair Import Investigations Information System No. 337-TA-849, *available at* http://1.usa.gov/YMqQzA.

U.S. DEP'T OF COMMERCE INT'L TRADE ADMIN., PROTECTING YOUR INTELLECTUAL PROPERTY RIGHTS (IPR) IN CHINA: A PRACTICAL GUIDE FOR U.S. COMPANIES (Jan. 2003).

US Presses China to Stop Growing Trade secret misappropriation, REUTERS (May 1, 2013), http://www.cnbc.com/id/100697434.

Weihua, Chen, *US, China Hopeful of BIT After Talks Reignited*, CHINA DAILY (July 13, 2013), http://www.chinadaily.com.cn/cndy/2013-07/13/content_16770417.htm http://www.whitehouse.gov/the-press-office/2013/02/12/executive-order-improving-critical-infrastructure-cybersecurity.

Wine, Mark P. and Christina Von der Ahe, *UPDATE: Sur-Sur-Sur Reply Highlights the Short Arm of U.S. Law in Trade secret misappropriation*, ORRICK TRADE SECRETS WATCH (Sept. 24, 2013), http://blogs.orrick.com/trade-secrets-watch/2013/09/24/update-sur-sur-sur-reply-highlights-the-short-arm-of-u-s-law-in-trade-secret-theft/# more-447.

Wood, Larry R. et al., *Trade Secret Law and Protection in India*, 20 INTELL. PROP. & TECH. L.J. 25 (2008).

WTO Successfully Concludes Negotiations on China's Entry (Sept. 17, 2001), WORLD TRADE ORGANIZATION, *available at* http://bit.ly/X9HOWZ.

8.   Who owns employee works? Pitfalls in a globally distributed work environment

Susan J. Marsnik and Romain M. Lorentz*

Two seminal questions in any nation's copyright law are: (1) Who has the right to claim authorship and ownership of a copyrighted work; and (2) what is the scope of those interests? Determining who owns a copyrighted work can be complex. In general, the person who creates a copyrightable work is both the author and the first owner of the work.

However, under the United States work-for-hire doctrine,[1] if an employee creates a work within the scope of employment, the employer is automatically both the author and the owner of the work. Certain statutory categories of commissioned works are also considered works for hire and are subject to similar default authorship and ownership rules. If a work is commissioned from an independent contractor in a category other than a statutory category, the independent contractor remains both the author and the owner, unless the parties agree otherwise by contract.

This is not the legal framework throughout the world. Copyright laws vary substantially from one country to another with little harmonization of key issues such as authorship and ownership. In a multinational context, the differences impact ownership and control of the work in unexpected ways. Thus, for a multinational corporation with employees

---

*   The authors wish to thank Lynda Oswald and Marisa Pagnattaro for organizing the April 2014 colloquium, "Managing the Legal Nexus Among Intellectual Property, Employees, and Global Trade," sponsored by the University of Michigan, Ross School of Business and the University of Georgia, Terry College of Business, and for their efforts editing this work. The authors are grateful to the other participants for their rigorous reading and thoughtful recommendations. Very special thanks to Lee Reer Geffre, University of St. Thomas Law School class of 2015 for her indefatigable research assistance and editing.
[1]   U.S. Copyright Act, 17 U.S.C. § 101 (1976).

and contractors located across more than one country, determining who may claim authorship and who owns rights to the work becomes exponentially more complex.

Consider this scenario: A U.S.-based company assembles a team to develop a new smartphone game application (app) consisting of software, graphic art, and music. If every member of the team is a U.S.-based employee hired to complete such work, the company is automatically both the author and the owner of the resulting app. None of the individuals involved in the team has a right to claim authorship and none own any aspect of the copyright. If some of the U.S.-based team are independent contractors, the ownership issues in the commissioned work will depend on whether the piece was commissioned as part of the audiovisual app or separately acquired.[2] If the music was specially commissioned for the app and the contractor and company executed a work-for-hire agreement, the U.S. company is the author and owner of the application. But if the company purchased an existing piece of music from a non-employee musician, depending on the nature of the contract, the composer could be the co-author and co-owner of the app as a joint work. For the company to own the work outright, the composer would be required to execute an assignment. The company would never be the author of the music, although it could require the composer to waive the right to claim authorship.

As complex as these rules appear under U.S. law, if the team creating the app included individuals located in the United States, France and India, matters of authorship and ownership become even more complicated. Depending on the country in which a particular task is performed, the rights of the U.S. company and the individual hired to complete the work vary considerably. While the United States recognizes corporate authorship, most countries do not. Furthermore, many countries recognize personal rights separate from the economic rights in the work. These moral rights, which include the right to be recognized as the author of the work and the right to object to a distortion or mutilation of the work, cannot be alienated.

---

[2] Video and computer games as a whole and all the component parts of the game application, including the software that operates the program and any audiovisual displays it generates, constitute an audiovisual work for purposes of U.S. copyright law. *See* Deborah F. Buckman, Annotation, *Intellectual Property Rights in Video, Electronic, and Computer* Games, 7 A.L.R. Fed. 2d 269, § 4 (2005); Tyler T. Ochoa, *Who Owns an Avatar? Copyright, Creativity, and the Virtual World,* 14. VAND. J. ENT. & TECH. L. 959, 969 (2012).

Failing to understand and address these complexities prior to commissioning the copyrighted work can result in substantial economic impact, if a U.S.-based multinational wrongly assumes that other countries have authorship and ownership rules similar to those in the United States or that U.S. law will apply. Moreover, the conflict of laws rules governing which law will apply to determine authorship, ownership, and liability do not provide clear answers, even if the parties have included a choice of law clause in their agreement.

This chapter does not attempt to provide a comprehensive discussion of variations among foreign laws impacting a work such as the application described above. Rather, it identifies some of the pitfalls facing multinational companies using internationally assembled teams to create copyrighted works. We have chosen a computer game application to illustrate these pitfalls because the game application example allows us to contrast the foreign copyright laws specific to software with more general copyright rules applying to artistic and musical works in those jurisdictions.

The chapter begins with an overview of the U.S. work-for-hire doctrine. We then place authorship and ownership rights in an international context, including the Berne Convention[3] and the World Trade Organization (WTO) Agreement on Trade Related Aspects of Intellectual Property (TRIPS).[4] To highlight differences between U.S. laws and the laws of foreign jurisdictions, we consider varying approaches to authorship and ownership in a number of legal regimes, including some of those in which U.S. multinationals might have distributed employees or commissioned contractors. These include a variety of European Union (EU) jurisdictions and India. The chapter analyzes potential conflicts among and between foreign laws, including how courts might choose which law to apply.

I. AUTHORSHIP AND OWNERSHIP: U.S. COPYRIGHT LAW

Classifying a work as "made for hire" under U.S. copyright law determines both initial authorship and ownership of the work, the

---

[3] Berne Convention for the Protection of Literary and Artistic Works, Sept. 9, 1886, as revised at Paris on July 24, 1971 and amended in 1979, S. Treaty Doc. No. 99–27 (1986)[hereinafter Berne Convention].

[4] Agreement on Trade-Related Aspects of Intellectual Property Rights, Apr. 15, 1994, Marrakesh Agreement Establishing the World Trade Organization, Annex 1C, 1869 UNTS 299; 33 ILM 1197 (1994)[hereinafter TRIPS].

duration of the copyright, the owner's renewal, and termination rights.[5] The contours of the doctrine carry significance not only for employers and employees, but for independent artists, designers, and computer programmers who create commissioned works. Inclusion of the modern work-for-hire doctrine in the Copyright Act of 1976 was meant to ensure predictability in authorship and ownership of the work.[6]

As a starting point, authorship and ownership are distinct concepts in U.S. copyright law. The Copyright Act defines "copyright owner" as "with respect to any one of the exclusive rights comprised in a copyright" the owner of that particular right.[7] Copyright initially vests in the author.[8] The Act does not define "author," although it is a term of art throughout the statute[9] and generally means the person who has fixed the work in a tangible medium of expression.[10]

The exception to the general rule that the author is the person creating the work is the work-for-hire doctrine in copyright. "A work prepared by an employee within the scope of his or her employment" is a "work made for hire."[11] In this situation, the author is not the employee who created the work. Rather, "the employer or other person for whom the work was prepared is considered the author."[12] Thus, the statute incorporates employers into the definition of author. This is not the typical approach to employer ownership in foreign jurisdictions. Congress could have followed a different approach, allowing an employer to gain an owner-ship interest through assignment, as with patents. Congress could also have granted an automatic transfer of ownership rights by operation of law from the employee to the employer.

Designating the employer as "author" by law possibly reflects a political compromise,[13] but has advantages. Drafting the Act to include

---

[5] MELVILLE B. NIMMER AND DAVID NIMMER, NIMMER ON COPYRIGHT § 5.03[A] (Lslf. ed. 2013) [hereinafter NIMMER].

[6] *Ibid.*

[7] 17 U.S.C. § 101 (2012).

[8] *Ibid.* § 201 ("Copyright ... vests initially in the author or authors of a work. The authors of a joint work are coowners of copyright in the work.").

[9] Catherine L. Fisk, *Authors at Work: The Origins of the Work-for-Hire Doctrine,* 15) YALE. J. L & HUMAN. 1, 5 (2003).

[10] Case law has defined "author" as "he to whom [a work] owes its origin." *Burrow-Giles Lithographic Co. v. Sarony,* 111 U.S. 253(1884).

[11] 17 U.S.C. § 101.

[12] *Ibid.* § 201(b).

[13] JAY DRATLER, JR. AND STEPHEN M. MCJOHN, INTELLECTUAL PROPERTY LAW: COMMERCIAL, CREATIVE, & INDUSTRIAL PROPERTY § 6.02 [3][b] (Lslf ed. 2013).

the employer as an author made revisions easier, since "author" is an otherwise undefined term of art within the Act.[14] Granting the employer authorship rather than mandating an assignment of ownership circumvented constitutional issues, since the copyright clause provides the exclusive rights belong to the author.[15] It also ensured that the employer would be the initial owner of the work rather than an assignee, which provides additional rights to the employer. While assignments may be subject to statutory termination or transfer, authorship continues for the life of the copyright.[16]

The work-for-hire doctrine applies to two mutually exclusive categories of works: (1) those created by an employee in the scope of his or her employment and (2) those commissioned from independent contractors in statutorily defined categories of works. Although the U.S. Copyright Act designates the employer as the author and initial owner of works created by employees in the scope of employment, it does not define "employee," "employer," or "scope of employment." The courts have been left to craft tests to define these concepts.

In 1989, the U.S. Supreme Court laid out the framework for analyzing whether a particular work falls within the statutory definition of work-for-hire in *Community for Creative Non-Violence v. Reid*.[17] The first step of the analysis requires the court to determine whether the person who created the work is an employee or an independent contractor. Reasoning that Congress used the term "employee" in the context of agency law's master-servant relationship, the Supreme Court adopted common law of agency principles to make the determination.[18] Courts consider the hiring party's right to control the means and manner through which the work is completed by applying factors such as: the skill required; the source of the instrumentalities and tools; the location of the work; whether the work is part of the hiring party's regular business; the duration of the relationship between the parties; whether the hiring party has the right to assign additional projects to the hired party; the extent of the hired party's discretion over when and how long to work; the method of payment; the hired party's role in hiring and paying of assistants; and the

---

[14] Fisk, *supra* note 9, at 62.
[15] US Const. art. I, §8.
[16] NIMMER, *supra* note 5, at § 5.03[B][2][a] (citation omitted).
[17] 490 US 730 (1989).
[18] *Ibid.* at 739.

provision of employee benefits and the tax treatment of the hired party.[19] No single factor is determinative[20] and courts apply the test with varying results.[21]

If the individual is an employee, the second part of the analysis addresses whether the work was within the "scope of employment." If an employee creates a work and the work product produced is not part of his or her employment duties (even though created during working hours using an employer's facilities), the employee retains authorship and ownership of the work.[22] Conversely, if an employee creates a work off-site that relates to employment duties, it will fall within the scope of employment, with the result being employer authorship.[23]

Parties may alter the default ownership rules of the work-for-hire doctrine by express agreement executed by both the employer and employee.[24] However, the copyright term differs based on whether the work is an individual work of authorship[25] or whether it is a work-for-hire.[26] Because the copyright term cannot be modified by the parties, the parties may not contractually vary the employer's legal status as the author.[27]

A second category of work-for-hire rules apply to certain works commissioned from non-employees. The Copyright Act enumerates nine categories of "specially ordered or commissioned works" as works for hire, including works for use as contributions to a collective work as part of a motion picture or audiovisual work, a translation, a supplementary work and instructional text.[28] If a specially commissioned work falls within one of the enumerated categories, the work-for-hire doctrine applies as long as the parties "expressly agree in a written instrument

---

[19]   *Ibid.* at 751–52, referencing RESTATEMENT (SECOND) AGENCY § 220(2) (citations omitted).

[20]   *Ibid.* at 752.

[21]   *See* NIMMER, *supra* note 5, at § 5.03[B][1][a] (analyzing subsequent cases). *See also* JULIAN S. MILLSTEIN, JEFFREY D. NEUGURGER AND JEFFRY P. WEIGARD, DOING BUSINESS ON THE INTERNET: FORMS AND ANALYSIS §3.03[6][a] (Lslf. 2013) (analyzing work-for-hire cases in digital context).

[22]   NIMMER, *supra* note 5, at § 5.03[B][1][b][i].

[23]   *Ibid.*

[24]   17 U.S.C. § 201(b).

[25]   17 U.S.C. 302(a) (in general, for works created after January 1, 1978, life of author plus 70 years after the author's death).

[26]   *Ibid.* § 302(c) (95 years from the date of first publication or 120 years from creation, whichever expires first).

[27]   NIMMER, *supra* note 5, at § 5.03[B][b][i].

[28]   17 U.S.C.. § 101.

signed by them that the work shall be considered a work made for hire."[29] If a work does not fall into one of the statutory categories for commissioned work, it cannot be a work-for-hire. The independent contractor remains the initial author and owner. Any rights transferred to the commissioning party must be expressly set forth in a writing signed by the author/owner of the copyright. Including work-for-hire language for a commissioned work that does not meet the statutory requirements can be detrimental.[30] A copyright assignment is more appropriate.[31]

II. AUTHORSHIP AND OWNERSHIP: AN INTERNATIONAL CONTEXT

Approaches to copyright are firmly rooted in historical and national traditions and, as such, vary significantly from country to country. The differing approaches have impacted the development of international copyright law and hindered the adoption of harmonized rules concerning authorship and ownership.

Although broad generalizations can be dangerous, there are similarities concerning features of copyright among common law nations that differ from those in civil law nations. In general, copyright laws in common law jurisdictions favor a utilitarian approach to copyright. In these legal traditions, the rights afforded by copyright tend to be freely alienable and of an economic nature. In the civil law tradition of continental European nations, author rights developed in the context of natural law. In addition to economic rights, these nations have long recognized that authors possess certain inalienable moral rights that stem from a perception of the work as an extension of the author's being. Civil law countries impose restraints on alienability of both economic and moral rights.[32]

---

[29] *Ibid.*

[30] J. Patrick Tober and Shawn C. Helms, *The "Work For Hire" Doctrine Almost Never Works in Software Development Contracts,* METROPOLITAN CORP. COUNS. 10 (June 2008) (If the California Labor Code (Section 3351 5(c)) applies to an independent contractor and the agreement uses work-for-hire language, the company must include the independent contractor under its workers compensation insurance.).

[31] *Ibid.*

[32] PAUL GOLDSTEIN & P. BERNT HUGENHOLTZ, INTERNATIONAL COPYRIGHT: PRINCIPLES, LAW, AND PRACTICE 203 (3d ed. 2012); RICHARD E. NEFF & FRAN SMALLSON, NAFTA: PROTECTING AND ENCOURAGING INTELLECTUAL PROPERTY RIGHTS IN NORTH AMERICA 26 (1994).

National copyright traditions also differ in terms of who may be considered an author. The U.S. position concerning corporate authorship is not typical worldwide.[33] Civil law countries have historically rejected the principle that legal persons may be authors.[34]

International treaties have become increasingly important as the world moves towards harmonization of intellectual property. For purposes of copyright law, the Berne Convention and TRIPS are the most important to modern national laws. Despite broad harmonization of substantive copyright law through Berne and TRIPS, many areas remain within the domain of national law. Among the areas in which international laws have not achieved harmonization, there are two primary areas of conflict: (1) who is the author and original owner of a work; and (2) whether a nation is obliged to recognize moral rights.

III. THE BERNE CONVENTION

The Berne Convention requires its 167 member nations to observe minimum standards for copyright protection, including automatically protecting the works of authors from Berne Convention states within their national boundaries.[35] Since the United States acceded to the Berne Convention, the Convention has arguably become the most important multinational treaty protecting U.S. nationals under foreign copyright law and vice versa.[36] A number of aspects of the Berne Convention confound adaption of an internationally harmonized work-for-hire doctrine. These include a lack of guidance on issues of authorship and ownership, and mandates that countries observe and enforce moral rights in national law.[37]

---

[33] Other countries do recognize corporate authorship. For example, under Chinese law, if a work is created under the auspices and direction of a legal entity bearing responsibility for the work, authorship resides with the entity. Copyright Law of the People's Republic of China (中华人民共和国著作权法), Art. 11 (promulgated by the Standing Committee of the Eleventh National People's Congress, Feb. 26, 2010, effective Apr. 1, 2010, available at http://www.wipo.int/wipolex/en/text.jsp?file_id=186569); Xue Hong and Guo Shoukang, *China* §4, in INTERNATIONAL COPYRIGHT LAW AND PRACTICE (Paul Edward Geller and Lionel Bently eds., 2013).

[34] NEFF AND SMALLSON, *supra* note 32, at 47.

[35] Berne Convention, Art. 5.

[36] NIMMER, *supra* note 5, at § 17.04[B].

[37] Much of the tension between moral rights and U.S. copyright law stems from the incompatibility of certain moral rights with the U.S. work-for-hire

The Berne Convention does not define authorship, provide rules for determining initial ownership in a work, or require countries to recognize legal entities as authors.[38] Additionally, the Berne Convention does not provide explicit rules for determining the nationality of the author nor choice of law in cross-border disputes.[39] Determining whether U.S. or foreign law governs matters of authorship and ownership in the area of work-for-hire is made more complex by a lack of international standards. This is particularly true when trying to apply U.S. work-for-hire standards in differing legal environments.

Moral rights, or personality rights, have long been a part of the tradition in continental Europe and many other copyright regimes. The purported international minimum standard for moral rights is expressed in Article 6*bis* of the Berne Convention, which requires national laws to include the rights of authors to claim authorship (the attribution right), and to object to any distortion, mutilation, or other modification of the work that would be prejudicial to the author's honor or reputation (the integrity right).[40] Both attribution and integrity rights are at odds with the work-for-hire doctrine.

The United States did not become a contracting party to the Berne Convention until 1988, a century after the Convention was created. The delay was primarily because of moral rights.[41] The scope of moral rights in the United States is limited, although the United States has taken the

---

doctrine. *See* Benjamin S. Hayes, *Integrating Moral Rights into US Law and the Problem of the Works for Hire Doctrine*, 61 OHIO ST. L.J. 1013, 1014 (2000).

[38] The exception is Article 14*bis*(2), containing special provisions for cinematographic works. GOLDSTEIN & HUGENHOLTZ, *supra* note 32, *at* § 4.4.1.1, 136 (2012). In addition, Article 15(2) has been interpreted as implicitly recognizing corporate authorship in cinematographic works. Robert A. Jacobs, *Work-For-Hire and the Moral Right Dilemma in the European Community: A US Perspective*, 16 BOSTON C. INT'L. & COMP. L.R. 29, 40 (1993).

[39] GOLDSTEIN & HUGENHOLTZ, *supra* note 32, at § 4.4.1.1, p. 126.

[40] Berne Convention, *supra* note 3, at Art. 6*bis*(1).

[41] The United States has long had concerns that moral rights would impact freedom of contract in copyright industries. The publishing industry was concerned that strong moral rights may cause authors and photographers to assert their integrity rights through litigation and interfere with publication. Producers and distributors were concerned that the cost of sales would increase if they were forced to purchase moral rights in addition to economic rights. NEFF AND SMALLSON, *supra* note 32, at 17 (discussing U.S. position on moral rights in the context of North American Free Trade Agreements (NAFTA) negotiations).

position that its common law moral rights and statutory provisions fully comply with Article 6*bis*.[42]

The Berne Convention is not self-executing in the United States; therefore, authors in the United States do not gain private rights under the treaty. In implementing the Berne Convention, Congress declared that the moral rights provisions of the Berne Convention did not "expand or reduce any right of an author of a work, whether claimed under Federal, State, or the common law," including attribution and integrity rights.[43] Since moral rights accrue only to natural persons, not legal entities, had the United States not included this declaration, U.S. employees would have gained the right to have their name attach to their work, even though the employer would be considered the legal author of the work.[44] This may have provided employee-authors with greater recognition and greater bargaining power in employment contexts.[45] However, industry perspectives prevailed. U.S. creative content industries have long been concerned that moral rights would impact their freedom of contract and increase costs if they were forced to purchase moral rights in addition to economic rights.[46]

IV. TRIPS

Given the increasing importance of intellectual property-based products to global trade, a primary motivation for including TRIPS in the constellation of WTO side agreements was to ensure all WTO members implemented international minimum standards of intellectual property protection into national law and provided effective national mechanisms for enforcing those rights. TRIPS incorporates the first twenty-one articles of the Berne Convention, but expressly excludes an obligation to incorporate Article 6*bis* moral rights into national law.[47]

---

[42] *Ibid.* at 18. The Visual Artist Rights Act of 1990 provides limited moral rights to a small category of visual arts. P.L. No. 101-650 (1990) (codified as amended in scattered sections of 17 U.S.C.). *See* Hayes, *supra* note 37, at 1014.

[43] The Berne Convention Implementation Act of 1988, Pub. L. No. 100-568, 102 Stat. 2853, Sec.3 (b).

[44] Hayes, *supra* note 37, at 1027.

[45] *Ibid.*

[46] NEFF AND SMALLSON, *supra* note 32, at 19.

[47] TRIPS, *supra* note 4, at Art. 9 (1).

Despite negotiations so intense as to be described as four and a half years of "bloodletting,"[48] TRIPS failed to resolve the authorship/ownership conundrum nor did it harmonize moral rights. TRIPS contains no standard for establishing authorship nor a standard for who enjoys initial ownership in a copyrighted work.[49] U.S. efforts to incorporate into TRIPS a transnational work-for-hire rule ensuring employer-author rights failed. Corporate authorship provisions did not survive the final draft of TRIPS.[50] The exclusion of a moral rights obligation from TRIPS was largely due to pressures from the U.S.[51]

Neither the Berne Convention nor TRIPS has successfully harmonized issues of authorship, ownership and moral rights. This area is rife with pitfalls for businesses that must navigate various rules in different countries. The next section considers how this lack of harmonization has manifested in differing approaches to these issues in national law.

V. AUTHORSHIP AND OWNERSHIP: THE EUROPEAN UNION

The legal environment regulating copyright or author rights[52] in the EU varies substantially from that in the United States. In the United States, copyright is strictly a matter of federal law based in the Constitution. For the twenty-eight EU member states, copyright is partially harmonized though a series of directives. Directives are a form of EU law requiring member states to implement a law that will achieve identified policy and legal goals. National legislatures are obligated to enact national law that meet the minimum requirements of the Directive, but are often allowed to impose additional obligations that do not conflict with the Directive's goals. In this way the law is harmonized, but is not identical across the EU, since implementing laws may differ in key aspects from country to country. Because the underlying historical, social, and cultural issues

---

[48] Ralph Oman, *Berne Revision: The Continuing Drama*, 4 FORDHAM INTELL. PROP., MEDIA & ENT. L. J. 139, 142 (1993).

[49] GOLDSTEIN AND HUGENHOLTZ, *supra* note 32, at § 4.4.1.1.

[50] Oman, *supra* note 48, at 143. The United States was successful in negotiating recognition for work-for-hire in the intellectual property provisions of NAFTA. NEFF AND SMALLSON, *supra* note 32, at 47.

[51] NEFF AND SMALLSON, *Ibid.* at 33.

[52] Many countries designate the law as "author rights," which does have a different theoretical basis. However, for purposes of reading and consistency, we use the term copyright to indicate both.

impacting copyright vary greatly in different member states, harmonization in key areas has remained elusive.

EU member states take various approaches to authorship and ownership of copyright and differ in their approach to alienation of rights. In general, national laws designate the natural person who created the work as author and initial owner. Exceptions to the rule are more frequent in EU countries with common law regimes than in civil law countries.[53] Approaches to how an employer comes to own an employee's copyright protected work vary. Some states require express contractual provision to transfer the economic rights to the employer.[54] Other states' laws imply a transfer of economic rights to the employer by virtue of the employment relationship.[55] Only one EU member state automatically recognizes the employer as the author and initial owner.[56]

The various national approaches to copyright and author rights within the EU preclude harmonization. At present, no EU directive harmonizes general approaches to authorship and ownership. The few copyright directives that have been implemented are limited to specific issues.[57] Thus, for the most part, copyright authorship, ownership, and control are matters of unharmonized national law. There is one exception. The 1991 Council Directive 91/250 on the legal protection of computer programs[58] expressly addresses ownership issues of computer programs. Article 2 (3) provides:

---

[53] GOLDSTEIN & HUGENHOLTZ, *supra* note 32, at 7.

[54] AGNÈS LUCAS-SCHLOETTER, "LES DROITS D'AUTEU.R DES SALARIÉS EN EUROPE CONTINENTALE" 49 – 54 (Cahiers de l'IRPI, No. 5, 2004) (France, Belgium, Romania and Latvia.).

[55] *Ibid.* at 35–48 (Germany, Austria, Italy, Sweden, Denmark, Finland, Norway).

[56] *Ibid.* at 10 (The Netherlands).

[57] For example, in 2001, the EU adopted a Directive on the Harmonisation of Certain Aspects of Copyright and Related Rights in the Information Society, Directive 2001/29/EC of the European Parliament and of the Council of 22 May 2001 on the Harmonisation of Certain Aspects of Copyright and Related Rights in the Information Society, 2001 O.J. (L. 167) 10. It did not address the work-for-hire question. Neither was the issue raised in the recent Directive on collective management of copyright and related rights and multi-territorial licensing. Directive 2001/29/EC of the European Parliament and of the Council of 22 May 2001 on the Harmonisation of Certain Aspects of Copyright and Related Rights in the Information Society, 2001 O.J. (L. 167) 10.

[58] Council Directive 1991/250/EEC on the Legal Protection of Computer Programs, 1991 O.J. (L 122) 42 [hereinafter Computer Program Directive]. *See also* Alan K. Palmer and Thomas C. Vinje, *The EC Directive on the Legal Protection of Computer Software: New Law Governing Software Development*, 2

Where a computer program is created by an employee in the execution of his duties or following the instructions given by his employer, the employer exclusively shall be entitled to exercise all economic rights in the program so created, unless otherwise provided by contract.[59]

The Directive's approach is similar to the U.S. work-for-hire doctrine in that the economic rights vest in the employer. However, it differs in that it addresses ownership and not authorship. In the United States, the employer would be both author and owner of the work. National copyright law in a particular EU member state will govern who is considered to be the author of a computer program. Computer programs are not *sui generis* rights.[60] They exist within the contours of copyright law,[61] but are treated differently than other works.

Furthermore, the Computer Program Directive expressly addresses only economic rights and not the moral rights vested in the work. Moral rights are not harmonized in the EU.[62] States take differing approaches to both the scope of moral rights and how an author's interests may be transferred.

For example, France takes a dualist approach to economic and moral rights. While the economic rights are freely alienable in France, moral rights are "perpetual, inalienable and imprescriptible."[63] In Germany and Austria, economic and moral rights are considered to be so thoroughly

---

DUKE J. COMP. & INT'L. L. 65 (1992) (general analysis of Computer Program Directive requirements).

[59]   Computer Program Directive, *ibid.* at Art.(2) (3).

[60]   Marc. A. Ehrlich, *Fair Use or Foul Play? The EC Directive on the Legal Protection of Computer Programs and Its Impact on Reverse Engineering*, 13 PACE L. REV. 1003, 1007 (1994) (proposals for the directive rejected a *sui generis* approach].

[61]   For example, under French law, computer programs are listed as a "work of the mind" CODE DE LA PROPRIÉTÉ INTELLECTUELLE [CPI] Art. L.121-2. Art. L.122-6 (Fr.), *available in English at* www.legifrance.gouv.fr/content/download/ 1959/13723/.../Code 35.pdf [hereinafter French Copyright Code). Under German Law computer programs are considered literary works. Gesetz über Urheberrecht und verwandte Schutzrechte [Urheberrechtsgesetz] [Copyright Act], Sept. 09, 1965, BGBl. I S. at 1273, Art. 2(1) (1.)(Ger.), *available in English at* http:// www.iuscomp.org/gla/statutes/UrhG.htm [hereinafter German Copyright Act].

[62]   Hayes, *supra* note 37, at 1019 (*citing* Council Directive 93/98/EEC of 29 Oct. 1993 harmonizing the term of protection of copyright and certain related rights, Preamble, para.4 exempting moral rights from harmonization).

[63]   GOLDSTEIN AND HUGENHOLTZ, *supra* note 32, at 254.

intertwined that the economic right may only be alienated through the grant of a privilege to use the work.[64] United Kingdom (UK) law prohibits assignment of moral rights,[65] but permits authors to waive them.[66] What follows is a brief overview of the copyright regimes in three EU member states to illustrate the different approaches taken and the lack of overall harmony.

A. France

In French law, only natural persons who create a work of the mind may be authors.[67] There can be no corporate authorship, although a legal entity may own the copyright through express or implied agreement. In the case of software, the transfer of ownership is implied at law. The author enjoys "an exclusive incorporeal property right which shall be enforceable against all persons" which includes both moral and economic rights.[68] Thus, ownership vests in the author. French law grants moral rights beyond the minimum required by Article *6bis* of the Berne Convention. In addition to the rights of attribution and integrity, French authors possess the right of divulgation (the right to decide when and how a work is disclosed to the public)[69] and a right of retraction (the right to recover the exploitation rights in the work).[70] Moral rights are

---

[64]   *Ibid.* at 265 (the privilege is similar, but not identical to licenses in other countries).

[65]   Copyright, Designs and Patent Act, c.V, §94 (1988) [hereinafter, U.K. Copyright Act].

[66]   U.K. Copyright Act, c.IV, § 87(2) (the waiver is in writing and signed by the person giving up the right).

[67]   André Lucas, Pascal Kamina and Robert Plaisant, *France* §4[1], in INTERNATIONAL COPYRIGHT LAW AND PRACTICE (Paul Edward Geller and Lionel Bently eds. 2013).

[68]   French Copyright Code, *supra* note 61, at Art. L. 111-1.

[69]   *Ibid.* at Art. L. 121–2; Lucas, et al., *supra* note 67, at §7[1][a] (divulgation requires a concrete act of disclosure by the author and encompasses the right to not disclose the work).

[70]   French Copyright Code, *supra* note 61, at Art.L.121-4; Lucas, et al., *supra* note 67, at § 7[1][d](the author may recover exploitation rights in the work that have been transferred, providing he indemnifies the transferee).

perpetual,[71] inalienable[72] and subject to limitations concerning whether they may be waived.[73]

These rules apply generally in an employment context. Article L.111–1 provides that "the existence or conclusion of a contract for hire or of service" does not impact an author's rights.[74] An employment contract is a contract of service.[75] Copyright vests initially with the author-employee, even if it is created at the direction of the employer. French law does not imply an automatic transfer of ownership of economic rights to the employer or the commissioning party.

Assignments are allowed, but will only be enforced if the assigned rights are expressly mentioned in a written agreement and comply with the formal requirements of the French Intellectual Property Code, including that each is defined as to scope and purpose, place and duration.[76] An assignment clause whose terms are too general and broad may be invalidated.[77] Because French law prohibits the total transfer of future works,[78] employers in France not only include a clause in employment agreements transferring rights from the employee author, but regularly revise and update to refer precisely to specific employee works to ensure the validity of the transfer clause.

In compliance with the Computer Program Directive, different rules apply to software created on the job. Article L. 113-9 provides: "[u]nless otherwise provided by statutory provision or stipulation, the economic rights in the software and its documentation created by one or more

---

[71] French Copyright Code, *ibid.* at Art. L. 121–1; Lucas, et al., *Ibid.* at § 7[3](the French Copyright Code is silent on the duration of divulgation rights, but it is assumed these rights are perpetual, however doubts exist as to the duration of the right of retraction).

[72] French Copyright Code, *ibid.* at Art. L. 111–1.

[73] Lucas, et al., *supra* note 67, at §7[4][b][i] and [ii] (an author may temporarily renounce the right of attribution, but it is questionable whether that may be done in favor of another person; the integrity right may be limited by agreement and an author may authorize modifications to the work after they have been made).

[74] French Copyright Code, supra note 61, at Art. L. 111–1(2).

[75] Lucas, et al., *supra* note 67, at §4[B][ii][A]5.

[76] Cour de cassation [Cass.] [Supreme court for judicial matters] Jul. 12, 2006, Bull. civ., No. 5-15472 (Fr.). *See also,* Lucas, et al., *supra* note 67, at § 4[ii][B](explaining that while some cases have held a "pre-assignment" in an employment contract to include a transfer of all rights created on the job to the employer, such findings contradict the letter and spirit of the law).

[77] French Copyright Code, supra note 61, at Art. L. 131–3.

[78] *Ibid.* at Art. L. 131–1.

employees in the execution of their duties or following the instructions given by their employer shall be the property of the employer and he exclusively shall be entitled to exercise them."[79] Economic rights in employee software automatically transfer to the employer by operation of law. The employer is not the original owner of the work, but a transferee who retains economic rights even after the employee is no longer working for the company.[80] The employee remains the author and possesses limited moral rights. The author may not oppose modification of the software by the employer if the modification does not prejudice either his honor or his reputation, and he may not exercise his right of retraction.[81]

B. Germany

German copyright law shares some commonalities with French copyright law, but also differs substantially. The German Copyright Act declares that authors "shall enjoy protection for their works."[82] An author, who is also the initial owner, can only be the natural person who created the work.[83] This includes works made as part of employment or specially commissioned. German law does not recognize a legal entity's ability to initially own a copyright.[84]

German law recognizes both moral and economic rights. But, unlike French law, which treats these rights separately, German law takes a monistic approach. According to this theory of copyright, economic and moral rights are inseparable, because economic rights may serve the author's personal interests and moral rights may serve his financial interests.[85] Unlike French law, moral rights are not perpetual, but are subject to the same term as economic rights.[86] German moral rights are broader than what is required by Article 6*bis* of the Berne Convention. Statutory rights include the rights of attribution, integrity, divulgation

---

[79]   *Ibid.* at Art. 113–9.

[80]   Lucas, et al, *supra* note 67, at § 4[D].

[81]   French Copyright Code, *supra* note 61, at Art. L. 121–7.

[82]   German Copyright Act, *supra* note 61, at Art. 1.

[83]   *Ibid.* at Art. 7; *see also* Adolf Dietz, *Germany* § 4][1][a], in INTERNATIONAL COPYRIGHT LAW AND PRACTICE (Paul Edward Geller and Lionel Bently eds. 2013)(for discussion of authorship issues in joint works).

[84]   Dietz, *ibid.*

[85]   *Ibid.* at § 4 [2][a] and § 7[1].

[86]   German Copyright Act, *supra* note 61 at, Art. 64 (copyright expires 70 years after the author's death).

(publication), retraction and the right to access the work.[87] German moral rights also incorporate general rights of personality beyond those enumerated in the German Copyright Act.[88]

Germany's monistic approach fuses economic and moral rights into an inseparable, inalienable bundle. German law has no provision equivalent to an assignment or license under U.S. law. Indeed, German law precludes transfer of copyright (with the exception of testamentary dispositions)[89] to protect authors from being deprived of core rights through contractual transfers.[90] Authors may only exploit their work through a grant of a privilege to use the work.[91] This exploitation right, or Nutzungsrechte, approximates an exclusive or nonexclusive license in other legal traditions.[92] But it does not grant an ownership interest. In general, contracts granting the exploitation right do not have to be in writing, with the exception that agreements granting rights in future works must be in writing and may be terminated by either party after five years.[93]

Article 43 of the German Copyright Act mandates these rules to apply both to works created by employees under contracts for employment and to a contract commissioning services.[94] German law contains no general work-for-hire concept in which initial ownership of the copyrighted work vests in the employer or commissioning party.[95] Article 43 does not create a presumption of transfer to the employer. Such transfers are possible but they must be provided for by contract.[96] The final clause of Article 43 supports this by stating "provided nothing to the contrary transpires from the terms or nature of the contract of employment or

---

[87]   *Ibid.* at Arts. 13, 14, 12(1) 41 and 25. For discussion of the contours of each of the rights and limitations, *see* Lucas, et al., *supra* note 67, at §7.

[88]   Dietz, *Ibid.* at §7[1] (rights of personality protected by the German Constitution are recognized as part of copyright law).

[89]   German Copyright Act, *supra* note 61, at Art. 29.

[90]   Dietz, *supra* note 83, at § 4[2][a].

[91]   German Copyright Act, *supra* note 61, at Art. 31; Dietz, *supra* note 83, at § 4[2][a].

[92]   GOLDSTEIN AND HUGENHOLTZ, *supra* note 32, at 265; Dietz, *supra* note 83, at §4[2][a].

[93]   German Copyright Act, *supra* note 61, at Art. 40(1).

[94]   *Ibid.* at Art. 43.

[95]   Dietz, *supra* note 83, at § 4[1][b].

[96]   LUCAS-SCHLOETTER, *supra* note 54, at 24–34 (the same rebuttable presumption is the rule in Spain, Portugal, Slovenia, Slovakia and Albania).

service."[97] At times, courts have interpreted this "vague and unsatisfactory clause" to find implied clauses in favor of employers.[98] However, the transfer will be only of exploitation rights, and not ownership.

Pursuant to Germany's implementation of the Computer Program Directive, the rules differ when the work is a computer program. Article 69b (1) of the German Copyright Act provides: "Where a computer program is created by an employee in the execution of his duties or following the instructions given by his employer, the employer exclusively shall be entitled to exercise all the economic rights in the program, unless otherwise agreed."[99] This section creates a stronger presumption of transfer of exploitation rights.[100] However, read in light of Germany's monistic tradition, the article limits the presumption: the employer is granted the exclusive right to exercise the economic rights in the software created by the employee, but the employee remains the author and owner of the rights.

C. United Kingdom

The United Kingdom, in the common law tradition, takes a more utilitarian approach to copyright, historically placing less emphasis on moral rights than its civil law counterparts. Under the U.K. Copyright Act, "author" is defined as "the person who creates" the work.[101] Unlike U.S. law, which allows for corporate authorship, U.K. law requires the author be a "flesh and blood" person.[102] Original ownership vests with the author, subject to exceptions for employment, Crown and Parliamentary copyright, and copyright held by certain international organizations.[103] Although U.K. law does not have a general work-for-hire provision, Article 11(2) of the U.K. Copyright Act provides that: "[w]here a literary, dramatic, musical or artistic work is made by an

---

[97] German Copyright Act, *supra* note 61, at Art. 43.

[98] Dietz, *supra* note 83, at § 4[1][b](citation omitted).

[99] German Copyright Act, *supra* note 61, at Art. 69b (1).

[100] Dietz, *supra* note 83, at §4[1]b].

[101] UK Copyright Act, *supra* note 65, at c.48, p.I, § 9; Lionel Bentley and William R. Cornish, *United Kingdom* §4[1], in INTERNATIONAL COPYRIGHT LAW AND PRACTICE (Paul Edward Geller & Lionel Bently eds., 2013) (The statute recognizes that authorship in various categories of works may be a person other than the one who created the work. For example, in the case of a film, the producer and principal director are the author.).

[102] Bentley and Cornish, *ibid.* (Special rules and presumptions apply to various categories of work, including computer-generated work.).

[103] U.K. Copyright Act, *supra* note 65, at c.48, p I, § 11.

employee in the course of his employment, his employer is the first owner of any copyright in the work subject to any agreement to the contrary."[104] Computer software is protected as a literary work.

By operation of law, ownership of an employee's work in those categories automatically vests in the employer unless the parties agree otherwise by contract.[105] The U.K. approach thus contrasts with the general approach in France and Germany, although other European countries have a similar approach to economic rights automatically vesting in the employer.[106]

To determine whether the employer exception applies, U.K. courts must determine whether an employment relationship exists and whether the work was created in the scope of employment. The first part of the test focuses on whether there is "mutuality of obligations" in which the employer is obligated to provide paid work and the employee to provide labor.[107] The employer must also be able to exercise control over the employee.[108]

Even if an employment relationship exists, the legal presumption applies only if the work was within the scope of the employee's duties.[109] As with the U.S. work-for-hire doctrine, whether the work was created outside the work place and office hours is not determinative of whether the work was created in the scope of employment.[110] If the work is commissioned from an independent contractor, copyright ownership may be assigned, as long as it is in a signed writing.[111]

Although the United Kingdom acceded to the Berne Convention in 1887, it did not recognize statutory moral rights until 1988. Chapter IV of the U.K. Copyright Act codifies the Berne Convention Article *6bis* rights of attribution and integrity.[112] These statutory rights are complex in terms of how they relate to particular works and numerous exceptions

---

[104] Jacobs, *supra* note 38, at 69.

[105] SANNA WOLK AND CHRISTINE KIRCHBERGER, OWNERSHIP OF THE COPY-RIGHT IN WORKS AND THE PATENT RIGHT IN INVENTIONS CREATED BY EMPLOY-EES: IN FINLAND, SWEDEN, GERMANY, AUSTRIA, THE UNITED KINGDOM, ESTONIA AND ARGENTINA 16 (2002).

[106] LUCAS-SCHLOETTER, *supra* note 54, at 10–23 (Poland, Hungary, Lithu-ania, Estonia, the Czech Republic, Greece, Bulgaria and Croatia).

[107] Bentley and Cornish, *supra* note 101, at § 4[1][b](citations omitted).

[108] *Ibid.*

[109] *Ibid.* at § 4[1][b].

[110] *Ibid.*

[111] U.K. Copyright Act, *supra* note 65, at c.48, p. 1, § 90(3).

[112] *Ibid.* at c.48, p. 1, §§ 77 and 80. The statute also recognizes a right against false attribution (§84).

exist. For example, the right to claim authorship does not apply to works where ownership originally vests in the employer[113] or to computer programs.[114]

The right of integrity does apply to works created in the scope of employment,[115] but does not apply to anything done in relation to the work by the copyright owner.[116] Moral rights may not be assigned[117] but they may be waived in a signed writing.[118]

This section demonstrates that even within the EU, which has harmonized certain aspects of copyright, issues of ownership and moral rights diverge greatly.

VI. AUTHORSHIP AND OWNERSHIP: INDIA

As a Commonwealth nation whose legal system developed from the English common law, India's approach to copyright has its roots in the English, utilitarian approach.[119] Indian copyright is governed by the Copyright Act of 1957 as amended by the 2012 Bill.[120] "Author" is defined particularly as it relates to various categories of works. For literary works, including computer programs, "author" is tautologously defined as "the author of the work."[121] The author is the natural person who created it.[122] There is no provision in the Indian Copyright Act for

---

[113] *Ibid.* at c.48, p. 1, § 79 (3).

[114] *Ibid.* at c.48, p. 1, § 79(2) (b).

[115] *Ibid.* at c.48, p. 1, § 82(1) (a).

[116] *Ibid.* at c.48, p. 1, § 82(2) (this exception doesn't apply unless the author has been identified).

[117] *Ibid.* at c.48, p. 1, § 94.

[118] *Ibid.* at c.48, p. 1, §8; Bentley and Cornish, *supra* note 101, at § 7[4](moral rights may also informally waived under contract law or estoppel).

[119] The rationale for protecting creative works is that economic and social development of society are dependent upon them. India: A Handbook of Copyright Law (Government of India Ministry of Human Resource Development) (1999) *available at http://www.wipo.int/wipolex/en/text.jsp?file_id=208016.*

[120] The Copyright Act, 1957 No. 14 of 1957; India Code (1957), *available at* http://www.wipo.int/wipolex/en/text.jsp?file_id=128098 [hereinafter, Indian Copyright Act].

[121] *Ibid.* at § 2(d) (i).

[122] Dev Gangjee and S. Ramaiah, *India* §4[1], in INTERNATIONAL COPYRIGHT LAW AND PRACTICE (Paul Edward Geller and Lionel Bently eds. 2013).

corporate authorship. In most instances, the first owner of the work is the author, subject to exceptions).

Article 17 (c) presentsa general provision akin to work-for-hire by providing that initial ownership of a work created in the course of employment "under a contract of service" shall vest in the employer, unless the parties agree otherwise.[123] The contract of service refers to an employment agreement. Key in determining whether the employment relationship exists is the degree of control the employer is entitled to exercise.[124]

These ownership provisions do not apply to works created under a "contract for service," such as that with an independent contractor.[125] If the work is commissioned from an independent contractor, Section 18(1) of the Act allows the owner to license or assign the rights attached to his work, including future works.[126] Section 19 imposes formalities and requirements, including a signed writing specifying the rights assigned, duration, and territorial extent of the assignment.[127] Indian law is not clear as to whether it is possible to assign or license the entire copyright without a limitation of term or territory, making the effectiveness of an assignment potentially problematic.[128]

The Indian Copyright Act recognizes the moral rights of attribution and integrity as "special rights"[129] that exist independently of copyright.[130] An author retains these rights even after the work has been assigned. Moral rights cannot be assigned. The statute provides that an author is entitled to an injunction or damages for the distortion, mutilation, modification, or other act prejudicial to the work.[131] India is

---

[123]   Indian Copyright Act, *supra* note 122, at §17 (c).

[124]   *Ibid.*

[125]   Indian courts have made the distinction between contracts of service, referring to employment, and contracts for service, to avoid applying this provision to independent contractors. Gangjee and Ramaiah, *supra* note 122, at § 4[1][b][i](citations omitted); *see also* MICHAEL A. EPSTEIN AND FRANK L. POLITANO, DRAFTING LICENSING AGREEMENTS §17.02[B][1] (2002, 2003 SUPPLEMENT).

[126]   Indian Copyright Act, *supra* note 120, at § 18(1).

[127]   *Ibid.* at § 19(1). There are further provisions limiting the assignment, including requirements that the assignee must exercise the rights (§ 19(4)) and that the assignment will be limited to five years, unless a different term is indicated (§ 10(5)).

[128]   EPSTEIN AND POLITANO, *supra* note 125, at §17.02[B][1].

[129]   Indian Copyright Act, *supra* note 119, at §§ 57(1) (a) and (b).

[130]   *Ibid.* at § 57(1).

[131]   *Ibid.* at § 57(1) (b).

"unique among common law countries" in how it deals with computer programmer moral rights.[132] Indian copyright contains a 'fair use' exception to infringement for copying or adapting a computer program for noncommercial purposes by the lawful owner of that copy.[133] The author of a computer program does not possess a right to enjoin or claim damages for the exercise of this exception. Normal use of a computer program by a purchaser will not be an infringement of moral rights. Indian law is unclear as to what extent an employer or commissioner of a software program will be exempt from liability for violation of the right of integrity.[134] Nor is it clear whether subsequent development of a software program by an employer or one who has commissioned the work would be violation of the programmer's moral rights.[135] The Indian statute is silent on whether moral rights may be waived and case law is inconclusive.[136]

VII. CONFLICT OF LAWS: WHICH LAW DETERMINES AUTHORSHIP AND OWNERSHIP?

Companies developing copyright protected products are concerned with retaining ownership and control over those products. In the U.S., ownership and control are facilitated by the work-for-hire doctrine which guarantees a great deal of control. Navigating copyright issues with a globally distributed workforce of employees or independent contractors is much more complex. The company must understand the contours of copyright law in each country in which a portion of the work is completed to better ensure ongoing ownership and control of the work.

The smartphone game application illustration presented early in the chapter demonstrates the complex nature of operating with a globally distributed workforce. Suppose the team includes a U.S. employee creating the graphics, a French employee composing the music, and an Indian employee designing the software. Under this scenario, by operation of law the U.S. employer is author and owner of the graphics, but may not legally be the sole author of the entire application. Given the

---

[132] MIRA T. SUNDARA RAJAN, MORAL RIGHTS: PRINCIPLES, PRACTICE AND NEW TECHNOLOGY 295 (2011).

[133] India Copyright Act, *supra* note 120, at § 52(1) (aa).

[134] RAJAN, *supra* note 132, at 296.

[135] *Ibid.*

[136] Nandita Saikia, *Indian Law: Getting Moral Rights Waived* (July 15, 2012) *available at* http://copyright.lawmatters.in/2010/07.

contours of French and Indian law concerning authorship, it is possible that the work would be one of joint authorship.[137] Without appropriate agreements, the company may not even own the economic aspects of components of the work created abroad. Under French copyright law, the composer, whether an employee or independent contractor, is the author. The composer may assign economic rights, subject to formalities and limitations, but is prohibited from assigning or waiving moral rights. The French composer will retain the right to claim authorship and object to a modification to the music that infringes his integrity right. If a French employee had created the software, the economic rights automatically transfer to the employer. In contrast, a French employee software developer, remains the author and retains limited moral rights.

Different rules apply to the software portion of the application created by an employee in India. Under India's version of work-for-hire, the employer is the first owner of the copyright, regardless of whether the employee creates the music, graphic design, or software portion of the application. The employee remains the author and cannot assign the moral rights in the work. Moreover it is doubtful whether the employee may waive those rights.

International disputes are often complicated by choice of law, and transnational work-for-hire cases present many difficult issues. The smartphone game application example illustrates the differences among legal regimes, and raises the questions of whether: (1) a court will choose to apply U.S., French, or Indian law to issues of copyright ownership, the scope of rights in the work, the validity of the assignment, and infringement; and (2) the person who created the work is an employee or independent contractor. In great part, the answer to the choice of law question depends on the forum in which the case is brought. But, given all of the issues at play in a transnational infringement case of this sort, resort to *dépeçage*, in which the court applies different laws to different issues in the case, is probable.

A choice of law clause in an international agreement can be an effective way to ensure the application of a particular country's laws. Yet, whether the U.S. work-for-hire doctrine determines authorship, ownership, and transfer of rights if a work is created by an employee or independent contractor in another country, even with a well-crafted choice of law remains uncertain. Problems relating to authorship and

---

[137] In the context of work-for-hire, issues of joint authorship become complicated. In the absence of an agreement to the contrary, all joint authors will equally share in the ownership of the joint work. Nimmer, *supra* note 5, at §§6.07[D] and 6.08.

ownership of copyright for purposes of U.S. conflict of laws are not well understood and it may not be possible to adequately address them in a contractual clause.[138]

Questions of which law will govern the transfer of a copyright interest is one of the most volatile conflict of law issues in international copyright.[139] Although parties are generally free to choose the law that will govern their contract, the choice is always subject to the conflict of law rules of the forum. European and U.S. courts favor enforcing the law chosen, on grounds of party autonomy or freedom of contract, subject to public policy considerations.[140]

A contractual choice of law may not be effective in international licensing and assignment agreements due to the overriding copyright-related public policy concerns in a particular forum. The copyright law of a country in which protection is sought may supersede the terms of a contract, particularly if the parties have attempted to transfer inalienable rights, such as moral rights.[141] When a conflict arises between the copyright law of the forum and the law governing the contract, copyright law generally prevails.[142]

The national treatment standard required under international law provides guidance on which law applies to infringement. A work created in a Berne Convention or TRIPS signatory country infringed in the United States receives the same protection as any U.S.-created work. The law of the forum applies to infringement within the forum.

No such international harmony exists concerning which law applies to questions of authorship, ownership, and transfer of rights.[143] While many countries will look to the law of the forum to answer these questions, courts in other countries will look to the country of origin or the country

---

[138] Douglas E. Phillips, *International Software Outsourcing* § 17.02[B], in DRAFTING LICENSING AGREEMENTS (Michael A. Epstein & Frank Politano, eds. 2013).

[139] GOLDSTEIN AND HUGENHOLTZ, *supra* note 32, at § 4.4.

[140] Paul Edward Geller, *International Copyright: The Introduction* §6[3][b]i], in INTERNATIONAL COPYRIGHT LAW AND PRACTICE (Paul Edward Geller and Lionel Bently eds. 2013); Regulation 593/2008 of the European Parliament and of the Council of 17 June 2008 on the Law Applicable to Contractual Obligations (Rome 1),2008 O.J. (L 177) 6.; American Law Institute, RESTATEMENT (SECOND) CONFLICT OF LAWS, §§ 186–188 (1988 revision) (criteria applicable to contracts).

[141] GOLDSTEIN AND HUGENHOLTZ, *supra* note 32, at § 4.4.2.

[142] *Ibid.* at § 4.4.3.

[143] *Ibid.*

having the closest connection to the work to answer questions of authorship and initial ownership.[144]

In the United States, issues of ownership and of substantive rights related to infringement are bifurcated into different conflict of law analyses. Courts generally determined ownership according to the law of the country with the most significant relationship to the property and parties, while deciding issues of infringement and remedies by the laws of the country where the infringement is alleged to have occurred. This rule was first articulated by the Second Circuit in *Itar-tass Russian News Agency v. Russian Kurier, Inc.*[145] The Court noted that U.S. copyright law contains no relevant conflict of law rules[146] and that previous courts had applied the work-for-hire doctrine without explicitly considering the conflict of law issues.[147]

The Second Circuit established, as a matter of federal common law, a choice of law rule for determining copyright ownership based on the *Restatement (Second) of Conflict of Laws*. The party's property interests are determined by the law of the state with "the most significant relationship" to the property and the parties.[148] Applying the rule, the court determined the work's "country of origin" was the appropriate law to apply in determining ownership of a work created by a foreign national and first published in its home country.[149] The court applied Russian law to determine whether the works were owned by the plaintiffs[150] and U.S. copyright law to govern issues of infringement and remedies.[151] Subsequent courts have followed this approach, applying foreign law to determine authorship or ownership. If the work is created by a foreign national and first published in a foreign country, then that is the country with the most significant relationship and the law of that country will be applied.[152]

---

[144]   *Ibid.*

[145]   153 F.3d 82 (2d Cir. 1998).

[146]   *Ibid.* at 90.

[147]   *Ibid.* at 88–89 (citations omitted).

[148]   *Ibid.* at 90 (*citing* RESTATEMENT (SECOND) OF THE CONFLICT OF LAWS § 222).

[149]   *Ibid.*

[150]   *Ibid.* at 92.

[151]   This is consistent with the Berne Convention regime conditioning choice of law in infringement in cross border cases on where the infringement occurred. Geller, *supra* note 139, at § 6[3].

[152]   *Fahmy v. Jay-Z*, 788 F.Supp. 2d 1072 (C.D. Cal. 2011); *Lahiri v. Universal Music and Video Distribution, Inc.*, 513 F. Supp. 2d 1172, 1176 (C.D.

The impact of *Iter-Tass* on software-based copyrighted products created with globally distributed teams is both considerable and unclear. The Second Circuit acknowledges that for purposes of conflict of laws, "ownership and infringement issues will not always easily be made."[153] The most difficult cases are those in which the cases involve questions not only of ownership, but of the nature of the ownership interest,[154] such as works created by multinational teams that may or may not be subjected to work-for-hire doctrine.[155]

The nationality of the person creating the work has been important in U.S. cases. The nationality of employer and where the work is first published may make a difference as well. "Insofar as the copyright ability of a work turns on the nationality or domicile of its author" the work-for-hire provision "may mean that the employer's nationality or domicile is determinative."[156] The work at issue in *Itar-Tass* was not first published in the United States nor had it been registered with the U.S. Copyright Office. The Second Circuit did not consider the interrelationship of foreign copyright law and the Copyright Act's presumption of validity for a timely registered work.[157] The law on this interrelationship is unclear. Given that a U.S.-based company will likely first publish its game application in the U.S. and register the work, the presumption of validity may be difficult to overcome.

Once the question of ownership has been decided, the next question is whether the work has been assigned. The *Itar-Tass* court did not clarify choice of law issues concerning the assignment of rights.[158] Nimmer suggests that the law of the country with the "most significant relationship" to the property and parties should also apply to assignments and licenses.[159] This may be what U.S. courts are tacitly doing. In *Saregama India Ltd.*, the Eleventh Circuit assumed, without deciding the issue, that Indian law governed both the ownership and the transfer of rights in that

---

Cal. 2007); *Saregama India Ltd. v. Mosley,* 687 F. Supp. 2d 1325,1334 (S.D. Fla. 2009), *aff'd* 635 F. 3d 1284, 1290 (11 th Cir. 2011).

[153]   153 F.3d at 91.

[154]   NIMMER, *supra* note 5, at § 17.05[B][2].

[155]   Geller, *supra* note 140, at § 6[2][b]ii](noting that joint or collaborative works and those created by collectives and teams also present difficult cases).

[156]   NIMMER, *supra* note 5, at §§ 5.03[A] and 5.10[A].

[157]   *See* 17 U.S.C. § 410(c); *Seoul Broadcasting v. Young Min Ro,* 784 F. Supp. 2d 611, 614–15 (E.D. Va., 2011) (finding that the nature of evidence of foreign law submitted did not overcome the presumption of validity in 17 U.S.C. § 410(c)).

[158]   153 F.3d at 91, fn 11.

[159]   NIMMER, *supra* note 5, at §17.05[B][2].

case.[160] The composer was Indian, the work was first published in India, and the agreements governing transfer of ownership provided that Indian law governed. In actuality, the case contained no conflict of laws issues since the result would have been the same under either Indian or U.S. law.[161] The court set down no rules for determining which law would govern in the event of an actual conflict of foreign laws. These issues have yet to arise or be resolved in a reported case concerning outsourcing software or computer-based applications using distributed work forces.

VIII. CONCLUSION

Companies recognize the benefits of incorporating employee and con-tractor talent from across the globe to create copyrighted works. They may not always appreciate the pitfalls that exist, as well. A carefully drafted choice of law clause in employment and contractor agreements designating U.S. law will not be enough to ensure ownership and control. It remains an open question which law a U.S. court will apply to determine issues of authorship for portions of the work created abroad.

Although most countries do not recognize corporate authorship, it is possible for a legal entity to obtain ownership in the economic aspects of employee works in most jurisdictions. This may be accomplished either by operation of law or by using assignment agreements that meet the requirements of host country law. In jurisdictions such as Germany, following a monistic theory of copyright, such ownership by an employer is never possible since assignments are prohibited. Given the inability of the international community to reach accord on how to define author and initial owner, and that the U.S. perspective on corporate ownership is at odds with many legal traditions, it is unlikely that this area will achieve harmony. Recognition of moral rights in many countries will remain an obstacle to applying U.S. work-for-hire rules in jurisdictions in which they cannot be assigned or waived.

This is an area of law in which international harmonization does not exist and is unlikely to occur. Therefore, understanding the contours of copyright laws in each country in which a person is hired to create or contribute to a copyrighted work is essential. If a company wants to ensure ongoing ownership and control over works created by globally distributed teams, it must take care to outsource the work to countries where the laws support that control.

---

[160]   635 F. 3d 1284 (11th Cir. 2011).
[161]   *Ibid.* at 1292.

BIBLIOGRAPHY

Treaties and International Conventions

Agreement on Trade-Related Aspects of Intellectual Property Rights, Apr. 15, 1994, Marrakesh Agreement Establishing the World Trade Organization, Annex 1C, 1869 U.N.T.S. 299; 33 I.L.M. 1197 (1994).

Berne Convention for the Protection of Literary and Artistic Works, Sept. 9, 1886, as revised at Paris on July 24, 1971 and amended in 1979, S. Treaty Doc. No. 99-27 (1986).

Statutes and Codes

The Berne Convention Implementation Act of 1988, Pub. L. No. 100-568, 102 Stat. 2853.

C. DE LA PROPRIÉTÉ INTELLECTUELLE [CPI] Art. L.121–2, Art. L.122–6 (Fr.).

The Copyright Act, No. 14 of 1957; India Code (1957) (India).

Copyright, Designs and Patent Act, 1988, c. 48, (U.K.).

Copyright Law of the People's Republic of China (中华人民共和国著作权法), (promulgated by the Standing Committee of the Eleventh National People's Congress, Feb. 26, 2010, effective Apr. 1, 2010)(China) *available at* http://www.wipo.int/wipolex/en/text.jsp?file_id=186569).

Council Directive 1991/250/EEC of May 1991 on the Legal Protection of Computer Programs, 1991 O.J. (L. 122) 42.

Directive 2001/29/EC of the European Parliament and of the Council of 22 May 2001 on the Harmonisation of Certain Aspects of Copyright and Related Rights in the Information Society, 2001 O.J. (L. 167) 10.

Directive 2014/26/EU of the European Parliament and of the Council on Collective Management of Copyright and Related Rights and Multi-territorial Licensing of Rights in Musical Works for Online Use in the Internal Market, 2014 O.J. (L. 84) 72.

Gesetz über Urheberrecht und verwandte Schutzrechte [Urheberrechtsgesetz] [Copyright Act], Sept. 09, 1965, BGBl. I S. at 1273 (Ger.).

Regulation 593/2008 of the European Parliament and of the Council of 17 June 2008 on the Law Applicable to Contractual Obligations (Rome 1), 2008 O.J. (L. 177) 6.

United States Code, Copyright Act of 1976, 17 U.S.C. §§ 101 *et seq.* (2012)

The Visual Artist Rights Act of 1990, Pub. L. No. 101-650 (codified as amended in scattered sections of 17 U.S.C.).

Cases

Burrow-Giles Lithographic Co. v. Sarony, 111 U.S. 253 (1884).

Community for Creative Non-Violence v. Reid, 490 U.S. 730 (1989).

Cour de cassation [Cass.] [supreme court for judicial matters] Jul. 12, 2006, Bull. civ., No. 5-15472 (FR).

Fahmy v. Jay-Z, 788 F.Supp. 2d 1072 (C.D. Cal. 2011).

Itar-tass Russian News Agency v. Russian Kurier, Inc., 153 F.3d. 82 (2d Cir. 1998).

Lahiri v. Universal Music and Video Distribution, Inc., 513 F. Supp. 2d 1172 (C.D. Cal. 2007).
Morris v. Business Concepts, Inc., 283 F.3d 502 (2d Cir. 2002).
Saregama India Ltd. v. Mosley, 687 F. Supp. 2d 1325 (S.D. Fla. 2009), *aff'd* 635 F. 3d 1284 (11th Cir. 2011).
Seoul Broadcasting v. Young Min Ro, 784 F. Supp. 2d 611 (E.D. Va. 2011).

Secondary Sources

Bently, Lionel and William R. Cornish, *United Kingdom*, in INTERNATIONAL COPYRIGHT LAW AND PRACTICE (Paul Edward Geller and Lionel Bently eds. 2013).
Buckman, Deborah F., Annotation, *Intellectual Property Rights in Video, Electronic, and Computer Games*, 7 A.L.R. Fed. 2d 269 (2005).
Dietz, Adolf, *Germany*, in INTERNATIONAL COPYRIGHT LAW AND PRACTICE (Paul Edward Geller and Lionel Bently eds. 2013).
DRATLER, JAY, JR. AND STEPHEN M. MCJOHN, INTELLECTUAL PROPERTY LAW: COMMERCIAL, CREATIVE, & INDUSTRIAL PROPERTY (Lslf. ed. 2013).
Ehrlich, Marc. A., *Fair Use or Foul Play? The EC Directive on the Legal Protection of Computer Programs and Its Impact on Reverse Engineering*, 13 PACE L.REV. 1003 (1994).
EPSTEIN, MICHAEL A. AND FRANK L. POLITANO, DRAFTING LICENSING AGREEMENTS (2002, 2003 SUPPLEMENT).
Fisk, Catherine L., *Authors at Work: The Origins of the Work-for-Hire Doctrine*, 15 YALE J. L & HUMAN. 1 (2003).
Gangjee, Dev and S. Ramaiah, *India*, in INTERNATIONAL COPYRIGHT LAW AND PRACTICE (Paul Edward Geller and Lionel Bently eds. 2013).
Geller, Paul Edward, *International Copyright: The Introduction*, in INTERNATIONAL COPYRIGHT LAW AND PRACTICE (Paul Edward Geller and Lionel Bently eds. 2013).
GOLDSTEIN, PAUL AND P. BERNT HUGENHOLTZ, INTERNATIONAL COPYRIGHT: PRINCIPLES, LAW, AND PRACTICE (3d ed. 2012).
Hong, Xue and Guo Shoukang, *China*, in INTERNATIONAL COPYRIGHT LAW AND PRACTICE (Paul Edward Geller and Lionel Bently eds., 2013).
INDIA: A HANDBOOK OF COPYRIGHT LAW (Government of India Ministry of Human Resource Development) (1999), *available at* http://www.wipo.int/wipolex/en/text.jsp?file_id=208016.
Hayes, Benjamin S., *Integrating Moral Rights into U.S. Law and the Problem of the Works for Hire Doctrine*, 61 OHIO ST. L. J. 1013 (2000).
André, Lucas, Pascal Kamina and Robert Plaisant, *France*, in INTERNATIONAL COPYRIGHT LAW AND PRACTICE (Paul Edward Geller and Lionel Bently eds. 2013).
LUCAS-SCHLOETTER, AGNÈS, LES DROITS D'AUTEUR DES SALARIÉS EN EUROPE CONTINENTALE, (Cahiers de l'IRPI, No. 5, 2004).
MILLSTEIN, JULIAN S., JEFFREY D. NEUGURGER AND JEFFRY P. WEIGARD, DOING BUSINESS ON THE INTERNET: FORMS AND ANALYSIS (Lslf. ed. 2013).
NEFF, RICHARD E. AND FRAN SMALLSON, NAFTA: PROTECTING AND ENCOURAGING INTELLECTUAL PROPERTY RIGHTS IN NORTH AMERICA (1994).
NIMMER, MELVILLE B. AND DAVID NIMMER, NIMMER ON COPYRIGHT (Lslf. ed. 2013).

Ochoa, Tyler T., *Who Owns an Avatar? Copyright, Creativity, and the Virtual World*, 14 VAND. J .ENT. & TECH. L. 959 (2012).

Oman, Ralph, *Berne Revision: The Continuing Drama*, 4 FORDHAM INTELL. PROP., MEDIA & ENT. L. J. 139 (1993).

Palmer, Alan K. and Thomas C. Vinje, *The EC Directive on the Legal Protection of Computer Software: New Law Governing Software Development*, 2 DUKE J. COMP. & INT'L. L. 65 (1992).

Phillips, Douglas E., *International Software Outsourcing*, in DRAFTING LICENSING AGREEMENTS (Michael A. Epstein and Frank Politano, eds., 2013).

RAJAN, MIRA T. SUNDARA, MORAL RIGHTS: PRINCIPLES, PRACTICE AND NEW TECHNOLOGY 295 (2011).

RESTATEMENT (SECOND) CONFLICT OF LAWS, vol. 1 (1988 revision).

Saikia, Nandita, *Indian Law: Getting Moral Rights Waived* (July 15, 2012), *available at* http://copyright.lawmatters.in/2010/07.

Tober, J. Patrick and Shawn C. Helms, *The "Work For Hire" Doctrine Almost Never Works in Software Development Contracts*, METROPOLITAN CORP. COUNS.10 (June 2008).

WOLK, SANNA and Christine Kirchberger, OWNERSHIP OF THE COPYRIGHT IN WORKS AND THE PATENT RIGHT IN INVENTIONS CREATED BY EMPLOYEES: IN FINLAND, SWEDEN, GERMANY, AUSTRIA, THE UNITED KINGDOM, ESTONIA AND ARGENTINA (2002).

9. Patent grant-back clauses in international license agreements: a survey and ethical analysis

David Orozco

This chapter will examine the topic of patent grant-back clauses in international patent license agreements. These clauses, which have greatest applicability to independent contractor agency relationships, have the potential to restrict innovation and violate international legal and ethical norms. Several international treatments of this issue will be examined to find a compromise that tempers the negative impacts of overly broad and restrictive grant-back clauses. A sample clause will then be offered as a compromise that represents an ethical solution that takes international norms and cultural differences into account

A patent is a set of exclusive rights granted to applicants for inventions that meet standards of novelty, non-obviousness, utility and full disclosure.[1] A patent grant-back is a contract term in a patent licensing contract that legally obligates the party licensing the technology (licensee) to transfer ownership of any improvements that the licensee makes with respect to the licensed technology back to the patent owner (licensor). This practice raises several interesting issues related to business strategy, international trade law and ethics. Each of these issues will be examined in this chapter.

In its broadest form, a patent grant-back extends to any improvement that relates in any way to the licensed and patented technology. An improvement patent builds from a prior patented technology and a license is required by the licensor to practice the improvement. A broad patent grant-back clause would require the licensee to notify the licensor of any improvements made, as in the following case:

---

[1] *See* 35 U.S.C. §§ 101, 103.

In the event Licensee or any of its employees shall make or acquire any invention or improvement relating to the licensed inventions, then the Licensee shall disclose and communicate such invention or improvement to Licensor and shall aid and assist in acquiring patent protection thereof.[2]

A patent grant-back may also be overly broad and restrictive if it forbids the licensee from using the improvement by assigning exclusive rights back to the licensor, for example in this case:

Licensee shall disclose to Licensor within thirty (30) days of the first use or embodiment thereof any improvements of the Licensed Technology, whether or not patentable, conceived and made by Licensee or its employees subsequent to the date of the agreement and shall grant to Licensor or its designee an exclusive license thereunder.

The issue of patent grant-back clauses has enormous practical significance given the trends associated with international trade, and cross-border intellectual property transfer agreements.[3] For example, companies in the United States have increasingly outsourced manufacturing overseas.[4] In the process, manufacturing outsourcing agreements with foreign suppliers include intellectual property agreements that seek to preserve the intellectual property rights of the outsourcing company. For example, trade secrets related to manufacturing processes and the trademark rights associated with products have been vigorously protected in outsourcing agreements.

Increasingly, companies partner with overseas companies to engage in joint research and development (R&D). These R&D partnerships may be viewed as another form of outsourcing related to knowledge, technology, and new product development instead of manufacturing. As outsourcing has matured, an opportunity has developed for companies to seek highly skilled talent in emerging markets.[5] The practice of finding alternative sources of knowledge and technology fits within the open innovation

---

[2] *See e.g.*, Zajicek v. Koolvent Metal Awning Corp. of America, 283 F.2d 127 (9th Cir. 1960).

[3] The terms intellectual property transfer and technology transfer are often used interchangeably in practice, and in this chapter, given that most technology transfers are negotiated and involve some intellectual property licensing terms.

[4] Gianmarco I.P. Ottaviano, Giovani Peri and Greg C. Wright, *Immigration, Offshoring and American Jobs*, 103 AMERICAN ECONOMIC REVIEW 1925-59 (2013).

[5] *See* Vinay Cuoto et al., *Offshoring 2.0: Contracting Knowledge and Innovation to Expand Global Capabilities*, Duke University Offshoring Resource Network Report (2007).

paradigm.[6] As companies seek the best, not just the cheapest, talent they enter into collaborative R&D arrangements abroad.[7] Both manufacturing and R&D outsourcing arrangements, however, raise the prospect that licensees will improve the underlying licensed technology, triggering the applicability of a patent grant-back clause.

Patent rights are powerful intellectual property rights since they offer the owner exclusive rights to make, use, or sell the claimed technology.[8] These broad rights establish infringement liability regardless of intent, and a strict liability standard is applied to virtually everyone in the distribution chain regardless of independent discovery, or culpability.[9] The exclusivity offered by patent rights is limited, however, to those jurisdictions where they have been registered.

Patents have gained prominent attention in media, policy, and academic circles given the scope of technologies that can be secured via this intellectual property regime.[10] Patents extend, for example, to genetic material, software, and biotechnology.[11] Patents are also controversial due to international trade considerations since they have been used in the U.S. to block imported goods manufactured overseas that have been found to infringe upon domestic patent rights. The International Trade Commission (ITC) has played a central role in stopping infringing goods from entering the U.S. ports by issuing exclusion orders involving the importation of infringing products. High profile cases in this area are *Apple v. Samsung* and other cases involving device manufacturers that have engaged in the so-called "smart phone patent wars."[12]

The World Intellectual Property Organization (WIPO), a United Nations-affiliated entity, annually measures the considerable growth in

---

[6] Open Innovation is the practice of finding innovation outside of the traditional confines of an organization. *See* HENRY CHESBOROUGH, OPEN INNOVATION: THE NEW IMPERATIVE FOR CREATING AND PROFITING FROM TECHNOLOGY (1995).

[7] Cuoto el al., *supra* note 5.

[8] Patent rights are negative rights that offer exclusivity against others.

[9] This standard differs from trade secrets or copyright liability standards.

[10] *See* David Orozco, *Administrative Patent Levers*, 117 PENN STATE L. REV. 1 (2012).

[11] *See* David Orozco, *Administrative Patent Levers in the Software, Biotechnology and Clean Technology Industries*, 9 J.L ECON. & POL'Y 615 (2013).

[12] Another controversial area of patent-related activity involves the strategic use of patents and other intellectual property. *See* Ashby Jones and Jessica E. Vascellaro, *Smartphone Patents: The Never-Ending War*, WALL ST. J., (April 12, 2012); *see also* Robert C. Bird and David Orozco, *Finding the Right Corporate Legal Strategy*, 56 MIT SLOAN MGMT. REV. 81 (Fall 2014),

global intellectual property registrations, and research and development flows. For example, China accounts for some of the highest growth in terms of domestic and foreign intellectual property filings. According to WIPO, in 2013 China accounted for 28 percent of the global share of patent filings within the top five patent offices.[13] China has also been the recipient of large foreign direct investment (FDI) inflows due to its status as a global manufacturing hub. China's FDI inflows for 2013 totaled a record high $117.6 billion. Much of the investment in China exploits its low cost and efficient labor force and supply chain capabilities, which have propelled its status as a global exporter.[14] In the United States, this has led to a decrease in manufacturing jobs from a high of 19.6 million manufacturing workers in 1979 to 11.8 million in 2012.[15] The focus of this article will be on the United States as a major global exporter of R&D, know-how, and manufacturing and business processes, and China and India since they are significant targets of these knowledge outflows.

Each of these three countries has a very distinct background related to intellectual property rights. This yields a complex international scenario that includes cultural norms, national laws, international treaties, and different development agendas. For example, one scholar questions whether intellectual property rights can find a suitable place in Chinese culture and society.[16] India has cultural norms that clash with Western notions of patent rights, particularly as they apply to agriculture[17] and healthcare.[18] With respect to the development issue, emerging economies like China and India are regarded as developing nations that can economically benefit from more liberal technology transfer practices. From an ethical perspective, some scholars argue that extending strict intellectual property laws to less developed nations is another version of

---

[13]   These patent offices include the United States Patent Office (PTO), the Chinese Patent Office (SIPO), European Patent Office (EPO), Korean IP Office (KIPO), and the Japanese Patent Office (JPO).

[14]   *See* David Orozco, *Will India and China Profit from Technological Innovation?* 5 Nw. J. Tech & Intell. Prop. 426 (2006). China's status as a low cost manufacturing center is diminishing due to higher wages. Increasingly, companies that seek to exploit lower wages are offshoring manufacturing in Southeast Asian countries like Vietnam.

[15]   Floyd Norris, *Manufacturing is Surprising Bright Spot in U.S. Economy*, N.Y.Times (Jan. 5, 2012).

[16]   *See* William P. Alford, To Steal a Book is an Elegant Offense: Intellectual Property Law in Chinese Civilization (1995).

[17]   *See* Vandana Shiva, Biopiracy: The Plunder of Nature (1997).

[18]   *Ibid.*

colonialism.[19] The problem of patent grant-backs is one additional challenge in this context, and national laws, treaties, business strategy, and ethical concerns all weigh in on this controversial and commonplace business practice.

I. PATENT GRANT-BACK CLAUSES

In its broadest form, a patent grant-back clause grants the licensor the exclusive rights to any improvement related to the licensed technology, or the actual title to the improvements. This can take the form of an assignment clause that requires the transfer of title to improvements, or an exclusive license awarded back to the licensor.[20] From a U.S. contract law perspective, these terms are permissible since they constitute consideration that induces bargaining related to the licensor's promise to license the patented technology.

From a strategic business perspective, a patent licensor would want to add a grant-back clause for several reasons. First, the licensor may be unwilling to license its technology because the technology may be improved upon in a manner that leads to downstream blocking patents that would prevent the licensor from practicing the improvement to its underlying technology. In the context of international technology transfer relationships, this takes on added risk since a low cost manufacturer may be able to engage in forward integration[21] and compete with the original licensor at a lower cost and with improved technology. Outsourcing companies in emerging markets have aggressively expanded into value-added products and services to avoid commoditization and to achieve superior margins.[22] Innovation, therefore, plays an ever-increasing role in

---

[19] *See* David Orozco and Latha Poonamallee, *The Role of Ethics in the Commercialization of Indigenous Knowledge*, 119 J. BUS. ETHICS 275 (2014).

[20] *See* Santa Fe Pomeroy Inc v. P&Z Corp, 569 F.2d 1084 (9th Cir. 1978) (discussing a case involving a grant-back clause that stated that if the licensee or any of its contractors or subcontractors made or acquired any improvements in the licensed invention, those improvements would immediately be disclosed to the licensor and the licensor would have the first right to attempt to patent them. The agreement also provided that the licensor could use any of those improvements without payment of additional royalties).

[21] *See* MICHAEL PORTER, COMPETITIVE STRATEGY: TECHNIQUES FOR ANALYZING INDUSTRIES AND COMPETITORS (1980).

[22] Outsourcing companies are now migrating to even lower cost areas such as southeast Asia (Vietnam) and Africa since Chinese wages have risen to the point that these lower cost areas are more efficient.

the outsourcing industry in developing nations.[23] Without a patent grant-back clause, these innovative efforts among outsourcing companies could lead to the licensor's loss of technology and the payment of higher royalty rates. From this perspective, patent grant-backs are considered an important risk management tool that actually encourages technology licensing.[24]

From a strategic perspective, one of the most important reasons for including the patent grant-back clause in international license agreements is to avoid creating a future competitor. This scenario has begun to occur in the U.S. auto industry after U.S. companies entered China to manufacture vehicles for the large Chinese auto market. A significant amount of patented technology and trade secret related know-how was transferred to Chinese partners in joint ventures that required foreign auto companies to transfer technology to domestic car companies under Chinese foreign investment laws that were meant to encourage indigenous innovation.[25] The companies created under these Chinese joint ventures are now seeking to expand the exports of Chinese-made vehicles to foreign markets, including emerging markets and eventually the U.S. market.[26]

Patent grant-back clauses are typically examined in the classic outsourcing scenario involving technology transfer into the market for goods and services. In this case, knowledge is licensed so that goods and services are produced abroad and then imported and re-integrated into the licensor's distribution chain. Another less-examined scenario that is increasingly common, as described above, involves patent grant-back clauses in cases that involve markets for knowledge such as R&D and new product development. In these cases, the licensor offers technology that is integrated as an input used in a third party's distribution chain. This occurred in the recent landmark case of *TianRui v. ITC*, a trade secret case.[27] In that case, an American manufacturer of steel railroad wheels (Amsted) licensed manufacturing trade secrets that it no longer practiced to Datong, a Chinese manufacturer. TianRui was Datong's

---

[23] Cuoto et al., *supra* note 5.

[24] Maria Isabella Leone and Toke Reichstein, *Licensing-In Fosters Rapid Invention! The Effect of the Grant-Back Clause and Technological Unfamiliarity*, 33 STRAT. MGMT. J., 965, 968 (2012).

[25] U.S. International Trade Commission, China: Effects of Intellectual Property Infringement and Indigenous Innovation Policies on the U.S. Economy, USITC Publication No. 4226, 5-37 (2011).

[26] *See* Colum Murphy, *Chinese Car Makers not Ready for U.S. Market,* WALL ST. J. (Jan. 9, 2014).

[27] TianRui Group Co. v. ITC, 661 F.3d 1322 (Fed. Cir. 2011).

competitor in China and tried unsuccessfully to license Amsted's trade secrets. TianRui then induced former Datong employees to disclose the trade secrets, which were used to manufacture railroad wheels that were exported to the U.S. In a landmark decision, the ITC and the Federal Circuit both held that trade secret misappropriation that occurs abroad may trigger liability if the infringing goods make their way back into the United States.[28]

Cases that involve traditional technology licensing to outsource manu-facturing and those that involve licensing for use as an R&D input in a third party's distribution chain often involve patent grant-backs. Both cases, however, present different societal risks and concerns. In the first case, regulators may discourage or forbid the use of patent grant-backs since they may lead to under-investment in the manufacturer's innovative capabilities. Knowing that any improvements related to manufacturing processes or the underlying technology will flow back to the licensor, the licensee will refrain from making any investments in innovation. This may lead to foregone investment opportunities that would yield more innovation. Also, if the manufacturer licensee engages in innovation that yields an improvement, a patent grant-back would offer no guaranteed payment, resulting in an unfair scenario. Both cases may result in lower social welfare. Empirical research confirms that in cases where grant-back clauses are present, licensees take longer to innovate given that their incentives to do so are lower when these contract terms are present.[29]

In cases that involve technology licensing as an R&D input for third party commercialization, the same problems persist; however, there is also the added problem of a potential patent hold-up. This occurs when a patentee upstream controls a key patent that is necessary to practice a more complex technology downstream. This scenario occurs most often in cases involving complex, or highly integrated technologies, such as electronics, software or technology standards.[30] A patent grant-back to a licensor that is unwilling to license may ultimately stifle innovation in complex technologies at the R&D stage.

---

28 *Ibid.*
29 Leone and Reichstein, *supra* note 24.
30 *See* David Orozco and James Conley, *Friends of the Court: Using Amicus Briefs to Identify Corporate Advocacy Positions in Supreme Court Patent Litigation*, 2 U. OF ILL. J. OF L. TECH., & POLICY 101 (2011); Rosemarie Ziedonis, *Don't Fence Me In: Fragmented Markets for Technology and the Patent Acquisition of Strategies of Firms*, 50 MGMT. SCI. 804 (2004).

Ultimately, policy-makers must decide how best to advance social welfare by striking an appropriate balance between protecting the patentee's property rights as an incentive to innovate and protecting the licensee's interest in advancing and diffusing the licensed technology. The comparative approach taken to address this question by lawmakers in the United States, China and India will be discussed next.

II. COMPARATIVE LEGAL ANALYSIS AND CONSIDERATIONS

A. The United States

In the United States, patent grant-back clauses have been legally challenged under antitrust laws. The antitrust statute that is relevant to licensing is Section 1 of the Sherman Act since it addresses bilateral conduct that prohibits "every contract, combination in the form of a trust, or conspiracy in restraint of trade or commerce."[31] A patent license with terms that restrain trade will, therefore, violate antitrust laws and will be deemed a patent misuse. The patent misuse doctrine is often applied in an antitrust analysis and arises when a patentee has "impermissibly broadened the 'physical or temporal scope' of the patent grant with anticompetitive effect."[32] A finding of misuse renders the patent unenforceable and is an affirmative defense to patent infringement.

When the courts or administrative agencies review license terms to determine patent misuse and anticompetitive behavior, they often apply a rule of reason analysis.[33] This analysis involves an inquiry into the specific facts and circumstances that are unique to the business and market in question, the nature and history of the restraint, its justification and its likely impact on competition.[34] This is in contrast to a per se illegality determination against certain practices. To date, the courts have

---

[31] Sherman Antitrust Act, 15 U.S.C §§1-7.

[32] Windsurfing Intl., Inc. v. AMF, Inc., 782 F.2d 995, 1001 (Fed. Cir. 1986).

[33] Commentators agree that a few patent license terms are likely to be analyzed under the alternate per se rule. For example, the Department of Justice and the Federal Trade Commission will employ a stricter approach when examining reverse payment agreements between brand-name and generic drug makers, and patent holders asserting standard-essential patents. *See* Kenneth M. Frankel and Mark S. Zhai, *A Return to the DOJ's "Nine No-Nos"?*, The AIPLA Antitrust News (Jan. 2013).

[34] Board of Trade v. U.S., 246 U.S. 231, 238 (1918).

held that patent grant-backs are not per se illegal, and instead they must be analyzed under the rule of reason.[35]

Generally, the courts have allowed grant-backs unless they work with other terms in the license to restrain trade.[36] When applying the rule of reason to grant-backs, the courts will look at the scope of improvements covered, the licensee's right to practice the improvements, and the duration of the grant-back obligation.[37] It is very rare for a court to invalidate a grant-back when there are no other license terms that restrain trade. Also, courts uphold patent grant-back clauses in the U.S. that are unsupported by additional consideration. If grant-backs are found to work with other restrictive license terms, however, they may be found to violate antitrust laws.

B. China

An important source of law in China that relates to patent grant-backs are the Regulations on Technology Import and Export Administration. These laws prohibit certain grant-back practices. For example, Article 27 states that "[w]ithin the term of validity of a contract for technology import, an achievement made in improving the technology concerned belongs to the party making the improvement." In a licensing context, this article establishes that the title to improvements and patent rights flows to the licensee absent any agreement to the contrary. Article 29 of this law foresees the issue of a patent grant-back and states the following: "A technology import contract shall not contain any of the following restrictive clauses: ... (3) restricting the receiving party from improving the technology supplied by the supplying party, or restricting the receiving party from using the improved technology." In China, therefore, a patent grant-back may not restrict the licensee from improving the technology, or its ability to use the improvement. If the grant-back does either of these things, it will be declared null and void under Chinese law.

As mentioned by one commentator, patent grant-backs must be carefully drafted to comply with Chinese law.[38] For example, licensors

---

[35] Transparent Wrap Machine, Corp., v. Stokes & Smith Co., 329 U.S. 637 (1947).

[36] Justice Douglas, writing for the Supreme Court majority in the Transwrap case held that grant-backs were lawful since they involved "using one legalized monopoly to acquire another legalized monopoly." *Ibid.* at 644.

[37] *See* Duplan Corp. v. Deering Milliken, Inc., 444 F.Supp. 648 (D.S.C. 1977); Santa Fe-Pomeroy, Inc., v. P&Z Co., Inc., 569 F.2d 1084 (9th Cir. 1978).

[38] J. Benjamin Bai, *Licensor Beware*, IP LAW & BUSINESS (2007).

who wish to implement a lawful and effective patent grant-back must take care to avoid the trappings of Article 27 by offering separate consideration to the licensee in exchange for the transfer of title to the improvement. Failing to do so invalidates the grant-back in China, and the licensee would own the improvement.[39] In China, therefore, licensees must be permitted to improve the licensed technology, practice the improvement and be offered additional consideration if title to the improvement is to be assigned back to the licensor. A defect in any of these requirements, e.g., an exclusive license or assignment back to the licensor, would negate the validity of the grant-back, and the licensee would have full ownership of the improvement.

C. India

In India, the patent laws are assessed relative to what policy-makers deem are the reasonable requirements of the public interest. The public interest, therefore, plays an important role in Indian patent law to a degree that distinguishes it from many other nations. Specifically, Section 84 (1) of the Indian Patent Act of 1970 lists various circumstances which constitute a failure to meet the reasonable requirements of the public and, therefore, merit a compulsory license.[40] Among the disfavored practices are exclusive license grant-back clauses. The specific language in the Act states that: "For the purposes of this Chapter, the reasonable requirements of the public shall be deemed not to have been satisfied – ... if the patentee imposes a condition upon the grant of licences [sic] under the patent to provide exclusive grant-back, prevention to challenges to the validity of patent or coercive package licensing ..." A patent grant-back clause would be challenged under this section of the Indian Patent Act by petitioning the patent authorities to grant a compulsory license.

Section 140 of the Indian Patent Act prohibits certain restrictive conditions outright. Among the license terms that are per se illegal under the Act are those that "provide exclusive grant-back, prevention to challenges to validity of Patent & Coercive package licensing." In India, a patent grant-back clause that extends an exclusive license back to the licensor is, therefore, illegal according to the Act, and may trigger a compulsory license under Section 84 of the Act. According to one commentator, the statute only prohibits exclusive license grant-backs; however, by implication, an assignment grant-back that transfers title to

---

[39] *Ibid.*

[40] A compulsory license is the authorization provided by the Government to a person for the exploitation of a patent without the patent holder's consent.

the licensor would be likewise prohibited.[41] Another implication according to the same source is that non-exclusive grant-backs are lawful in India.[42]

III. THE UNCTAD'S CODE OF CONDUCT ON THE TRANSFER OF TECHNOLOGY AND TRIPS ARTICLE 40

Technology transfer was first raised as an international issue in 1961 when the United Nations Secretary General received a request from developing nations to prepare a study on the role of international treaties in protecting intellectual property rights in developing nations.[43] In 1976, the United Nations Conference on Trade and Development (UNCTAD) engaged in a multi-year negotiation effort between countries to implement a code of conduct related to international technology transfer agreements.[44] This effort was initiated by developing nations as a way to preserve access to technology and stimulate development on fair terms.[45] For example, one restrictive license term that would have been forbidden under the code involved exclusive patent grant-back provisions. Specifically, the code would have prevented:

> [r]equiring the acquiring party to transfer or grant back to the supplying party, or to any other enterprise designated by the supplying party, improvements arising from the acquired technology, on an exclusive basis [or] without offsetting consideration or reciprocal obligations from the supplying party, or when the practice will constitute an abuse of a dominant market position of the supplying party.

Although the code was criticized and challenged by developed nations and was ultimately unsuccessful, the UNCTAD's draft code illustrates various important points of contention between developed and developing

---

[41] Amarchand and Mangaldas & Suresh A. Shroff & Co., INTELLECTUAL PROPERTY AND COMPETITION LAW (2011).

[42] *Ibid.*

[43] Padmashree Gehl Sampath and Pedro Roffe, *Upacking the International Technology Transfer Debate: Fifty Years and Beyond, International Centre for Trade and Sustainable Development (ICTSD)*, Working Paper, 6 June 2012.

[44] UNCTAD is governed by United Nations member states and its purpose is to deal with international trade issues as a driver of development.

[45] Ton J. M. Zuidjwijk, *The UNCTAD Code of Conduct on the Transfer of Technology*, 24 McGILL LAW J. 562 (1978).

nations. Many of the issues highlighted during the code's negotiation are still being debated to this day. Some of these issues relate to ethical concerns raised by developing nations concerning their ability to access technologies under fair terms as part of their development agenda.

The World Trade Organization (WTO) Agreement on Trade Related Aspects of Intellectual Property Rights (TRIPS) came into effect in 1995 and introduced intellectual property law into international trade agreements for the first time. TRIPS has generated considerable controversy since it is perceived by some as an attempt to impose intellectual property laws and standards that favor the economic and trade agendas of industrialized vis-à-vis developing nations. One area of contention involved patent grant-backs. Article 40(2) of TRIPS discusses patent grant-backs and specifically states:

> Nothing in this Agreement shall prevent Members from specifying in their legislation licensing practices or conditions that may in particular cases constitute an abuse of intellectual property rights having an adverse effect on competition in the relevant market. As provided above, a Member may adopt, consistently with the other provisions of this Agreement, appropriate measures to prevent or control such practices, which may include *for example exclusive grantback conditions*, conditions preventing challenges to validity and coercive package licensing, in the light of the relevant laws and regulations of that Member (emphasis added).

This chapter was adopted at the request of less developed countries in part so they could enact legislation that would be TRIPS-compliant, yet, protect the right of their domestic companies to innovate and practice technical improvements.

IV. ETHICAL ISSUES

There is a vigorous and ongoing debate about the role that ethics should play in issues involving intellectual property.[46] At one end of the spectrum are groups that analogize intangible property with tangible property and seek to protect intellectual property rights as vigorously as tangible property rights. The opposing view regards intangible property as conceptually distinct,[47] and regards treating the two types of property

---

[46] *See* D.B. Resnik, *A Pluralistic Account of Intellectual Property*, 46 J. BUS. ETHICS 319 (2003).

[47] Intellectual property, unlike tangible property, is both non-rivalrous and non-excludable.

as a mistake that has serious social and ethical consequences.[48] Parties who favor the first perspective tend to identify with a libertarian ideology and they view the freedom of choice concomitant with property rights as a paramount principle in society. They also regard the incentive offered by exclusive monopoly rights as a necessary condition for promoting the progress of science and useful arts. Those who fall into the second category tend to identify with either a utilitarian group that assesses intellectual property in relation to economic efficiency and social welfare, or a humanistic perspective that regards deontological interests such as human rights as a vital counterforce to the demands of intellectual property rights holders. These competing perspectives emerge in debates held in developed nations,[49] and prove to be as, if not more, divisive in an international context.

Advocates for less developed nations make various arguments about why intellectual property rights should not be applied forcefully in an international context. Advocates for developed nations, on the other hand, often take the opposite viewpoint. These concerns and arguments became apparent in the UNCTAD negotiations discussed earlier, which began in 1976 and were led by developing nations. This ongoing debate has continued within the context of TRIPS, most recently during the Doha round of negotiations at the WTO. The 2001 Doha Declaration on TRIPS and Public Health states that the TRIPS agreement should not prevent measures by WTO members to protect public health. This has been used by developing nations to engage in the compulsory licensing of pharmaceuticals to meet the needs of public health crises, including the AIDS epidemic.[50]

Another contentious ethical issue relates to traditional knowledge, which is knowledge held by indigenous communities. It often has cultural and ecological significance. A point of contention in multilateral

---

[48] *See* David Levin and Michele Boldrin, *The Case Against Intellectual Property*, 92 AM. ECON. REV. 209 (2002); Michael A. Heller and Rebecca S. Eisenberg, *Can Patents Deter Innovation? The Anticommons in Biomedical Research*, 280 SCIENCE 698 (1998).

[49] For example, within developed nations there is an ongoing debate about the role of intellectual property in fields like software, creative media and biotechnology. *See* Yochai Benkler, *Coase's Penguin, or, Linux and the Nature of the Firm*, 112 YALE LAW J. 369 (2002); LAWRENCE LESSIG, FREE CULTURE: THE NATURE AND FUTURE OF CREATIVITY (2004); Heller and Eisenberg, *supra* note 48.

[50] *See* Robert Bird and Daniel R. Cahoy, *The Impact of Compulsory Licensing on Foreign Direct Investment: A Collective Bargaining Approach*, 45 AM. BUS. L.J. 283 (2008).

trade agreements is whether there should be a ban on patenting that draws from traditional knowledge sources or some form of informed consent and benefit sharing among indigenous communities.[51] One viewpoint, shared by the author, is that traditional knowledge represents an aspect of communal rights that are ultimately linked to human rights.[52]

According to one scholar, a strong case can be made for pluralism.[53] This perspective has appeal given that different countries approach intellectual property issues differently due to a broad range of political, economic, historical, and cultural differences. Any system that is flexible is ultimately going to be more resilient than one that is rigid, externally imposed or overly formalistic. Given the wide range of differences observed with respect to the very narrow issue of patent grant-back clauses in the United States, China and India it appears that a pluralistic set of principles can be gleaned that would offer room for compromise. For example, a review of the three legal systems on this one topic indicates that patent grant-back clauses should not be declared per se illegal across the board. Instead, at a minimum, a licensor should allow and perhaps even encourage the licensee to improve the licensed technology as a way to partner and share the benefits of distributed innovation. The Indian legal system dictates that the grant-back should not be exclusive but shared between the parties. Also, the Chinese perspective teaches that the licensor must provide some additional and adequate compensation for access to the improvement rights. To comply with all of these perspectives in a pluralistic sense, the following grant-back clause may be suitable:

> In the event Licensee develops any improvements, whether or not patentable, to technology covered by the Licensed Patents, upon the Licensor's written request the Licensee shall grant to Licensor a nonexclusive, worldwide license to such improvements. Licensor shall pay Licensee a reasonable royalty for such licenses so requested upon terms to be negotiated in good faith.

---

[51]   Orozco and Poonamallee, *supra* note 19.

[52]   DAVID OROZCO, KEVIN MCGARRY AND LYDIE PIERRE-LOUIS, *The Human Rights-Related Aspects of Indigenous Knowledge in the Context of Common Law*, in LAW,

[53]   Resnik, *supra* note 46.

V. CONCLUSION

This chapter examined the common practice of including patent grant-back clauses in international license agreements. A survey of various international jurisdictions highlights important legal issues and differences with respect to this licensing term. Patent grant-back clauses are used by patent owners to minimize competitive risks. These terms can be overly broad and, therefore, an abusive practice that deprives the licensee of the incentive to innovate and the rewards of any such efforts. This chapter surveys various international treatments of this issue to find a compromise that tempers the negative impacts of overly broad and restrictive grant-back clauses by offering a sample clause. This compromise represents an ethical solution that takes international norms and cultural differences into account.

BIBLIOGRAPHY

BUSINESS AND HUMAN RIGHTS: BRIDGING THE GAP (Robert C. Bird, Daniel R. Cahoy and Jamie D. Prenkert eds. (2014)).

Statutes and Codes

35 U.S.C. §§ 101, 103.
Sherman Antitrust Act, 15 U.S.C §§ 1-7.

Cases

Board of Trade v. U.S., 246 U.S. 231 (1918).
Duplan Corp. v. Deering Milliken, Inc., 444 F.Supp. 648 (D.S.C. 1977).
Santa Fe-Pomeroy, Inc. v. P&Z Co., Inc., 569 F.2d 1084 (9th Cir. 1978).
TianRui Group Co. v. ITC, 661 F.3d 1322 (Fed. Cir. 2011).
Transparent Wrap Machine, Corp. v. Stokes & Smith Co., 329 U.S. 637 (1947).
Windsurfing Intl., Inc. v. AMF, Inc., 782 F.2d 995 (Fed. Cir. 1986)
Zajicek v. Koolvent Metal Awning Corp. of America, 283 F.2d 127 (9th Cir. 1960).

Secondary Sources

ALFORD, WILLIAM P., TO STEAL A BOOK IS AN ELEGANT OFFENSE: INTELLECTUAL PROPERTY LAW IN CHINESE CIVILIZATION (1995).
AMARCHAND AND MANGALDAS AND SURESH A. SHROFF & CO., INTELLECTUAL PROPERTY AND COMPETITION LAW (2011).
Bai, J. Benjamin, *Licensor Beware*, IP LAW & BUSINESS (2007).
Benkler, Yochai, *Coase's Penguin, or, Linux and the Nature of the Firm*, 112 YALE LAW J. 369 (2002).

Bird, Robert and Daniel R. Cahoy, *The Impact of Compulsory Licensing on Foreign Direct Investment: A Collective Bargaining Approach*, 45 AM. BUS. L.J. 283 (2008).

Bird, Robert C. and David Orozco, *Finding the Right Corporate Legal Strategy*, 56 MIT SLOAN MGMT. REV. 81 (Fall 2014).

CHESBOROUGH, HENRY, OPEN INNOVATION: THE NEW IMPERATIVE FOR CREATING AND PROFITING FROM TECHNOLOGY (1995).

Cuoto, Vinay et al., *Offshoring 2.0: Contracting Knowledge and Innovation to Expand Global Capabilities*, Duke University Offshoring Resource Network Report (2007).

Frankel, Kenneth M. and Mark S. Zhai, *A Return to the DOJ's "Nine No-Nos"?*, The AIPLA Antitrust News (Jan. 2013).

Heller, Michael A. and Rebecca S. Eisenberg, *Can Patents Deter Innovation? The Anticommons in Biomedical Research*, 280 SCIENCE 698 (1998).

Jones, Ashby and Jessica E. Vascellaro, *Smartphone Patents: The Never-Ending War*, WALL ST. J., (April 12, 2012).

Leone, Maria Isabella and Toke Reichstein, *Licensing-In Fosters Rapid Invention! The Effect of the Grant-Back Clause and Technological Unfamiliarity*, 33 STRAT. MGMT. J., 965 (2012).

LESSIG, LAWRENCE, FREE CULTURE: THE NATURE AND FUTURE OF CREATIVITY (2004).

Levin, David and Michele Boldrin, *The Case Against Intellectual Property*, 92 AM. ECON. REV. 209 (2002).

Norris, Floyd, *Manufacturing is Surprising Bright Spot in U.S. Economy*, N.Y.TIMES (Jan. 5, 2012).

Murphy, Colum, *Chinese Car Makers not Ready for U.S. Market*, WALL ST. J. (Jan. 9, 2014).

Orozco, David, *Administrative Patent Levers*, 117 PENN STATE L. REV. 1(2012).

Orozco, David, *Administrative Patent Levers in the Software, Biotechnology and Clean Technology Industries*, 9 J.L ECON. & POL'Y 615 (2013).

Orozco, David, *Will India and China Profit from Technological Innovation?*, 5 NW. J. TECH & INTELL. PROP. 426 (2006).

Orozco, David and Latha Poonamallee, *The Role of Ethics in the Commercialization of Indigenous Knowledge*, 119 J. BUS. ETHICS 275 (2014).

Orozco, David and James Conley, *Friends of the Court: Using Amicus Briefs to Identify Corporate Advocacy Positions in Supreme Court Patent Litigation*, 2 U. OF ILL. J. OF L. TECH., & POLICY 102 (2011).

OROZCO, DAVID, KEVIN MCGARRY AND LYDIE PIERRE-LOUIS, *The Human Rights-Related Aspects of Indigenous Knowledge in the Context of Common Law*, in LAW, BUSINESS AND HUMAN RIGHTS: BRIDGING THE GAP (Robert C. Bird, Daniel R. Cahoy and Jamie D. Prenkert eds., (2014).

Ottaviano, Gianmarco I.P., Giovani Peri and Greg C. Wright, *Immigration, Offshoring and American Jobs*, 103 AM. ECON. REV. 1925 (2013).

PORTER, MICHAEL, COMPETITIVE STRATEGY: TECHNIQUES FOR ANALYZING INDUS-TRIES AND COMPETITORS (1980).

Resnik, D.B., *A Pluralistic Account of Intellectual Property*, 46 J. BUS. ETHICS 319 (2003).

Sampath, Padmashree Gehl and Pedro Roffe, *Unpacking the International Technology Transfer Debate: Fifty Years and Beyond, International Centre for Trade and Sustainable Development (ICTSD)*, Working Paper, 6 June 2012.

Shiva, Vandana, BIOPIRACY: THE PLUNDER OF NATURE (1997).

U.S. International Trade Commission, China: Effects of Intellectual Property Infringement and Indigenous Innovation Policies on the U.S. Economy, USITC Publication No. 4226 (2011).

Ziedonis, Rosemarie, *Don't Fence Me In: Fragmented Markets for Technology and the Patent Acquisition of Strategies of Firms*, 50 MGMT. SCI. 804 (2004).

Zuidjwijk, Ton J. M., *The UNCTAD Code of Conduct on the Transfer of Technology*, 24 McGILL LAW J. 562 (1978).

10. Political, economic, and public policy constraints on the use of human resource practices to protect intellectual property in China and the United States

Christine M. Westphal

Firms doing business in China have had serious concerns about the protection of intellectual property in China from the beginning of the 1990s[1] when China first began its rapid economic expansion by focusing on attracting direct foreign investment.[2] Initially concerns were limited to the Chinese practice of illegally reproducing copyrighted material such as movies and software. As companies began manufacturing consumer goods in China, firms were threatened by a proliferation of counterfeit goods that misappropriated trademarks, design patents, and trade dress. China's acceptance into the WTO brought with it promises that China would put more uniform and standardized protections for intellectual property in place[3] but, as the Chinese economy evolved, the threats to intellectual property have become more complex. Companies and, in some instances, whole industries are being threatened by Chinese competitors who appear to have appropriated or misappropriated patented information, trade secrets, and confidential business methods and practices. In some instances, it appears that the Chinese government is working in tandem with both state-owned and privately-held companies

---

[1] William O. Hennessey, *Proceedings of the Annual Meeting of the American Society of International Law*, 91 AM. SOC'Y INT'L L. 402, 402–407 (1997).

[2] Daniel C.K. Chow, *Enforcement Against Counterfeiting in the People's Republic of China*, 20, NW. J. INT'L L. & BUS. 447, 447–75 (2000).

[3] Kamal Saggi and Joel P. Trachtman, *Incomplete Harmonization Contracts in International Economic Law: Report of the Panel, China-Measures Affecting the Protection and Enforcement of Intellectual Property Rights*, WT/DS362/R, adopted 10 March 2009, 10:1 WORLD TRADE REV. 63, 63–86 (2011).

to provide competitive advantage and political protection to Chinese firms as they compete with Western firms in the global marketplace.[4] It also appears that the Chinese government may be intervening in the global marketplace in order to further its public policy objectives. It should be understood that for the Chinese government the policy objectives go beyond simply supporting the expansion and local control of industries within China. Controlling inflation as demand for goods increases in China, meeting social welfare goals set by the Communist Party and extending China's influence in the global economy are incorporated into the Chinese government's public policy considerations.

Western firms with high-value intellectual property are increasingly confronted with a serious dilemma when considering business transactions in China. Companies that have already shifted their manufacturing plants to China and companies that are contemplating new expansions into the growing Chinese consumer markets all need to evaluate, or in some instances re-evaluate, the potential profits that can be made in China against the cost of possible loss or misappropriation of their intellectual property. When China was simply a location for manufacturing that offered low-wage workers and lax environmental enforcement as its competitive advantages, Western firms could offshore production to China, or if China became problematic, to other Asian or developing regions. Vietnam, the Philippines, Indonesia, and India sometimes provided attractive alternatives to China's low-cost manufacturing. Now, however, China is increasingly seen as a market where Western firms must be successful if they are to remain competitive in the global economy. With its rapidly expanding middle class and still expanding economy, firms as diverse as retailers Ikea and Walmart, heavy equipment manufacturer Caterpillar and European and American car companies, pharmaceutical giants such as SmithGlaxoKline, consumer electronics firms such as Apple and Google all recognize that expansion into the Chinese market is essential to their continued success. The Chinese government has encouraged this belief by regularly announcing plans to make extraordinary investments in economic sectors such as infrastructure, solar power, and healthcare; and by emphasizing the growth of the Chinese middle class.

Section I of this paper will discuss some of the issues that Western firms with high-value intellectual property will need to consider when

---

[4] *Lew Warns China on Antritrust Probes*: WSJ, CNBC (Sept. 14, 2014), http://www.cnbc.com/id/101999091; *see also* Steven Pearlstein, *China is Following the Same Old Script – the One that Gives It All the Best Lines*, WASH. POST, Jan. 19, 2011, at A11.

making decisions about doing business in China (whether they are considering new expansion or continuing existing operations). Section II will review how Chinese government policies might impact those decisions. Section III will suggest ways that companies doing business in China might protect their intellectual property, including how those companies might align their human resource practices. If multinational companies are going to continue to do business in China they must have a clear understanding of the possible threats to the value of their intellectual property and align their policies and practices to provide maximum protection.

I. STRATEGIC CONSIDERATIONS

When China was seen primarily as an offshore location for manufacturing, the strategic considerations for Western companies seemed more straightforward. How much initial investment, plus transportation and training costs, would a company have to spend in order to realize a cost savings, based on lower labor and production costs? Occasionally there were also significant economic and political costs associated with closing home country facilities, but these costs were familiar to Western companies and their calculation was easily understandable. The availability of an alternative, low-cost provider in China also gave companies economic leverage when they were negotiating with their local governments and labor groups. While some authors argued that Chinese labor might not be cheap if companies had to comply with Chinese labor laws[5], enforcement by the Chinese was lax and a majority of companies realized their expected savings. The 1990s and the first decade of the new millennium saw a major shift in manufacturing from the United States and Europe. Off-shore production was lowering the cost of consumer goods, making markets more competitive, and forcing companies to develop new business models.

Although companies were concerned about the potential loss of value of their intellectual property, particularly copyright and trademark infringements, protection efforts were often focused on their own national boundaries. If the company could help home country authorities prevent pirated and counterfeit goods from being sold in home markets then the intellectual property's value would be preserved. When China

---

[5] Marisa Anne Pagnattaro, *Is Labor Really "Cheap" in China? Compliance with Labor and Employment Laws*, 10 SAN DIEGO INT'L L.J. 357, 357–79 (2009).

came to be viewed as a consumer market in its own right, many organizations had to rethink protection of their intellectual property. It was no longer sufficient to protect home and Western markets from being flooded with pirated and counterfeit goods, companies also needed to pressure the Chinese government into removing the goods from the Chinese markets.

Although China has joined the WTO, signed the TRIPS agreement, entered into other international agreements for the protection of intellectual property, and codified international standards into Chinese law, enforcement is still a major problem.[6] Initially, in the 1990s, there was some consensus that the Chinese government did not have a sufficiently developed legal system, particularly at the local level, to provide effective protection against misappropriation of intellectual property.[7] Finally, even if a company could succeed in a claim that its intellectual property rights had been infringed, recovery of its loss seemed inadequate by Western standards.[8]

In this environment, the strategic considerations necessary for the protection of the value of a company's intellectual property began to evolve. For media and software companies concerned with pirating of copyrighted material, the main issue was still keeping the infringing material off the market, both in the Western marketplace and in China. By cooperating with and assisting local Chinese regulators, media and software companies could often have pirated material confiscated and destroyed in China.[9] They already had extensive networks and cooperative relationships with their home country and other Western regulators.[10]

Manufacturers of consumer goods face a more complex strategic landscape. They are often simultaneously grappling with trying to stem the sale of counterfeit goods, and build brand loyalty for their products in China. In this case, some companies began to recognize that "knockoffs" of their products might actually help build brand recognition and loyalty in China.[11] The process can be described using the iconic Gucci handbag as an example. In a large Chinese organization, only top employees can

---

[6] Peggy Chaudhry, Victor Cordell and Alan Zimmerman, *Modelling Anti-Counterfeiting Strategies in Response to Protecting Intellectual Property Rights in a Global Environment*, 5 MKTG. REV. 59, 69–72 (2005).

[7] Chow, *supra* note 2.

[8] *Ibid.*

[9] *Ibid.*

[10] Chaudhry, Cordell and Zimmerman, *supra* note 6.

[11] Kai Raustiala and Christopher Sprigman, *Fake It Till You Make It*, 92 FOREIGN AFF. 25, 25–30 (2013).

afford "real" Gucci handbags. The top employees own and proudly display authentic Gucci merchandise, usually purchased through legitimate channels like the Gucci Company sponsored store at the local high-end shopping area. Mid-level workers have good "knock-off" copies purchased at local Chinese discount stores. Clerical workers have cheap "knock-offs" often purchased from street vendors. In this model, there is very little or no brand confusion. Clerical workers and mid-level workers aspire to be successful enough to own "real" Gucci bags and shop at upscale establishments. Everyone in the organization recognizes that these lower level workers do not have actual Gucci bags; rather, they have articles that are embossed with the Gucci trademark as a sign of respect for the brand. From a strategic perspective, companies like Gucci might decide that it is better to focus resources on reinforcing the brand's high-end, exclusive nature in China, and not on working with the Chinese authorities to have "knockoffs" removed from the market place. Such companies and industries must still devote resources to limiting the impact of counterfeit goods on home and Western markets.

This calculation changes when the existence of imitation or counterfeit products hurts the value of the brand instead of enhancing brand loyalty. Premium liquors are experiencing significant difficulty in China.[12] In the case of premium liquors, counterfeiters are re-using legitimate packaging or counterfeiting packaging, trade dress, and trade mark labeling, then filling the containers with products that are concocted to "look" right but lack characteristics of the original (with the possible exception of alcoholic content). Chinese consumers who are not familiar with the authentic product, but have purchased the bottle based on advertising for the brand may become ill after consuming the counterfeit product, which damages the image and value of the brand. In these cases it is important for the company and trade organizations representing the manufacturers to keep working with and pressuring the Chinese authorities to get the counterfeit products off the Chinese market.

For manufacturers of heavy equipment, automobiles, electronics, basic machinery, and pharmaceuticals the strategic calculation is also complex. In the first instance, these manufacturers must decide if manufacturing their products in China is worth the risk of having their patents infringed and their trade secrets and business practices pirated. Filing for patent protection in China may also subject American and European firms to the

---

[12] *China Food & Drink Report*, Bus. Monitor Int'l. Ltd. 51–60 (2010).

risk of having the Chinese authorities force them into licensing agreements with potential competitors.[13] They will need to determine how much research and development, if any, they want to have in their Chinese facilities. The manufacturing decision often hinges on the perceived value of capturing significant market share in China. The calculation of the value of capturing market share is fairly complex. The Chinese are concerned about the price structure of goods sold within China. The Chinese government has devoted resources to studying how the United States and European countries regulate the monopoly power of Western manufacturing[14] and has recently forced a number of European and American companies to lower their prices in China.[15] This puts pressure on Chinese manufacturers to keep pricing in China lower, which helps control inflationary pressures on the economy. China has been engaged in a careful process of raising wages, particularly of factory workers,[16] over the last decade and in order for this process to be successful in improving the standard of living for workers inflation needs to be controlled as the economy expands. The political cost of pressuring Western firms in China is likely to be small, the government is seen as protecting the Chinese consumer and the indirect pressure that this puts on Chinese manufacturers is unlikely to provoke local resistance. For Western firms the lower profit margins that government pressure creates may still be sufficient to make expansion into the Chinese market attractive, but it will be a tougher decision, especially if firms have to factor in the potential losses of intellectual property. The Chinese government's pressure on pricing and profit margins has caused some

---

[13] Patricia E. Campbell and Michael Pecht, *The Emperor's New Clothes: Intellectual Property Protections in China*, 7 J. BUS. & TECH. L. 69, 69–115 (2012); *see also* Brett M. Neve, *China, Google, and the Intersection of Competition and Intellectual Property*, 38 N.C. J. INT'L L. & COM. REG. 1091, 1091–1128 (2013).

[14] Michelle Price and Norihiko Shirouzu, *How Firms Learn to Live with China Antitrust Raids*, CNBC (Sept. 3, 2014), http://www.cnbc.com/id/101909294.

[15] Tom Mitchell, *European Companies Slam Chinese Antitrust Probes*, CNBC (Aug. 13, 2014), http://www.cnbc.com/id/101918483.

[16] Christine M. Westphal and Susan C. Wheeler, *Increasing Wages in China: Government Manipulation of Wage Rates Without Direct Regulation*, 18 N.E. J. LEGAL STUDIES 1, 5 (2007).

financial analysts to warn American investors that American and European companies that are projecting significant growth of market share in China may be disappointed.[17]

II. THE IMPACT OF CHINESE GOVERNMENT POLICIES

The solar panel industry serves as a cautionary example.[18] A number of European manufacturers moved production facilities to China in order to lower labor costs. The Chinese government announced that it would make significant investments in renewable energy including solar panels in order to power rural villages.[19] The logic, on the part of the Chinese government seemed to be that many of the outlying areas would be too expensive to connect to a centralized power grid but placing solar panel arrays at the villages would allow for a faster, more cost-effective way to improve the lives of rural villagers. The Chinese government pressured the European manufacturers to source components locally, which caused the European manufacturers to lose control of significant parts of their intellectual property. European and American manufacturers initially calculated that capturing even 10 percent of the emerging Chinese market would more than double their sales and profits. They did not foresee Chinese companies entering the marketplace with significant government subsidies,[20] which led to rapid increases in worldwide production and a rapid price drop for the panels.[21] A number of companies were forced into bankruptcy.[22]

---

[17] Michael Yoshikami, *China is Muscling Tech Firms – Investors Need to Pay Attention*, CNBC (Jul. 30 2014), http://www.cnbc.com/id/101879646.

[18] Stephen Lacey, *How China Dominates Solar Power*, THE GUARDIAN (Aug. 30, 2014), http://www.theguardian.com/environment/2011/sep/12/how-china-dominates-solar-power/.

[19] Solidiance, *Solar Power in China*, ECOLOGY.COM (Aug. 30, 2014), http://www.ecology.com/2013/03/15/solar-power-in-china/.

[20] Ucilia Wang, *China Tops the World in Solar Panel Manufacturing*, DAILY FINANCE (Feb. 23, 2014), http://www.dailyfinance.com/2010/06/03/china-solar-panel-manufacturing.

[21] *Marc Roca, China Drives Record Solar Growth Becoming Biggest Market*, BLOOMBERG (Aug. 30, 2014), http://www.bloomberg.com/news/print/2013-03-08/china-drives-record-solar-growth-becoming-biggest-market/.

[22] Lacey, *supra* note 18.

The WTO determined that China was dumping solar panels on the U.S. and European markets.[23] The U.S. instituted penalties under the WTO guidelines.[24] The Chinese government gradually removed its subsidies, causing a consolidation of Chinese manufacturers, who will capture the bulk of the Chinese market.[25] The Chinese government will be able to obtain panels at a significantly reduced cost. The European companies who lost control of their intellectual property are presently complaining to the European Union authorities that the Chinese are trying to take over the entire global market. The actions of the Chinese government, in concert with Chinese firms, have completely disrupted the market, leading to a quicker, less-costly implementation of the Chinese public policy initiative to provide electric power to rural villages. When the production capability of the Chinese firms exceeded worldwide demand, the central government of China increased its investment in solar power[26] and began creating larger solar arrays that are connected to its power grid.[27] The expansion of the Chinese government's investments in solar power will probably offset any actions that the United States and European countries take to protect manufacturers from dumping as China becomes the largest consumer of solar panels in the world.[28]

Although U.S. companies have signed a number of agreements to sell their solar panels in China, they are often hit with long delays in obtaining the necessary permits to complete installations.[29] There is speculation in the American media that government entities in China may be delaying expansion into the Chinese market by U.S. solar manufacturers in order to support their domestic manufacturers.[30] Public policy initiatives in Europe and the United States were designed to stimulate

---

[23] Janie Hauser, *From Sleeping Giant to Friendly Giant: Rethinking The United States Solar Energy Trade War with China*, 38, N.C. J.INT'L L. & COM.REG. 1061, 1061–1088 (2013).

[24] *Ibid.*

[25] Ucilia Wang, *First Solar, SunPower Ink Major Deals in China*, FORBES (Mar. 31, 2014), http://www.forbes.com/sites/uciliawang/2012/12/03/first-solar-sunpower-ink-major-deals-in-china/.

[26] Roca, *supra* note 21.

[27] Solidiance, *supra* note 19.

[28] Roca, *supra* note 21.

[29] Wang, *supra* note 25.

[30] *Ibid.*

demand for solar panels by subsidizing consumer purchase and installation; the Chinese were focused on capturing market share[31] by providing low-cost loans and subsidies to Chinese manufacturers.[32]

A similar pattern may be about to appear in the pharmaceutical industry. The Chinese government has announced a significant investment in health care.[33] Several Chinese agencies have also launched investigations into the practices of pharmaceutical companies that some writers believe are a prelude to forcing the industry to share patents and trade secrets if they hope to continue participating in the Chinese market.[34] This may be the first move on the part of the Chinese government to disrupt the pharmaceutical industry in order to maximize the benefits of their investment in health care.

China is now the largest car market in the world.[35] Starting in the 1990s, China began an aggressive campaign to build highway infrastructure that would allow for greater movement of both goods and people. The Chinese used this infrastructure to draw foreign investment into their Western provinces and greatly improve worker mobility.[36] With the highway construction programs on track and an emerging middle class with the resources to purchase private automobiles, China is poised for rapid growth in its domestic automotive sector. This led to increased scrutiny by Chinese authorities and increased pressure on foreign automobile manufacturers.[37] European and American companies that manufacture automobiles in China must do so in joint ventures where they control less than 50 percent of the company. The Chinese have allowed parts manufacturers to be owned entirely by American and European companies. Many foreign car manufacturers have attempted to increase the profitability of their Chinese operations by increasing their margins

---

[31] Keith Bradsher, *China Benefits as US Solar Industry Withers*, N.Y. TIMES, Sep. 1, 2011, at B1.

[32] Lacey, *supra* note 18.

[33] Megan Shank, *Specialty Drugmaker Sinobiopharma Takes on Big Pharma in China*, BLOOMBERG.COM (Nov. 12, 2010), http://www.bloomberg.com/news/2010-11-12/specialty-drugmaker-sinobiopharma-takes-on-big-pharma-in-china.html.

[34] *China Syndrome: Crackdown on Foreign Firms No Coincidence*, CNBC-.COM (July 12, 2013), http://cnbc.com/100879812.

[35] Paul A. Eisenstein, *World's Largest Auto Market Plans to Restrict Car Purchases*, CNBC.COM (July 11, 2013), http://www.cnbc.com/id/100879726.

[36] Westphal and Wheeler, *supra* note 16.

[37] Mitchell, *supra* note 15.

on parts and services.[38] The Chinese authorities have staged a number of raids on car companies including Mercedes-Benz (Daimler AG) claiming that they are manipulating prices for parts and services and over-charging Chinese consumers.[39] This has caused some Western car companies to lower their prices in China.[40] The Chinese government has also announced that some automotive parts manufacturers can no longer operate without Chinese "partners," which raised fears that the Chinese will misappropriate their intellectual property.[41] There is concern that China is hoping to copy the "knowhow and innovation"[42] of American and European parts manufacturers. The Chinese government is interested in increasing the use of innovative technologies to continue its rapid economic expansion. Part of their plan was included in a 2006 report, "National Medium and Long-Term Program for the Development of Science and Technology 2006–2020." Scott Cendrowski reports that James McGregor believes that the Chinese "plan" is simply to engage in the theft of technology from European and American firms.[43] There is also a sense that in a joint venture the main goal of the Chinese partner is to obtain access to the technology and intellectual property of the participating firm.

Chinese companies have also been able to purchase American and European companies in order to obtain existing technology. Geely Holding, a Chinese company, acquired Volvo Cars in 2010 and they are already producing both cars and engines in China, in addition to their European plants.[44] By purchasing Volvo cars from Ford they acquired the expertise needed to export cars that meet both the American and European standards. If the Chinese can capture the entire supply chain for automotive production they will be poised to enter the global automotive market aggressively. By suppressing the profit margins of

---

[38] *Mercedes-Benz Found Guilty for Price Manipulation*, CNBC (Aug. 18, 2014), http://www.cnbc.com/id/101925991.

[39] *Ibid.*

[40] *German Auto Suppliers Asked to Form JVs in China*, CNBC (Aug. 24, 2014), http://www.cnbc.com/id/101942991.

[41] *Ibid.*

[42] *Ibid.*

[43] Scott Cendrowski, *Tesla's Big Gamble in China*, FORTUNE (May 8, 2014), http://fortune.com/2014/05/08/testlas-big-gamble-in-china/.

[44] Volvo Car Group Global Media Newsroom Press Release, *End of an Era as Swedish Production of Volvo XC90 Stops After 12 years*, VOLVOCARS.COM (Aug. 25, 2014), https://www.media.volvocars.com/global/en-gb/media/press realeases/147889/end-of-an-era-as-swedish-production-of-volvo-sc90-stops-after-12-years/.

Western companies selling goods in China, the Chinese government will make those companies less able to respond to the competition of Chinese manufacturers in the global marketplace. For the Chinese government this is a win-win situation; Chinese manufacturers can potentially obtain the systems and innovations of Western parts manufacturers at little or no cost, and the government receives credit for protecting Chinese consumers.

Chinese labor practices have also been evolving as the economy grows. The Chinese government has used both regulatory and market forces to increase wages.[45] The passage of the 2008 Revisions of the Labor and Contract Law of the People's Republic of China was intended to help stabilize labor relations in China. For management employees, the law requires written contracts; for workers, the law requires that employers with more than twenty-five employees allow the All-China Federation of Trade Unions to represent the workers. The Chinese want to enforce their labor and contract laws to both maximize economic growth and avoid widespread labor unrest. From a public policy perspective, "(t)he new law emphasizes greater employee rights and participative labor relations that are supposed to emulate the German labor model."[46] The combination of regulatory action and manipulation of market forces has resulted in significant wage increases in China over the last ten years. Because wage increases in China have made China less attractive for manufacturers it will be interesting to see how the parts manufacturers respond to these new Chinese demands for joint venture partners.[47] It is possible that companies such as Bosch will simply return manufacturing to their plants in Europe or the United States rather than risk creating Chinese competitors who have the advantage of R & D savings because they have been able to misappropriate intellectual property by participating in joint ventures. The Boston Consulting Group estimates that it is now only "4 percent more expensive to manufacture in America versus China,"[48] and even that gap may be closing.

Research and Development is another area that involves complex calculations when developing a strategy for investing in China, and other countries with weak intellectual property rights protections. Minyuan Zhao, an Associate Professor at Wharton, who has written extensively on

---

[45] Westphal and Wheeler, *supra* note 16.

[46] Xiaoya Liang, Janet H. Marler, and Zhiyu Cui, *Strategic Human Resource Management in China: East Meet West*, 26, ACAD. MGMT. PERSP. 55, 70 (2012).

[47] Heesun Wee, *Why the 'Made in China' Model is Weakening*, CNBC (Aug. 19, 2014), http://www.cnbc.com/id/101920959.

[48] *Ibid.*

research and development strategies, estimates that companies can reduce the cost of R&D by up to 50 percent by moving significant parts of their facilities to countries such as China.[49] She suggests a framework that uses internal company resources to discourage imitation and protect the value of intellectual property developed in countries without significant protections. Specifically she suggests that "by developing technologies that require complementary knowledge and resources not readily available to potential imitators" companies can preserve the ability to profit from their innovations. Her framework suggests that there be no reliance on legal enforcement efforts. She establishes that a country has weak intellectual property rights, she accepts that situation as a given, and suggests a framework for companies that will work in the absence of legal protection.

III. PROTECTION OF INTELLECTUAL PROPERTY

Once a company understands the risks to its intellectual property that are inherent in doing business in China and has developed a strategy for handling those risks, it can then develop a strategy for meeting its human resource requirements in the global business environment.

   While Zhao and others[50] would simply accept that a country has weak intellectual property protections and move forward, other writers have focused on addressing ways to use the existing legal structures in both the developing world and the international community.[51] As countries seek acceptance into the WTO they are supposed to address issues of intellectual property protection as part of the process. American and European companies need to have a nuanced response to a country's acceptance into the WTO. China serves as a good example of the possibilities. It would be naïve to assume that protection of intellectual property can be adequately addressed by relying on the Chinese legal system to consistently enforce the laws that it has enacted as part of the WTO acceptance process. But, simply ignoring the possibility of enforcement leaves a company with significantly less protection than it can

---

[49]   Minyuan Zhao, *Conducting R&D in Countries with Weak Intellectual Property Rights Protection*, 52, MGMT. SCI. 1185, 1186 (2006).

[50]   *See*, e.g., Michael J. Burstein, *Exchanging Information Without Intellectual Property*, 91:2 TEX. L. REV. 227, 227–282 (2012).

[51]   Marisa Anne Pagnattaro, *Protecting Trade Secrets in China: Update on Employee Disclosures and the Limitations of the Law*, 45 AM. BUS. L.J. 399, 399–415 (2008).

achieve. It is also important to realize that the Chinese legal system is transitioning toward international standards of business practice and this includes expanded use of the international treaties and legal protections for intellectual property. As has often been the case historically, in a rapidly industrializing nation, the Chinese began with a focus on engineering, then the focus shifted to business practices, and more recently some of the focus has shifted to law. This transition can be seen in the students China sends to American and European universities. Initially the majority of these students came to study STEM disciplines, but in the early 2000s there was a significant shift toward management disciplines[52]. Recently, anecdotal evidence suggests that American law schools have seen an increase in Chinese students. As the leadership cohort in China becomes more conversant with international laws and enforcement mechanisms, it seems likely that enforcement of international obligations will become more predictable and useful.

American and European companies should take a multi-pronged approach to the protection of intellectual property in China and other WTO member counties with weak intellectual property protections. In China, successful strategies will have to include a clear understanding of Chinese law as it is written, as it is presently enforced, and as it may be enforced in the foreseeable future. Contracts should be drafted as if the Chinese law will be enforced as written, even if enforcement is not presently anticipated. Moreover, supplemental, non-legal adjustments should be made in company policy to minimize any damage that might be caused by lax enforcement. The primary areas where employment contracts might be effective in protecting intellectual property are trade secrets and confidential business practices. As noted above, companies may be forced to license patented technology to competitors under Chinese law. Minyuan Zhao suggested a framework for exploiting R and D capabilities that might also be used when exposing patented innovation to Chinese control, but keeping the required "complementary knowledge and resources"[53] from potential imitators poses a number of problems.

The use of restrictive covenants in the employment contracts of employees in China would be the logical way to protect trade secrets and

---

[52] Institute of International Education, *Open Doors Data*, http://www.iie.org/resarch-and-publications/open-doors/data/international-students/fields-of-study-by-place-of-origin.

[53] Zhao, *supra* note 49.

confidential information. Marisa Ann Pagnattaro[54] has suggested a number of steps that companies can take in order to maximize the chances that they will be able to protect their trade secrets under Chinese law. Although her focus is China, the practices she recommends would be considered best practices for any company wishing to protect trade secrets and confidential information in the current global business environment. She recommends having clear, written policies on confidential information that restrict access to trade secrets and confidential information; clearly identifying the information that is confidential; written policies that clearly define the ownership of trade secrets and other intellectual property developed by employees; and having employees sign contracts that include confidentiality and non-compete clauses that comply with Chinese laws.[55] All of these practices are necessary for companies seeking enforcement in the courts in China, but they would also enhance enforcement efforts in the United States if jurisdiction in the U.S. court system is possible. Pagnattaro also recommends that employment contracts require employees to notify management whenever they are going to take a position with a potential competitor;[56] that employees who are leaving the firm have their access to trade secrets and confidential information limited; and that the organization keep track of where key employees go when they leave the firm.[57] Enforcement of restrictive covenants designed to protect intellectual property may be limited in China, but the rapid expansion of Chinese companies in the global economy may provide a number of other enforcement options. As Chinese companies seek to expand their businesses into the United States by either buying American and European firms or simply creating their own subsidiaries in the West it will be easier for the U.S. Courts to take jurisdiction over disputes between U.S. Companies and their Chinese competitors. If the dispute is to be litigated in China, Pagnattaro also suggests that international companies consider the inclusion of arbitration clauses in their contracts with employees in China because, among other reasons, it may avoid the perceived or real bias that international companies are said to experience in the Chinese court system.[58]

---

[54] Marisa Anne Pagnattaro, *Preventing Know-how From Walking Out the Door in China: Protection of Trade Secrets*, 55 BUS. HORIZONS 329, 329–337 (2012).

[55] *Ibid.*

[56] *Ibid.*

[57] *Ibid.*

[58] *Ibid.*

American and European companies have adapted to the variations in the content and enforcement of restrictive covenants in their own countries (for example California does not allow enforcement of non-compete clauses in employment contracts). China's labor law uses the European model of "garden leave" when companies include non-compete clauses in employment contracts: the employee continues to receive substantial compensation during the non-compete period, which cannot exceed two years.[59] The Chinese labor law also limits restrictive covenant contracts to managers, but a carefully drawn contract will be enforceable. To the extent that individual employees may be deterred from revealing trade secrets and confidential information obtained during employment by the placement of restrictive language in a contract, whether enforcement is likely to be successful or not, such language should be included. While the dangers inherent in joint ventures with Chinese partners have been identified, it should be noted that, even though contracts that create joint ventures can be drafted to protect intellectual property, they face the same enforcement difficulties in China as individual employment contracts. Additionally, it has been noted that in China "in a joint venture, political power often trumps controlling stakes."[60]

Because Chinese firms have become so adept at competing in the global economy, it is often difficult for American and European firms to remember that China is an authoritarian state still governed by the Chinese Communist Party. In many respects, the Chinese economy still possesses aspects of the old-style command economy. The state still owns a significant part of the country's productive capacity, still controls all political and union activity, and still sets development goals.[61] This has simplified the construction of infrastructure and has sometimes allowed the government to appear significantly more efficient than democracies, such as India, in encouraging economic growth. The rapid economic expansion of the Chinese economy has led to an historic reduction of poverty in China.

The Chinese version of an economic "social contract" – the Communist Party retains political control of the country as long as the economic wellbeing of the population continues to improve – puts substantial pressure on Chinese bureaucrats to meet public policy goals. The government in China is willing to make large investments, and it is also

---

[59]   DLA Piper, *Doing Business in China* (2012). http://www.dlapiper.com/en/us/sitesearch/?q=doingbusiness%20in%20china

[60]   Cendrowski, *supra* note 43.

[61]   Robert Taylor, *China's Labour Legislation: Implications for Competitiveness*, 17 Asia Pac. Bus. Rev. 493, 493–510 (2011).

willing to manipulate market forces to aid in achieving those public policy goals. When the Chinese government decided that wages need to be raised, they pressured "captive" foreign firms, such as Walmart and McDonalds, to accept representation of workers by the All-China Federation of Trade Unions and raise wages.[62] Walmart executives had been assured by local Chinese government representatives that they would not need to accept union representation of their workers.[63] However, once they were sufficiently committed to expanding their business in China, they were informed that they would need to comply with the Chinese labors laws, and accept union representation.[64] While it often takes the Chinese authorities several years to transition to a new standard, Western and European firms need to be aware of policy announcements. The government in China is both capable of, and willing to, cause market disruption in order to further its public policy initiatives. It is especially willing to do so when it will also allow Chinese firms to be more competitive both in the Chinese market, and the global market, which is why financial writers are concerned about the bribery and price-fixing investigations that are currently underway with pharmaceutical, automotive, and software firms.[65]

The "centrally managed capitalism"[66] that China has developed seems poised to limit the competitive ability of American and European firms in China and makes decisions to try to capture market share in China more complex. The potential for loss of intellectual property coupled with the Chinese government's enforcement of regulations that seems to focus on limiting the profit that foreign firms can realize may cause the loss of some direct foreign investment, but it is unlikely that any international business can afford to ignore the potential of Chinese consumers or completely abandon expansion into the Chinese market. It is therefore important that American and European firms avail themselves of every opportunity to prevent the loss of their intellectual property as they expand into the Chinese market.

The Chinese government exercises great flexibility when enforcing its regulations and foreign firms are often the focus of enforcement efforts.

---

[62] Carl Goldstein, *Wal-Mart in China*, 277 NATION, 7, 7–10, (2003).

[63] *Ibid.*

[64] *Ibid.*

[65] China Syndrome, *supra* note 34; and Scott Cendrowski, *Headache for Tesla as China Lets 1,000 Electric Flowers Bloom*, FORTUNE (July 3, 2014), http://fortune.com/2014/07/03/headache-for-tesla-as-china-lets-1000-electric-flowers-bloom/.

[66] Xiaoya Liang, Janet H. Marler, and Zhiyu Cui, *supra* note 46, at 57.

It would not be surprising if China started to tighten enforcement of its environmental laws in the near future, especially when it can identify foreign-owned firms causing pollution. If local firms are given advanced notice of the intent to enforce environmental regulations more strictly, or if they simply respond more quickly to public announcements of increased enforcement, they will have an opportunity to gain significant market advantage. As the Chinese legal system matures, and the Chinese government faces more discontent on the part of the Chinese people over pollution, working conditions, and uneven levels of prosperity, it can be anticipated that China will increase regulation and government enforcement of the Chinese laws in a wide range of issues from bribery, to environmental pollution, to labor and contract law enforcement.

If the Chinese government increases enforcement of the laws protecting intellectual property this may help Western companies protect their intellectual property by allowing them to enforce employee and licensing contracts, provided they have had the foresight to draft their contracts to carefully comply with the requirements of the Chinese legal system.

IV. CONCLUSION

Over the last twenty years, China has industrialized and entered the global economy. It has had to adopt international standards in order to both encourage direct foreign investment and to become a full member of the WTO. It has looked to both American and European laws as models[67] but it has moderated its implementation and enforcement of those laws if it feels that that will aid it in achieving economic expansion or meeting its stated public policy goals. While American and European companies cannot rely on Chinese law to protect their intellectual property, they would be foolish to ignore the benefits that legal safeguards, such as restrictive covenants in employment contracts and carefully drafted joint venture agreements, might provide. It seems likely that the Chinese government will begin to consistently enforce both its intellectual property laws and labor laws as its economy matures, and its businesses and manufacturers seek to protect their intellectual property. American and European firms may also be the beneficiaries of increased and consistent enforcement of the Chinese laws designed to protect intellectual property if they have drafted appropriate language into their contracts.

---

[67]   Taylor, *supra* note 61.

BIBLIOGRAPHY

Bradsher, Keith, *China Benefits as US Solar Industry Withers*, N.Y. TIMES, Sep. 1, 2011, at B1.

Burstein, Michael J., *Exchanging Information Without Intellectual Property*, 91:2 TEX. L. REV. 227 (2012).

Campbell, Patricia E. and Michael Pecht, *The Emperor's New Clothes: Intellectual Property Protections in China*, 7 J. BUS. & TECH. L. 69 (2012).

Cendrowski, Scott, *Headache for Tesla as China Lets 1,000 Electric Flowers Bloom*, FORTUNE (July 3, 2014), http://fortune.com/2014/07/03/headache-for-tesla-as-china-lets-1000-electric-flowers-bloom/.

Cendrowski, Scott, *Tesla's Big Gamble in China*, FORTUNE (May 8, 2014), http://fortune.com/2014/05/08/testlas-big-gamble-in-china/.

Chaudhry, Peggy, Victor Cordell and Alan Zimmerman, *Modelling Anti-Counterfeiting Strategies in Response to Protecting Intellectual Property Rights in a Global Environment*, 5 MKTG REV. 59 (2005).

China Food & Drink Report, BUS. MONITOR INT'L. LTD. 51 (2010).

China Syndrome: Crackdown on Foreign Firms No Coincidence, CNBC.COM (July 12, 2013), http://cnbc.com/100879812.

Chow, Daniel C.K., *Enforcement Against Counterfeiting in the People's Republic of China*, 20 NW. J. INT'L L. & BUS. 447 (2000).

DLA Piper, *Doing Business in China* (2012), http://www.dlapiper.com/en/us/sitesearch/?q=doingbusinesspercent20inpercent20china.

Eisenstein, Paul A., *World's Largest Auto Market Plans to Restrict Car Purchases*, CNBC.COM (July 11, 2013), http://www.cnbc.com/id/100879726.

German Auto Suppliers Asked to Form JVs in China, CNBC (Aug. 24, 2014), http://www.cnbc.com/id/101942991.

Hauser, Janie, *From Sleeping Giant to Friendly Giant: Rethinking The United States Solar Energy Trade War with China*, 38 N.C. J. INT'L L. & COM. REG. 1061 (2013).

Hennessey, William O., *Proceedings of the Annual Meeting of the American Society of International Law*, 91 AM. SOC'Y INT'L L. 402 (1997).

Institute of International Education, Open Doors Data, http://www.iie.org/resarch-and-publications/open-doors/data/international-students/fields-of-study-by-place-of-origin.

Lacey, Stephen, *How China Dominates Solar Power*, THE GUARDIAN (Aug. 30, 2014), http://www.theguardian.com/environment/2011/sep/12/how-china-dominates-solar-power/.

Lew Warns China on Antritrust Probes: WSJ, CNBC (Sept. 14, 2014), http://www.cnbc.com/id/101999091; see also Steven Pearlstein, *China is Following the Same Old Script – the One that Gives It All the Best Lines*, WASH. POST, Jan. 19, 2011, at A11.

Liang, Xiaoya, Janet H. Marler and Zhiyu Cui, *Strategic Human Resource Management in China: East Meet West*, 26 ACAD. MGMT. PERSP. 55 (2012).

Mercedes-Benz Found Guilty for Price Manipulation, CNBC (Aug. 18, 2014), http://www.cnbc.com/id/101925991.

Mitchell, Tom, *European Companies Slam Chinese Antitrust Probes*, CNBC (Aug. 13, 2014), http://www.cnbc.com/id/101918483.

Neve, Brett M., *China, Google, and the Intersection of Competition and Intellectual Property*, 38 N.C. J. INT'L L. & COM. REG. 1091 (2013).

Pagnattaro, Marisa Anne, *Is Labor Really "Cheap" in China? Compliance with Labor and Employment Laws*, 10 SAN DIEGO INT'L L.J. 357 (2009).

Pagnattaro, Marisa Anne, *Preventing Know-how From Walking Out the Door in China: Protection of Trade Secrets*, 55 BUS. HORIZONS 329 (2012).

Pagnattaro, Marisa Anne, *Protecting Trade Secrets in China: Update on Employee Disclosures and the Limitations of the Law*, 45 AM. BUS. L.J. 399 (2008).

Price, Michelle and Norihiko Shirouzu, *How Firms Learn to Live with China Antitrust Raids*, CNBC (Sept. 3, 2014), http://www.cnbc.com/id/101909294.

Raustiala, Kai and Christopher Sprigman, *Fake It Till You Make It*, 92 FOREIGN AFF. 25 (2013).

Roca, Marc, *China Drives Record Solar Growth Becoming Biggest Market*, BLOOMBERG (Aug. 30, 2014), http://www.bloomberg.com/news/print/2013-03-08/china-drives-record-solar-growth-becoming-biggest-market/.

Saggi, Kamal and Joel P. Trachtman, *Incomplete Harmonization Contracts in International Economic Law: Report of the Panel, China-Measures Affecting the Protection and Enforcement of Intellectual Property Rights*, WT/DS362/R, adopted 10 March 2009, 10:1 WORLD TRADE REV. 63 (2011).

Shank, Megan, *Specialty Drugmaker Sinobiopharma Takes on Big Pharma in China*, BLOOMBERG.COM (Nov. 12, 2010), http://www.bloomberg.com/news/2010-11-12/specialty-drugmaker-sinobiopharma-takes-on-big-pharma-in-china.html.

Solidiance, *Solar Power in China*, ECOLOGY.COM (Aug. 30, 2014), http://www.ecology.com/2013/03/15/solar-power-in-china/.

Taylor, Robert, *China's Labour Legislation: Implications for Competitiveness*, 17 ASIA PAC. BUS. REV. 493 (2011).

Wang, Ucilia, *China Tops the World in Solar Panel Manufacturing*, DAILY FINANCE (Feb. 23, 2014), http://www.dailyfinance.com/2010/06/03/china-solar-panel-manufacturing.

Wang, Ucilia, *First Solar, SunPower Ink Major Deals in China*, FORBES (Mar. 31, 2014), http://www.forbes.com/sites/uciliawang/2012/12/03/first-solar-sunpower-ink-major-deals-in-china/.

Volvo Car Group Global Media Newsroom Press Release, End of an Era as Swedish Production of Volvo XC90 Stops After 12 years, VOLVOCARS.COM (Aug. 25, 2014), https://www.media.volvocars.com/global/en-gb/media/pressrealeases/147889/end-of-an-era-as-swedish-production-of-volvo-sc90-stops-after-12-years/.

Wee, Heesun, *Why the 'Made in China' Model is Weakening*, CNBC (Aug. 19, 2014), http://www.cnbc.com/id/101920959.

Westphal, Christine M. and Susan C. Wheeler, *Increasing Wages in China: Government Manipulation of Wage Rates Without Direct Regulation*, 18 N.E. J. LEGAL STUDIES 1 (2007).

Yoshikami, Michael, *China is Muscling Tech Firms – Investors Need to Pay Attention*, CNBC (Jul. 30 2014), http://www.cnbc.com/id/101879646.

Zhao, Minyuan, *Conducting R&D in Countries with Weak Intellectual Property Rights Protection*, 52, MGMT. SCI. 1185 (2006).

Index